BOOKS BY JESSE FINK

The Eagle in the Mirror (2023)
Pure Narco (2020)
Bon: The Last Highway (2017)
The Youngs: The Brothers Who Built AC/DC (2013)
Laid Bare (2012)
15 Days in June (2007)

THE
EAGLE
IN THE
MIRROR

IN SEARCH OF WAR HERO, MASTER SPY AND ALLEGED TRAITOR
CHARLES HOWARD 'DICK' ELLIS

JESSE FINK

Black&White

Black&White

First published in the UK in 2023
This edition first published in the UK in 2024 by
Black & White Publishing Ltd
Nautical House, 104 Commercial Street, Edinburgh, EH6 6NF

A division of Bonnier Books UK
4th Floor, Victoria House, Bloomsbury Square, London, WC1B 4DA
Owned by Bonnier Books
Sveavägen 56, Stockholm, Sweden

First published in 2023 by Viking, Penguin Random House Australia Pty Ltd

Cover images by CollaborationJS/Trevillion Images and ullstein bild/Getty Images
Cover design by Luke Causby/Blue Cork © Penguin Random House Australia Pty Ltd
Maps by James Mills-Hicks, Ice Cold Publishing

The publisher has made every reasonable effort to contact copyright holders of images
and material used in this book. Any errors are inadvertent and anyone who
for any reason has not been contacted is invited to write to the publisher so
that a full acknowledgement can be made in subsequent editions of this work.

A CIP catalogue record for this book is available from the British Library.

ISBN: 978 1 78530 525 2

1 3 5 7 9 10 8 6 4 2

Typeset by Midland Typesetters, Australia
Printed and bound in Great Britain by Clays Ltd, Elcograf S.p.A

MIX
Paper | Supporting
responsible forestry
FSC® C018072

www.blackandwhitepublishing.com

For Fred, who had the idea

'Doth the Eagle know what is in the pit,
Or wilt thou go ask the Mole?'
– William Blake, 'The Book of Thel', 1789

'He had moved from the realms of speculation into the dangerous,
paranoid "wilderness of mirrors", in which even the most
experienced of counterintelligence officers start putting a sinister
interpretation on the most innocent of incidents.'
– Nigel West, *Molehunt*, 1987

CONTENTS

DICK ELLIS'S NORTH AMERICA AND THE CARIBBEAN

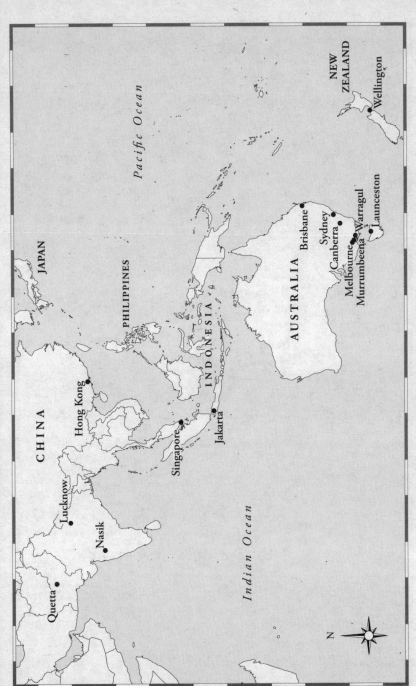

DICK ELLIS'S SOUTH, EAST AND SOUTH-EAST ASIA, AND AUSTRALASIA

DICK ELLIS'S BRITAIN AND EUROPE

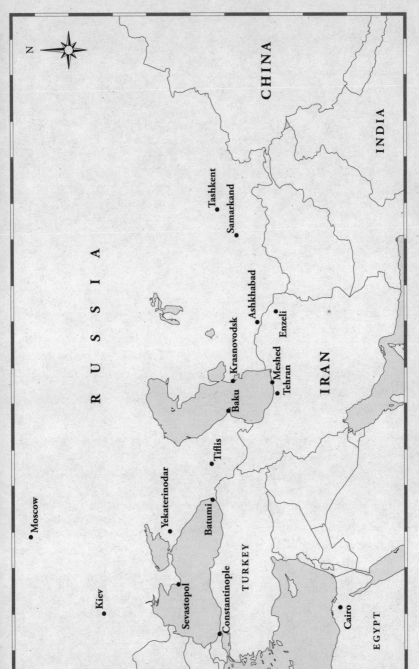

DICK ELLIS'S WEST ASIA, MIDDLE EAST AND RUSSIA

TWIST SLOWLY IN THE WIND

'Obscurity was his nature, as well as his profession. The byways
of espionage are not populated by the brash and colourful
adventurers of fiction.'
– JOHN LE CARRÉ, *A MURDER OF QUALITY* (1962)

ONE OF THE WAYS I'D CONNECT with my father, Lawrence Fink,
known to friends and family as 'Fred', was to meet for a coffee
on a weekday afternoon. We'd chat for about half an hour then drive
off to browse the bookshelves of the opportunity shop of St Vincent
de Paul in Leichhardt, Sydney, Australia.

Most days we'd buy two or three secondhand paperbacks each,
$3 apiece, and take them to our respective homes, where they'd
faithfully gather dust for six months. Then it would be time to pack
them up in a cardboard box and hand them back to Vinnies, largely
unread. (There were a *lot* of James Lee Burke novels among them.)
Our thinking was that if you can't read a book the least you can do is
let it sit on your shelf so you can absorb it by osmosis. You also helped
a charity.

One day in July 2021, while failing to read yet another book
during Australia's never-ending COVID-19 lockdown – nothing much
was grabbing me – I got a text message from Fred. It was short and
intriguing: 'Jess, have you heard of Dick Ellis? Look him up.'

Dad, then 74, had read a line in one of the paperbacks he'd bought
at Vinnies that mentioned an Australian-born colonel, Charles Howard

'Dick' Ellis, who'd worked at a very senior level for the intelligence services of the United States, the United Kingdom and Australia. Ellis had been born into impoverished circumstances in the suburb of Annandale, right next door to Leichhardt and where Fred lived.

Annandale today is a well-heeled neighbourhood where not a hell of a lot goes on other than dogs being walked. Its streets are uncommonly wide for Sydney and its Federation houses largely preserved. It seemed strange that after living in the area for a couple of decades between us, neither Dad nor I had even heard mention of Dick Ellis. Who on earth was Dick Ellis? As a non-fiction writer and biographer always on the lookout for new book ideas, I was immediately interested.

One American newspaper called Ellis 'Britain's number-three spy at the end of World War II'. Brian Toohey and William Pinwill, co-authors of *Oyster: The Story of the Australian Secret Intelligence Service*, described him as 'the most intriguing figure who has crossed the often-surprising landscape of Australian intelligence'. Fellow spy-writing duo Desmond Ball and David Horner called him 'one of the most shadowy figures of all'.

The doyen of espionage non-fiction, the late Phillip Knightley, saw in Ellis the prototype for 007: 'His adventures not only rival those of James Bond; he *was* James Bond.' Knightley claimed Ian Fleming had based the character of Bond on a mix of Ellis, 'one of the most remarkable secret service agents in the history of espionage', and the legendary Serbian double agent and ladies' man Duško Popov.[1] American journalist C. L. Sulzberger, who met Ellis in the 1960s, wrote that the Australian had 'gained a reputation as tough, ruthless and brilliant. In World War II he was a big shot in intelligence.' Ellis has also been called 'the Grand Old Man of British espionage . . . the oldest living professional agent'.

Beyond the praise and hyperbole, Ellis – a university dropout – was certainly an accomplished individual: classical musician, scholar, journalist, author, historian, diplomat, consul, polyglot (he spoke Russian, French, German, Urdu, Farsi, Turkish and some Mandarin, and is credited with a passing knowledge of other languages, including Italian and Spanish),[2] respected intelligence officer, Cold War warrior and decorated soldier who saw battle in France and Belgium (where he served on the Western Front), British India, Egypt, Afghanistan, Persia, Transcaspia (modern-day Turkmenistan), southern Russia and the Caucasus.

Ellis collected a swag of medals and honours including the US Legion of Merit, an OBE (Officer of the Most Excellent Order of the British Empire), CBE (Commander of the Most Excellent Order of the British Empire) and CMG (Companion of the Most Distinguished Order of St Michael and St George). He had been present at or involved behind the scenes in some of the biggest conflicts and events of the 20th century (World War I, the Russian Civil War, World War II, the Japanese bombing of Pearl Harbor, the creation of the Central Intelligence Agency and Australian Security Intelligence Organisation, the Vladimir Petrov affair, Kim Philby's defection to the Soviet Union), was friends with or worked with some of the most fascinating people of the century (Roald Dahl, Ian Fleming, Noël Coward, Reginald Teague-Jones, Duško Popov, J. Edgar Hoover, William Donovan, H. G. Wells, Stewart Menzies, William Stephenson), and whose personal narrative involves four undisputed titans of World War II (Franklin D. Roosevelt, Joseph Stalin, Adolf Hitler and Winston Churchill). Ellis's personal journey was quite staggering in its richness of experiences and people encountered.

But much more sensationally, after his death in 1975 the ruddy-cheeked Ellis, drily described by CIA historian Thomas F. Troy as a 'short (5'5" in his prime), slightly rounded, white-haired, proper person', was publicly accused of being a traitor. Not just any garden-variety traitor, either: a *triple* agent who in the 1960s had apparently secretly confessed to his treasonous crimes. It was grave stuff.

*

According to Troy, Dick Ellis was 'widely believed to have been both a Nazi and a Soviet agent'. British espionage journalist and author Henry ('Harry') Chapman Pincher, who went by the abridged name Chapman Pincher, wrote in 1981 that Ellis had been the beneficiary of 'the most blatant cover-up' and 'broke down after interrogation in 1965 and confessed to having spied for Germany before and during the early stages of the war.[3] This would have been a capital offence in wartime.'

Pincher passed away in 2014, aged 100. He went to his deathbed maintaining Ellis was guilty, his case against the man an encapsulation of the old idiom 'there's no smoke without fire'. Ironically, though, Brigadier Denis Blomfield-Smith observed that Pincher himself was a perfect candidate for a Soviet mole.[4] (Over his writing career, Pincher certainly accused a good many people of being Soviet agents, mostly with scant foundation.)

Adding to all this intrigue, one of the legendary 'Cambridge Five' of British traitors, Anthony Blunt, had 'inferred [sic] during his 1964 confession' that there was a 'link between [Kim] Philby and Ellis', a matter that would have ramifications for Ellis when he was interrogated himself in London the following year.[5] Blunt, however, never actually named Ellis, and was publicly outed as a traitor in the House of Commons by Prime Minister Margaret Thatcher on 15 November 1979 – despite a deal that, in exchange for his confession, he would not be exposed.[6] Blunt reportedly said before his death in 1983, 'It's amusing to see the security services spinning round like mad dogs chewing their own tails.'

Kim Philby, of course, who became a Russian spy in 1934, joined the Secret Intelligence Service (SIS or MI6) in 1940 and crossed over to the Soviet Union in 1963, was the most notorious traitor of all time. The mere mention of his name has become a synonym for betrayal and spawned dozens of books. Phillip Knightley, who interviewed Philby at his home in Moscow before Philby's death aged 76 in 1988, called him 'the most remarkable spy in the history of espionage . . . the most successful penetration agent ever . . . professionally, as a spy, he is in a class all by himself'.

Could Ellis, this unassuming, almost anonymous Australian, have been his secret accomplice?[7] Philby never gave any indication during his exile in the Soviet Union the pair had worked in tandem, yet they well knew each other and served on an MI6 reorganisation committee together after World War II. No mention is made of Ellis in Philby's 1968 autobiography, *My Silent War*, but Ellis was still alive at the time and no allegations of treason against him had yet to surface in the public domain.[8] Ellis was even considered a possible candidate for the infamous Soviet mole ELLI, whose codename was first mentioned in the 1940s but has never been positively and conclusively identified, despite claims to the contrary.

*

So how has Dick Ellis, such a huge figure in the history of Western espionage, practically been forgotten? It's rotten enough betraying your country for an enemy state – but to do so for the two most evil empires of the 20th century, fascist Nazi Germany *and* the communist Soviet Union? It puts you in a category all of your own. Ellis potentially was a bigger traitor than Philby and the FBI's Robert Hanssen, who in 2001 was caught spying for the Russians.

Ellis would be widely talked of as being 'a spy for both Hitler and Stalin', though that is preposterous: he didn't meet either the German or Russian dictator and is not known to have had contact directly with them or any of their subordinates. Both men, however, feature indirectly in his story. Available sources show that Ellis flatly denied ever being a Soviet mole. It seems though that reports of his alleged connections to the Nazis warrant closer examination.

Let me be plain. Even if Ellis had been simply feeding 'chicken-feed', or low-value information, to the Third Reich before World War II under orders from MI6 superiors – or out of penury: by many accounts Britain didn't pay its secret agents enough as well as give them enough money to pay other agents[9] – the charge that he *in any way* worked for Nazi Germany is deeply shocking. We're talking about Nazis, after all: history's greatest villains and Hollywood's go-to personification of badness.

Indeed, cast as a Nazi agent, Ellis's name has been publicly connected to a catalogue of betrayals: revealing MI6's bugging of the German Embassy in London; 1939's notorious Venlo Incident in the Netherlands (where two British agents were kidnapped by the Nazis on the Dutch–German border); being the source for Waffen-SS Major General Walter Schellenberg's infamous arrest list prepared prior to the Battle of Britain, *Sonderfahndungsliste G. B.* ('Special Wanted List Great Britain', popularly called 'The Black Book'), and its accompanying SS handbook *Informationsheft G. B.* ('Information

Brochure Great Britain'); and feeding intelligence to Adolf Hitler's number two, Martin Bormann.[10] It's as bad as it gets.

It has been alleged that Ellis 'sold vast quantities of information to the Germans' before the invasion. Pincher insinuated Ellis was responsible for the wartime killing of English actor Leslie Howard: the plane he was travelling in from Lisbon to Bristol was shot out of the sky off the coast of northern Spain by the *Luftwaffe*. Ellis has even been linked to the attack on Pearl Harbor in Hawaii in 1941. In the 1980s there was no end to Axis-collaboration accusations made against Ellis; but most – and this is an important qualification – had very little to no substance at all. How much actual *evidence* was needed to make a convincing case that the boy from Annandale had been up to no good? Or didn't proof matter anymore?

The MI5 intelligence officer Peter Wright, who died in 1995 aged 78, was in the interrogation room with Ellis when he allegedly confessed; Wright subsequently gave Pincher the inside scoop the latter needed for his books demonising Ellis (1981's *Their Trade is Treachery* and 1984's *Too Secret Too Long*).

Wright wrote the following in his own book, the 1987 global bestseller *Spycatcher*: 'Ellis was a venal, sly man. He sat there, stripped of his rank, white-faced and puffy. But never once did I hear an apology. I could understand how a man might choose the Soviets through ideological conviction. But to sell colleagues out to the Germans for a few pounds in time of war? I told him that had he been caught in 1939–40 he would have been hanged.'[11]

Ellis's life appeared to be an incredible, untold tale; it was astonishing that no biographer before me had attempted to write a proper book on this enigmatic individual (Phillip Knightley, to his credit, had tried to get a film made about Ellis but it never materialised). But what if, after all the relentless smearing and character assassination from the *Daily Mail* to *Newsweek* to the *Washington Post*, there was another explanation for Ellis's confession? Could he have made a 'false confession' and, like the soldier he was, professed guilt to protect someone else? What if he was actually innocent?

What if there was more to the story of Pincher and Wright themselves and their motivation to 'nail Ellis'?

Was Ellis an evil spy and a traitor of epic proportions or a hero of freedom and liberty? Four decades before the term even entered our lexicon, could he have been a posthumous victim of cancel culture, where truth doesn't matter and an allegation is enough to condemn someone in the court of public opinion?

Like any writer of serious non-fiction worth his or her salt, I wanted to explore these questions. I'd written challenging books before – on dead rock stars and Miami cocaine traffickers – and was used to investigating stories where people didn't want to talk. What I didn't realise was just how profoundly difficult it would be.

*

From the outset, the internet wasn't much help. Online, Dick Ellis barely registered. There was one picture of Ellis on Google Images and in the months of frenetic searching that followed I was to turn up only three other photographs – two from a book he'd written in the 1960s, *The Transcaspian Episode, 1918–1919*, and one from *The Second Oldest Profession* (1986) by Phillip Knightley.

That was it. For a man who had worked at the most senior levels for MI6, been involved in the setting up of the Office of Strategic Services – the World War II progenitor of the CIA – and later created the Australian Secret Intelligence Service, essentially running three separate intelligence services in three English-speaking countries, Ellis was a complete mystery, a wraith. Constructing a timeline of his life would take some doing. Indeed, the story you're about to read spans nearly 130 years.

In the preface to his book *Desperate Deception: British Covert Operations in the United States, 1939–44*, Thomas E. Mahl quotes Thomas F. Troy's advice on the challenges facing any author writing a book about a spy: 'What you're looking for, what I've looked for, is the file with the whole story in it. That file doesn't exist. The material you want has been scattered to the winds – a sentence here, a paragraph there. You'll have to hunt them out just as I've had to.'

A deeper plunge into online archives returned suitably scattered mentions of Ellis in various theses, newspapers and books, but there was nothing substantial on him all in the one place, save for a modest

Wikipedia entry, a short biography on historian John Simkin's excellent Spartacus Educational website, some interview footage of Ellis shot for an unaired 1973 Canadian television documentary, Ellis's own handful of obscure books and pamphlets,[12] and an impassioned defence of Ellis in two chapters of Canadian author William Stevenson's 1983 book *Intrepid's Last Case*.

This latter account of Ellis was Stevenson's sequel to 1976's *A Man Called Intrepid*, a biography of Ellis's former British Security Coordination (BSC) boss in the United States, fellow Canadian William Stephenson aka 'Intrepid'. For that book, a huge hit around the world, Ellis had written the foreword though he died before publication.

Millions of copies were sold and dozens of translations published of *A Man Called Intrepid*; a mini-series was made starring David Niven and Michael York; a video-arcade game was even released.[13] Today, there is hardly a place on Earth where a dog-eared old edition can't be found. In October 2022, on a rainy day in Chiang Mai, up in the hills of northern Thailand, I chanced upon two deeply aged, travel-worn Ballantine paperbacks – *A Man Called Intrepid* and *Intrepid's Last Case* – wedged into the bulging shelves of Shaman Bookshop, a charmingly cluttered secondhand bookstore on Kotchasarn Road.

Its impressive worldwide sales numbers notwithstanding, the first *Intrepid* book was roundly (and rightly) criticised for historical inaccuracies and wild embellishments.[14] The distinguished historian Hugh Trevor-Roper called it a 'grotesque myth . . . one of the most ludicrous works ever to be written . . . on such a subject' and an 'egregious publication'. He also claimed a May 1940 letter of invitation from Winston Churchill to William Stephenson quoted in the book was nothing short of a fabrication.[15] A photo reproduced in *A Man Called Intrepid* purportedly of Churchill and Stephenson together 'among the bombed ruins of the Houses of Parliament' in 1941 is highly dubious. The image definitely shows Churchill but the 'dark figure' who is supposedly Stephenson has his back to camera and could well be anyone. Stephenson biographer Bill Macdonald, in his book *Intrepid's Last Secrets*, called *A Man Called Intrepid* 'inaccurate'.

Despite the book's critical shellacking, Stephenson and Stevenson (a sort of espionage version of Thomson and Thompson from Hergé's

Tintin and who were then neighbours in Paget, Bermuda) obviously thought it was worth releasing a sequel seven years later, *Intrepid's Last Case*, with Ellis a leading character in the story. Stephenson wouldn't have a bar of anyone impugning his old colleague, calling Ellis 'one of the very few you could be certain about' and so certain of his talents that he 'could have, should have, moved up to the number-two, or even the number-one, spot in MI6'. Stephenson confidently maintained, 'I knew everything about him.'

After retiring from BSC, Stephenson had moved to Montego Bay, Jamaica, and started the Caribbean Cement Company (Carib Cement) in 1952, remaining chairman for almost 20 years. By the time *A Man Called Intrepid* came out in 1976 he was in declining health after suffering a 'major stroke' in the early 1960s and was reportedly 'an invalid by 1964'.

Thomas F. Troy, who met both Stephenson and Ellis in Bermuda in 1969, recalled of Stephenson: 'He shuffles about, tires easily, is slightly forgetful, but is still alert and coherent, remains active in the conduct of his affairs, and retains an interest in world affairs.' But he had 'obvious physical disabilities . . . his left eye seemed half-closed, and the right corner of his mouth was slightly contorted, especially when he spoke'.

Either way, without help from the ailing Stephenson, Stevenson would have been stretched to write extensively about the by-then-dead Ellis, who had left very little by way of documents to mount his own defence. Stevenson made the point that Ellis 'signed nothing, avoided all written commitments. That was the mark of a good agent', but the Australian had 'left himself unprotected by memos'.[16]

Major General Richard Rohmer, at time of writing this book Honorary Lieutenant General of the Canadian Armed Forces, wrote the foreword to *Intrepid's Last Case*. He said Ellis had been a victim of a classic 'KGB character assassination'. It was KGB practice to 'neutralise enemies of the Soviet Union by sowing seeds of mistrust and discord among members of the intelligence or counterintelligence services': the same *dezinformatsiya* (disinformation) we are so familiar with today when it comes to mudslinging in US politics, the China–Taiwan issue, or the Russian invasion of Ukraine.

Stephenson took a similar view, writing in his foreword to Harford ('H.') Montgomery Hyde's 1982 autobiography *Secret Intelligence Agent* that any charges Ellis spied for the Nazis and Soviets amounted to 'pure disinformation by the KGB' and had any confession taken place 'I would have known about it, because I would have been the first person the Security Service in London (MI5) would have got in touch with. No documentary evidence in support of the charge against Ellis has yet been forthcoming; if it exists it should be produced instead of relying on hearsay.'[17] Hyde, too, shared Stephenson's opinion about Ellis being a victim of Soviet 'disinformation'.[18]

But as we shall see, both men also had their doubts about Ellis.

*

Since William Stephenson died in 1989, the mythology around him has only grown – becoming, frankly, outlandish. In 2022 a lake in his home state of Manitoba, Canada, was named in his honour and memory. To this day, the University of Winnipeg in Manitoba has an annual Sir William Stephenson Scholarship. It has been going since 1984.

After the death of William Stevenson in 2013, his papers were donated to the University of Regina in Saskatchewan. I emailed its archives department to see if anything on Dick Ellis was among the collection – there was – but was told any letters between Stevenson and Ellis were 'currently restricted materials on request of the donor. Stevenson requested a closure of certain files in the collection for a period of 30 years after his death, which would take us to 2043, and the correspondence between himself and Colonel Ellis is part of those closed materials.'

Taken aback, but hopeful of finding a way around the embargo, I got in touch with Monika Stevenson, the second wife and widow of William Stevenson, to ask why.[19]

'Because of unsuccessful attempts to use my husband's research and personal experience to slander people like Colonel Ellis, Sir William himself and even my husband, I have become very careful in vetting everyone who has an interest in seeing his papers,' she wrote. 'For all these reasons I need to know more from you.'

Fair enough. But when I carefully explained what I was doing – keeping an open mind about Ellis and hopefully constructing a standalone biography of the man – she issued an extraordinary caveat.

'This is clearly a multi-year commitment on your part, a commitment which I very much respect. In making such a commitment, one has to consider the risk of a single disclosure or document that could pull the rug out from under you. That game-changing document would be Colonel Ellis's alleged written confession. Both you and I need that minimum degree of certainty, one way or the other.

'As a skilled investigative author, can you get that document? And if you cannot, you will have a thoroughly documented record of investigation and evasion, which would establish the non-existence of such confession. This is a certainty that we both need before proceeding.'

Essentially, Mrs Stevenson was asking me to find what had eluded her own husband and all others over the past 70 years – incontrovertible, documentary proof establishing Ellis's innocence or guilt. Pull that off and she would grant me permission to get my hands on the Stevenson–Ellis letters. No biggie.

The problem, of course, is MI5 and MI6 aren't subject to the Freedom of Information Act, and aren't legally or morally obliged to cough up anything, especially a confession – written, recorded, apocryphal or otherwise. MI6 never releases anything. Whatever clues I could find would be deeply embedded, if not hidden, in hundreds of incredibly dense, barely legible personal files from the interwar and World War II periods released by MI5 and held by Britain's National Archives. Mrs Stevenson even conceded at one point, 'I think it is a given that you will never find Ellis's confession, simply because it doesn't exist,' but the pointlessness of the task didn't matter, apparently.

'The outcome of your well-documented efforts to find the confession will be a story of dogged, focused research on your part, and transparent denials, lies and evasions by those who ever claimed it existed. That part of the story will ensure that there will not be a future disclosure that pulls the rug out from your project, and if something suddenly surfaces post publication, it could only be seen as a forgery, else why would it not have been made available to you earlier?'

That Mrs Stevenson thought the powers-that-be would find it necessary to create a forgery of a document 50 years *after* Ellis died was astonishing in itself. Subsequent emails between the two of us led nowhere, even when the head archivist at the University of Regina's library attempted to intervene to broker a resolution to the impasse.

'I am very much aware of what has been written about Colonel Ellis and the complete lack of backup for the smear job that has been done on him,' Mrs Stevenson wrote to me. 'What is particularly reprehensible is that after my husband died, access was given to some of my husband's papers without my permission and the material was completely falsified by writers [it is not clear who Mrs Stevenson is referring to] you seem to take seriously. I was told later that they could not reach me. I have had the same house address and telephone number (shared with my husband for 35 years). When I tried to rectify matters, I was told I could sue. Laughable, right? . . . all of the material on Colonel Ellis in the archives has precisely to do with BSC, of which he was deputy head. And those who wish to ruin Ellis's reputation, wish to do so precisely to smear the entire BSC effort.

'Suffice it to say that *A Man Called Intrepid*, including the information about Colonel Ellis in it and by him, continues to do very well. The readers who still write letters [to me] have no doubt about the integrity of everyone who sacrificed so much to win that war [and] are proof of its impact. I doubt that any of the books you tell me to Google still have that kind of staying power.'

As I saw it, Mrs Stevenson, perhaps understandably, was being obstructive and difficult. Whatever her reasons, the end result was the same: she formally denied my request to access her late husband's correspondence with Ellis.

'I do not wish to make the materials available to you . . . I will leave things as they are. I do wish you luck in persuading your countrymen of the simple fact that if there were an authentic confession, which has never materialised in over 50 years, it would long ago have been made public. With your obvious talent, if you put your mind to it, you will certainly be able to prove that the overall success of BSC would not have been possible if its deputy director was working for the enemy. Any future narrative asserting otherwise could easily be crushed both by the unchallengeable success of BSC and by the inability of the detractors to produce the signed confession that is the basis of their slander.'

We were going around in circles. Fortunately, I didn't come up empty-handed. Without my asking, the kindly librarians in Saskatchewan sent me – gratis – what they could of the collection that didn't require Mrs Stevenson's permission.

*

When I contacted the National Library of Australia in Canberra about Dick Ellis's own handful of papers and photographs, I was told they were available for research but that access to some documents similarly required the permission of his then-octogenarian daughter, Ann Veronica Salwey (née Ellis), a widow and former teacher. Ellis's only other child – a son, Olik Cyril 'Peter' Ellis, born ten years before Salwey and who went on to become an intelligence officer just like his father, but for Canada not Britain – had passed away in Ottawa in 2012.[20]

Salwey, who married John Arthur C. Salwey in Sydney in 1955 and was widowed in 1972, had left some interesting handwritten notes in Ellis's collection at the NLA. Among what she had documented were Dick Ellis's love of cats and C. J. Dennis's *The Songs of a Sentimental Bloke*. That there were any papers to be accessed seemed like something of a miracle given that an American writer, the late Robin W. Winks, had written in 1987: 'Ellis is dead; any papers, to which I have not had access, are said to be in the possession of his daughter, though she states that she has none.'[21]

Maybe I could approach her and ask if she'd be interested in co-operating with a prospective biography of this intrepid Australian who also happened to be her father? Not wanting to cold-call Salwey and give her a fright, I decided to see if I could approach her through an intermediary: Australian academic James Cotton, who'd written a paper about Ellis's authorship of a book on the League of Nations. The most interesting thing about the paper was the curious case Cotton made – largely on the basis of Ellis's daughter's full name – that Ellis was good friends with the esteemed science-fiction writer H. G. Wells.[22]

Ellis's friendship with Wells had been hinted at before, first by President Franklin D. Roosevelt's wartime adviser Ernest Cuneo and then by William Stevenson. (The latter appeared to borrow a lot of Cuneo's writings on Ellis.)[23]

Initially Cotton seemed supportive but warned me, 'Ann is very elderly but such a nice lady to meet in person. The spy-literature writers made her life uncomfortable so she may not wish to correspond. Nevertheless, I will contact her by forwarding your message and she may reply. She lives in New York. If you are interested in Dick Ellis – a rare talent – his papers in the NLA are worth examining.'

A second email from Cotton sounded ominous: 'I believe Ann would prefer not to be involved. There are some materials of his in various UK archives – especially Churchill College, Cambridge, and also the British Library – and other scattered materials, but any life would involve a lot of conjecture. He knew Moura Budberg . . . but what to make of that.'[24]

After that, Cotton pretty much stopped answering my emails. Eventually a friendly librarian in Canberra advised me that Salwey's daughter, Ellis's granddaughter, handled correspondence and supplied me with an email address. After my first email was ignored, I emailed again and got this reply:

Mr Fink, I have received your emails. I know nothing about Mrs Salwey's life with her father. Mrs Salwey passed all papers to the Australian Library [sic] some years ago. She does not wish to be interviewed. Please do not contact me again.

The electronic version of having a door slammed in your face. *Twice*. Monika Stevenson had done it; now, so too had what remained of Ellis's family, though I have no idea whether Salwey even saw my email. Perhaps Salwey was being shielded by her daughter? Regardless, I wasn't getting access to some of those materials at the NLA if they required Salwey's permission. Paradoxically, encountering these obstacles only made me more determined to write *The Eagle in the Mirror*.

*

When Dick Ellis looked at himself in espionage's famous 'wilderness of mirrors', described by former CIA counterintelligence head James Jesus Angleton as an 'ever-fluid landscape where fact and illusion merge', what did he see?[25] Where did his loyalties lie? For a man whose name was inextricably linked to the Soviet Union, Nazi Germany and the United States of America, what national eagle – Russian, German, American – was staring back at him? Was he truly innocent or guilty?

The case for the prosecution has never been comprehensively tested and proven because Ellis's supposed 1960s confession has never seen the light of day. Even if a confession was made by Ellis that he betrayed MI6 to the Nazis, the collective circumstantial case against him (driven principally by West, Wright and Pincher) is flawed and weak, and only gives rise to further questions about who Ellis may have been really working for, what his motivations were, what information he might have been receiving in return, and what the ultimate endgame was. Indeed, I'd argue the Dick Ellis case should be considered one of the great whodunits of espionage to this day – except it was Ellis, no one else, who was the biggest victim.

London's *Times* newspaper reported in 1981: 'A former member of MI6 and a close friend of the [Ellis] family said . . . Mr Ellis himself had told him of his interrogation. No mention was made of any confession.'

Saying something exists is one thing. Accepting its existence without seeing it is another. But, as Ernest Cuneo wrote: 'If the charge against Ellis is true . . . it would mean that the OSS, and to some extent its successor, the CIA, in effect was a branch of the Soviet KGB.'

Could this be why the Dick Ellis story has been obscured, if not covered up, for so long? That was Pincher's hard-nosed view: 'The security and intelligence authorities decided that a court case against a man who had been undetected for so long and was deeply suspected of having continued his treachery for the Soviet Union would damage the reputation of the secret services, especially with the USA and other allies who were therefore kept in ignorance of it . . . Ellis was allowed not only to remain free on full pension but to enjoy honour as a patriot, save among the very few of his former MI6 colleagues who knew the truth about him.'[26]

Thomas F. Troy had an even more cynical take: 'The British government has certainly allowed Ellis, who died in 1975, to twist slowly in the wind. The United States, an interested – possibly an injured – party, has likewise said nothing.'

*

The Eagle in the Mirror has been written not as a traditional biography but as a sort of biographical cold-case investigation. It's as honest a telling of Ellis's life story as possible in the face of some unavoidable obstacles: a narrative composed of factual and circumstantial evidence. In this book the charges that Ellis was a traitor are scrutinised in an attempt to determine the truth about his guilt or innocence, once and for all. On a personal level, I feel like I went down a very deep rabbit hole attempting to piece together Ellis's movements over the 80 years of his life, but it was worth it. To be his first biographer became, in the end, not just a kind of authorial duty but a privilege.

It was also a step back into a world that's been lost. Travel used to fill me with a sense of wonder. I grew up in Sydney in the 1980s and '90s reading battered old copies of *National Geographic*. Before the internet changed everything, walking down an unfamiliar street in a foreign city was an adventure. Now, in the 2020s, travel is often a ticket to somewhere else merely to look at other people looking at their iPhones. Telling Ellis's story – with its gazetteer of faraway lands and exotic locations, his love of languages, his personal interest in Central Asian history – renewed that sense of wonder. It's remarkable to think he saw so much of the world by sea passage.

Of necessity I have quoted from numerous other books that mention Ellis, even in passing: this scattering of clues help form the story arc of this book. *The Eagle in the Mirror* is endnoted but it is not necessary to read these notes in tandem with the main text; they are there for anyone who is interested in the many side branches of the Ellis story. Some valuable groundwork has been done on Ellis by other writers. I humbly acknowledge them.

Equally, works have been published that directly contributed to the distortion of Ellis's good name over a period of half a century since his death. Many authors, journalists and scholars, dead or alive, could and should have done better by a man who had achieved so much and left behind a remarkable if totally hidden legacy. I give credit to those men and women who I believe did the right thing by Ellis and weren't persuaded by rumour and scuttlebutt.

Was Ellis a traitor or forgotten war hero or both? That is ultimately for the reader to decide. In any event he was a significant Australian and globetrotter who led a singularly extraordinary life. No lake, mountain or other geographical feature in Australia has ever been named in Ellis's honour but it should be, in light of the case I present and what I believe, on balance, ultimately amounts to his vindication.

It has come too late for Ellis and what is left of his family but the historical record has now been rewritten. The year 2025 will mark the 130th anniversary of his birth, the 50th anniversary of his death and 80 years since the end of the greatest event in human history, World War II. Dick Ellis's story should be known to one and all.

Jesse Fink, August 2023

CHAPTER 1

THE PURGE

'If the day ever comes when there are no enemies left in the world, governments will invent them for us.'
– JOHN LE CARRÉ, *THE SECRET PILGRIM* (1990)

LIKE A LOT OF PEOPLE whose lives come to sticky or ignominious ends, Dick Ellis's time on Earth was ruined by the butterfly effect. All it took was the bodies of two Russian secret agents to be discovered – one machine-gunned to death at point-blank range and dumped on a lonely road in Lausanne, Switzerland, the other a supposed suicide by self-inflicted gunshot in a Washington DC hotel room – for his reputation to begin to unravel completely.

It would take time, decades, for that to happen but there was no escaping Ellis's ultimate fate. It mattered not that he was widely admired, possessing 'a most refreshing sense of humour which made being in his company always a most enjoyable and rewarding experience' or that he was 'greatly liked and trusted in his day'. Ellis's achievements as a soldier and intelligence agent would evaporate into irrelevance. No matter what he said or didn't say, no matter how much evidence he presented to prove his case, it made no difference because simple suspicion of collaboration with the enemy was enough to ruin him both in life and in death, for perpetuity. That is the fate of spies accused of such an unforgivable crime.

Soviet secret agent Ignace Reiss, codename LUDWIK or LUDWIG, aka 'Ignace Poretsky' and 'Hans Eberhardt', had vowed never to go back to Moscow. In 1937 World War II was on the distant horizon and Russian dictator Joseph Stalin was picking off his rivals and perceived enemies one by one in the unprecedented purges that had started the year before. For Reiss – then based in Paris but who'd served in Berlin, Vienna and Amsterdam, an idealistic Trotskyite – any return to the Soviet Union would mean certain death. He'd be far better off taking his chances in exile but he wasn't going to exit quietly.

His 'old friend and comrade', Walter Krivitsky – who in his 1939 book *In Stalin's Secret Service* described himself as 'chief of the Soviet Military Intelligence in Western Europe' – would write that Reiss had 'worked for years in our secret service abroad' and 'had been deeply shocked by the purge of the Old Bolsheviks and the "treason trials" and was already determined to break away from Moscow . . . those were the days when ambassadors and ministers, to say nothing of special agents, were being recalled from all over the world to be shot or imprisoned in Moscow, when even the leading generals of the Red Army were bound for the firing squad.'

Some 35,000 Soviet army officers were killed in 1937 alone, hundreds of thousands of people were exiled and millions more interned in concentration camps. Despite knowing the risks, Reiss effectively signed his own death sentence by brashly sending Stalin a letter on 17 July that year, admonishing his leader for betraying the ideals of the Russian Revolution:

```
Up to now I have followed you. From now on, not a
step further. Our ways part! He who keeps silent
at this hour becomes an accomplice of Stalin,
and a traitor to the cause of the working class
and of Socialism . . . let no one be deceived.
Truth will find its way. The day of judgment is
nearer, much nearer, than the gentlemen in the
Kremlin think.
```

Wrote Krivitsky: 'Reiss was a thorough idealist who had enlisted heart and soul in the cause of communism and world revolution, and Stalin's policy appeared to him more and more obviously an evolution toward fascism. He spoke to me of his crushing disillusionment, of his desire to drop everything and go off to some remote corner where he could be forgotten.'

Instead on 4 September, futilely hiding away from roving assassins with his wife Elsa and son Roman in Lausanne, Reiss was murdered. He'd been taking an evening stroll with a fellow Soviet secret agent, Gertrude Schildbach, whom he thought he could trust. That trust was misplaced. The treacherous Schildbach had at least declined to kill him with the strychnine-laced chocolate in her possession but had agreed to participate in the ambush that would end Reiss's life at the age of 38. It has been inferred that the chocolate was 'doubtless intended' for Roman.

'He went out with her to dine in a restaurant near Chamblandes to discuss the whole situation,' recalled Krivitsky. 'So he thought. After dinner they took a little walk. Somehow they wandered off into an obscure road. An automobile appeared and came to a sudden stop. Several men jumped out of it and attacked Reiss. He fought the attacking band, but with the aid of Schildbach, whose strand of hair was found in his clutch, they forced him into the car. Here one of them, Abbiat-Rossi, assisted by another, Etienne Martignat, both Paris agents of [the Russian secret police] the OGPU,[1] fired a submachine gun point-blank at Reiss. His body was thrown out of the car a short distance away . . . there were five bullets in his head and seven in his body.'

What makes this account so credible is that Krivitsky – at the time of Reiss's assassination ostensibly a bookseller in The Hague, the Netherlands, but working undercover for the Soviets (he was living in France when he wrote his book) – had himself been asked to help kill Reiss but had refused. Upon learning of Reiss's death, he wrote, 'I realised that my lifelong service to the Soviet government was ended . . . I could not pass the criminal test now put to those who wished to serve Stalin. I had taken an oath to serve the Soviet Union; I had lived by that oath; but to take an active hand in these wholesale murders was beyond my powers.'

In 1938 Krivitsky defected to the United States. The 41-year-old planned to apply for American citizenship and settle in Virginia.

He'd already survived one kidnapping attempt by Stalin's agents and knew his life and those of his wife and family were in mortal danger. Nevertheless, he told what he knew of Stalin's secrets – and Russia's network of double agents – to the secret-intelligence services of France, United States, Canada and Britain, as well as the readers of the *Saturday Evening Post* in America. Sure enough, being so open and public about the Soviet Union's inner workings and espionage activities abroad ensured Krivitsky would meet the same grisly end as Reiss and another Soviet defector, Georges Agabekov, who had been assassinated in the Pyrenees the same year.

Of course, it was made to look like a suicide – Kim Philby called it a suicide,[2] and the coroner officially found it so – but the manner of Krivitsky's death bore all the hallmarks of expert Russian assassins. On the morning of 10 February 1941, Krivitsky's body, with a head wound from a .38 calibre revolver, was discovered by a chambermaid on his bed in a pool of blood at the Bellevue Hotel on 15 East Street, Washington DC. The gun lay next to him on the floor. The fifth-floor room was locked from the inside – both door and windows – and there were three separate suicide notes.

'If they ever try to prove I took my own life, don't believe it,' he'd told an American investigator before his death.

*

Krivitsky, whose real name was Samuel Ginsberg and codename 'Walter Thomas', was notable for having given British intelligence its first hint of infiltration by notorious Soviet mole Philby, though the tip-off wasn't followed up.[3] Information he supplied did directly lead to the arrest of another traitor, Captain John Herbert King, however.

MI5's Jane Archer began debriefing Krivitsky in late January 1940 in London and extracted from the Russian a trove of valuable intelligence.[4] Among it was a reference to an obscure figure called Vladimir von Petrov (aka Waldemar von Petrow). Codenamed T100, Von Petrov was a secret agent who'd operated in Western Europe in the 1920s. He was a valued source for British intelligence and had an indirect association with Australian-born MI6 intelligence officer Dick Ellis in the 1930s.[5]

Ellis had married into a Paris-based White Russian (anti-Bolshevik) family, the Zelenskys, in 1923 and it was Ellis's brother-in-law, Aleksei (Alexander), who had a personal connection to Von Petrov. Through the conduit of Aleksei, Ellis had allegedly traded information with Von Petrov, a Nazi agent, and for this reason Ellis would later be accused of giving over secrets to Nazi Germany in return for money. It was suspected Ellis had also been blackmailed into service for the Soviet Union.

Von Petrov was a very big fish – a different individual to the Soviet official Vladimir Petrov who later defected to Australia.[6] He was, it transpired, a Nazi/Soviet/Japanese triple agent.[7] Like any spook worthy of the name, Von Petrov used various aliases: Petroff, Petrow and Otto von Bohl, among countless others.[8]

'Sometime between 1921 and 1929 the third section [Russian secret police] had what they considered a most valuable agent for British colonial matters who was a member of the staff of the Japanese Embassy in Berlin,' wrote Archer in her report. 'His name was PETROFF – agent no. 401 – a White Russian. No. 401 was much relied upon as a source of information on British colonial problems. He not only had access to Japanese sources but himself wrote reports on the subject. He would never disclose his source.'[9]

In 1945, when the war was over, the same Von Petrov (T100) appeared in the British interrogation files of a captured senior Nazi, Walter Schellenberg, the chief of *Sicherheitsdienst* or SD, the intelligence division of SS (*Schutzstaffel*). Schellenberg was an *oberführer* (senior leader) who became *brigadeführer* (brigade leader) and number-two man in the Gestapo.

'Agent T100 was [a] Chilean White Russian [called] Petroff in Switzerland who was also used by [SS police chief Ernst] Kaltenbrunner to transfer his funds there.'[10]

Another reference to Von Petrov is made in the same files ('I presume Kaltenbrunner will be asked about Petrow')[11] and Schellenberg states in his interrogation that he last met Von Petrov in his office in Berlin in 1944 and that Von Petrov had 'direct relations with [Reinhard] Heydrich', the head of the Reich Security Main Office or *Reichssicherheitshauptamt* (RSHA).[12]

This detail shows that Von Petrov was networked into serious power because around 1941, the RSHA under Heydrich and his boss, *Reichsführer-SS* Heinrich Himmler, had supplanted the Abwehr (the military intelligence service of Nazi Germany) as the Nazis' top department for 'espionage, sabotage and repression'. Schellenberg's Amt VI, the foreign political intelligence department of SD, had been absorbed into RSHA.

In the CIA files in Washington DC, a document dated 28 June 1945 says that Von Petrov was the highest paid agent Schellenberg had on the Nazis' books: 'Despite meagre results, Schellenberg continued to reward him with the highest pay of any agent of Amt VI ... Kaltenbrunner thought that T100 worked also for the Japanese or the Russians and Schellenberg did not deny this possibility as far as the Japanese were concerned.'[13] The Chilean-born White Russian was regarded as 'something of a protégé of Schellenberg's'.[14]

Schellenberg also took Von Petrov's reports 'directly to Himmler without ever showing them to Kaltenbrunner'. The fearsome Himmler, of course, was not just head of the SS but one of Hitler's most trusted henchmen.[15]

Taken together, all these documents confirm for the first time that the elusive, phantom-like Von Petrov – a British intelligence asset – had been working for the Soviets *and* the Nazis as well as the Japanese, and in each case at the highest levels. Indeed, further investigation by the British secret services established beyond doubt that Von Petrov was no less than an 'emissary for Himmler'.

This friend and close contact of Dick Ellis's brother-in-law was not your run-of-the-mill intelligence operative. Who exactly was this Chilean White Russian Ellis had allegedly been selling information to, where was that information going, where was he exactly, and how was he about to alter the course of Ellis's life?

*

In September 1945, a Soviet defector in Ottawa, Igor Gouzenko, told representatives of the Canadian government that there was a mole called 'ELLI' inside MI6 working for Stalin. Who ELLI is remains a mystery; his identity has never been unanimously agreed upon. Ellis, with his similar-sounding name and specific details that seemed to match ELLI's personal background, was at one point considered one of three possible suspects, only to be eventually ruled out, despite Gouzenko himself saying right before his death from a heart attack in Mississauga, Ontario, in June 1982 that he thought ELLI might be Ellis after all.[16]

Then, somewhat ominously for Ellis, in April and May 1946, an *Abwehroffizier* (Abwehr officer) under interrogation at Fort Blauwkapel in Utrecht, the Netherlands, came into the picture. Referred to by his peers as 'Onkel Richard' (Uncle Richard), Traugott Andreas 'Richard' Protze spilled the beans on a British double agent called 'Captain Ellis' operating in Brussels who had met supposed Russian agents.[17] Brussels is 160 kilometres from The Hague, where Krivitsky had been based.

Protze was no minor Nazi. A former Kriegsmarine *kapitän zur see* (naval captain), he was a close confidant of the Abwehr's former director, the recently executed Admiral Wilhelm Canaris (one of the leaders of a failed plot against Hitler), and served as head of the Abwehr III F, the counterespionage unit of Abwehr III, the Abwehr's counterintelligence department. From 1927 to 1938 Protze had lived in Berlin. He'd been personally sent to The Hague in 1938 by Canaris, working undercover as a travel agent for German railways. There he set up his own espionage unit, Stelle P.

In his 1971 book *The Game of the Foxes*, Ladislas Farago wrote that 'Canaris considered Protze his mentor and aide' and Protze was 'a troubleshooter in the old *Marinenachrichtendienst* [German Naval Intelligence Service] ... then continued as the ace spybuster of the Abwehr. A fox among the foxes and a cynic with a strong stomach, he was an odious old pro who regarded every man as guilty even when proven innocent. He could be affable and charming. His personal diplomacy consisted in doing and saying the nastiest things in the nicest way ... dedicated, diligent, and self-effacing on the one hand but eccentric, iconoclastic, and rather sinister on the other.'

A cable was promptly sent in June 1946 to the desk of none other than Harold Adrian Russell Philby, head of a section in MI6 handling counterintelligence, who signed his letters 'H. A. R.' but was known to all by his nickname, 'Kim'. (The previous year Philby, yet to be exposed as a Soviet spy, had given up aspiring defector Konstantin Volkov to the Russians forestalling Volkov's chance to tell the British secret services what he knew in exchange for protection. Volkov, then Soviet vice-consul in Istanbul and an NKVD agent, disappeared and was presumably executed.)[18] Philby, bizarrely, replied that he didn't know who this 'Ellis' could be – even though he and Ellis were both members of the same SIS committee on the service's postwar reorganisation.

'I am afraid,' Philby wrote in a letter to MI5 officer Major John Gwyer, 'that I cannot make any suggestions on the spur of the moment as to the possible identity of ELLIS and suggest that all we can do is to await the result of PROTZE's further interrogation. Yours sincerely, H. A. R. Philby.'[19]

A battery of questions had been drafted by British intelligence to press Protze on his spectacular claim about a 'Captain Ellis' but the German, then almost 70, took ill and was mysteriously released; in any case Protze had begun backpedalling, making out Ellis had been a Russian who had simply used the British name 'Ellis'. An SIS agent in the same intelligence file warned: 'PROTZE will probably deny further knowledge of the matter and profess that he cannot answer any of the questions.'[20]

By the following year, Philby and his MI5 counterpart, future MI5 boss Roger Hollis, had shut down the Protze probe. That, so it seemed, was where the investigation of 'Captain Ellis' wrapped up until the spectacular defection of Philby to Moscow in 1963 prompted British intelligence and a group of 'young Turks' in MI5 to launch an unprecedented internal 'molehunt'. An unsuspecting Dick Ellis would be comprehensively ensnared.

*

One of those young Turks was MI5 intelligence officer Peter Wright who'd become a confidential source for crusading British espionage journalist Chapman Pincher. On his own account Wright would author (with future *Bourne Supremacy*, *Bourne Ultimatum* and *Jason Bourne* director Paul Greengrass as his ghostwriter) one of the bestselling books of the 1980s, *Spycatcher*, in which he laid out the circumstantial case against Ellis (whom he dismissively called 'Dickie'). While some thought Wright's 'knowledge was on an altogether different scale', not everyone was impressed with his modus operandi: 'Behind the guarded doors of Leconfield House, Peter Wright was behaving like a Witchfinder-General.'

Serious charges would be levelled against Ellis by Wright; that effectively, as late British historian Donald Cameron Watt summarised, he 'was a double agent working both for the German Abwehr and the Russians', 'that he betrayed to the Germans the MI5 tap on the German Embassy telephone to Berlin', 'that he continued to work for the Abwehr when he was posted to Washington in December 1939', 'that Ellis "betrayed" the entire MI6 organisation in Western Europe to the Abwehr' and 'that Ellis was a Soviet mole in the pre-war years'.

None of it, however, convinced Watt. He was absolutely scathing about Wright's *Spycatcher*, especially the purported confession Wright claimed to have witnessed Ellis make under interrogation.

'The more one reads Wright's account, the sorrier one becomes for the unfortunate Ellis. One is even left to doubt whether Ellis's interrogation ever took place (though I am assured by persons who claim to have spoken with the interrogating officer that it did), or that he could have admitted one tenth of these accusations.'

Nor was anything ever *proven* against Ellis while he was alive but he remained actively under scrutiny and suspicion till his death in 1975.[21]

As for Wright, he was supremely confident Ellis had been a triple agent all along: 'The first thing which convinced me Ellis was always a Russian spy was the discovery of the distribution of the Abwehr officer's report in which he claimed Von Petrov's British source was a Captain Ellis.[22] The report was sent routinely to Kim Philby, in the Counterintelligence Department. He had scrawled in the margin: "Who is this man Ellis? NFA,"[23] meaning "No further action", before burying the report in the files.[24] At the time Ellis's office was just a few doors down the corridor, but it seemed to me to be a most suspicious oversight by the normally eagle-eyed Philby.'

Roger Hollis, it should also be noted, died in 1973 and was posthumously accused of being a Russian mole himself. Some espionage experts went so far as to finger him as the fabled ELLI. It has been suggested Hollis even supplied Archer's report on Krivitsky to Moscow before Krivitsky's murder.[25]

Had Philby and Hollis, as early as 1946, attempted to cover the tracks of a hitherto unknown and most unlikely Australian-born Nazi and Soviet spy? Had Philby, having learned Ellis had worked for the Nazis, blackmailed Ellis himself, as was suggested by the late British historian John Costello in his book *Mask of Treachery*?[26] Or was Chapman Pincher's and Peter Wright's joint campaign against Ellis (one seemingly supported by Nigel West) simply a paranoid witch-hunt that all but destroyed the reputation of an innocent man?

CHAPTER 2

THE TOILS OF CHILDHOOD

'The eye that mocketh at his father, and despiseth to obey his
mother, the ravens of the valley shall pick it out, and the young
eagles shall eat it.'
– PROVERBS 30:17, THE HOLY BIBLE, KING JAMES VERSION

THE WORLD OF BRITISH SECRET AGENTS before the 1970s conjures
up images of double-decker buses, black cabs, Pall Mall gentlemen's clubs, stale cigarette smoke, middle-aged men in trench coats and
bowler hats who look like Alec Guinness, red phone booths, creaking
floorboards, green desk lamps, manilla folders, clapped-out Trabants,
and East German border crossings manned by humourless communists
in fur hats. It's clichéd but true. Where did Colonel Charles Howard
Ellis, Dick to most people who knew him, fit in to all of it, and, more
intriguingly for a man born without connections, without a silver spoon
in his mouth, how did he get to the very top of the spy game?

What's more, if Ellis had been an ideological triple agent for the
Nazis and Soviets, surely there would have been clues in his past? There
were plenty in Kim Philby's, among them his formative time in Vienna
and marriage to a known communist, Alice 'Litzi' Friedmann.[1] Had
Ellis done anything that might betray the true political allegiances
of a peripatetic Australian-born intelligence officer whom Phillip
Knightley regarded as a 'lifelong anti-communist'?

Well, typical for a spy, firstly it appears even his own birth date
was concocted. On various travel documents Ellis gives his birth

date as 15 March 1894, while the official record for his home state of New South Wales has him born on 13 February 1895.[2] Throughout his life Ellis made a point of calling himself English (which he was, by his father) rather than Australian and spoke with a clipped English accent (what's called 'received pronunciation'). He even took to putting London as his place of birth on departure and arrival cards, although he came into the world in another hemisphere, at 110 Annandale Street in the inner-western Sydney suburb of Annandale. It must have been so much easier just passing himself off as a born-and-bred Englishman.[3]

Ellis's father, William Edward Ellis, emigrated to Australia from Devonshire, England, in 1849.[4] Ellis said his father's side 'originally came from the Welsh border country, probably Monmouthshire'.[5] Ellis's mother, New Zealander Lillian Mary Hobday, was half the age of William when they wed on 15 January 1892 at St Philip's Church in Sydney. William was a two-time widower who had variously been a well-to-do goldsmith, jeweller and watchmaker before turning his hand disastrously to the fashion industry and ending up broke.

His first wife, Annie, had died of pulmonary tuberculosis in 1884 and his second, Sophia, of cancer in 1891. Lillian was in her early 30s, William was in his mid 60s, a father already of two girls. Within a year of marriage Lillian had given birth to William's third child and first son, William Stanley or William Jr, but known to all as Stanley. Charles Howard – who answered to Dick – became William's and Lillian's second son in 1895 and a daughter – Lillian Mary, or Maisie – followed in 1898. Their residence was 'Tyagarah', Charles Street, Leichhardt.[6] But tragically, William's new wife and mother of his youngest three children appears to have died during the birth of Maisie. She was aged just 39.[7] Ellis, only four years old, had barely got to know his own mother and his elderly father was a broken man. The *Sydney Morning Herald* of 19 March 1898 published her funeral notice by undertakers Wood and Company of Petersham.

Wrote Ellis: 'The loss of three wives, in such circumstances, would have shaken any man, and there is no doubt that my father was badly upset by the disaster, as disaster it was for a man in his sixties to be left with three small children to care for, particularly at a time when his affairs were not going well.'

Maisie was taken to Christchurch, New Zealand, with Lillian's family and William Ellis was refused all access to his youngest child. Stanley and Charles went to Brisbane briefly with their father. After returning to Sydney, they lived in Melbourne and Launceston, where Ellis first went to school.[8]

'The Boer War was in progress,' wrote Ellis, 'and we children played "Britons and Boers", the smaller ones invariably being designated Boers. I recollect all the talk of disasters in S. Africa, the battles of Colenso, Magersfontein and Spion Kop, and saw and heard all the excitement of Australian troops going to the war . . . the little school on Cataract Hill must have been a good one as I was reading long before we left Tasmania.'

William Ellis, who had become a 'fashion artist and designer of clothes',[9] eventually returned with his two sons to Melbourne.[10]

It couldn't be said that Dick Ellis had a great start in life. His father was already elderly when he was born and was struggling financially; he had three sisters, none of whom he knew; and his mother died when he was four. Following her death, not only were he and his brother Stanley shuttled between relatives in different states, they were even shunted for a nine-year stretch to an Irish family, the Dunlops, in Warragul in Gippsland and Murrumbeena (a suburb of Melbourne). Ellis's childhood wasn't exactly *My Left Foot* but the Ellis boys would have been conditioned to endure much hardship and because of this became largely self-sufficient.

'Although father must have been hard put to cope with us, he gave us a good deal of attention,' wrote Ellis. 'We were badly fed (he had no idea of feeding children) which sowed the seeds of later ailments, and in Stan's case, no doubt hastened his death at 58 from colitis . . . [my father owing to his age] was almost entirely dependent on Stan and myself . . . it was a gravely limiting factor on our own development and efforts to obtain something of an education, and to break away from the rut that we found ourselves in as a result of the neglect and lack of opportunity from which we suffered.'

*

Stanley Ellis left school at 12 to work as a store boy. Dick Ellis, however, stayed on a few more years and benefited from an education from a 'curious teacher' from Dublin at Rosstown State School, which became Carnegie State School. It is situated next to Murrumbeena and near Malvern.[11]

The man in question was Thomas Boardman, the head teacher, who started work at the school in 1900 and was to die in office in 1908. Glen Eira Historical Society in Melbourne told me he was 'noted for establishing a cadet corps'. A memorial was later erected to him.[12] Boardman, wrote Ellis, had 'descended in the academic scale through drink' and 'often failed to appear', but 'had his good side. If he spotted a child with intelligence, he gave that child some attention . . . I learned masses of poetry and prose at his behest.'

Ellis was enraptured by the work of Charles Dickens 'and acquired an image of London from his novels that was one of the determining factors in my decision to go there as soon as I could escape from the toils of childhood'. Ellis also discovered an aptitude for languages and music: at the age of ten, his father gifted him a violin. Ellis's time in Murrumbeena evoked vivid memories.

'The Russo-Japanese war was raging, causing scares of possible raids by Russian battleships on Australian ports. Why this should have been feared, I am unable to say, unless it was because popular opinion in Australia as in England was pro-Japanese. The Russians were very unpopular, and all the Japanese victories in Manchuria, and later the naval victory at Tsushima in which the Russian fleet was destroyed,[13] was applauded . . . I remember very hot summers, the smell of the gum trees in the surrounding paddocks, bathing in the creek, fishing for "yabbies" in waterholes, mushrooming in the autumn mornings, and feuds with some of the local boys.

'We played cricket in the paddock, flew kites of our manufacture, and on special occasions, had bonfires at which we exploded mines made from gunpowder extracted from large crackers, purchased for half-pence at the neighbouring store. I earned odd pennies delivering newspapers, chopping wood for neighbours, and from the sale of bones and bottles to itinerant "rag and bone" men.'

In 1909 Ellis got his first career break, working as a 'messenger boy and "ink boy"' at Stott & Hoare's Business College at 428 Collins Street, Melbourne.[14] Ellis's job was 'keeping ink wells [sic] full and ringing the bell between classes', for which he received a token salary but also 'permission to attend classes in shorthand, English, book-keeping and typing', whereupon he 'made new contacts and mixed with a less bucolic class of people'.

'I gained a good deal of practical knowledge to enable me to earn my living as a clerk, but there were many gaps in my education, and in more ways than one, I was innocent and ill-equipped for life,' wrote Ellis. He added that because of his upbringing he was at a 'disadvantage with most boys my age' and 'suffered from neglect' and lack of 'robust health', especially with his teeth. (He had never been to a dentist and suffered from toothache throughout his life.)

He also had zero contact with his full sister, Maisie, who had been taken to England in 1907. '[Stanley and I] had a brief glimpse of Maisie as she passed through Melbourne, a shy little girl of eight or nine. She had not met her father, and it was clear that she knew little or nothing of him or of us.'[15]

*

Ellis left Stott & Hoare's to work for a bookseller, Melville & Mullen, on Collins Street. There he 'worked in the office, ran messages and delivered books'.[16] Outside of paid employment, he was busy: he sold his violin, took up the cello and oboe, graduated (allegedly) from Malvern Grammar School (now Caulfield Grammar School) in 1911,[17] left Murrumbeena and rejoined his father and brother in the city until 1914: they lived in a succession of boarding houses. His last known address in Melbourne was 308 City Road, South Melbourne.[18]

During this period Ellis performed in local orchestras as a cellist and 'also played from time to time in dance bands'; he found himself 'torn between the desire to be a professional musician or a writer'. Night classes in literature and history at the University of Melbourne yielded Ellis an unexpected opportunity: he won a 'small scholarship' through the 'generosity of one of the lecturers',[19] which gave him 'the possibility of taking a course at one of the English universities, provided a small sum of money could be found to cover the cost of the journey and sojourn in England'.[20]

Ellis wasted no time packing his bags. He'd had enough of the 'limited outlook of suburbia and the dull country towns' of Australia.

'I decided that the time had come to make a break with my existing environment, and take full advantage of the opportunity now offered to strike out on a new path.'

The future number three in MI6 sailed to England third class on the Orient Line steam ocean liner RMS *Orontes* in June 1914.[21] The same month Archduke Franz Ferdinand was assassinated in Sarajevo. The rumblings of war were about to interrupt Ellis's academic plans.

CHAPTER 3

FRONT TO FRONTIER

'The essence of war is destruction, overcoming resistance,
killing, and the strain in modern war is terrific and bears on
the whole population. It is a denial of all that makes life worth
living, a flat contradiction of the bases on which our civilisation
ostensibly rests.'
– DICK ELLIS, THE ORIGIN, STRUCTURE AND WORKING OF THE
LEAGUE OF NATIONS (1928)

DICK ELLIS'S DAUGHTER, ANN SALWEY (NÉE ELLIS), left a short,
handwritten note about her father in the piecemeal Ellis papers
at the National Library of Australia: 'He did not write about his WWI
experiences nor his later life, marriages, etc.' The paucity of documentary sources makes reconstructing Ellis's time during World War I
and its aftermath somewhat difficult, not least because of contradictory information and fuzzy timelines. By all available accounts
his distinguished military-service record included stints in Europe,
Russia, North Africa, and West, Central and South Asia, in addition
to his later service for Britain and the United States during World
War II.[1]

Conflicting reports abound. Take for instance what Ernest Cuneo
wrote of Ellis: 'He had fought in Egypt and France. He was a survivor
of the slaughter of the Second Battle of the Somme. Some 400,000
British soldiers in 40 days were sacrificed to Field Marshall [sic] Sir
Douglas Haig's folly.'

This seems highly unlikely as the Second Battle of the Somme took place in August–September 1918 and by then Ellis was known to be in Central Asia.

What is known for certain is that Ellis arrived from Australia in London after the start of the Great War and stayed with the Roberts family – his aunt and uncle from his mother's side – in Highams Park near Epping Forest, 'devoting as much time as possible to finding my way about London and visiting all the sights which were already familiar to me from books and pictures'.

He was decidedly underwhelmed.

'London in some ways disappointed me; I expected it to be more impressive as a city and found the streets narrow, many of the more famous buildings dirty and smaller than I had anticipated, and crowds in the street dull and even shabby. In those days, pubs were open at all hours and there was still a great deal of poverty and drunkenness. The West End region was more impressive, but I had neither the money or [sic] the courage to venture into the portals of the great hotels and restaurants, although I quickly made the acquaintance of the theatres (cheap gallery seats) the Albert Hall and the Queens Hall, and the parks and gardens.'

Despite claims to the contrary, there is no evidence that Ellis enrolled at the University of Oxford in 1914: the archivists at Oxford found no record.[2] The following year, to quote from H. Montgomery Hyde in *Secret Intelligence Agent*, Ellis 'enlisted in the Royal Fusiliers as a private', and he appears as number 201989 in the City of London Regiment.

He had, according to his son Olik's recollection, 'missed being sent to Gallipoli owing to [a] bout of influenza' but took his place in the 100th Provisional Battalion, based in Aldeburgh, Suffolk, part of the Territorial Force Battalions (part-time soldiers). This later became 29th (City of London) Battalion. An approach to originally enlist in the Australian Army – and perhaps save himself the cost of passage to England – had seen him allegedly knocked back for being 'too delicate'. This last detail is highly doubtful, as the first recruitments for the Australian Expeditionary Force started in August 1914 – six days after the United Kingdom declared war on Germany; two months after Ellis left Australia. Olik adds that 'after special treatment his health improved so much' Ellis managed to convince the British he had the right stuff for battle.

'My regiment went to France late in 1915,' Ellis wrote in a letter to some Australian friends, 'and I followed with reinforcements shortly afterwards.'[3]

Ellis's service record from the National Archives says he entered the actual 'theatre of war' on 19 October 1916 in France, where he fought in the First Battle of the Somme commanded by Douglas Haig (which ended on 13 November 1916), got promoted to lance corporal (second-in-command of a section), was repeatedly maimed and, according to Hyde, while serving on the Front 'his favourite cousin and many of his comrades were killed'.[4] (Forty years later Ellis was awarded a Battles of the Somme Commemorative Medal by France's Ceux de la Somme Association.)

Of Ellis's specific physical injuries (the mental scars would become apparent later),[5] nothing is known but at a 'line [northeast] of Albert', a commune in the Somme behind British lines where the first weeks of the battle had been fought that July, 'he was wounded while on a raid' and before Christmas that year 'came out of [the] line and [was] sent on [a] refresher course'.

Soon he was 'back in [the] line near Ypres' in Belgium, 100 kilometres from the town of Albert, 'where he was badly wounded' and taken to convalesce in a British hospital, released and wounded again on the Front. Out of this pain – and stoicism – came Ellis's first exposure to the world of intelligence and the Russian and French languages.

'[I] served [on the Western Front] until the Somme battle finished, when I was given a commission and returned to England to work at the War Office and on censorship work in London and the Midlands. My department was in connection with Russian affairs, and the interesting character of the work induced me to take up the language. I worked at this in London and Paris for 13 months.'[6]

During this period – precise dates are elusive – Ellis was sent to an Officers Training Unit at Gailes Camp, near Troon, Scotland, whence-forth he joined the 4th Battalion Middlesex Regiment and 'received his first pip – a subaltern' (junior officer/lieutenant) in September 1917; one rung below the rank of captain, which he also attained before long. Soon Ellis was back in hospital, this time in the south of France, after being injured at Etaples, a coastal port town in northern France: it had become infamous for its mutiny of British, Australian and New Zealand soldiers in the course of September 1917.

Circa late 1917 and early 1918 Ellis left France, travelling with a brigade to Italy, escorting a group of 'sappers' (military engineers) to Alexandria in Egypt. From the Middle East he voyaged east with injured soldiers to Bombay (Mumbai), Maharashtra, India. There he attended a 'mountain warfare course' in Nasik (Nashik), a city north-east of Bombay; was stationed briefly in Lucknow, 1000 kilometres away in Uttar Pradesh; and was then sent to a British Army garrison, the South Lancashire Regiment 1st Battalion, in Quetta in Balochistan (Baluchistan), now modern-day Pakistan, near the border with Afghanistan.[7]

'Apart from minor brushes with Marri tribesmen along the Afghan frontier, this was garrison soldiering,' he wrote, meaning he was confined to his garrison and didn't see conflict. Largely idle as a result, Ellis used his free time and allayed his boredom by studying Farsi (Persian) and the local language, Urdu, while honing his command of Russian. The self-reliance he'd learned as a child had never left him, even in this most foreign of environments.

He continued: 'Early in 1918 there were rumours of operations against gun-runners and raiders in Seistan in south-east Persia. A short period of service in that desolate and forbidding area was followed by staff duties in the course of which my attention was drawn to developments in Russian Turkistan and the Caucasus arising from the collapse of the Russian armies in north-west Persia and along the Turkish frontier of Transcaucasia.'[8]

Positively itching for action and adventure, and by then fully recovered from his injuries on the Western Front, Ellis duly volunteered to join the British Army's Intelligence Corps (its intelligence-gathering department) in Persia and Transcaspia.

'A British Political Mission, which had been working in [North] Persia for some few months, was sent up to Transcaspia,' Ellis wrote to friends back home in Australia. 'I had just passed the Army exam, in Russian and French, and was at once given staff grade and sent up through Persia to Russia.'[9]

The geopolitical landscape was changing dramatically. On 7 November 1917 the Bolsheviks had stormed the Winter Palace, Vladimir Lenin then seizing power in Russia. Anti-communist émigrés, or 'White Russians', and 'Mensheviks', or non-Leninist socialists, subsequently formed locally in opposition to the 'Reds', leaving the region in chaos, civil war and open to predations by German and Turkish forces. In July 1918, the month Tsar Nicholas II and his family were slain in Yekaterinburg, Ellis fronted up in Meshed (now known as Mashhad), the second biggest city in Persia.

Wrote H. Montgomery Hyde in *Secret Intelligence Agent*: 'Following the developments in Russian Turkestan and the Caucasus owing to the collapse of the Tsarist armies in that region, the British planned to send a military mission to Meshed in north-east Persia to co-operate with the White Russians and other anti-Bolshevik elements such as the Mensheviks. Ellis volunteered to serve with the mission.'

His focus was Turkestan (also spelled Turkistan) in Central Asia,[10] which Ellis described as a 'great tract of country north of Persia and Afghanistan, stretching in the North towards Russia proper, and bounded on the East and West by the Pamirs and the Caspian Sea'. Turkestan, home to various discrete Turkic peoples, had some big-hitting neighbours: Russia, Persia, Afghanistan, British India, Tibet and China. It was divided up into Russian Turkestan and Afghan (or Southern) Turkestan in the west and Eastern (or Chinese) Turkestan.

Within Russian Turkestan, the city of Ashkhabad (now Ashgabat) in Transcaspia (Turkmenistan) was the home of the Menshevik-backed Transcaspian government. Turkmenistan even today is one of the least visited countries on Earth. It must have seemed like another planet in 1918.

It was also a time of much turbulence. The aftershocks of the Great Game were still reverberating in the region. As Ellis himself explained: 'After the Russo-Japanese war, which obliged Russia to change her foreign policy entirely, an agreement was arrived at between England and Russia, which divided Persia up into spheres of influence, Russia controlling the North, and England the South. This was signed in 1907, and Russia lost no time in turning her "influence" into absolute control, as the events in Teheran [Tehran] in 1908 testify.[11]

'In the meantime Russian rule in Turkistan and in the Transcaspian province had prospered. A railway had been built between Krasnovodsk on the Caspian Sea and Tashkent, the capital of Turkistan proper, and a large number of Russians, Armenians and Persians settled in the country. The Russians are excellent colonists, and build well. Askhabad [sic], Merv and Bairam Ali [all in Transcaspia] quickly grew into large towns. In the first two a garrison of nearly 10,000 troops was stationed, and great military depots created.'

The original campaign to thwart German and Turkish incursions in Central Asia and India was two-pronged: Major General Lionel Dunsterville's 'Dunsterforce' led a British Indian Army brigade in Baku, capital of the newly formed and oil-rich Azerbaijan, and Major General Wilfrid Malleson, assistant quartermaster-general for intelligence, focused on the area from Meshed in Persia to Merv in Transcaspia: a distance of about 400 kilometres. Ellis was appointed one of Malleson's three staff officers, or captains, accompanied by 'a small guard of Indian cavalry'.

But Malleson's primary aim switched to preventing the Bolsheviks from taking over the railway Ellis had described: the Trans-Caspian Railway, or Central Asian Railway, which roughly followed the route of the old Silk Road from Samarkand (now part of Uzbekistan) west to Krasnovodsk (now Türkmenbaşy) in Transcaspia.[12]

'The mission's first task in Meshed,' wrote Hyde, 'was to open negotiations with the dissident group of Mensheviks, which had set up a government at Ashkhabad on the Central Asian Railway and was consequently in a position to block communications by that route with the Bolsheviks in Samarkand and Tashkent [both now part of Uzbekistan].'

By September 1918, however, things hadn't quite gone to plan. On the 15th of that month, Baku fell to the Turks and Dunsterville retreated to Enzeli (now Bandar-e Anzali) on Persia's Caspian Sea coast and Krasnovodsk, the terminus of the Trans-Caspian Railway.[13] Five days later, on the 20th, an event occurred that would dog Ellis for the rest of his life.

A young Joseph Stalin called it 'the savage murder of responsible officials of Soviet power in Baku by the British imperialists . . . savages'.

H. Montgomery Hyde, with typical understatement, would call it an 'unhappy incident'.

Either way, 26 people were dead and someone was to blame.

CHAPTER 4

STALIN AND THE KING'S MESSENGER

'Sowing suspicion is the classic KGB tactic. They've got a name
for it, *dezinformatsiya*, and a department to direct it.'
– DICK ELLIS, QUOTED BY WILLIAM STEVENSON,
INTREPID'S LAST CASE (1983)

THE MASSACRE TOOK PLACE, according to Paris-based author and academic Taline Ter Minassian, on 20 September 1918 'at the 207th *verst* of the Transcaspian line to Ashkebad [sic], between the stations at Pereval and Asha-Kuyma'.[1] The victims were a group of Bolshevik prisoners – 26 commissars (or political officers of the Soviet Communist Party) – who'd been arrested on the 17th of that month after the fall of Baku while attempting to flee by boat to Russia. They were accused of plotting against the local anti-communist government, then, as Ter Minassian describes, taken out into the desert by train and shot dead in cold blood by a railway line near Krasnovodsk.

The Bolsheviks accused the British of being the culprits, though they had little to do with the killings: the real perpetrators were Mensheviks based in Ashkhabad and Krasnovodsk.[2] This didn't stop the Reds turning it into a legend 'raised to epic rank by a voluminous and unanimous Soviet historiography'. In the process, Dick Ellis was named: thus was born his wildly inflated legend.

In *Intrepid's Last Case*, William Stevenson overplays it a touch: 'Ellis had been a personal enemy of Stalin . . . engaged in a secret war with Stalin.' He even went so far as to say Ellis's espionage activities 'during the Russian Revolution had earned him Stalin's personal hatred as a British spy fomenting "counter-revolutionary forces"'.

There is absolutely zero evidence for this absurd statement and in all his writings Ellis never disclosed any personal beef with the future Soviet dictator. Stalin did write about the desert executions in April 1919 in the Bolshevik newspaper *Izvestiya*, and was nothing if not colourful in his depiction of the event: 'It must be taken as proven that our Baku comrades, who had quitted [sic] the political arena voluntarily and were on their way to [the Russian city of] Petrovsk as evacuees, actually were shot without trial by the cannibals from "civilised" and "humane" Britain . . . only imperialist cannibals who are corrupt to the core and devoid of all moral integrity need to resort to murder by night.'

Critically, too, Stalin never once publicly mentioned Ellis by name. This hasn't stopped various spy writers parroting the same nonsense as Stevenson, the basis of which is a painting by Isaak Brodsky, 'The Execution of the Twenty-Six Baku Commissars', which became a Soviet propaganda tool before and during the Cold War.

Five British officers appear in Brodsky's painting, none of whom resemble Ellis, yet Stevenson boldly states in his book of the same artwork, 'a Soviet painting showed Ellis helping to direct the shooting party'. In 1932 a Russian film was made about the massacre by Nikolaï Chenguelaïa, *Twenty-Six Commissars*. A Soviet monument to the commissars commissioned in 1923 by Stalin was demolished in 2009.

In 1961 H. Montgomery Hyde – a former British secret agent, barrister, Member of Parliament, and at the time a professor in the Department of History at the University of the Punjab in Lahore, Pakistan – wrote a letter to *The Times* in London: 'While on a recent visit to Soviet Central Asia I happened to be in the State Museum in Samarkand, where I could not help noticing a huge painting by the Soviet artist I. I. Brodsky depicting in graphic detail the shooting of the commissars. In the foreground, immediately behind the firing party, I could see the figure of a British Army officer looking on, if not actually directing the operation. It may well have been intended for Colonel Ellis himself, who was known by the Bolshevik authorities to be in Transcaspia at the time.'[3]

Hyde repeated the story, with a slight variation, in his 1982 autobiography, *Secret Intelligence Agent*: 'Two British officers were looking on, if not actually directing the executions, and one of them bore a striking resemblance to Ellis, who was known by the Bolsheviks to be operating in Transcaspia at the time.'

The normally dependable Phillip Knightley even added to the fiction: 'Ellis was present at the execution and Stalin accused him of having organised it. Although Ellis denied this charge, the Stalin version has become part of official Soviet history and Soviet reference books to this day blame Ellis for the massacre.'[4]

Knightley, however, never actually named which 'Soviet reference books' mentioned Ellis. The truth is that a fellow British officer, Reginald Teague-Jones, was blamed by the Russians – not Ellis. Historian and Great Game expert the late Peter Hopkirk quoted Leon Trotsky in his 1922 work *Mezhdu Imperializmom i Revoiutsiei* (English title: *Between Red and White*) as calling out Teague-Jones by name as the 'direct practical organiser' of the massacre. Teague-Jones, who like Ellis wasn't present at the massacre but rightly feared assassination, promptly went into hiding and changed his name to Ronald Sinclair. To all intents and purposes, he vanished from the face of the earth. In reality, he ended up in Miami, Florida, and died in Plymouth, England, in 1988.[5]

Hopkirk, who by then had visited Azerbaijan, wrote in Teague-Jones's obituary that he 'was officially assured . . . [Teague-Jones was] singled out as [the] principal villain'.[6] This was echoed by Teague-Jones's biographer Ter Minassian, who said Stalin had mentioned Teague-Jones – again, not Ellis – by name: 'Teague-Jones, cast as the central figure in the inquiry mounted by the Soviet authorities, was demonised by propaganda as the principal culprit, incarnating all the misdeeds of British imperialism' yet 'no British authority, nor Teague-Jones himself, had been involved in the tragedy of the 26 Commissars, an affair which had been exclusively Russian from the outset.'

The British historian Antony Beevor disagrees, claiming Teague-Jones was given advance warning the previous day: 'He almost certainly could have stopped the executions if he had insisted.'

*

Russian-speaking Teague-Jones, a good friend of Ellis's who would also marry a Russian, and whose diary was posthumously turned into the book *The Spy Who Disappeared,* was working as a spy or, as he called himself, British 'political representative' in Transcaspia.

On 24 November 1918, less than two weeks after the armistice of 11 November that brought World War I to an end, Teague-Jones wrote about Ellis in his diary – one of the few printed mentions of the globe-trotting Australian at this most formative juncture in his life – calling him and a fellow officer, Captain Sydney Jarvis, 'cheery' individuals whose 'presence acted on me like a tonic'.

'It is two years since I have seen a play or any kind of show,' Ellis wrote in a letter from Transcaspia to two sisters he knew who worked in dancehalls in Sydney, 'excepting a music-hall in Bombay and a couple of badly performed Russian operas at Tiflis [Tbilisi] in the Caucasus. The only amusement here is revolution, occasional scraps, and a certain amount of game shooting in the hills. We get very little time for the latter on account of the frequency of the former.' But, he said, it was altogether 'interesting work, [which] has taken me all over South Russia, the Caucasus and Turkistan. We have had a good deal of fighting against Bolsheviks and odd tribes on the frontier.'[7]

*

In retirement, and soon after the death of Stalin, what Ellis did was write a thorough, big-picture but exceedingly dry book about British military activities in Transcaspia: *The Transcaspian Episode, 1918–1919.* Ter Minassian – in her biography of Teague-Jones, *Most Secret Agent of Empire* – noted 'the light it sheds on [Ellis's] political even-handedness'. Yet, as with most of Ellis's published writings, he conspicuously failed to write anything much about himself. His descriptions of the local people of Ashkhabad are vivid and colourful: a snapshot of a lost world.[8]

Russian historian Ian Grey wrote that in *The Transcaspian Episode* Ellis gave an 'authoritative and fascinating account of the Malleson mission . . . the most acceptable account of the shooting of the 26 Bolshevik commissars in Ashkhabad in September 1918, which Soviet propaganda has magnified as a British atrocity'.[9]

Ellis denied categorically any involvement in the incident: 'No British officer was in the vicinity, nor was any British officer or official aware of what was happening to the prisoners'. Teague-Jones, he added, 'was, in fact, in Ashkhabad, several hundred miles away'.

In 1979 Teague-Jones said this himself, writing to Russia historian Brian Pearce, 'the British authorities, including myself, had no part whatever [sic] in or connected with the tragedy of the 26 . . . on the contrary, they made every possible effort to avert it'.

But out of the association between Ellis and Teague-Jones around the time of this atrocity, writes Ter Minassian in *Most Secret Agent of Empire*, the pair forged an enduring bond. Ellis 'occupied a special place' in Teague-Jones's life.[10]

'The friendship was made in 1918 in the area between Ashkhabad and Meshed, where Malleson's mission, to which Ellis was directly answerable, was based. In the sixties, well after the Second World War, when Ellis's book on the Transcaspian episode appeared, the two men were still exchanging letters replete with political and strategic matters relating to Iran and Central Asia . . . as both men were fluent in Russian, they used Russian to write about confidential topics in their letters.'

Hopkirk, too, writes of the pair's 'lifelong' friendship: 'The two men, I learned from Ellis's son [Olik], saw a great deal of one another over many years, suggesting, in that world anyway, a professional bond as well as a social one. But even Ellis's own son, who was himself to become an intelligence officer, never realised who Ronald Sinclair, whom he regarded almost as an uncle, really was. He told me that he was as astonished as anyone when he picked up a copy of *The Spy Who Disappeared* and learned the truth.'[11]

The longstanding friendship of these two former spies is extraordinary in and of itself. It also belies the hypothesis that Ellis was recruited as a double agent for the Soviets. Given that Teague-Jones was a man some old-guard Reds regarded as public enemy number one for his role in the 26 Commissars massacre, had Ellis been loyal to the Soviets he would have given them the location and new identity of Teague-Jones so Soviet assassins could eliminate him – as they did several other operatives, such as Ignace Reiss and Walter Krivitsky.

But Ellis did the exact opposite. Years later, during the Allied intelligence campaign of World War II, he even employed Teague-Jones in New York.

Teague-Jones managed to live to the age of 99, dying in 1988. As Ter Minassian wrote, the incident of the 26 Commissars 'was a matter of anxiety for the rest of [Teague-Jones's] long life. He saw a lot of change: in 1918, as a secret agent, he was an eyewitness to the shattering of the Russian empire and the collapse of the Ottoman empire. He lived long enough to also witness the decline of the British empire.'

Three empires had fallen under Teague-Jones's watch. The fact that Ellis, as a potential Soviet double agent, had so much time and opportunity to betray his friend yet didn't do so speaks for itself. It shows how nonsensical it is to make the case that Ellis ever betrayed Britain or any other Western nation to the Communists. Further, if Ellis really was the man who directed the executions of the 26 Commissars, why would the Soviets have had anything to do with him? They would have shot him on the spot when they had the chance.

There was a good reason Teague-Jones spent his life in hiding under a false identity.

*

As 1919 dawned, with Europe at peace, Ellis remained stationed in Transcaspia. Within months he was taking part in the Anglo-Afghan War (6 May 1919 to 8 August 1919). His extensive military service saw him awarded an Officer of the Most Excellent Order of the British Empire (Military Division) the same year. Malleson had withdrawn his forces from Transcaspia by mid-April 1919 and by 1920 the region was in the hands of the Bolshevik Tashkent Soviet.

'Shortly after [Transcaspia] I returned to North Persia, and was then sent to the Caucasus as military attaché,' he wrote. 'When the Bolsheviks from Tashkent broke through, I went back to Meshed, and stayed there until June, when I managed to obtain leave. It was a narrow squeak getting through to Caucasia, as the Bolsheviks were pouring down towards the Caspian; but after a little difficulty (and a great deal of bribery), I got across to [Batumi].[12]

'Whilst in the South Caucasus, [Major] General [George Norton] Cory, of the General Staff at Constantinople, got hold of me and sent me up on a mission to [Anton] Denikin.[13] I stayed at Ekaterinodar [sic, Yekaterinodar now Krasnodar] and Sevastopol [in Crimea] for nearly a month, and then got away to Constantinople. I arrived [in London] a little over a month ago, and have since then been at the Foreign Office as Liaison Officer and King's Messenger between Paris, Stockholm, and London.'[14]

The Foreign Office oversees the Secret Intelligence Service.

In Sydney's *Sunday Times*, a headline appeared on page 17, the chatty 'Every Woman's Page', on 14 December 1919.

FROM OFFICE CLERK TO KING'S MESSENGER: THE ROMANTIC STORY OF AN AUSTRALIAN BOY'S PROGRESS – STAFF WORK IN RUSSIA

'May and June Henry, the Tivoli twins, are highly delighted with the success of their friend, Captain C. H. Ellis, M.B.E.,' it gushed. The Henrys were twin sisters and vaudeville dancers at the Tivoli Theatre in Castlereagh Street, Sydney. The story went on to detail Ellis's meteoric rise from lowly office clerk at Stott & Hoare's Business College to courier for the King of England. He'd come a long way from Murrumbeena.

In April 1920, Ellis applied for a training grant to study Russian language and literature at St Edmund Hall, or 'Teddy Hall', at the University of Oxford, after which 'I was granted leave to Australia pending demobilisations.'[15] In May, he arrived in Australia on the HMAT *Euripides*, along with other returning imperial troops. By July, still in Australia, his application had been approved (Award No. 20826). Having relinquished his commission as captain, on the 24th of that month Ellis had an article, 'The British in Central Asia', published in Melbourne magazine *Stead's Review* about his time in Transcaspia.

'Captain Ellis, now in Australia on leave, was a member of the British mission to Central Asia, where his knowledge of Russian came in exceedingly useful,' wrote the editor, Henry Stead.[16]

It was evident that even this early in his life – he was just 25 years old – Ellis held some virulently anti-communist views. This is most telling for someone who would later be accused of being a Soviet mole, as Ellis was articulating these views years before he would have any reason to dissemble.

His prose was full of anti-Russian venom – 'a young and particular blood-thirsty specimen of the genus Bolshevik', 'Bolshevik terror in Transcaspia' – hardly the language of a man who was allegedly to become a committed double agent for Stalin and accomplice to Kim Philby.[17]

'However little British intervention in Russia has been justified elsewhere,' Ellis wrote, 'it would seem that here [in Central Asia] it was well warranted. Our good name never stood so high as during those months when a handful of British and Indian troops held the Merv Oases [sic], and never has it been so low as it is now. Bolshevik forces are now free to penetrate Persia and Afghanistan with pernicious pan-Islamism and pseudo-Socialism, and men turn to each other in the bazaars of Meshed, Herat and Bokhara, and talk of broken promises, and how the British were forced to flee before a rabble of Austrian prisoners, Chinese and Kalmuks. Russians, to whom formerly the name of England stood for everything trustworthy and honourable, now turn to the Bolsheviks in despair. And Simla sleeps on, waking with a start sometimes, when the name of Afghanistan is mentioned, and dreaming troubled dreams of a new aggressive Russia pouring her legions through the passes to Peshawar and across the swamps of Seistan.'

*

Later in life, because of his wartime experiences and travels in Egypt, British India, Turkestan, Afghanistan, Persia and Turkey, Ellis became something of a scholar of Islam. In *Intrepid's Last Case*, William Stevenson, borrowing from Ernest Cuneo, wrote: 'Ellis was known as a specialist in the histories of the ancient Persian, Babylonian and Egyptian empires. He had, it was said, an encyclopaedic knowledge of Islam.'[18]

He was also a fan of the work of author, Turkestan independence agitator and alleged traitor Baymirza Hayit (1917–2006) and a great admirer of Imam Shamil or Shamyl (1797–1871), 'the Caucasian patriot who kept the Russians at bay for 30 years . . . a great Moslim [sic] hero, one whose exploits and whose renown perplexes the boys in Moscow a lot as they go hot and cold on him'.[19]

In a letter to H. Montgomery Hyde on 5 November 1960, Ellis – writing from 68 Courtfield Gardens in Kensington, London – talks of a book reviewer, 'Miroshnikov' (probably L. I. Miroshnikov, of the Academy of Sciences, Moscow, author of *British Expansion in Persia*), who 'in typical Soviet fashion . . . quotes out of context and distorts the picture by making dogmatic statements'.

In his book *MI6*, the late Keith Jeffery quotes Ellis appraising one double agent as 'no fool and, like most Russians of his type, played both ends against the middle'. Indeed, James Cotton, who spoke to Jeffery before he died, writes in his Ellis essay footnotes: 'The official historian of MI6 could find no convincing evidence that [Ellis] had been an agent for another power.'

When Nigel West reviewed Jeffery's book, he seemed to take exception to Jeffery's position: 'Ellis . . . was perhaps an even worse traitor [than Philby], making Philby look like a rank amateur. Yet Jeffery, who says that he was allowed to look at Ellis's file, concludes that he was guilty of nothing more than indiscretion and a poor choice of White Russian friends in Paris before the war.'

In summary, then, according to Jeffery, the charges against Ellis could well have had no substance at all. No wonder West was ticked off: his whole case against Ellis had been shown up by MI6's official historian as unpersuasive. If Ellis really had been a spy for the Russians, he'd chosen some odd heroes.

CHAPTER 5

A STRANGER IN A STRANGE LAND

'The world changes so fast nowadays that events in the '20s
and '30s of this century, newly related, seem to belong to
another century. As for the Edwardian period, it might be the
18th-Century Augustan period, and I am sure it seems so to the
post-war generation.'
– LETTER FROM DICK ELLIS TO H. MONTGOMERY HYDE
(26 DECEMBER 1960)

DICK ELLIS LEFT AUSTRALIA, apparently with his brother
Stanley according to shipping records, on 11 August 1920
on the SS *Benalla*, bound for London via South Africa.[1] Writing
from Durban, he told Alfred Brotherston Emden, the principal
of St Edmund Hall, with whom he would continue to correspond:
'I obtained passage on the very first available steamer which was due
to arrive in England in early September.' However, due to 'innumerable delays', Ellis did not arrive in England until 10 October. With no
time to waste, he unloaded his bags at Highams Park then went on
to Oxford, 80 kilometres northwest of London.[2] Where Stanley went
in England is unknown.

Perhaps the trip back home to Victoria had been made so Ellis
could say goodbye to his father for the last time. The day after he'd left
Port Melbourne, 12 August, William Ellis died in Ivanhoe, aged 91;
he had been a widower three times and had fathered five children.
He was buried on the 14th alongside his first wife, Annie, and their

eldest daughter, Annie Lancaster. Their grave can be found at St Kilda Cemetery on Dandenong Road.

The Australian was hardly in the best frame of mind to be a student, later reflecting on his experience that he was 'a somewhat war-scarred and not particularly bright student of Slav languages'. Interestingly Ellis had been economical with the truth when he filled out his paperwork on 13 October for university. While he correctly gave his place of birth as Sydney, Australia, he gave his birth date as 14 February 1895: a day off from the correct date of the 13th. Why he would do that is anyone's guess, but he would continue to do it for the rest of his life. His profession was entered as 'Intelligence Service (Foreign Office)'.

Ellis was admitted for Michaelmas term (October to early December) and matriculated on 14 October 1920.[3] He went into shared digs – at Staircase 4, Room 28 – with fellow Russian-language student A. A. Gordon,[4] but it was a brief stay. In 1921 he was back for Hilary term, but as summer approached and Trinity term drew to a close, so too did Ellis's time at Oxford University. The call of the spy world would prove too irresistible. Besides, Britain's top foreign-intelligence target was communist Russia: there was hot demand for military men who knew the Russian language and were ready to work for King and Country.

That year, 1921 – not 1924 as put forward by Chapman Pincher – is the year Ellis officially joined SIS (MI6).[5] Keith Jeffery, who wrote the official history of MI6 and had access to 'the holy grail of British archives', its top-secret files, confirmed Ellis joined that October and shortly thereafter went out to Turkey (now known as Türkiye). Ellis had even nipped over to New York for reasons unknown in December 1920, presumably intelligence work.[6]

'C. H. Ellis has been absent in Constantinople on Intelligence Service under the Foreign Office,' *St Edmund Hall Magazine* stated in print in 1922. Ellis would never return to complete his degree.[7] There's a photo of Ellis, presumably from his time at Oxford, held by the National Library of Australia, which someone has embellished so Ellis appears to be wearing a monocle. An inscription underneath in Russian translates to 'Anarchist'. He was a university dropout but he had learned what he needed to learn in the field.[8]

In *Secret Intelligence Agent*, H. Montgomery Hyde claimed Ellis 'left without taking a degree in order to continue his language studies at the Sorbonne in Paris' but this is misleading. He had already been recruited (albeit informally) by SIS, evidently before he even got to Oxford. Ellis did go to Paris but it was just a stopover on his journey east. Yet again there are discrepancies in other people's accounts of Ellis's movements around this time. Olik Ellis insisted his father took a 'long vacation' and studied 'French courses at [the] Sorbonne' and that one day he 'received [a] call from [the] War Office from one Col. Shakespeare who offered [Ellis] reinstatement [to rank of captain] on active list for a two-year term of service in [the] Black Sea area.'[9]

By November 1921, Ellis had left St Edmund Hall, on his way to Paris and Constantinople.[10] His London address – between finishing Oxford in June and going abroad that November – had been 5 Gledhow Gardens, South Kensington, a considerable step up from Highams Park. In order to foot the rent, he must have been on a good salary.

In a letter to Brotherston Emden in Oxford, Ellis commented: 'I hoped to be able to return to Oxford for a few days before setting out on my travels but the F.O. [Foreign Office] have kept me so busy that I've hardly had a moment to spare. I have to leave for Paris tonight and I doubt if I shall be able to return to England before going to Constantinople.'

Ellis indicated his return 'should be within six or eight months' and 'when I come back to the Hall, it will be very different to me from when I came up a year ago – a stranger in a strange land and a pretty sick stranger at that!'

*

Why had Ellis been sent to Constantinople, today's Istanbul? Presumably because Ellis, who turned down a consular posting in Mukden (now Shenyang) in Manchuria, China, knew it well from time he spent there during the war, plus it was the biggest major city in Europe close to the region with which he was even more familiar, his area of expertise: Russia and Central Asia.

In the rough timeline Olik Ellis constructed of his father's life, he wrote that Ellis was 'attached to Intelligence Branch working under

Maj. Gen. Sir Charles Harrington [sic] helping out in dealing with the presence of thousands of Russian refugees'.[11] But Constantinople was also, says Keith Jeffery in *MI6*, a critical station in Britain's foreign-intelligence operations because 'there was a real possibility of British forces in the region having to resume active operations' as the Turkish nationalist movement of Kemal Atatürk grew in popularity. The Republic of Turkey was to come into being on 29 October 1923.

Jeffery writes that Ellis, who was reinstated as a captain in the British Army on 21 February 1922, 'became the contact for a number of Russian agents. Long afterwards Ellis reflected on the over-close relationships between SIS's Russian-speaking officers, using their own names, and their Russian agents, and the socialising between both groups which led to a most unprofessional level of interconsciousness.[12] As these individuals spread out over Central and Eastern Europe, the Russian cadre of SIS case-officers and their head agents became far too well known to the White Russian communities, and thus, in turn, to the [Soviet secret police, the] OGPU.'

*

This part of Ellis's career is largely a blank but I uncovered an interesting document dated 8 October 1920 in the National Archives of India regarding SIS operations in Constantinople. At the time Major Valentine Vivian of the Indian Police, special intelligence officer, future deputy head of MI6, led operations in Turkey. Under him was Ellis's friend from Transcaspia, section officer Major Reginald Teague-Jones, also of the Indian Police, on a one-year contract – he was responsible for 'Caucasus and Trans-Caspia' – and a Mr Gibson, appointed by SIS in London, who was detailed with 'Local Russian Intelligence, Southern Russia, etc.'[13]

'Between them,' wrote Vivian, 'they control Russian, Caucasian, Trans-Caspian and Central Asiatic sources of information.'

There were also separate SIS branches for local Turkish intelligence, 'Pan-Islamic' intelligence ('Muhammadan relations with Bolshevism, etc') and 'Egypt and the Arab-speaking countries'.[14] It was quite the nascent spying operation and Ellis was welcomed with open arms.[15] Vivian was also on the lookout to hire a personal assistant, 'any regular officer found suitable to all parties concerned'.[16] Vivian and Teague-Jones wrapped up their appointments in May 1922.[17]

It's tempting to think Ellis could have become Vivian's assistant but the official cover for Ellis's spying activities was working for the British High Commission. He lived in 'a fine house' in Pera (Beyoğlu), the expat quarter, and by his second year in Turkey had a live-in girlfriend, a Ukrainian teenager called Lilia (Elizabeth or Elisabeth) Zelensky,[18] whom he originally met while in Paris. In Peter Wright's *Spycatcher*, he claims Ellis 'joined MI6 in the 1920s, and was based in Paris, where he was responsible for recruiting agents in the White Russian émigré community . . . a cesspool of uncertain loyalties'. This may or may not be true: his studies at the Sorbonne could well have been a cover for his espionage, but Ellis couldn't have been in Paris for long.

Lilia was from a White Russian (anti-Bolshevik) family: father Nikolai (Nicolas) Guermanovitch Zelensky, mother Aleksandra (Alexandra) Sakhnovitch, sister Elena (Nelly) and brother Aleksei (Alexander).[19] They were of aristocratic stock: Elizabeth's grandmother was Baroness Elena Nikolaevna von Holmann.

On 12 April 1923, the relationship was formalised: Ellis married Lilia, then only 17, at the British consulate in Constantinople.

*

In *MI6*, Keith Jeffery writes that Ellis was called from Constantinople to go to Berlin in October 1923 to 'work under [Berlin SIS station chief Frank] Foley on the Soviet target' and 'where he was given a list of Russian agents to run and was himself approached by several White Russians who had heard of his transfer from friends in Turkey. Provided with little specific briefing or preliminary training – a typical experience for the time – Ellis was largely left to fend for himself and learn on the job.

'Afterwards he complained that desk officers at Head Office, who had no agent-running experience and seldom visited stations, knew very little about the realities of work in the field and frequently nursed unrealistic expectations of what could be achieved.'

Ellis's cover job in Germany, as it had been in Turkey, was working for the British government: this time as a passport control officer (PCO), acting vice-consul/vice-consul at the British Passport Control Office.[20] It was a typical dummy position for British agents in the field, and not particularly well paid, because SIS didn't directly pay their salaries.

'PCO salaries were paid out of visa fees, and not out of the dwindling SIS budget,' wrote Philip H. J. Davies in *MI6 and the Machinery of Spying: Structure and Process in Britain's Secret Intelligence*. 'This meant that the SIS had to recruit mainly from former servicemen who already had a basic military pension.'

Worse, it was obvious what the British were up to, argued R. G. Grant in *MI5 MI6: Britain's Security and Secret Intelligence Services*: 'The PCO cover was a thin disguise. Hostile intelligence services could identify all the MI6 station heads once they had penetrated this one transparent stratagem.'

In 1924 Ellis and Lilia would have a son, Olik (variously given as Oleg and Olick, or anglicised as Peter or Pete) in Berlin and they stayed in Berlin until 1926, when Ellis was transferred to Vienna, working under MI6 station chief Thomas Kendrick, but remained largely based in Berlin. In Vienna, says Kendrick's biographer Helen Fry in *Spymaster: The Man Who Saved MI6*, Ellis 'worked on German and Russian targets for Kendrick' and was busy 'penetrating White Russian circles'.

By then Ellis had a new cover – as a foreign correspondent for London's *Morning Post* (he'd become a member of the British Chamber of Commerce at Kärntnerstrasse 41,[21] his ID card issued 8 May 1927). According to Nigel West in *MI6: British Secret Intelligence Service Operations, 1909–45*, Ellis 'remained on Foley's staff for the following 14 years, although he undertook missions all over Europe during this period'.[22]

In *Intrepid's Last Case* William Stevenson observed that Ellis, while operating as an agent in Turkey, Germany and France, witnessed first-hand 'the growth of an unholy alliance between defeated German generals and the infant Soviet Union, a strange realm of whirling political fogs and shifting loyalties'.

Working out who was working for whom and who was taking money from whom in exchange for information would have tested even the most well-briefed intelligence agent. But Ellis was nothing if not self-sufficient. Despite having been left largely to his own devices, without the resources to do his job properly and on poor remuneration in cover positions his enemies could detect a mile off, he got on with things. As he had done when mastering each of his foreign tongues, Ellis was adapting in the field.

*

In 1927 Ellis was spending much time at his Geneva residence, 6 Quai des Eaux-Vives, where he was a 'sometime press correspondent for [the] League of Nations secretariat', the progenitor of the modern-day United Nations. He began finessing his first book, 1928's *The Origin, Structure and Working of the League of Nations*, a work three years in the making.

H. Montgomery Hyde in *Secret Intelligence Agent* says Ellis 'frequently [visited] Geneva, where he covered the League of Nations Assembly meetings and conferences, including the abortive conference on naval disarmament in 1927'.

But Ellis's real mission continued to be espionage, according to Russian double agent Aleksandr Nelidov (not to be confused with the Russian diplomat of the same name who died in 1910). He claimed under NKVD interrogation to have replaced Ellis at the Berlin station: '[Captain D. O. 'Charles'] Seymour had sent [Ellis] to Geneva, where he was attached to the League of Nations in order to target Comintern [Communist International] agents in Europe.'

Nelidov was involved in the selling of forged documents in Berlin in the early 1930s and connected to Aleksei Zelensky.[23] He'd worked with the British in Constantinople in 1921, would end up being arrested by the Soviets in 1940 and committed suicide in 1942.

In the 2009 book *TRIPLEX: Secrets from the Cambridge Spies*, editors Nigel West and Oleg Tsarev describe Nelidov as 'a skilled agent handler for SIS' and 'a long-term SIS source who was probably betrayed by Anthony Blunt'. The official MI6 history by Keith Jeffery dismisses Nelidov as a 'dubious White Russian character' and a 'purveyor of faked intelligence'.

They're quite opposing characterisations. Either way, a confession was extracted from Nelidov before his death. Published in *TRIPLEX*, it gives a valuable insight into the kind of high-stakes game of intelligence horse-trading Ellis had become involved with and which would soon land him in so much trouble.

'I went from Constantinople to Berlin in order to replace Captain Ellis, who was transferred to Switzerland for work with the League of Nations. I was told from London that Soviet intelligence in Berlin was very strong and that I had to try and penetrate it . . . after I had arrived in Berlin and taken over from Captain Ellis, I realised that there was no material at all that might be used to interest Soviet intelligence . . .

'Captain Ellis's work was not at all difficult. His main job had been to collect material about the Soviet Union from German sources in exchange for British information or for payments. His secondary task was to keep an eye on Indian students in Germany, for which he relied exclusively on the evidence of the German police. Ellis had established connections.'

Nelidov makes it as plain as day: Ellis's job at MI6 was to gather intelligence on the Soviet Union from his German sources in *exchange for British information or for payments*. In other words, whatever Ellis was doing was being done with the knowledge of a higher authority and he was given a budget to do so.

CHAPTER 6

THE LEAGUE OF GENTLEMEN

'In all cases espionage is illegal and the clandestine services'
job is to break those laws without being caught. Espionage is
deceptive, covert, underhand. It is probably the second oldest
profession in the world.'
– ROBERT MARSDEN HOPE AKA JUSTICE HOPE (1981)

COULD DICK ELLIS'S COVER in Geneva – as a journalist for the
Morning Post – and Kim Philby's cover before World War II, also
as a journalist, have come from the same spy playbook?

As Phillip Knightley wrote in *Philby: KGB Masterspy*, Philby's job
as a war correspondent in Spain was 'part of Philby's plan to construct
a right-wing façade to hide his earlier, public, socialist stance'. Philby
joined MI6 in 1940, having secretly worked for Soviet intelligence for
six years to that point.

Yes, the *Morning Post* was a conservative London newspaper; it
would be merged with the *Telegraph* in 1937. But unlike Philby, Ellis
had not only worked *against* Soviet agents in the field but had been
expressing unambiguously anti-Bolshevik sentiments since the Great
War. *Origin*, a work of 528 pages – it was to have been the first of
three volumes, but numbers two and three never happened – continued
in that vein. Ellis wrote it while Philby was still in public school. In the
book Ellis talked of the Bolsheviks' 'militant and destructive communism rightly feared by its neighbours' and, in totality, the work was
nothing short of a plea for an end to war and an era of lasting peace,

41

not socialist revolution or armed struggle. An impressive if also impenetrable work for the ages, well ahead of its time.[1]

'To anyone who reflects it becomes fairly clear that peace is not to be had by aiming at it directly, by conceiving of it as merely the absence of war,' wrote Ellis. 'War is a hideous and self-destructive attempt to do things that we will have to do by other and civilised means. War is the terrible symptom of evils which we must tackle. War is an institution that has outlived whatever usefulness it may have had and become an evil so deadly as to menace the very existence of civilised society; it must be replaced by other institutions. War is a vast breakdown, a consequence of the failure to adjust society to the realities in which we have our being. We must make the adjustment – we must make a world society morally and politically, for we are already living in a world society materially.'

Ellis really put in the work as a writer: he was no casual observer of events. C. Delisle Burns in the *International Journal of Ethics* was impressed by this 'journalist in Geneva' and wrote that Ellis 'has been in close and continuous contact with the Secretariat and has attended all the chief League meetings'.[2] Burns praised *Origin* as 'an important book, not merely because it is the only adequate record of the working of the League system, but also because it includes criticism of the moral practices and theories on which war and peace depend'.

Other reviews were similarly laudatory.

Saturday Review: 'This book is undoubtedly the nearest approach to a perfect text book [sic] for the more serious student that has been produced . . . undoubtedly the fullest account of the origin, composition and working of that body that has ever appeared in print.'

New Statesman: 'It is such a mine of useful information that the present reviewer is tempted to recommend it to the exclusion of all others on the subject of international relations.'

The Economist enthused that the book was an 'important publication . . . well documented, the nature of the subject has obliged the author to rely for much of his matter upon observation and personal contacts, and this method adds vividness to his narrative'. In a longer, separate review it called the book 'exhaustive . . . Mr Howard-Ellis [sic] is a dispassionate and discerning critic, a profound believer in the

League in theory, and a convinced admirer of the League in practice, but at the same time fully conscious of its weaknesses, and always alive to the dangers besetting it.'

Only barrister Wyndham Anstis Bewes, in the *Journal of the Royal Institute of International Affairs*, demurred. Appearing to appraise Ellis as an upstart colonial, he said the book was 'defective' but was a 'good work . . . it is unfortunately necessary to draw attention to the tendency of the author to make depreciatory and often insulting remarks about public men and institutions, which certainly cheapens his book . . . still, I shall retain the volume in my library, and expect to consult it.'

*

In 1930, when Ellis turned 35, he had been an agent of SIS for nearly ten years – in Constantinople, Berlin, Vienna and Geneva. He was well established in his cover as a journalist for the *Morning Post*. Prematurely grey, Ellis was 'a small man, slender, wiry, blond, keen-eyed and fine-boned' with 'graceful movement of his hands'.

This unlikely yet striking figure was no Jason Bourne but he was well on the way to becoming one of the most important and useful agents Britain had working on the Continent. As an Australian, Ellis was an outsider to the British class system and Establishment, a man of 'maverick ways . . . the very model of eccentric creativity essential to any successful intelligence service'. He also 'worked alone in the field, dealing with agents from both sides [Nazi and Soviet] and reporting back to London'.

In *Intrepid's Last Case* William Stevenson contends that Ellis felt his role was to be a point man for both these sides, with Moscow in particular keenly interested in 'whatever he might disclose about British ambitions in Central Asia'.

Early in 1930 Ellis spent time in Australia and New Zealand (according to intelligence historian Christopher Andrew, he visited Canberra 'to reorganise the SIS network in the Far East') and by June he had departed on the RMS *Makura* for Liverpool via San Francisco. Well versed in the art of subterfuge (or a victim of cultural cringe), he was giving his nationality as English on travel documents, and his place of birth as England.

'They're very good at duchessing you, the British Establishment,' said Ellis. 'You're duchessed when you get bowled over by invitations to take tea with a duchess – or a duke, baron, bishop or king. You've entered the magic circle, and after that you're frightened to say something that shows you don't belong inside the circle.'

While Ellis's career was going well, the same could not be said of his marriage and in 1931 he and Lilia divorced. Olik was just six or seven years old. Ellis wasted little time getting married again and exchanged vows with the 160cm-tall 21-year-old Barbara Mary Burgess-Smith on 19 April 1933 at St Peter's Parish Church, in Cranley Gardens, London. The couple had a daughter, Ann, the following year in Steyning, West Sussex. His brief first marriage, however, would haunt him the rest of his days.

*

Where exactly Ellis lived in the 1930s is a matter of conjecture and debate: Berlin, Paris, London. It might seem trivial but it's important because of the accusations of collaboration with the Nazis levelled against Ellis after his death and the role Paris plays in his alleged confession.

According to his good friend and fellow Australian Alban M. (A. M.) 'Bill' Ross-Smith, Ellis spent all of the 1930s right up to the war living in London. There are references in Australian archives that he holidayed or was afield at various points in the French Riviera and the Kiel Canal, Germany. Smith maintained that Ellis 'never lived or worked in Paris from 1921 to 1940'. He also specified that Ellis lived in Berlin from 1923 to 1926, Vienna from 1926 to 1927, Geneva from 1927 to 1930, and London from 1930 to 1938, and was not in Paris or Berlin for the times claimed by Nigel West, Peter Wright and Chapman Pincher in their respective 1980s books, all of which accused Ellis of being a traitor.[3] The timeline of his father's life put together by Olik Ellis – held by the National Library of Australia – reads, '1931 to 1939 based in UK engaged in journalism and associated with SIS'.

There is some evidence to suggest this is correct. In 1932 Ellis was attending meetings of the Royal Geographical Society in London.[4] (He was made a fellow that year, resigned in 1937, got reelected in 1957 and resigned again in 1960.)[5] He divorced his first wife and married his second wife in London. He had known addresses in Kensington – 11 Durward House, 31 Kensington Court; 39 Roland Gardens; 54 Wynnstay Gardens – and was sending his son, Olik, to a school in Winchester, England. Ellis had hopes of sending Olik to King's School (in Canterbury) and St Edmund Hall. But, intriguingly, Ellis's Geneva address was supplied in the 1933 and 1934 editions of *Who's Who in Literature*.

In 1937 Ellis wrote to Alfred Brotherston Emden at Oxford regarding Olik: 'The time has now come to consider the education of my own boy. [Olik] is now 13 and is at West Hayes, a small prep school at Winchester.'

Ellis spoke of Olik being abroad with him on his travels and because of this 'he came late to English schooling and even to the language. For this reason he is a little backward (though not unintelligent) and has not been doing as well at West Hayes as I could wish. He knows French and Russian well' but has 'shortcomings', namely, 'mainly the knowledge of facts – he is quite erudite on continental affairs, but somewhat hazy about English kings and the exact geographical situation of say, Manchester'.

It would have been tough being Ellis's kid.

Furthermore, in MI6's official history, Keith Jeffery mentions an agent in Italy, unnamed, who was a 'high-status Baltic German with social connections across Europe, who was run from London by Dick Ellis and whom [SIS's political section head Major Malcolm] Woollcombe described as "first class", though with "limitations" as he could not be "a permanent agent for German information".'

From London. All this would indicate Bill Ross-Smith was right: Ellis *was* based in England. An 18 May 1984 letter from Antony D. Cliff, a friend of Ellis and his first wife, to Chapman Pincher also states: '[Ellis] was a frequent visitor to our house in London up to 1938.' But the prevailing Ellis narratives in spy lore (as written by Hyde, West, Wright, Pincher, et al.) have Ellis either living in Paris or Berlin during this time and running his vast networks of White Russian spies from the Continent.

Nigel West even suggests in his book *MI6: British Secret Intelligence Service Operations, 1909–45* that Aleksei Zelensky, who was born in 1913, introduced Ellis to the head of MI6 in Paris in 1924: 'Ellis was an Australian who had been recruited as an SIS agent in 1924 after he had studied French at the Sorbonne in Paris. His introduction to the Paris Station, then headed by Major T. M. Langton, had been made by his future brother-in-law, Alexander Zelensky, who had many contacts in the White Russian community in the French capital.' He also states that Ellis's 'first [marriage was] in 1923 in Paris'.

This is patently false. For a start, Aleksei would have been 10 or 11 years old in 1924, so he wouldn't have been introducing Ellis to anybody. Ellis only briefly attended classes at the Sorbonne; it was the same pattern he had followed in Melbourne and Oxford. He was in Turkey from 1921–23 and married Lilia in Constantinople. He joined MI6 in Turkey in 1921, not France in 1924.

West goes on: 'Ellis recruited [Lilia's] brother, Alexander, as an agent, and continued to meet him in Paris even after his marriage to Lilia had broken up ... he attempted to cover the traces of his first [marriage], to Lilia Zelensky. In his *Who's Who* entry, Ellis (who wrote it) describes his marriage to Barbara Burgess-Smith as his first.'

This last part, at least, is completely true. Ellis did omit Lilia from his relationship history in *Who's Who*, when he first appeared – in the 1955 edition.[6] Why he would do that is at least intriguing if not damning, yet provides evidence of nothing. It might have just been a bad marriage and Ellis regretted it. There could be a more sinister interpretation, too, especially given the crisis over the defections of Guy Burgess and Donald Maclean to Russia in 1951 and the suspicions over Kim Philby, who was only fully exposed after he defected in 1963.

Ellis omitted Lilia from his biography well before his interrogation in 1965 and would have had ample reason to, given any perceived connection to the Soviet Union could be misconstrued and, in the wrong hands, weaponised to kill his career. Which it was. He also took the step of listing Olik as his son by Barbara, his second wife.

Meanwhile, Phillip Knightley said that from the early 1920s the Australian had been posted to Paris 'using the cover of a journalist' where 'his assignment was to try to expose those members of White Russians [sic] organisations who were really KGB agents . . . as the Nazi menace grew, this network changed its emphasis from Soviet affairs to German ones and by the mid-thirties Ellis had managed to establish a spy link that led right to Hitler.' Knightley even boldly asserts that siblings Lilia and Aleksei Zelensky were the foundation for Ellis's 'espionage network' in Europe. Zelensky's reputed contact, of course, was Vladimir von Petrov, the same Von Petrov who would spark the MI5 investigation into Ellis that would culminate in his interrogation in 1965.[7] William Stevenson wrote in one of his books that Ellis's various covers 'included that of a newspaper correspondent in Europe. Ellis cultivated both White Russian and German contacts.'

There is universal agreement among spy writers about one thing: that Ellis, without a family inheritance and on measly remuneration, was at some point 'hard up' for money and would remain so for the rest of his days.[8] Being short of cash wasn't an uncommon problem for secret-service agents: the Soviets were known to lure British agents with money. John Herbert King is one example.

Writes Philip H. J. Davies in *MI6 and the Machinery of Spying: Structure and Process in Britain's Secret Intelligence*: 'The financial strictures of life as a PCO appear to have resulted in at least one penetration by the German Abwehr, which recruited a cash-strapped Dick Ellis in Berlin as a source.'

Knightley's version of events is that Ellis borrowed money from Aleksei so he could pay for Lilia's convalescence in hospital from an unspecified ailment. Ellis became indebted to his brother-in-law and then, as Knightley tells it, began coughing up information that Aleksei and his contact, T100 or Von Petrov, could sell to the Nazis but which 'the Germans would know anyway'.

'Now the trap snapped shut,' he says, dramatically.

CHAPTER 7

THE SPY FROM SANTIAGO

'The world of secret intelligence is a world apart and, like any
other insulated world, it generates, or can generate, its own
mentality . . . secrecy breeds fantasy, and fantasy, feeding on itself
at a high altitude of self-importance, can breed more fantasy.'
– HUGH TREVOR-ROPER (BARON DACRE OF GLANTON),
SUNDAY TELEGRAPH (1989)

THE SHADY VLADIMIR VON PETROV (aka Waldemar von Petrow),
T100 or agent no. 401, of whom no pictures are known to exist,
had various forged passports – Nicaraguan and Bolivian, among
others – and had come to the attention of British intelligence as early
as 1923.

He claimed he was born Waldemar Federico de Petrov de Alexander in Santiago, Chile, in 1896, spent his early life in Moscow, and
served in the Russian imperial army in World War I. After the death
of his military-general father, he received an inheritance. Von Petrov
lived in Berlin between the wars, which would have put him in Dick
Ellis's viewfinder when the Australian worked as a PCO in the 1920s
or on roving duty as an agent for MI6 in the 1930s.

Von Petrov lived at Villa La Tanzina[1] in central Lugano,
Switzerland, and married a fabulously wealthy older heiress named
Elly Therese Oppenheimer-Hirschhorn (aka Elly Fassnacht or Lydia
Fassnacht) in Lugano in 1947. He left Europe for Chile on 8 March
1952. Four years later, investigators in Santiago interrogated Von

Petrov about Richard Protze's revelations about a 'Captain Ellis'. The transcripts of those 1956 interrogations (in Spanish and English) form most of what is held in Von Petrov's nearly 200-page file at the National Archives in London.

When he'd lived in Berlin in the 1930s, Von Petrov had worked for Japanese intelligence. The Gestapo demanded he submit his reports for the Japanese to them. His Japanese overseers in Berlin would not give Von Petrov permission to do that. In the event, he left for Paris around July 1938 and instead spied for the Japanese there.

In 1953 agent Ronnie Reed at MI5 was told there was 'no record whatsoever' of a Von Petrov family in Santiago and 'the records of the Chilean Ministry of Foreign Affairs contain no information on the grant of a Chilean passport' to Von Petrov; 'there is therefore a strong presumption that PETROV is not a Chilean and that the passports were forged'.

However, my own investigation proved that wasn't the case: there is an American court record of a 'Mrs von Petrow' living in Santiago in the 1950s, serving as a witness in a trial after World War II regarding Swiss property that had been confiscated under the Trading with the Enemy Act.[2] A Von Petrov family *had* lived in Chile.

*

Vladimir von Petrov is critical to the story of Dick Ellis because without him none of the charges that Ellis had been a double agent for the Nazis (and by extension, the Soviets) would have ever stuck. The basis for those charges seems to be Ellis's brother-in-law Aleksei Zelensky's purported association with Von Petrov, of which there is scant mention in Von Petrov's file.

It's unmistakable that Von Petrov's interrogators in Chile were fishing for Von Petrov to spill Ellis's name. At one point, there is a reference to a person called Atle – 'enemigo de Heydrich' ('Heydrich's enemy') in the Spanish transcript of the interrogation. Atle is likely a mistranscription. Right next to Atle is a handwritten '? ELLIS' in ink.[3] It's the only mention of Ellis in the entire file.

Presenting 'Atle' and Heydrich as adversaries is an intriguing if tenuous link to Ellis, however, especially after Walter Schellenberg's statement that Von Petrov, Ellis's source in Berlin, had a direct connection to Heydrich. The latter was assassinated in Prague in 1942 by operatives trained by the Special Operations Executive (SOE). William Stephenson bizarrely took credit for the Heydrich killing – it's laid out in *A Man Called Intrepid* – but it was a claim that was disproven.[4]

*

Something that interested Von Petrov's interrogators in Santiago in 1956 was that the head of the Abwehr's counterintelligence department, Richard Protze, had spoken about the city of Brussels while being interrogated at Fort Blauwkapel in 1946. In what appears to be a ploy to get Von Petrov to say the name 'Ellis', his interrogators accused the Chilean White Russian of buying British secret-service documents in Brussels in 1933. But Ellis's name didn't pass Von Petrov's lips.

'Petrov admitted having visited Brussels in 1932/33 but he denied having bought any documents dealing with the British Secret Service from any Englishman in Brussels, and having sold such a document to the German counterintelligence . . . [Von Petrov] denied having worked for the Germans and Russians.'

What Von Petrov did own up to was working for the Japanese and he said he'd been in Brussels at that time for a sporting tournament. Von Petrov also admitted knowing a White Russian colonel – variously given the name Neporoschny/Neporozhny/Neporozhni – who ran a garage in Berlin and worked for the Americans. Von Petrov occasionally went hare hunting with him; the colonel had died in Germany in 1953.

It's at this point in the interrogation that Von Petrov talks about Ellis's brother-in-law (referred to as Zelenky, Zelenski and even Terenti) and he also makes a clear reference to Ellis, though there is no indication Von Petrov even knew his name.

'Zelenky [sic] was a great friend of Neporozny [sic] . . . I do not know if a relation of his married an Englishman.'

H. Montgomery Hyde in *Secret Intelligence Agent* states that Zelensky was an agent or informer: '[Ellis] recruited his brother-in-law as a British agent, and Zelensky succeeded in providing some useful information for the British SIS.'

This is corroborated in MI5 personal files, which include summaries of German intelligence documents seized after the war.[5] These had belonged to Abwehr agent Helmuth Wehr, a subordinate of Richard Protze, the high-ranking Nazi who while under interrogation had spoken of a 'Captain Ellis' as a German intelligence source. An MI5 summary of one document buried in Wehr's file reads, 'ZILISNKI [sic] is really Alexander SELENSKI [sic] . . . he is in touch with ELLIS', and that Ellis is Zelensky's 'chief' and 'comes from GENEVA and is in the Intelligence Service'.

The relevant Abwehr report is dated 24 October 1931,[6] which would make Aleksei Zelensky about 18 years old. Another MI5 summary of an Abwehr report dated 20 December 1931 refers to 'buying and selling, double-crossing, etc, etc, etc, involving various personalities' and names 'PETROFF' and 'ELLIS'. One dated 17 February 1932 talks of the interception of a letter from Ellis in Geneva 'sealed' with nothing but the letter 'E' and says, 'RW [report writer] has reason to think that this is Ellis, and that SELENSKI's [sic] cables to England are all connected with ELLIS'.

The Helmuth Wehr file makes it plain Aleksei Zelensky was heavily involved in selling forgeries of documents to the Nazis – he's referenced as being a member of 'a gang of forgers'[7] run by Ellis's alleged MI6 replacement in Berlin, Aleksandr Nelidov – and that the Abwehr was well aware of this.[8] The Abwehr was surveilling Zelensky and Ellis. A report dated 23 January 1932 speaks of the Abwehr giving over 'false, valueless material' to Zelensky 'to test him' while a report from Berlin dated 20 February 1932 says, 'SELENSKI has a visitor (RW guesses it to be ELLIS).' Both men were obviously compromised. Zelensky's name appears in a list of identities 'connected with espionage' in Helmuth Wehr's file, from '1932 onwards'. Ellis's name is not among them.[9]

But how much (if at all) was Zelensky working for the Soviets? In *Intrepid's Last Case*, William Stevenson says that Russian intelligence agent and Rote Kapelle (Red Orchestra) Soviet spy network head Leopold Trepper 'had mingled in Paris with the family of Dick Ellis's White Russian wife'. Trepper's allegiances are well documented. Tom Bower writes in his book *Klaus Barbie: Butcher of Lyons* that notorious Lyon Gestapo chief Barbie was 'assigned a delicate mission . . . to kidnap . . . an agent working for Moscow with Leopold Trepper'.

The Zelenskys kept interesting company, for sure, but that is not proof of anything nefarious. Then again, it is noted in Wehr's MI5 personal file that the Germans were monitoring Zelensky not only for his 'cables to England' but for 'KPD-MOSCOW-BERLIN interests'.[10] KPD was the German Communist Party, which was banned upon the Nazis' ascension to power in 1933.

In his interrogation, Vladimir von Petrov colourfully described Zelensky as a 'dancing master' and said he had lessons from him; Von Petrov last saw him '30 years ago' and thought he possibly went to Antwerp in Belgium. Zelensky, he claims, was supposedly a lieutenant in the Russian Army, but no basis is supplied for this statement. (According to Ellis's friend and BSC agent Bill Ross-Smith, Zelensky 'after schooling led a quiet adult life as an industrial chemist in Paris, with no intelligence or political background'. That, however, is contradicted by MI5's files and its captured Abwehr intelligence.)

That was all Von Petrov could tell his interrogators about Ellis's former brother-in-law. It wasn't much to build a case against Ellis.

*

In 1940 Von Petrov's name was mentioned – according to Peter Wright in *Spycatcher* – by Walter Krivitsky during his debriefing by MI5's Jane Archer. Krivitsky, Wright wrote, alleged the Chilean White Russian 'had been an important agent for the Fourth Department, the GRU [*Glavnoye Razvedyvatelnoye Upravleniye* or Soviet Military Intelligence Department], during the prewar period, with good sources in Britain as well as Germany, where he was operating as a double agent for the Germans and the Russians'.

Von Petrov certainly had known connections to some of the most notorious Nazis of World War II: Heinrich Himmler, Reinhard Heydrich, Walter Schellenberg, Ernst Kaltenbrunner. But I discovered some hitherto unknown details about Von Petrov in the file of Carl Marcus aka 'Dictionary', the former personal assistant of Kurt Jahnke of Jahnke Büro, a private spy agency in Germany that did work for the Nazis.

Marcus surrendered to the Allies in 1944, was brought to England for interrogation, and Keith Jeffery in *MI6* says he went on to become 'SIS's most productive human source of the war in German counter-intelligence matters'. Von Petrov freely disclosed his own Jahnke Büro connections but explained that he cultivated those relationships – and even paid bribes to German officers who were also with Jahnke Büro – solely to protect his future wife, who was a 'Swiss Jewess'.

The relevant part of the Marcus file reads as follows: 'PETROFF, who is now furnished with a South American passport, is the son of a Czarist general who migrated to Japan, where [Von Petrov] made many friends in the Japanese Intelligence Service, and from there came to Germany. He was attached to KNOCHEN as technical adviser and was taken by the latter to Paris, still in an advisory capacity. Through PETROFF, whose vast influence Source [sic] conceivably over-rates, it is possible that Amt VI maintains some relation with the Japanese IS. This, says Source [sic], is the only possible exchange mart.'

The picture that emerges is that the shady Von Petrov was working for the British, Japanese, Germans and Russians. He was effectively a *quadruple* agent. The game he was playing and the personalities he was involved with were also extremely dangerous.

The mention of Knochen is somewhat alarming. Helmuth Knochen was another evil Nazi from central casting: Gestapo chief in Paris and aide to *Obergruppenführer* Carl Oberg, 'The Butcher of Paris'.[11] Although both Knochen and Oberg were sentenced to death by the War Crimes Court in 1954, they were released in 1963.[12] In Walter Schellenberg's interrogation, he refers to Von Petrov being 'on a good footing' with Knochen.[13]

Von Petrov was 'JAHNKE's principal agent in Western Europe and ... his main task was the penetration of French government circles. DICTIONARY [Marcus] knows that he controlled a source in the French Admiralty and that he made use of his fiancée [Elly], the daughter of the diamond king, to establish contacts in British circles.'[14]

It appears the British intelligence services had trouble working out exactly who Von Petrov was sleeping with or married to. A letter dated 5 January 1956 from agent Ronnie Reed to MI6 reads: 'We believe [Von Petrov] to be married to, or at any rate living with the wife of Paul HARDT and both PETROV and his wife undoubtedly have information of very considerable counter-espionage interest.'

On 14 June 1950 an MI6 officer reported Carl Marcus had seen a woman called Lydia Hardt 'in the company of PETROFF in Germany before the war. PETROFF was another of the Amt VI agents who, like JAHNKE (and possibly URBAN), seems to have been in Russian service at one time. PETROFF has been reported as having a mistress called Lydia FASSNACHT. It seems likely that Lydia FASSNACHT may be identical with Lydia HARDT.'

An unidentified woman was seen with Von Petrov at Wilhelmstrasse in Berlin and his flat on the corner of Augsburger and Motzstrasse.[15] Were Elly Therese Oppenheimer-Hirschhorn (aka Elly Fassnacht or Lydia Fassnacht, Von Petrov's future wife) and Lydia Hardt the same person, as the MI6 officer surmised, or two different people?

It's of great import because Lydia Hardt was the wife of Hungarian-born OGPU agent Paul Hardt, the alias of Theodore (Teodor) Stepanovich Maly, a man who with other Russian operatives was instrumental in recruiting Kim Philby and the other four members of the 'Cambridge Five' into the service of the Soviet Union.

Maly is characterised in John Costello's book *Mask of Treachery* (1988) as 'one of the most remarkable non-Russian Comintern agents who ever served as undercover Soviet intelligence officers'.[16] Not only was Maly complicit in the 1937 assassination of Ignace Reiss in Lausanne but he was connected to the 'espionage activities' of British communists George Whomack, Albert Williams and Percy Glading, who were jailed under Section 1 of the Official Secrets Act in 1938. Maly left England in June 1937 for Paris, living at 28 Avenue de Friedland, then disappeared into Russia and is presumed to have been executed there in 1938.[17]

Philby never uttered Maly's name, telling Phillip Knightley in *Philby: KGB Masterspy* (1988): 'I was approached by a man who asked me if I would like to join the Russian intelligence service. For operational reasons I don't propose to name this man, but I can say that he was not a Russian although he was working for the Russians.'

So this introduction of Maly and his wife, Lydia, into the Ellis narrative because of Ellis's association with Von Petrov and Von

Petrov's relationship with Lydia does open up an intriguing if remote link to the greatest Russian spy of all: Philby. Could Ellis have had contact with Maly too? It's definitely possible.

The critical issue is this: no one has actual *proof* that Ellis ever met Von Petrov, Hardt or Maly, or that he at any stage directly communicated, let alone *sold*, anything to them at all. The best anyone has been able to come up with against Ellis is verbal testimony from captured Abwehr officers mentioning the name 'Captain Ellis'. It's hardly a smoking gun. Even Ellis's relentless persecutor, Chapman Pincher, concedes there is no evidence of Ellis ever having contact with Von Petrov. Pincher does however document Ellis's personal relationship with former brother-in-law Aleksei Zelensky, who in *Their Trade is Treachery* Pincher describes as an 'intermediary' between Ellis and Von Petrov.

There's really nothing with which to mount a solid case that Ellis was a Russian spy. Counting against the idea that Ellis could have been recruited as a double agent for Moscow, too, is the fact Philby was, in the words of Anthony Cave Brown, a 'terrific snob' and his contemporaries were 'all of exactly the same social grouping and age'. Ellis was nearly 20 years older than Philby, from a completely different background to the 'Cambridge Five', and fought in the trenches in World War I against the Germans when Philby was a toddler. A penniless Australian who'd had to fight for an education, passed himself off as a higher class Englishman to get ahead in his career, and come to loathe Bolshevism and all it stood for while fighting the Communists in the Russian Civil War was not a likely candidate for a Soviet super-mole.

CHAPTER 8

THE GENERAL

'Talking about laws of war is about as sensible as preaching the
chastity of prostitution.'
– DICK ELLIS, *THE ORIGIN, STRUCTURE AND WORKING OF THE
LEAGUE OF NATIONS* (1928)

So VLADIMIR VON PETROV HAD CLEAR LINKS not just to the
Nazis but, it appears, also to the Soviets, through his mysterious
girlfriend/fiancée/wife. Dick Ellis had his own links, knowingly or
unknowingly, to the communists through Von Petrov and also Von
Petrov's powerful associate Anton Vasilyevich Turkul (or Turkhul).

The latter was an alleged prince[1] and former Tsarist major general
described as 'a head of the White Russian émigrés' in David Kahn's
book *Hitler's Spies*. Reputedly 'one of Ellis's key agents', Turkul
was in fact a spy on the Soviets' payroll and double agent for Nazi
Germany.[2] Turkul denied being a traitor ('I have not been, I am not
and I shall never be a Bolshevik agent')[3] but his MI5 file character-
ises him as 'more than a spy; he was an *agent provocateur*'.[4] He's
been called by Mark Aarons and John Loftus, authors of *Unholy
Trinity: The Vatican, the Nazis, and the Swiss Banks*, 'perhaps the
most extraordinary communist double agent – far more valuable than
[Kim] Philby'.

Turkul ran a White Russian resistance group in Paris called the
Russian All-Military Union (ROVS), which had a counterintelligence unit called the Inner Line. 'Both were supported and helped

financially by [head of MI6 Stewart] Menzies', according to Stephen Dorril in *MI6: Fifty Years of Special Operations*. Turkul was also involved with an anti-communist, pro-American kidnapping group backed by ROVS called *Narodnyi Trudovoy Soyuz* (National Labour Council, or NTS), which 'was supported by MI6 ... at its core an anti-Bolshevik organisation'.[5] The problem was that at some point Turkul was corrupted and, in the words of Aarons and Loftus, 'had turned NTS into the most deadly weapon of Soviet espionage ... British intelligence had sold a communist net to the gullible Americans'.

In *The Bedbug*, a biography of Peter Ustinov's father, Jona 'Klop' von Ustinov, Peter Day adds that Turkul 'had been recruited in the 1920s in Paris by Dick Ellis' and 'been suspected of involvement in the kidnap and disappearance of the White Russian leader General [Yevgeny] Miller by agents of the NKVD'. Miller was drugged and spirited back to the Soviet Union in 1937 and executed in 1939. Even though Turkul was eventually the subject of a French expulsion order in 1938 and exiled to Germany, he was considered a valuable source by MI6 and supported financially by the service.[6]

'Paris was then the centre of White Russian hopes of overthrowing the Soviet regime and one of the White Russian leaders was a certain General Turkhul [sic], with whom Von Petrov was friendly,' writes Chapman Pincher in *Their Trade is Treachery*. 'The advantage of this gossip chain to British intelligence in the '30s lay in the fact that Turkhul ... had ingratiated himself with Heinrich Himmler and Alfred Rosenberg, who were both close to Hitler.'

Reichsführer Himmler and *Der Führer* Adolf Hitler need no introduction. After 1941, Rosenberg was *Reichsminister* for the Occupied Eastern Territories, being those lands in Eastern Europe and Russia captured by the German unified armed forces, the Wehrmacht.[7] Serious Nazis then.

'Such a complex chain is typical of the sources on which secret services depend for "raw" intelligence, which then has to be cross-checked at other points. As the Second World War drew near, Ellis used the chain to send back a mass of confidential information about Nazi affairs to his headquarters in London. Unfortunately, much of this intelligence turned out to be faked, and, though Ellis managed to blame his sources, he fell out of favour with his secret service chiefs. Gradually, he rehabilitated himself and was forgiven.'

Presumably the bogus information Ellis passed to MI6 in London was from his brother-in-law, Aleksei Zelensky.

'From this complex web of ties which reached into German, French and, seemingly, Russian intelligence services, Ellis was able to forward to London a mass of information,' writes Stephen Dorril. 'Unfortunately, headquarters was to discover that much of it was faked, produced by the many exile "paper mills" that proliferated in Paris. The majority of these organisations were riddled with double agents working for either the Germans or the Russians or had been discredited by the numerous scandals that surrounded the émigré community. Inevitably, reliance on the émigrés as a source was to lead Ellis into a world of double-dealing and blackmail.'

Even if Ellis had sent through some faked intelligence, the work he was doing in the field was perfectly legitimate – whether in Berlin, Paris, Geneva or London. It's not clear exactly where he was, even to all these spy writers, though London seems the most likely location. In the run-up to World War II, Ellis – along with many other British agents (such as Ian Fleming, of future James Bond fame) – was working for Permanent Under-Secretary of State for Foreign Affairs Robert Vansittart, who, along with Winston Churchill, strongly opposed the appeasement of Hitler.

Vansittart is described by Ben Macintyre in *A Spy Among Friends* as 'the Foreign Office mandarin ... who ran what was, in effect, a private intelligence agency, outside the official orbit of government but with close links to both MI6 and MI5 ... his network of spies gathered copious intelligence on Nazi intentions, with which he tried (and failed) to persuade Prime Minister Neville Chamberlain of the looming confrontation'.[8]

*

Various writers have spoken of Turkul being 'one of [Ellis's] most trusted contacts'. Ellis is purported to have 'secured the support of Stewart Menzies, the chief of SIS' in his dealings with the White

Russian general. Indeed, 'Ellis claimed that it was Menzies who ordered him to keep up Turkul's Nazi contacts in the first place'.

After a time as acting chief, Menzies became chief of MI6, codename C, in November 1939 after the death of Hugh Sinclair, having been head of its military division since 1919 and deputy to Sinclair from 1929. Turkul was expelled from France in 1938. So the timelines don't quite add up. Menzies didn't have complete authority at MI6 until Turkul had left Paris but was active in counterintelligence from about 1925, according to his biographer Anthony Cave Brown, the only author to have interviewed Menzies, in 1964, the year before Ellis was interrogated.

Cave Brown writes in 'C': The Secret Life of Sir Stewart Graham Menzies, Spymaster to Winston Churchill that Menzies was 'responsible for a number of espionage operations of consequence' before World War II against the Germans and Russians, including 'infiltrations of the Abwehr . . . Menzies discovered that the Germans were violating almost every clause written into the Versailles Treaty to keep them disarmed'.

In March 1936, the Nazis had seized back the Rhineland. In March 1938 Nazi Germany absorbed Austria in the Anschluss and by that September Prime Minister Chamberlain and French Prime Minister Édouard Daladier had assented at the Munich Conference to the occupation of the Sudetenland. A Canadian diplomat, Charles Ritchie, later remarked: 'Chamberlain spoke of the disappearance of Czechoslovakia like a Birmingham solicitor winding up an estate.'[9] Hitler was gobbling up new territory and a shot hadn't been fired.

Ellis had written a universally acclaimed, near 600-page book ten years earlier urging world peace and an end to all wars.[10] Rather than aiding and abetting the enemy, as Ellis's critics like to make out retrospectively, his high-stakes game of running double agents in Europe – like Von Petrov and Turkul – could be seen as a valiant attempt to avoid another global conflict. Intelligence was power.

According to William Stevenson in Intrepid's Last Case, 'Ellis . . . encouraged [Turkul] to keep up his powerful Nazi connections. The Nazi Germans had secret plans for using White Russians and Ukrainians to overthrow Stalin, although during the 1930s they were still working clandestinely with Soviet military intelligence.' Ellis, he says, 'was the SIS expert on what Stalin called the nationalities question – the euphemism for unrest among non-Russians making up half the population of the USSR.'

In the course of maintaining this valuable contact, and perhaps to atone for his accepting of faked information, Ellis had to play ball.

'Andrei Turkhul [sic] ... told Ellis that he had contacts with German intelligence and could probably obtain information from them,' wrote Phillip Knightley in *The Second Oldest Profession*. 'But he would need to offer them something in return. He suggested that he should tell the Germans that he knew a British SIS officer who had secrets to sell and then see what reaction this produced. The scheme appealed to Ellis on two levels. On a professional level, he felt that he could appear to be disenchanted with SIS and prepared to betray it at a price. In this role, any contact with the Germans was bound to be rewarding.'

Pushing to the side questions over Turkul's true character, there is no evidence Ellis was aware that Turkul was working for the Soviets. There is evidence, however, that Ellis well knew Turkul was dealing with the Germans. In Turkul's MI5 personal files a document dated 15 September 1938, addressed to Hugh Sinclair, then head of MI6, says, 'Ellis is of [the] opinion that General TURKUL and Co. have been getting support from the Nazi party, but doubts very much whether the Nazis are sincere in using these people to advance their plans for an attack on Russia. The White Russians are willing to serve anyone for money, and it is possible that the Germans are using them to some extent for espionage, though they doubtless do not put much faith in them.'[11]

Both Ellis and Turkul had had a connection to White Russian resistance leader Anton Denikin (as previously mentioned, after the Russian Revolution Ellis had been Major General George Norton Cory's envoy to Denikin, while Turkul had fought under Denikin), so conceivably the pair had a longstanding acquaintance.

William Stevenson's claims in *Intrepid's Last Case* – that Turkul was a Soviet spy 'sending chickenfeed to the Nazis to maintain his credibility', that Turkul masqueraded as a White Russian in the company of Ellis, and that Turkul's personal association with Ellis has been unfairly cast as 'damning evidence of [Ellis's] disloyalty' – do seem to be believable and factually sound. That hasn't stopped a narrative forming about Ellis and this period in his life that at worst he knew Turkul was a Soviet agent or at best had been fooled by his duplicity.

This is writ large in books such as *Unholy Trinity* by Aarons and Loftus, who have called Ellis 'a Nazi agent with ties to General Turkul's Soviet net' and brazenly introduce Kim Philby as a co-conspirator in a massive cover-up directed straight from the Kremlin.

'When MI6 discovered German documents proving that Turkul's friend Ellis was a Nazi agent, Philby ordered that the investigation be closed. No top KGB agent would have risked the inevitable exposure, except under orders from Moscow. If Ellis had been exposed in 1945, it would have jeopardised Turkul, who was far more valuable than Philby. Because of Philby's cover-up, Turkul and Ellis were safe for several more years.'[12]

Chapman Pincher, who really didn't like Ellis at all (in the book *Traitors*, he stuck the boot in hard: 'Ellis was short – "a horrible little man", according to one colleague'), also ran with the ridiculous conspiracy line.[13]

In *Too Secret Too Long*, Pincher expanded on Turkul's friendship with Von Petrov, implying Ellis had poor judgement: 'Von Petrov was friendly with two leading generals in [the White Russian community], who were really Soviet spies – Nikolai Skobline and Prince Turkul.'[14] Von Petrov's name comes up in MI6's Turkul files as a 'White Russian courier' in Turkul's network.[15]

But in his 1984 book Pincher went further than he did in its 1981 predecessor, *Their Trade is Treachery*, with the supposition (again without evidence) that Ellis himself may have faked the information that he passed (wherever it came from) to MI6, that it was 'dreamed up by Ellis himself to improve his standing at headquarters'.

It was bad enough that Ellis was apparently dealing with severely bent double agents. Now he was fabricating their reports.

*

Whether or not Ellis knew all along Turkul was a Soviet spy, it appears the general's personal effectiveness, influence and acumen was seriously called into question by one of his postwar American interrogators in Austria, Arnold M. Silver.

'In the spring of 1946 CIC [Counter Intelligence Corps] in Salzburg foiled a Soviet attempt to kidnap an Austrian who had served German military intelligence (Abwehr) during the war by providing it with information on the Soviet military,' he recalled. 'The man the Soviets tried to kidnap was Richard Kauder, alias Klatt. He and two of his wartime associates were sent to Oberursel for their protection and for detailed interrogation. The two associates were the White Russian émigré Gen. Anton Turkul, and another Russian émigré, Ira Longin, alias Lang, alias several other names. I was assigned to interrogate all three of them . . .

'SSU (Strategic Services Unit – the successor to the OSS until the CIA was established) in Frankfurt, with which I had close liaison, somehow became fascinated with "the Turkul case". Turkul was in fact a useless oaf who had lent his name to the Klatt network as the man who allegedly recruited sources in the USSR. He never recruited even one source, although Klatt managed to convince the Abwehr that Turkul was one of his principal agents.'[16]

In mid-1947 Kauder, Turkul and Longin were released by the Americans. The cataloguing description for Kauder's MI5 personal file at Britain's National Archives reads: 'After the war it was concluded that Ira Longin and possibly Turkul had been under Soviet control all along.' But if you read Stevenson's *Intrepid's Last Case*, you would think Turkul mysteriously vanished after the war.

'After the outbreak of World War II, Turkhul disappeared. Many Ukrainians thought that if Moscow were defeated by the Germans, they would have a free Ukraine. So they donned German uniform and fought against the Red Army . . . General Turkhul showed up unexpectedly in Central Europe, having been traced through a secret transmitter which provided the Germans with intelligence on Soviet military formations and movements.'

The truth is Turkul died on 19 August 1957 in Munich and is buried at the Russian Orthodox Cemetery at Cimetière de

Sainte-Geneviève-des-Bois in the southern suburbs of Paris. Like Ellis, he has been all but forgotten by history. He left behind a 1937 memoir published in Belgrade, *Drozdovtsy v ognie* (*Drozdovians on Fire*).[17]

Was Turkul an extraordinary communist agent or unjustly smeared? Either way, the general unwittingly inflicted immense damage upon Ellis's future legacy. As Phillip Knightley surmised in *The Second Oldest Profession*: '[Ellis's] contact with Turkhul made him one of the targets of a "Red mole hunt" that was to wrack Western intelligence agencies in the 1970s and 1980s.'[18]

The world of hurt for Ellis was just beginning.

CHAPTER 9

A DANGEROUS GAME

'Spies of fiction lived like kings but the authentic British agent
lived on little save a sense of serving his King.'
– WILLIAM STEVENSON, *A MAN CALLED INTREPID* (1976)

WHAT SECRETS HAD DICK ELLIS ALLEGEDLY OFFERED to Vladimir von Petrov through his brother-in-law, Aleksei Zelensky? Ellis, his army of detractors would have you believe, had sold the Germans the so-called order of battle for MI6, namely 'the addresses of the operation, the safe houses, the floors on which each section worked, and the names of the heads and deputy heads of each section' or 'the exact hierarchical structure of the organisation and who occupied what post – knowledge that intelligence organisations prize because it helps them to identify their exact rivals but which, over the whole intelligence spectrum, is only of minor importance'.

Nigel West reproduces an English translation of part of the 11-page document *Der Britische Nachrichtendienst* ('The British Intelligence Service') in his book *MI6: British Secret Intelligence Service Operations, 1909–45*, saying it was 'a summary prepared by the Reich Security Agency [sic, Reich Security Main Office] early in 1940, in preparation for the German invasion of Britain and discovered after the war by Allied intelligence officers amongst Nazi records . . . [it] identifies Broadway Buildings as the headquarters and even reproduces the passport photographs of many of its principal officers . . . as well as accurately giving the SIS order of battle, it also

64

states on which floors particular sections were located. Thus Section III, the naval section, is mentioned as being on the sixth floor and headed by Captain Russell.'

West calls the leak an 'appalling breach of SIS security' and does not hesitate to say who was to blame: Ellis. In another book, *At Her Majesty's Secret Service: The Chiefs of Britain's Intelligence Agency, MI6*, West writes that Ellis 'sold out to the Germans in Paris' and 'as a spy for the Germans, Ellis had obviously done immense harm'.

Potentially damaging, yes; but rather than being *immensely* harmful, the leak was arguably chickenfeed, what William Stevenson in *Intrepid's Last Case* described as information 'offered to convince the other side [Ellis] was corruptible' and possibly information they already had or information that Ellis *thought* they *should have* already had. Even Peter Wright in *Spycatcher* acknowledged it was such: '[Ellis] was sent out into the field with no training and no money, and began providing chickenfeed, odd scraps of information about MI6 plans, to his agent Zilenski (his brother-in-law), who was in touch with Von Petrov, in order to obtain more intelligence in return. It was a dangerous game, and soon he was being blackmailed. He claimed that his wife was ill, and he needed money, so he agreed to supply Zilenski with more information.'

With Ellis operating in the shadows between MI6 and the Nazis, Stevenson argued that Ellis was 'aware of both sides, plugged into the traffic and took out whatever intelligence seemed valid and useful to London'. Ellis's actions weren't seen in a negative light either by the late Australian writer Richard Hall in *A Spy's Revenge*, one of the few writers to defend Ellis after his death.

'[Ellis was] cleared to the highest level. He knew about the successful codebreaks at Bletchley Park and Operation Double Cross, which successfully turned almost all Nazi agents in England . . . there is not a shred of evidence in the extensive captured [Nazi] archives to show they knew the success of these operations. What there is in the German records[1] is the claim that Ellis was a source of some material in 1939 in Paris . . . specialising in the White Russian émigré community, a bearpit of double, triple and even quadruple agents . . . the operational world of running agents is more complex than the desk analysts comprehend.

'Of course he "confessed", although the leaker [of Ellis's interrogation] showed exasperation that they didn't get him to confess spying during the war and for the Russians. On this flimsy foundation of play in double-agentry among the émigrés of Paris, a vast structure has been built to make poor Ellis one of the spies of the century.'

Another Ellis defender was Canadian politician, journalist and historian John Bryden. In his book *Fighting to Lose: How the German Secret Intelligence Service Helped the Allies Win the Second World War*, he made this perspicacious observation: 'Ellis, it must be said, was surely no Nazi . . . [he] was likely acting as liaison between MI6 and anti-Nazi conspirators in the Abwehr.'

Which is absolutely plausible, though Chapman Pincher had earlier dismissed such a theory as nonsensical, since 'there was no official [MI6] liaison with [the Abwehr] in the late 1930s'. Whether any liaison was official or unofficial is immaterial. Could Ellis have actually been *helping* or seeking to aid anti-Hitler elements inside the Abwehr?

F. H. Hinsley's 1979 official British government history *British Intelligence in the Second World War* mentions that MI6 was 'under increasing pressure from the Foreign Office to obtain as much political intelligence as possible, even on such matters as whether the German opposition groups could form an alternative German government'.

Numerous assassination attempts were made on Hitler, including one by Johann Georg Elser at the Bürgerbräukeller, Munich, on 8 November 1939. Elser planted a time-bomb, but Hitler left the venue earlier than expected and the bomb detonated, killing eight people.[2] One elaborate plot against Hitler, the 20 July Plot, or Operation Walküre – widely known from the 2008 Hollywood film *Valkyrie*, starring Tom Cruise – was hatched as far back as 1938. Richard Protze, who mentioned a 'Captain Ellis' in his 1946 interrogation in Utrecht, was good friends with conspirator Admiral Wilhelm Canaris, who was executed among 5000 other Nazi officials and individuals deemed to be either plotters or sympathisers.

As Bryden explains: '[Ellis's] contact was Richard Protze, one of Canaris's most trusted deputies. Protze ran his own espionage agency covering Belgium-Holland and reported directly to the admiral.'

Even the authors of *Unholy Trinity*, who brazenly claim Ellis 'later admitted selling the rosters of British intelligence agents', theorised Ellis may have had good intentions. After all, the Anti-Comintern Pact, officially called Agreement Against the Communist International, had been signed by Germany, Italy and Japan in November 1937.

'Perhaps Ellis thought he was doing the right thing in helping Admiral Canaris prepare for war against the hated Communists. To this day, there is some question whether Ellis aided the Nazis on his own or under instructions from SIS chief Menzies. Before 1939 it made sense to share British networks with the Germans in the common anti-Soviet struggle. Unfortunately, Ellis was also using Turkul's German connections for personal gain, augmenting his meagre salary by working on the side for Admiral Canaris.'

Interestingly, Ellis himself expressed positive views about Canaris in a short historical article written for his daughter, Ann, titled 'Opposition to the Nazis'. Ellis said that Canaris was 'as strong a nationalist as many other German officers but was a realist and strongly critical of the aims and methods of the Nazis and Hitler in particular. Canaris was associated with other officers, including General [Ludwig] Beck,[3] with similar views and on several occasions [passed] warnings to foreign government [sic] regarding impending actions by Hitler which he disapproved of. Canaris was no traitor, and not, as some people have stated, a "foreign agent".'

They are hardly the words of a sympathetic Nazi.

So it is apposite at this point to consider the political and tactical manoeuvring of Ellis's superior at MI6, Stewart Menzies, with regard to Canaris. The latter might have been a good guy in the final analysis but he was still a Nazi.

One Canaris biographer, Richard Bassett, writes in *Hitler's Spy Chief*: 'There is much in print to help those wishing to focus on links between Canaris and his opposite number in the British secret service, Sir Stewart Menzies, and there can be no doubt that both men worked together for an understanding between Britain and Germany, with Churchill's tacit encouragement, which could, by 1943, have led to the war ending far sooner than it did . . .

'Menzies would have appreciated Canaris as they were both "terrific anti-Bolsheviks". The incomparable Soviet section of the

Abwehr was the best-informed intelligence department in the world on the activities of Soviet Russia. Several times, even when Britain and Russia were allied . . . Menzies would gratefully receive Abwehr intelligence on the Soviet forces and the Abwehr would receive appreciations of Churchill's political intelligence from SIS. In one case, Menzies – sensationally – even supplied the Abwehr, via Finnish signals intelligence, with the latest wireless intercept equipment to compile a list of the Soviet order of battle days ahead of the German invasion [of Soviet Russia].[4]

Biographer Richard Deacon (the pen name of the late Donald McCormick) adds that one of Menzies's successors as head of MI6, Maurice Oldfield, 'made the point again and again in private conversation that "without aid from our friends inside the German Abwehr, we shouldn't have won the war quite so soon"'.

In his autobiography, *Spy/Counterspy*, Serbian double agent Duško Popov wrote, 'Menzies was contemplating a dialogue with Canaris or those close to him with a view to ousting Hitler.'

So if Menzies had a mutually beneficial relationship with Canaris, then it stands to reason that Ellis, Menzies's man in the field, had a mutually beneficial relationship with Canaris's man in the field, Protze.

But had Ellis crossed a moral line?

*

Why would Ellis involve himself in a strategy as risky as allegedly accepting payment for 'solid secrets'? (According to Stevenson in *Intrepid's Last Case*, that was how Ellis's enemies viewed his horse trading.) A number of theories for his motives have been put forward, all with varying degrees of substance and veracity.

'His wife was ill, he was underpaid, and he needed money,' argued Phillip Knightley in *The Second Oldest Profession*, a description Wright pinched almost word-for-word for *Spycatcher*. 'Since, in order to establish his credibility, he would have to take German payment anyway, why not keep it – a not unusual practice. Unfortunately his plan went wrong for several reasons. It seems that Ellis went further than he intended.'

Richard Hall in *A Spy's Revenge*: 'Dick Goldsmith White [later head of MI6], who discussed the matter with Ellis after his "confession", has told friends that Ellis should have kept London better informed of his tricks and not pocketed the cash. White accepts his later denials [of treachery].'

Observed William Stephenson: 'Today people are more careful, but in those days you didn't get a signed chit telling you to go ahead. After World War II there was a frightful tangle – everybody had been playing double agent, and German spies tried to prove their anti-communism through false accusations.'

In his alleged 1965 confession, Ellis himself is said to have remarked that White Russians were 'a double-crossing lot of bastards who would sell intelligence to whoever would pay them'.

Which seems to be a fair assessment. The problem for Ellis, like a lot of people accused of bad things and cancelled as a result, was optics. The details didn't really matter. Decades after the fact, to the likes of West, Wright and Pincher, Ellis accepting anything from or selling anything to the Nazis, whatever the motive, whatever the endgame, was proof of bad intentions. They were of one mind in deciding Ellis had made himself ripe for exploitation by Britain's enemies, the biggest of all being the Soviet Union. If someone was potentially capable of being exploited, then the natural corollary is they *were* exploited. To their way of thinking, now Ellis's former brother-in-law Aleksei Zelensky could easily blackmail Ellis for either the Nazis or Soviets and extract more information from him.

When Walter Krivitsky had defected to the West, scores of Russians were executed by state-sponsored assassination squads. Operatives were right to be scared for their lives. With White Russian agents so compromised by Soviet penetration, naturally there was speculation Ellis was compromised, too. The big question is what MI6 – and Ellis's then superior at MI6, Stewart Menzies – knew about Ellis's activities at the time, not how it looked 20 or 40 years later. Was Ellis giving the Nazis chickenfeed – useless info/false info – with the knowledge of his superiors? I believe this was the case. Was Ellis involved in a dangerous game which then came back to haunt him? I also believe this was the case. Menzies was obviously well aware of Ellis's activities, though the titular head of MI6 at the time of the relevant events was Hugh Sinclair.

Wrote Phillip Knightley: 'Only at the highest levels of the Secret Service would the truth be known and Ellis would have to depend on his chiefs to protect him if ever MI5 became suspicious of him.'

*

By early 1938, Ellis had become a fluent German speaker and a full-time intelligence officer without a cover job. Along with the Russian-speaking Captain Henry 'Bob' Kerby, later a Conservative MP who was himself suspected of being a Russian mole by Chapman Pincher,[5] Ellis was intercepting calls between Adolf Hitler and Nazi Germany's ambassador to London, *Obergruppenführer* Joachim von Ribbentrop, and translating them into English for MI6. The operation had purportedly been underway for three years.[6] He was living at 54 Wynnstay Gardens, Kensington; the German Embassy was less than five kilometres away at 9 Carlton House Terrace in the St James district of Westminster, not far from Buckingham Palace.

It's unclear exactly who Ellis was directly working for while bugging the embassy's phone lines, whether it was the 'secret Security Division of the Post Office' or Robert Vansittart, or whether he was doing this on his own initiative. The by-now well-trusted Ellis had his own intelligence network within MI6. It was the nattily titled but shadowy 22000 Organisation (22000 was the internal SIS country code for Atlantic islands). John Bryden described it as 'his own espionage service'.

Ellis's 22000 Organisation existed parallel to Claude Dansey's better known SIS-sponsored spy group, Z Organisation,[7] according to Keith Jeffery, yet 'operated within the main SIS establishment' not apart from it, like Z.

'Its primary tasks were the penetration of Germany and Italy . . . agents were recruited mostly from the business, journalistic and academic world.'

It was around this time Ellis met a wealthy European-based Winnipeg businessman and former RAF 73 Squadron fighter pilot named William 'Bill' Stephenson, who was providing information to

Winston Churchill on German rearmament and 'had created his own private clandestine industrial intelligence organisation, the services of which he offered to the British government'. According to Bryden, the 22000 Organisation 'utilised Bill Stephenson's international industrial intelligence network as well as agents in Europe of Ellis's own', which included 'two White Russians [presumably Vladimir von Petrov and Aleksei Zelensky] who Ellis had run against the Soviets during the 1920s. In 1938–39, he used this same pair to feed information to the Abwehr.'

Peter Wright says the Russian mole–hunting joint MI5–MI6 Fluency Committee of the 1960s 'traced the records of the prewar operation to tap the Hitler–Von Ribbentrop link. The officer in charge of processing the product was Ellis.' Wright's literary ally, Chapman Pincher, says the operation ran 'almost up to the outbreak of the war' and on 'a list of the six translators of German who had been involved' in the operation 'the top name on the list was that of Captain C. H. Ellis'. Pincher put forward no documentation to support these assertions.

Von Ribbentrop had arrived at Carlton House Terrace in October 1936 following the death of his predecessor, Leopold von Hoesch. In February 1938 he became Hitler's Minister of Foreign Affairs and left the post, so he was there for only about 16 months. According to H. Montgomery Hyde in *Secret Intelligence Agent*, when Von Ribbentrop arrived, the embassy – two adjoining houses – was refurbished inside by specially hired German workmen and MI6 seized the opportunity to install listening devices.

'The horde of workmen necessary to carry out this operation were imported from Germany, and they installed a number of listening devices, burglar alarms, and a special direct telephone line to the Chancellery in Berlin so that Ribbentrop could speak to Hitler without going through the normal telephone exchange ... English workmen were necessarily employed to supplement the work of their German counterparts, and some of these succeeded, so Ellis told me, in installing counter devices. In this way the direct London–Berlin telephone line was tapped and the embassy was bugged for the benefit of the British SIS.'

This is vouched for in MI6's official history, Keith Jeffery writing that from the mid-1930s 'a branch (Section X) was set up to tap telephone lines of embassies in London'[8] and 'successfully listened in to conversations to and from, and within, a large number of foreign embassies ... conversations, for example between the German military attachés in London and Berlin appear to have been particularly revealing, and included "details of a reconnaissance that the former was to carry out of possible landing beaches along the South and West coasts of Ireland".'

However, it has been claimed by the anti-Ellis troika of West, Wright and Pincher[9] that soon after Ellis's appointment the German Embassy began shutting down its outgoing communications and 'suddenly abandoned the telephone link for no known reason': they'd been tipped off by someone and that person, allegedly, was Ellis. Unnamed Abwehr officers interrogated after the war had, in the words of Pincher, 'recorded that this Captain Ellis had warned the Germans, before the war, that the British were listening in'.

Pincher's books are short on verifiable sources, poorly footnoted, and I could not find any evidence of these telephone records in National Archives files in London. Interestingly, he conceded in one of his books, 'senior secret service officers ... denied that Ellis had ever been involved in the operation and insisted that there was no way he could possibly have known about it'.

We don't know who Ellis's defenders were because Pincher never revealed the names of these senior officers and nor did Wright. The fact that Pincher disclosed this information, perhaps begrudgingly, indicates that they existed. Yet Pincher remained resolute there'd been a cover-up of sorts – that MI6 had blocked MI5's investigators, and that the latter were 'satisfied that Ellis had been a spy for Germany, at least until the British were driven out of Europe in 1940' and 'decided to investigate the possibility that he had continued to spy for the Nazis afterward or had been recruited by the Russians'.

Writes Pincher in *Too Secret Too Long*: 'In 1953, when the MI5 officers had progressed as far as they could [with their investigation into Ellis], they asked MI6 to look at their old records of it, not having any right of access to them themselves. The first reaction from MI6 was that nobody there could recall any such operation and that the Abwehr information in the MI5 files must have been "disinformation". Under pressure, however, the records were found, and while agreeing that somebody must have warned the Germans that the line was being tapped MI6 denied that Ellis had ever been involved in the operation or had any access to information about it. There is no doubt now that in 1953, incensed at MI5's suspicions against [Kim] Philby, which his colleagues believed to be unwarranted, MI6 was totally opposed to supporting any suspicions against another MI6 officer as senior as Ellis then was.'

Yet, importantly, Jeffery's history of MI6 makes no mention of the leaking of the phone taps on the German Embassy, which is unusual, given how serious a breach it must have been for MI6. If the bugging operations on the various embassies had been 'successful', as Jeffery said, surely such a catastrophic leak would have been documented?

The logical scenario, applying Occam's razor, is there was no leak to the Germans. H. Montgomery Hyde had it right: 'A more likely explanation is that Ribbentrop left London to become Reich Foreign Minister in March 1938 and the [telephone] link was no longer required.'

CHAPTER 10

THE VENLO MYTH

'Spies do not sprout in the enemy's lands like soldiers grown
from dragon's teeth. They have to be found, trained, equipped,
assigned missions, disguised, inserted, communicated with,
paid, and sometimes withdrawn. Their reports must be
evaluated and forwarded. Their files must be maintained.'
– DAVID KAHN, *HITLER'S SPIES* (1978)

DICK ELLIS'S FIRST ENCOUNTER with William Stephenson would
change the course of his life – and, in many ways, change history.
Ellis shared his recollections of that encounter for a 1973 Canadian
television documentary on Stephenson.

'I met him about the end of '38 when I was engaged on some
research work on German rearmament, and he was introduced to me
by a Member of Parliament, Sir Ralph Glyn.'

Lord Glyn, 1st Baron Glyn, was the Conservative MP for Abingdon
and one-time parliamentary private secretary to former prime minister
James Ramsay MacDonald.[1] Glyn had business interests in Sweden –
much of that country's iron ore ended up in Hitler's war machine – and
was a director, with Stephenson, of the now-demolished Earls Court
Exhibition Centre in London.[2]

Stephenson, Ellis said, 'was engaged in a similar kind of activity
[to Glyn] in Scandinavia and Germany', referring to Stephenson's
International Mining Trust (IMT), a cover for his fledgling private
intelligence network, Business Industrial Secret Service (BISS). Ian

Fleming, an intelligence officer before he found fame as the creator of James Bond, explained, 'Stephenson's cover story was that he had to go to Sweden on business. He had commercial interests there. The secondary cover, for intelligence types who needed to know his movements, was that he would destroy the source and the supply lines of iron ore which Germany's steel industries depended upon.'

As H. Montgomery Hyde wrote in *The Quiet Canadian*: 'The German output of high-grade steel for armament manufacture depended on the Bessemer process in which iron ore of high phosphorus content from the Gallivare mines in northern Sweden was used. Normally this was shipped in winter through Narvik on the west coast of Norway, and, in the spring and summer when they were free from ice, through Lulea and other Swedish ports on the Gulf of Bothnia.

'When Hitler launched his *blitzkrieg* against Poland at the beginning of September 1939, Germany had about nine months' supply of ore, sufficient only for the short war on which the Nazis were gambling. With the immediate entry of Britain and France into the conflict and the likelihood that it would be prolonged well into the following year, it became imperative for Germany that the Swedish supplies should continue and if possible be increased . . . the war would be won by the side which secured control of the Swedish ores.'

Ellis recalled: '[Stephenson] had been providing a great deal of information on German rearmament to Mr Churchill at that time he was not in office [prior to May 1940] but was playing quite an important role in providing background information to members of [the] House of Commons who were much more concerned with what was happening than the administration [of Prime Minister Neville Chamberlain] seemed to be at the time . . . that was the beginning, I think, of my official connection to him.'

Stephenson's work was 'all being done through his personal relationship with people like Mr Churchill and Lord Leathers[3] and others . . . I introduced him to my own channels, to heads of intelligence. And that led to his being asked if he was going to America . . . if he would do what he could to reestablish a link between security authorities here and the FBI.'

*

Around this time, after the bugging of the German Embassy in London, Nigel West says Ellis was sent to Liverpool for 'a brief spell in cable censorship', though I found no mention of this anywhere other than in one of West's numerous espionage books. Olik Ellis's timeline makes no mention of Ellis being in Liverpool. But 1939 would see Ellis, formerly a captain, rejoin the British Army as a major, according to Olik, though the date of his promotion is not known; nor are later promotions to lieutenant colonel and colonel.[4] Colonel is one of the most senior positions in the British Army; only brigadier, major general, lieutenant general, general and field marshal outrank it.

What is known is that on New Year's Eve, 1938 Ellis left Southampton for Villefranche-sur-Mer in the Côte d'Azur on the MS *Johan van Oldenbarnevelt*. He gave his occupation on shipping records as 'journalist'. A few months later he left England for France again, this time with his 25-year-old wife, Barbara, heading to Marseille on the MS *Dempo*. He gave his address as Travellers Club, Pall Mall.

On 23 August 1939 the Molotov–Ribbentrop Pact was signed and according to Jeffery in *MI6* 'just days before the outbreak of the Second World War, Dick Ellis reported a rather unconvincing series of steps taken by the service to warn of an impending German attack'. This would suggest he was working *against* the enemy not aiding it.

On 1 September Germany had invaded Poland and three days later the United Kingdom and France had declared war on Germany. World War II had begun. Just over two weeks later the Soviet Union invaded Poland from the eastern side.

In this excerpt from his diaries, MI5 counterespionage chief Guy Liddell writes, 'I saw Commander Rex Howard of SIS. He is anxious to start working on our internees as soon as possible and has appointed Dick Ellis to be in charge of this work. Ellis will have the assistance of Superintendent Jempson of Special Branch and also Thomas Kendrick who is kicking his heels at the Tower of London while waiting for the arrival of German prisoners of war. I suggested we might perhaps pool our resources with SIS in the matter of the interrogation of prisoners, of whom there are over 200. Howard was quite in agreement. I suggested to him that he might perhaps like to interrogate some of the German sailors whom we have already taken off neutral ships.'[5]

In November, the Soviet Union entered Finland. That month was when the infamous Venlo Incident occurred in the Netherlands. A Dutch intelligence officer, Lieutenant Dirk Klop, was shot dead and two British MI6 agents, Major Richard Henry Stevens and Z Organisation man Captain Sigismund Payne Best, who'd thought they were about to meet anti-Hitler resistance figures inside the German Army, were instead kidnapped by the Nazis' industrial and political intelligence agency, *Sicherheitsdienst*, the SD. It happened just a matter of metres from the German border. The event would feature prominently in Chapman Pincher's 1980s vendetta against the memory of Ellis. This vendetta was egged on by Peter Wright. Despite there being little foundation to his story – Pincher didn't present much of a slam-dunk case against Ellis – he went ahead and published it anyway, with the caveat that it 'might incriminate Ellis'. It was an egregious example of pure Pincheresque scapegoating.

'In the early days of the war,' Pincher wrote in *Their Trade is Treachery*, 'when Holland was still neutral, two British intelligence officers from the secret service, Maj. H. R. Stevens and Capt. S. Payne Best, based at The Hague, were lured across the border at Venlo into Germany. There they were captured by the Gestapo, grilled and held prisoner, finally ending up in a concentration camp.

'When they returned to Britain, they reported that it was evident from the questions they were asked that German intelligence had detailed knowledge of the organisation of the British secret service and of the personalities running it.[6] This was confirmed by another captured German officer, who volunteered the information that a source inside British intelligence had told them how to get hold of Stevens and Best and how best to question them.

'There was no proof that the source was Ellis, but he had been in the right position in the secret service to have provided the information. Furthermore, there has been no trace of any other spy working for the Germans at that time.'

Nigel West in his 2006 book *Historical Dictionary of International Intelligence* went further, laying the blame squarely at the feet of Ellis: 'Upon their release in 1945 Best and Stevens blamed each other for having disclosed too much detailed information about the SIS, unaware that the real culprit had been an SIS colleague, Dick Ellis.[7] The SIS did not become aware of Ellis's duplicity until 1966, by which time Stevens had died in ignominy and a bankrupt Best had tried to make some money by publishing his memoirs, *The Venlo Incident*. Their interrogations had been handled with considerable skill by the enemy, who deliberately gave each the impression that the other was cooperating, without revealing the true source of the information.

'The loss of two such well-informed SIS officers so early in the war was a considerable blow for the [Secret Intelligence] Service and a significant coup for the *Sicherheitsdienst*, which had masterminded the operation. When he was questioned in 1945, Walter Schellenberg acknowledged his role [at Venlo], as he did later in his memoirs, *The Schellenberg Papers* [sic], but was unable to identify Ellis as the SIS officer who had caused so much damage.'

This, in my opinion, is an insufficient account by West. Stevens died of cancer, having worked for NATO as a translator in the postwar years, in 1967 and not in 'ignominy' in 1966. One of his predecessors as PCO in The Hague, Major Ernest Albert Llewellyn Dalton, committed suicide in 1936 after accepting bribes and allegedly being blackmailed by a fellow officer, William John 'Bill' Hooper, who then became an agent for the Abwehr.[8] His successor and Stevens's immediate predecessor, Major Montagu 'Monty' Chidson, hired the Nazi double agent Folkert Arie van Koutrik, who worked not just for the British but for the Abwehr III F's chief, Richard Protze, the very same man who gave so much information on 'Captain Ellis' while being interrogated in 1946.[9]

As R. G. Grant writes in the book *MI5 MI6*, 'Stevens took over a station already penetrated by the Abwehr through Van Koutrik, and made things worse by absurdly re-employing the blackmailer Hooper.' In other words, the Hague MI6 station was riddled with crooks and moles. Hooper and Van Koutrik were thus prime candidates for any leak about Britain's intelligence apparatus.

Schellenberg, who ran Von Petrov as an agent, was a pivotal figure in the events leading up to the Venlo Incident and on the day of Best's and Stevens's capture posed as a monocled German general called 'Hauptmann Schämmel', makes no identification of Dick Ellis by name in the thousands of pages of documents in his MI5 personal files or his posthumously published biography. So for West to say Schellenberg was 'unable to identify Ellis' is correct. But after West in his book prefaces that statement by nakedly calling Ellis the 'real culprit' without any evidence, the implication is Ellis was guilty with or without Schellenberg's input.

The 'Captain Ellis' spoken of by interrogated Nazi officers could be anybody. It *could* be Ellis, granted, as details about Ellis's personal life, his Australian background and his tremendous facility with foreign languages seem to have been common knowledge among some officers, but 'Captain Ellis' could also be someone posing as Ellis or someone wanting to frame Ellis. None of the claims made in various books about Ellis's alleged link to what happened at Venlo are adequately referenced.[10]

Indeed, one of Ellis's most active defenders, Bill Ross-Smith, maintained the real culprits (to borrow West's terminology) of the 'order of battle' leak commonly attributed to Ellis and which got him into so much trouble with the Fluency Committee of 1964–69 were in fact Best and Stevens themselves.[11]

Phillip Knightley says as much in *The Second Oldest Profession* but doesn't exactly preclude Ellis from involvement: 'Best and Stevens . . . had been the Germans' main source of information for the SIS order of battle. (Ellis . . . was another.)' Ben Macintyre in *A Spy Among Friends* writes that 'the meeting was a trap, personally ordered by *Reichsführer* Heinrich Himmler' and 'Stevens had been carrying in his pocket, idiotically, a list of intelligence sources in Western Europe. MI6 scrambled to extract its network of agents before the Germans pounced.'[12] Keith Jeffery in *MI6* has a slightly different version: 'Stevens was carrying some coding material, and Best had a list of agents' names and addresses with him.' Notably, Jeffery makes no mention of Ellis being a source for the Germans.

These accounts should cast reasonable doubt on the proposition that Ellis was to blame. An MI5 report of Schellenberg's interrogation dated 19 September 1945 regarding his 'Knowledge of the Organisation of the British Intelligence Service' even says 'Amt IV [the Gestapo] was never particularly successful regarding England, and certainly nothing about the Intelligence Service was ever supplied . . . the only

British agents with whom SCHELLENBERG came into contact were BEST and STEVENS.'[13]

Another earlier interrogation report dated 27 June–12 July 1945 says Schellenberg 'knows absolutely nothing' about British intelligence and 'was not able to produce a single name belonging to the British Service'.[14] So naturally if Ellis were so damaging a double agent it stands to reason Schellenberg would have been in possession of highly detailed and much more explosive material.

The only piece of evidence which seems to suggest there *may* have been a link between the 'order of battle' leak and Ellis is *Sturmbannführer* Helmuth Knochen's file,[15] which confirms in a 9 February 1945 interrogation report from Camp 020 – MI5's London interrogation centre for enemy agents, also known as Latchmere House – that Knochen and Schellenberg came into contact with Stevens and Best 'either in Poland or Holland some six or nine months' before the kidnapping that led to the Venlo Incident, 'with [Reinhard] Heydrich's consent . . . and finally conceived a plan to kidnap them and bring them to Germany'.

Knochen worked with Vladimir von Petrov, Ellis's alleged contact in Paris or Berlin. Schellenberg also worked with Von Petrov. This indicates a path between Von Petrov, Knochen, Schellenberg and the Venlo Incident – and by logical extension, Ellis. That is *if* he had the contact he's claimed to have had with Von Petrov via his brother-in-law, Zelensky. Which perhaps explains why on 27 June 1946 the FBI wanted MI6 to grill Knochen on Von Petrov, stating in a cable: 'FBI requests KNOCHEN be interrogated in detail regarding WALDEMAR VON PETROW.'[16]

But that's highly tenuous and insufficient to prove anything. You would think. Not to Chapman Pincher in *Too Secret Too Long*.

'The MI5 officers who debriefed [Stevens and Best] were convinced that the Abwehr had indeed been in possession of a mass of highly secret information which could only have come from a source inside MI6. This conclusion was endorsed when they were able to question the Abwehr officers who had grilled Stevens and Best. To their horror, the MI5 men learned that it was a British intelligence source that had advised the Abwehr on how to lay hands on the two Britons.

'Ellis had been in a position to supply the information so MI5 again asked for permission to examine the relevant MI6 files. Again this was refused. The MI6 management argued that the White Russians with whom Ellis had been in contact before the war had proved to be double-crossers and fabricators of "intelligence", so Von Petrov and the rest must have convinced the Abwehr that Ellis had been their agent when, in fact, they had been his. This argument did not explain how the MI6 secrets had leaked.'

Must have might be logical reasoning but it's not proof of anything. There is still no evidence it was Ellis.

CHAPTER 11

THE BLACK BOOK

'Very often the eagles have been squalled down by the parrots.'
– WINSTON CHURCHILL, HOUSE OF COMMONS (1945)

IT WAS WHILE BEING DEBRIEFED by MI5's Jane Archer in London during the first two months of 1940 that Russian defector Walter Krivitsky gave what is alleged to be the first clue that Dick Ellis had been up to no good: connecting an unnamed British source to Vladimir von Petrov.

In March 1940, Archer's report was issued. The next few months saw a torrent of critical events in the course of the war. In April, Germany invaded Denmark and Norway. In May, Neville Chamberlain resigned as prime minister and Winston Churchill replaced him. Germany invaded Belgium and the evacuation of Dunkirk commenced.

As Ellis remembered: 'After Dunkirk there was . . . a strong wave of pessimism regarding British chances of survival, much of which derived from official appraisal of logistic and other objective factors, but also from the defeatist attitude on the part of certain diplomatic representatives in London and Paris. We were, not unnaturally, disturbed by the extent and the comparatively unhindered scope of Axis intelligence and sabotage potential in the western hemisphere.'

On 10 May 1940, the day Churchill became prime minister, William Stephenson attended a celebratory dinner at Stornoway House – the London home of Canadian newspaper baron and

Churchill's new appointee as Minister of Aircraft Production William Maxwell Aitken aka Lord Beaverbrook.[1] There, Stephenson claimed, his 'old friend' Churchill asked him to be his 'personal representative' and form and lead British Security Coordination. Stephenson warmed to the task and would later describe the 'unique special-intelligence organisation which I created and financed in the US to the extent of $3,000,000 and which operated throughout World War II, with headquarters in Rockefeller Center, New York'.[2]

Said John le Carré: '[Stephenson] was Churchill's secret intelligence ambassador to President Roosevelt, who, no thanks to [United States ambassador] Joseph Kennedy[3] in London, supported Churchill's view of Hitler even when Churchill himself was in the wilderness.'

By 21 June, Stephenson had landed in Manhattan under the guise of Passport Control Officer (PCO), taking a penthouse apartment at the Hotel Dorset on West 54th Street, where over martinis he held court with various luminaries, including businessman Vincent Astor, lawyer and presidential adviser Ernest Cuneo, former world heavyweight boxing champion Gene Tunney, industrialist Errett Lobban Cord and Republican presidential nominee Wendell Willkie. By dint of their introduction by Lord Glyn two years earlier, Stephenson chose Ellis as his second-in-command at British Security Coordination, located in Room 240 of the Rockefeller Center's Palazzo d'Italia at 626 Fifth Avenue. Apparently, this was against the protests of Stewart Menzies in London, who was reluctant to let him go.[4] The Australian would use the cover of His Britannic Majesty's Consul at New York.[5]

On 6 September 1940, the British Embassy in Washington DC wrote to United States Secretary of State Cordell Hull to inform the White House of the appointment and enclosed Ellis's official signature and seal. In America, Ellis reunited with his old friend from Transcaspia and Constantinople, Reginald Teague-Jones aka Ronald Sinclair, who was appointed vice-consul the following year.[6]

Chapman Pincher deals with Ellis's World War II years in two paragraphs in *Their Trade is Treachery*, while Peter Wright in *Spycatcher* all but admits he came up with nothing on him: when he looked at Ellis's 'wartime record . . . some of the American VENONA [decrypts of Soviet coded cables] showed clearly the Soviets were operating a number of agents inside BSC, but although we tried exhaustive analysis to link Ellis with each of the cryptonyms, we could never be certain'.[7]

*

A few months before his move to Manhattan, Ellis had called on Stephenson at his offices in London. This passage from William Stevenson in *Intrepid's Last Case* about their meeting illuminates the relationship between the two men.

'Ellis put on a military uniform and ... visited Little Bill Stephenson in his business office on St James's Street, between Piccadilly and Buckingham Palace. One of the few pieces of art decorating Stephenson's private quarters was a short-barrelled pistol. Ellis had obtained it from the Cossacks fighting around Baku in 1918, though it had been fashioned for the imperial Persian cavalry ... Ellis had become involved in the so-called Baku Project. In 1940, this was part of a study for the British Chiefs of Staff, officially entitled "Military Implications of Hostilities with Russia". If Baku was knocked out, 90 per cent of Soviet oil resources would be unavailable to Stalin's customers, Hitler and the Nazi war machine.'

The plan was to bomb Russia's oil facilities in Azerbaijan and, if needed, send 60,000 British troops into the region and 'spread subversion and sabotage'. Ellis, a man 'who knew where Stalin's physical weaknesses were to be found along the borders, starting from the first mission to Baku' was the logical person to write it. Ellis's Baku report was prepared in March 1940 but the project was shelved for being 'simply beyond British resources'. There was also suspicion it had been deliberately leaked to the Russians, conceivably by Ellis.

As Stevenson explained in *Intrepid's Last Case*, at the time the Soviet Union was providing Nazi Germany with large supplies of metals and other resources needed for the production of armaments. Stevenson posited that Ellis could 'have leaked the Baku Project ... to frighten Stalin into reducing aid to the Nazis. Such a leak could be made to seem sinister if there should be no paperwork proving official sanction.'

Weeks before Ellis visited Stephenson, the Nazis captured Dunkirk, Italy declared war on Britain and France, the Nazis entered

Paris without resistance, and the Soviets had begun their invasion of the Baltic States. For Stephenson, Ellis was far from under suspicion; he was the man for any crisis. In fact, according to Thomas F. Troy, Stephenson issued a caveat: he'd only accept the job in New York if Ellis would join him: '[His] services [were] demanded from SIS as a *sine qua non* for his own acceptance of the PCO [Passport Control Officer] post.'

The situation facing the West was dire, as Ellis wrote in his unpublished 1972 manuscript, *The Two Bills: Mission Accomplished*: 'The Dunkirk disaster and the fall of France signalled the beginning of a profound change in the climate of American public opinion. The possibility of a British defeat and of German naval dominion of the Atlantic, the implications of which were clearly understood by the President and by many American naval and military leaders, now began to be voiced by a section of the press and by a number of influential radio commentators.'

The Ellises – Dick, 45; his wife, Barbara, 29; their daughter, Ann, aged six; and Ellis's son from his first marriage, 16-year-old Olik – arrived in New York on board the RMS *Scythia* from Liverpool on 7 July 1940.[8] Around the same time, in London, a 28-year-old Kim Philby joined MI6.

Ellis was about to begin work for what he described as 'the most intricate integrated intelligence and secret-operations organisation in history'. British Security Coordination, a name suggested by FBI director J. Edgar Hoover, would have stations in Montevideo, Rio de Janeiro and New York.[9]

'I had been 20 years in the professional secret-intelligence service when in 1940 London sent me to British Security Coordination headquarters in New York to help maintain that secrecy,' wrote Ellis in his introduction to *A Man Called Intrepid*, a book in which he barely rates a mention. 'BSC networks were manned by amateurs, and it was thought that my special experience was required there. Such concern proved unwarranted. The British Secret Intelligence Service had been rendered useless in Europe when our professional agents were cut down almost in a single stroke after conventional armed resistance to the Nazis ended on the Continent and Hitler entered Paris. But the amateurs who flocked to replace the professionals were well able to take care of themselves.'

Together Stephenson and Ellis, heading BSC's dedicated secret-intelligence unit, recruited the likes of Roald Dahl, Ian Fleming, Noël Coward, H. Montgomery Hyde and other luminaries to Britain's spy ranks.

It was a baptism of fire for Ellis. Shortly after his arrival in New York the Nazis attacked England. From the beginning of August through to the end of October the Battle of Britain raged. When that didn't end well for the Germans, starting on 7 September and for 57 consecutive nights, they bombed London in The Blitz, from the German word *blitzkrieg* (lightning war). On 21 August, Stalin's mortal enemy Leon Trotsky was assassinated with an ice axe by an NKVD agent in Mexico City. On 16 October, R-Day, 16.4 million American men between the ages of 21 and 35 registered for the draft. On 17 December President Franklin D. Roosevelt held a press conference floating the concept of the United States loaning military supplies to Britain under what later became known as the Lend-Lease plan. America was getting ready to go to war.

Roosevelt's emissary, the 'World War I combat hero and self-made Wall Street millionaire lawyer' Colonel William 'Big Bill' Donovan,[10] had already visited Churchill in July in London, met Ellis the following month in New York, and from December 1940 to March 1941 was based full-time in Europe.[11] America would soon have its very own spy service, with Stephenson's and Ellis's help.

As Bill Macdonald wrote in *Intrepid's Last Secrets*: 'Stephenson's first assignments included getting needed supplies and weaponry for Britain, implementing means to protect British shipping, and providing assistance and guidance in setting up an all-encompassing American intelligence agency.'

But the idea that Stephenson singlehandedly established British relations with the FBI didn't wash with his deputy, Ellis.

'Relations with [J.] Edgar Hoover's boys started long before BSC's time. The famous [Jessie] Jordan case in 1938, in which the arrest of a woman of that name in Scotland engaged in naval espionage on behalf of the Nazis, led to disclosure of a group of spies in the States and close collaboration between "5" here and the FBI in bringing them to book. The FBI man in charge of the case, Leon. G. Turrou, later resigned and wrote a book called *Nazi Spies in America* in Mar '39, also published here by Harraps. This book caused something of a flap in the "5" and "6" dovecotes here. There was some correspondence between our charge d'affaires Victor Malet and Pres Roosevelt in '38 in connection with this case in which the latter expressed his determination to "clean up the Nazi nests" and mentioned the need for collaboration with the British services.

'Bill [Stephenson] seems to think everything started with him. It didn't really. The link existed but owing to [the] US Neutrality Act it was "working to rule" only in 1939 and early '40.[12] What Bill achieved was a coordinated service and a basic organisation that enabled the Yanks to start their own services with working lines and have material after Pearl Harbor . . . [the US–British] link was already in existence; Bill revived its activity and extended its scope.'[13]

So Ellis was busy enough with America on the cusp of entering the war, running BSC as Stephenson's deputy and hiring personnel, and helping the 'quiet and urbane' but 'forceful' Colonel William Donovan set up what would soon become America's first foreign-intelligence agency: Office of the Coordinator of Information (COI), which became Office of Strategic Services (OSS).

'With headquarters at Rockefeller Center, thousands of our agents and experts passed under the statue of Atlas on Fifth Avenue, yet their identities and activities remained effectively masked,' he wrote in his introduction to *A Man Called Intrepid*. 'The story of BSC was that of a great Anglo-American enterprise that began when President Roosevelt and his like-minded colleagues saved the British Isles from Nazi occupation despite the United States then being technically at peace.'

Ellis has been deservedly described as 'OSS's tutor and mentor' but typically he deflected any credit to his boss: 'BSC inspired COI (later OSS) and Bill [Stephenson] talked Donovan into starting it.' Part of Ellis's wide remit was writing spy how-to memos for the Washington DC-based Donovan, such as one titled 'Working of a secret service organisation'.[14]

The 14-page document notes that 'the function of an intelligence organisation is to secure information' in four categories (political; naval, air and military; enemy activities and counterespionage; economic) and a 'good SS man should have the best qualities of a competent foreign correspondent of a good newspaper. He must be energetic, patient, discreet and intelligent. The "cloak and dagger" mentality is useless, as it masks the romantic temperament that colours and distorts facts, and distorts cool and accurate judgment.'

Ellis also has advice on agents being 'well advised to allow the local authorities (when they have to be considered) and "enemy" agents to get accustomed to his presence before running the risk of making himself conspicuous. It is usually better to employ a good trustworthy "cut-out" or intermediary, well paid and firmly but generously handled, to work on the lines required.'

<u>Pitfalls and Hints</u>

Agents of other countries are likely to be on the watch for activities of their real and potential opponents, and are bound to employ the time-honoured stratagems, among which are the following:

(1) Placing their own agent in their opponent's service

(2) Putting out false information

(3) Arranging for the disposal of faked documents and of reports purporting to come from 'opposition elements' among their own nationals

(4) Provocation, ie leading an opponent's agent on a false scent in order to compromise him with the local authorities

But to the conspiracy-minded, all the while Ellis was also actively aiding the Nazi war effort, for instance through his alleged 'order of battle' leak, which found its way as *Der Britische Nachrichtendienst* ('The British Intelligence Service') into a Nazi publication called *Informationsheft G. B.* ('Information Brochure Great Britain', the SS handbook for the invasion of Britain).

'At the end of June 1940, I was ordered to prepare a small handbook for the invading troops and the political and administrative units that would accompany them, describing briefly the most important political, administrative, and economic institutions of Great Britain and the leading public figures,' wrote Walter Schellenberg in his posthumously published memoir, *The Labyrinth*, later retitled *Hitler's Secret Service*. Soon after he was awarded the Iron Cross, First Class, Nazi Germany's top military honour – bestowed personally by Hitler for his role in the Venlo Incident – and prior to the Battle of Britain, Schellenberg was asked to compile an SS document. He produced *Informationsheft*, which he refers to as a 'small booklet'. (It was published in English in 2000 as *Invasion 1940: The Nazi Invasion Plan for Britain*.) *Informationsheft*'s companion piece, *Sonderfahndungsliste G. B.* (better known as 'The Black Book') – effectively an arrest list of 2820 prominent British people – was to be actioned immediately after a successful invasion. Ellis's name, no first or middle names, solely as a 'journalist', was on the list: 'Ellis, brit. Journalist, RSHA IV E 4.'[15]

Continued Schellenberg: 'It was also to contain instructions on the necessary measures to be taken in occupying the premises of the Foreign Office, the War Office, the Home Office, and the various departments of the Secret Service and Special Branch. This task occupied a great deal of my time, involving the collection and assembly of material from various sources by a selected staff of my own people. When it was finished an edition of 20,000 copies was printed and stored in a room next to my office. They were burned in 1943 in a fire started in one of the air raids, an ending that is symbolic of the ultimate failure of the German opportunity in the West.'

As one of the principal characters involved in the Venlo Incident, it would be logical that Schellenberg, the man who lured Stevens and Best to their capture, plundered them for information for *Informationsheft G. B.* It's a point hammered home by Keith Jeffery in his official history of MI6, even though MI6's late official historian can't get the name of the document right.

'How much actual information [the Nazis] got from the two SIS officers, and how much from their double agent [Folkert Arie] van Koutrik, remains uncertain . . . by mid-December 1939, however, the

Germans were able to construct detailed and largely accurate charts of both Stevens's and Best's agent networks and in the autumn of 1940 their *Informationschaft GB* [sic] provided some fairly accurate information about SIS head office and the Z Organisation, quoting both Stevens and Best.

'Postwar interrogation of German intelligence officers suggested that, while Van Koutrik had provided names and addresses of Stevens's Hague station agents, "they knew nothing of the Best organisation prior to the Venlo incident".[16] Whatever the truth of the matter, it is clear from the German interrogation reports on Stevens and Best that both men provided plenty of information about SIS, if only because they believed the Germans already knew a lot.'

There is no mention by Jeffery of Dick Ellis having anything to do with it. But in Nigel West's telling of 'The Black Book' story in his book, *MI6*, he says that an Abwehr officer, who'd undergone debriefing at Camp 020 after the war, had claimed that a White Russian source in Paris provided much of the information used in *Informationsheft Grossbritannien*. The officer 'confirmed that the SIS order of battle had come from Alexander Zelensky, who had in turn obtained it from an Australian married to a Russian'. To make certain, the investigators tracked down the notes taken by the SIS interrogator who had debriefed the officer in 1945, which 'even mentioned the name Captain Ellis. Evidently, an error in the translation had obscured the correct spelling of the surname.'

As a result, claimed West, Ellis was now suspected of having been the Abwehr's source on SIS. 'A check in the *Sonderfahndungsliste* provided another clue. At the end of each entry was a departmental reference for the particular section (Amt) of the Reich Security Agency which [would have] been responsible for requesting the arrest. The designation RSHA IV referred to the Gestapo and the sub-section responsible for journalists was VI G 1.' Ellis's entry was unique 'because, although he is described simply as a British journalist, the Gestapo section which supplied the information about him was IV E 4, the unit which dealt with SIS. In other words, the Gestapo had tried to obscure the fact that this "journalist" was known to them as an SIS officer.'

West noted that this was the only instance in which the agency's entry failed to reflect a person's true status as an intelligence officer. As an example, he observed that on page 86 of the document, entry number 173 for William John Hooper 'describes him as a British agent . . . like all other SIS officers Ellis also used a cover-name, and his was Howard. A check on the two male Howards listed failed to find Ellis . . . the omission of Ellis's details was entirely circumstantial, but it lent weight to the evidence of the former Abwehr officer.'

Although no one reveals who this Abwehr officer is and what his bona fides are, when West writes that *the Gestapo had tried to obscure the fact that this 'journalist' was known to them as an SIS officer* – his meaning could not be plainer: he has no doubt that it was an act of deliberate concealment by the Nazis. Couldn't be accidental or a clerical oversight, then, right? Or poor intelligence-gathering? Which begs the question why the Nazis would list Ellis in the first place. What would be gained by omitting his true profession as an intelligence officer? If he were a true double agent, surely it would be better cover to list him as an intelligence officer known to the Gestapo like all the other known British agents on the list rather than draw attention to a missing but obvious detail? One MI6 agent, Thomas Kendrick, is simply listed as a 'British captain': no reference is made to his status as an intelligence officer. Why suppose then that Ellis was being protected or being treated differently to everyone else?[17]

Instead, interpretations like West's have allowed conspiracy theories around Ellis to spread all over print media and the internet. The following accusations are unfounded in fact:

'The Gestapo captured two British intelligence agents in Holland and drew on their knowledge in compiling the handbook; information also came from an Australian, Dick Ellis, who had links with British intelligence.'
- York Membery, *Sunday Times*, 30 May 1999

'A rogue British intelligence officer, Colonel Dick Ellis, admitted after his retiral [sic]

that he had sold "vast quantities of informa-
tion" about the British secret service to the
Germans.'
- James Dalrymple, *Independent*, 3 March 2000

'Major Stevens and Captain Best, along with
Colonel C. H. ("Dick") Ellis, were significant
contributors to the intelligence part of the
handbook. Ellis later confessed that he had
betrayed England to Germany . . . it is probable
that material provided to the Germans by Ellis
gave the interrogators the pertinent questions
to ask Stevens and Best, giving the captives
the impression that the SD already knew most of
the material under consideration and that their
mere additions would not add significantly to the
total picture.'
- Kenneth Campbell, *American Intelligence
Journal*, 2007

The stories are never-ending. One of the worst of them all is that
Ellis was directly implicated in the 1 June 1943 death of British actor
and *Gone with the Wind* star Leslie Howard, who was on a KLM
flight shot down over the Bay of Biscay. Seventeen people were killed.

Postulated Chapman Pincher in *Their Trade is Treachery*: 'The
Germans had known, for instance, that Leslie Howard, the film actor,
had been carrying out secret war missions for Sir William Stephenson.
They had been told that he would be on a certain aeroplane and had
been able to shoot it down over the Bay of Biscay. Had Ellis been one
of these spies?'

It's abundantly clear from this passage that Pincher's journalistic
modus operandi is to make a false assumption in order to lead the
reader: like the classic loaded question, 'When did you stop beating
your wife?'

In his foreword to Hyde's autobiography, Stephenson denied
having any involvement with Howard ('I never had anything to do

with Leslie Howard') or any 'secret war missions', yet bizarrely there in black and white in *A Man Called Intrepid*, written five years before Pincher's book, is a reference to Howard being on a 'secret mission for Stephenson' and an admission that 'the Germans knew about it and shot down the unarmed plane', even though the 'British knew beforehand that the Germans knew, but to protect the secret of how they knew, Bletchley [Park], which had monitored the German Air Force orders, let the plane go down.' Howard's son Ronald Howard makes no mention of Ellis or Stephenson in his 1982 memoir, *In Search of My Father: A Portrait of Leslie Howard*.[18]

An even more bizarre conspiracy is the one connecting Ellis to *Gruppenführer* Heinrich Müller and *Reichsleiter* Martin Bormann in former American soldier Paul Manning's 1981 cult book *Martin Bormann: Nazi in Exile*.[19] Manning's sources were never disclosed – it's doubtful there were any. He provides no proof, no references.

'In 1941 a Gestapo agent within the British intelligence structure sent a coded report to General Mueller in Berlin that top secret information affecting the course and outcome of the war was being regularly exchanged over the ether between Churchill and Roosevelt. Although it is true that British intelligence had penetrated the German General Staff, it is equally true that General Mueller had his mole inside Britain's Secret Intelligence Service, a fact unknown to either the British or Admiral Canaris of the Abwehr, who was leaking information secretly to General Sir Stewart Graham Menzies, head of MI6.

'General Mueller's agent was Charles Howard Ellis, a top-level British career intelligence officer who also served as a Nazi double agent throughout World War II. At the time of his tip-off to General Mueller, Ellis was in New York as second in command to Sir William Stephenson ("A Man Called Intrepid"), who was doing his best to move the US into war against Germany with a combined propaganda and British spy operation . . . Ellis learned of the Roosevelt–Churchill telephone conversations from Stephenson, who was a frequent visitor to the White House. Ellis sent his message to Mueller through Gestapo channels via Mexico City to Buenos Aires, where it was beamed to Hamburg by one of the clandestine German transmitters in that capital. The Ellis report was quickly taken by General Mueller to

Reichsleiter Bormann, who promptly told Hitler about it. The Fuehrer [sic] ordered Bormann to do whatever was necessary to unscramble these conversations and provide him with transcripts within hours of their occurrence.'

The late celebrity biographer Charles Higham also preposterously charged that Ellis, as British consul in New York, had deliberately sabotaged the passport and visa of British actress and Howard's *Scarlet Pimpernel* co-star Merle Oberon on a 1942 tour to entertain US and British troops in Britain.[20] On top of all that, said Higham, no less than alleged Nazi sympathiser Errol Flynn had enjoyed 'the powerful protections of the Nazi agent, Charles Howard Ellis'.[21]

All of which is balderdash. As an anonymous 'special correspondent' wrote in the *Canberra Times* in 1981: 'According to [Chapman Pincher], Colonel Charles Howard Ellis, an Australian-born member of British intelligence, began his treachery by spying for the Germans. In which case, he must have had the deepest of deep covers, because the Germans seem to have been unaware of him. Researchers such as [John Cecil] Masterman failed to uncover him, as have biographers of Admiral Canaris, who headed the German intelligence services, Ladislas Farago, whose monumental book on the failures of the German secret services in *The Game of The Foxes* is a textbook on the era, and Günter Peis, in his *Mirror of Deception* . . . one can only wonder if John le Carré or Frederick Forsyth might not have done it better.'[22]

CHAPTER 12

OUR MAN IN NEW YORK

'In wartime, truth is so precious that she should always be
attended by a bodyguard of lies.'
– Winston Churchill to Joseph Stalin, Tehran Conference
(30 November 1943)

On 10 February 1941 Soviet defector Walter Krivitsky
had been found dead in his Washington DC hotel room. Dick
Ellis, meanwhile, was shuttling around the United States and Mexico.
On 20 May he arrived at Brownsville Municipal Airport, Texas, on a
Pan American World Airways aeroplane from Mexico. Less than four
weeks later, Germany invaded the Soviet Union.

On 11 July the Office of the Coordinator of Information (COI),
an American military-intelligence and propaganda agency, was established by President Franklin D. Roosevelt with William Donovan
at its head, its creation largely stemming from justifiable concern
over the Nazis' *blitzkrieg* in Europe. Within a year COI had mutated
into the Office of Strategic Services (OSS). The OSS is now recognised
as the organisation that evolved into the Central Intelligence Agency
(CIA), which officially came into being in 1947.

Donovan's right-hand man at COI/OSS in Washington DC and
chief adviser was Ellis, then living at the Hotel Weylin, on 54th Street
and Madison Avenue in Manhattan, but the avuncular Australian
effectively 'ran the organisation'. Ellis was sent from New York by
William Stephenson 'to Washington to open a sub-station to facilitate

daily liaison with Donovan, who reciprocated by sending [future Director of Central Intelligence, DCI] Allen Welsh Dulles to liaise with BSC in the Rockefeller Center'. According to Thomas F. Troy, paraphrasing Stephenson, Ellis 'was the tradecraft expert, the organisation man, the one who furnished Bill Donovan with charts and memoranda on running an intelligence organisation'.

Ellis writes about all this in his introduction to *A Man Called Intrepid*.

'I was soon requested to draft a blueprint for an American intelligence agency, the equivalent of BSC and based on these British wartime improvisations . . . detailed tables of organisation were disclosed to Washington . . . among these were the organisational tables that led to the birth of General William Donovan's OSS.'[1]

It's been a matter of debate who exactly came up with the 'blueprint' for the establishment of America's first spy agency; James Bond creator Ian Fleming has also been credited.[2] Ellis rejected the idea outright: 'It's simply not true; [Fleming] had nothing to do with it.' But if it was indeed Ellis, it would mean an Australian later accused of being a Nazi and Soviet double agent had been instrumental in the setting up of what would become the CIA, the world's foremost, most powerful and popularly recognised secret service.

Ellis said he 'gave no formal lectures but had many talks with individual officers of COI on work "in the field", the handling of agents, methods of reporting, etc . . . I spent some months in Washington in close liaison with D [Donovan] and members of his staff, and during this time was frequently called upon to advise on this or that "I" [intelligence] problem . . . I had frequent contact with D, both in his office and at his home in Washington.'

Naturally, the conspiracy brigade has duly theorised that if Ellis had been such a well-placed double agent 'it might explain why many OSS operations unravelled without apparent reason'. One individual likened Ellis to a low-level mafia lieutenant figure straight off *The Sopranos*, a sort of secret-service Paulie Walnuts, 'an associate of the MI6 cabal of Philby, Burgess and Maclean', with Philby cast as Tony Soprano: 'OSS was set up for "Wild Bill" Donovan by Dickie Ellis, an MI6 official and member of the Philby gang, and the CIA was organised on a scheme by Philby himself.'

What's irrefutable is that testimonies from American political and military heavyweights of the period elevated Ellis, widely regarded as MI6's chief in North America, to a position of great importance within the fledgling US spy apparatus. Former OSS Europe head and later US ambassador to France, Germany and the United Kingdom Colonel David K. E. Bruce, who was trained as a spy by Ellis,[3] said Ellis was so significant, that 'without [his] assistance . . . American intelligence could not have gotten off the ground in World War II'.[4]

Further, Bruce declared that Ellis was a 'remarkable, unpublicised individual' whom he credited with 'helping him set up COI's Secret Intelligence branch'.[5] William Casey, who headed up OSS's Europe-based human-intelligence operations, the Secret Intelligence Branch, and went on to become director of the CIA, wrote in his autobiography, *The Secret War Against Hitler*, that Ellis was not only writing blueprints but involved in on-the-ground, logistical programs: 'Dick Ellis, [an] experienced British pro, helped establish training centres, mostly around Washington.'[6] United States Assistant Secretary of State Adolf Berle commented: 'The really active head of the intelligence section in [William] Donovan's [OSS] group is [Ellis] . . . in other words, [Stephenson's] assistant in the British intelligence [sic] is running Donovan's intelligence service.'

But Ellis wasn't a huge fan of Donovan, summing up the American thus: 'Intense personal ambition . . . bad strategist: crystallises opposition and underrates political enemies. Indiscreet. Inclination to flashy work.'

Ellis also found Donovan too impetuous.

'He was apt to call one at unusual hours to discuss organisation problems, projects or simply to exchange ideas. He liked one to argue with him, to submit ideas and schemes, to criticise and to comment freely. One had to be cautious in suggesting schemes, as he was apt to seize upon them at once and start the wheels rolling without sufficient preparation or study.'

According to Guy Liddell, Ellis was criss-crossing the Atlantic, having meetings with Valentine Vivian in London, having 'flown over from New York at 26,000 feet in an atmosphere of sixty degrees below zero. He had eaten a large meal and drunk half a bottle of brandy before starting since he could not get any food on account of having to wear an oxygen mask the whole way. The journey took eight and a half hours, starting from some desolate spot in Newfoundland.'[7]

There was virulent opposition to the idea of a new service, according to Anthony Cave Brown, who spoke of 'one of the most violent and prolonged interdepartmental battles in modern Washington history, as all the established intelligence departments in Washington closed rank and opposed both man and concept'. Ellis was among Donovan's inner circle, who were ostensibly 'all the senior representatives of the British secret services in the United States', including 'Stephenson, [Rex] Benson, David Bowes-Lyon (brother of Queen Elizabeth and chief of the Political Warfare Executive),[8] Colonel Ellis, and Professor J. W. Wheeler-Bennett of the New York office of PWE [Political Warfare Executive]. It was a war council the purpose of which was to establish a US secret service with Donovan as its chief.'

On 2 December 1941 Ellis arrived in Halifax, Nova Scotia on the *Pasteur* from Greenock, Scotland. He was 47 and travelling with British broadcaster Howard Percival Marshall, director of public relations at Britain's Ministry of Food, and film editor Sidney Stone. It's not totally clear why Ellis was in Canada, but from the background of his travelling companions it would appear it had something to do with BSC propaganda for the effort to get the United States into the war.

Halifax, according to Thomas F. Troy, 'was a major starting point of convoys heading across the Atlantic. Canadian intelligence on the identification and movement of known or suspected spies, saboteurs, and couriers, and disaffected workers, sailors, cargo handlers, and others was essential to the establishment of a pool of intelligence without which the security job could not be done.' The Canadian government had provided four destroyers to protect shipping 'in and out of Halifax' and the port 'had become a central point of enemy espionage'. Historian David Stafford has also said that Nova Scotia was considered a possible site for Camp X, or STS (Special Training School) 103, a kind of British-led commando boot camp for American secret-service agents.[9]

Four months earlier, the Atlantic Conference between the United States and the United Kingdom had taken place on the USS *Augusta* in Newfoundland. The Allies' declaration, or charter, was released on 14 August. At this point in the chronology of World War II, the American public generally opposed their nation becoming involved in a war it didn't need or wish to fight but the British aggressively wanted the US involved, as has been argued in various books, most recently Henry Hemming's *Our Man in New York: The British Plot to Bring America into the Second World War*. The title refers to William Stephenson but the same phrase was used by British intelligence officer and BSC agent Major John A. R. Pepper in Serbian spy Duško Popov's autobiography to describe Ellis.[10]

Hemming calls Britain's efforts to lure the United States 'the largest state-sponsored influence campaign ever run on American soil' and Ellis's own words in a 1970s Canadian Broadcasting Corporation documentary backed this argument, yet Ellis, somewhat oddly, only gets a single mention in Hemming's book.[11] Ellis said Stephenson was in America 'to do what he could of course to bring the United States in the war' and 'on a mission for Churchill . . . to arouse the sentiment in the United States in favour of joining the Allies'. BSC achieved that through propaganda: '[Stephenson's] greatest achievement was through [William] Donovan, starting a very widespread campaign throughout the United States, through the press and by radio, drawing American attention to the dangers of a Nazi victory; the effects it would have on the United States.'

But Ernest Cuneo countered this, writing that 'the charge that BSC endeavoured to involve the US in war was absurd. The President knew we would be forced to stop Hitler long before the British realised it . . . a "pilot" program was started in 1938 under Louis Johnson, Under Secretary of War, and 250 millions [sic] diverted from [Secretary of Commerce Harry] Hopkins's and [Secretary of the Interior Harold] Ickes's domestic programs to refitting of Army bases.'

Hemming argues otherwise: 'The US commander-in-chief was deploying American sailors in the hope that they would be attacked, so that he could have a better chance of taking the country to war' and that he was working on getting America into the war 'as early as March 1941'.

Less than a week after Ellis arrived in Canada, on 7 December 1941, over 350 Japanese planes bombed almost the entire United

States Pacific Fleet at Pearl Harbor in Oahu, Hawaii, killing over 2400 people, and the following day the United States declared war on Japan. Germany then declared war on the United States. But how much had BSC, its American partners the FBI, President Roosevelt and FBI–BSC go-between Ellis himself known of the Japanese attack before it happened and how much of that information had been passed on to FBI boss J. Edgar Hoover and President Franklin D. Roosevelt? It has been reported Ellis advised Hoover on 'counter-espionage measures before Pearl Harbor'.

It has also been grist for the conspiratorial mill since the 1940s. Hemming denied there was any forewarning of the attack, despite his ideas about Roosevelt wanting war.

'If either Roosevelt or Churchill had known that an attack was planned at Pearl Harbor, let alone the date, it would have been in their interests to pass this on. Even if the Americans had been forewarned, and as a result the raid had been less successful, the country would have clamoured for war. Their anger had less to do with the severity of the defeat than the scale and nature of the assault. The only advance warning of Pearl Harbor received by any Briton or American was the one picked up at Opana Point Radar Station less than an hour before the assault began.'

Yet Duško Popov, codename TRICYCLE, who was working for MI6's Stewart Menzies and isn't mentioned at all in Hemming's book, wrote an autobiography featuring extensive passages laying out his case that he had warned the Americans months in advance. Ellis was Popov's handler or 'US case officer' in New York. BSC agent, Ellis's friend and later world-famous children's-book author Roald Dahl thought 'the whole thing doesn't make sense' but said that William Stephenson 'swears, he did to me' that he had audio tapes of Japanese government officials discussing the attacks and these tapes were given to President Roosevelt. 'He swears that they knew therefore of the oncoming attack.'

Ellis himself said it was all true and the Americans, including President Roosevelt himself, had been warned at the highest levels. His account goes against the prevailing narrative the President knew nothing about the coming attack.

'[Stephenson] was convinced from the information that was reaching him that this attack was imminent, and through Jimmy Roosevelt, President Roosevelt's son, he passed this information to the President. Now whether the President at that time had other information which corroborated this . . . it's impossible to say.'

CHAPTER 13

A SLEDGEHAMMER IN SEARCH OF AN ANVIL

'There was a very considerable Anglo-US effort, behind the
scenes, before Pearl Harbor.'
– LETTER FROM DICK ELLIS TO H. MONTGOMERY HYDE
(26 DECEMBER 1960)

IN THE SECOND WEEK OF AUGUST 1941 DuŠKO POPOV arrived in
New York from Lisbon, Portugal. The Serbian had been asked
in his capacity as an agent for the Berlin-headquartered Abwehr to
gather intelligence about American air force and navy installations
and their capacities, specifically Pearl Harbor.

'Popov's mission from the Abwehr was to bring back a laundry
list of data about American military defences and industrial capacity,'
wrote John Koster in *Operation Snow*. 'His mission from the British –
eager to have America in the war and eager for American help should
Japan attack British and Dutch colonies – was to tip off the Americans
about Japan's sinister interest in Pearl Harbor . . . the whole first page,
minus the introductory paragraph, was a request for military data
about Pearl Harbor.'

Popov's biographer Larry Loftis says, 'Forty per cent of [the
document] pertains to investigation of Pearl Harbor's defences.'[1]

It was a powerful warning something big was coming.

'I communicated the news of the impending attack on Pearl
Harbor to Lisbon MI6 post-haste. They got on to London, and I was

instructed to carry my information personally to the United States, since I was leaving in a few days,' Popov wrote in *Spy/Counterspy*. 'Apparently, they thought it preferable that I be the bearer of the tidings since the Americans might want to question me at length to extract the last bit of juice.'

Popov's point man in Manhattan was BSC's Dick Ellis, who was coordinating weekly with Percy Foxworth, head of an FBI counterintelligence unit called SIS (Special Intelligence Service) and head of the FBI in New York. Ellis was also meeting with FBI boss J. Edgar Hoover, whom he gave 'some useful lessons in counterespionage techniques as well as passing on important domestic security intelligence which they could not otherwise have obtained', though their relationship later soured. In his autobiography, Popov quoted Double Cross head Colonel Thomas Argyll 'Tar' Robertson: 'We're not letting you out of our hands. The FBI will be running you, but you'll go to New York as our man. You'll report to our representative there, Colonel Ellis.'

At this point BSC had 1000 agents.[2] Popov was met at an airfield by the FBI and taken to the Waldorf-Astoria to await what would be an eventual meeting with Hoover. According to Loftis, 'in Popov's briefcase was a treasure trove worthy of an international spy', including 'a German questionnaire with an English translation' about what Popov was to find out about Pearl Harbor for the Nazis' allies, the Japanese, and 'a vial of white crystals for making secret ink'. President Roosevelt was at the same time in Newfoundland for the Atlantic Conference with Prime Minister Churchill.

'Ellis, the most senior officer for MI6 in America, turned up at the New York office of Percy Foxworth, chief of the FBI's Special Intelligence Service and principal liaison with BSC, to inform him that the expected British double agent had arrived, was staying at the Waldorf, and that the FBI were welcome to take him over,' wrote John Bryden in *Fighting to Lose*. 'He had been Britain's "number-one agent", Ellis told Foxworth, and with his help the British had been able to "locate all of the radio stations used by the Germans and also to identify a large number of their agents".

'This was a huge fib, but it drew Foxworth in, especially as Ellis had brought along samples of [Popov's] secret ink and copies of his code, his wireless instructions, and a photo-enlargement of a list of questions in English the Germans wanted their spy to get answers to.'

The Abwehr's questionnaire about America's military capacity was hidden in a microdot – miniaturised text or photographs that can be seen only with microscope – embedded in a telegram. It could be enlarged for reading. Popov was known to write letters in specially made invisible ink.[3] Bryden cannot resist having a sarcastic dig at Ellis's origins when he writes: 'Within the first week of the FBI taking [Popov] over [from MI6] . . . Ellis was asked to prepare his first invisible-ink letter reporting to the Germans that he had arrived safely. It was probably thought that Ellis had a better chance of composing it in proper Englishman's English, even though he was an Aussie.'

The questionnaire clearly troubled Popov's FBI contact, Foxworth, according to Bryden.

'Foxworth sent the questionnaire on to Hoover with the strong recommendation that the FBI take Popov on. If, by any chance, Roosevelt and Churchill did not get Popov's Pearl Harbor questionnaire at their Atlantic meeting [in Newfoundland], Hoover got it now . . . while [Stephenson] certainly did lead the security and counter-espionage function of BSC, Charles Ellis was the actual MI6 chief for North America.

'Until Ellis called on Foxworth, the FBI had understood that Popov was only passing through the United States on his way to Egypt. The Bureau had also been told by the British to expect him on August 12 at La Guardia Airport, but he had landed at nearby North Beach instead. This had led to the mix-up with the army and navy intelligence officers, embarrassing in an organisation that prided itself on being methodical. A makeup meeting was swiftly arranged.'

It took place at the Commodore Hotel, almost four months before Pearl Harbor.

'FBI assistant director Earl Connelley sat down with Popov on August 18, along with Ellis and FBI special agent Charles Lanman.[4] The session lasted three hours . . . [Ellis] brought with him photo-enlargements of the microdots containing the English-language questionnaire and Popov's wireless-transmission instructions. These Connelley attached to his report, not knowing that Hoover had already received the copies Ellis had given Foxworth. The next day, Lanman went around to Popov's hotel and collected what microdots Popov still had, and his other espionage paraphernalia.'

Loftis continues the story and underlines the gravity of what had just taken place.

'Connelley sent to Hoover a 12-page letter recapping the discussion. Providing J. Edgar with a full account of Dusko's work as a double agent, Earl wrote: "Mr Popov was furnished with a letter of instructions in German, which letter was turned over to the British authorities here, and Mr Ellis furnished me with an English translation of these instructions ... reference to these instructions indicates considerable information as to what the German authorities already have ... and ... indicates the detailed information which they expect him to obtain while in the United States" ... as of August 19, 1941, then, almost four months before the Pearl Harbor attack, J. Edgar Hoover and the FBI were on notice of the German/Japanese interest in the Hawaiian naval base, and Dusko's assignment to investigate its defences.'

While in his book Bryden cheekily refers to Ellis at that moment being 'apparently, Admiral Canaris's top agent inside British intelligence', it is evident he does not believe Ellis spied either for the Nazis or the Soviets, though brings up a curious letter written before Pearl Harbor by Popov's underage teenage lover, Mady, 'his supposed 15-year-old girlfriend in Portugal.' Much of it seemed innocent chit-chat, but then:

```
My dear uncle . . . has been travelling abroad
but has returned now. He too sends you a lot of
greetings because, as you well know, he is very
fond of you. I was very anxious about Dicky, but
he is really a nice chap. I got a letter from him
some days ago. I would be glad if we could arrange
to meet all of us together in some nice place.
```

'When the FBI asked Popov who this "Dicky" might be, he quickly replied that it was "the name of one of the British intelligence officers in London who was acting as a German spy for that organisation."

'And so there was; except another person nicknamed "Dickie" was standing right there at Popov's elbow. One can imagine Charles Ellis's forehead beading with perspiration. It may have been a threat, of course, but it also may have been an open-code instruction for Ellis to attend a meeting set up by his Abwehr contacts.'

As Popov writes in *Spy/Counterspy*, he told Connelley 'you can expect an attack on Pearl Harbor before the end of this year' but when he eventually met Hoover in New York weeks later, Hoover instantly dismissed Popov.

'J. Edgar Hoover encountered me. I use the word advisedly. There was no introduction, no preliminaries, no politesse ... there was Hoover sitting behind the desk looking like a sledgehammer in search of an anvil.'

It was a disastrous meeting. Popov told Hoover he was carrying a 'serious warning indicating exactly where, when, how, and by whom your country is going to be attacked' but Hoover branded Popov 'a bogus spy' and shouted 'good riddance' after him as Popov left Hoover's office in disgust at the way he was being treated. He immediately sought out the counsel of Ellis, who 'was aghast as I was at Hoover's transparent artifice and utter disregard for the exigencies of the war'.

'I rang Colonel Ellis to report on the fiasco with Hoover and to prepare a strategic retreat. He asked for a day or two to see what went wrong and to seek advice from William Stephenson ... I roamed my apartment like the caged animal I had become. Leaving seemed the only solution. I told Ellis as much when we met for lunch two days later.

'"Hoover is a very difficult man," Ellis understated diplomatically, "but you have to understand that he rescued the FBI from the corruption into which it had fallen during the [Warren G.] Harding administration. That was in 1924, but I think he is still obsessed with the idea that it may have a relapse. He is very mistrustful of anyone who tries to mix in his affairs."'

Ellis was prescient in his character analysis of Hoover. But Ellis's consultation with Stephenson came to nothing.

'"Any intervention from us would do more harm than good," Ellis estimated. "Hoover is very jealous about any interference with his organisation, especially from the British."'

A month before Pearl Harbor, Ellis was in England.

'Charles Ellis arrived in London on November 3 for talks with the head of MI6(V), Valentine Vivian, and the following week discussed Popov over lunch with Major [sic] [Thomas Argyll] Robertson and Guy Liddell,' writes Bryden in *Fighting to Lose*. 'The first two had definitely read the entire Pearl Harbor questionnaire, and with relations between Japan and the United States worsening, they surely would have speculated on the implied threat to the Pacific Fleet. Liddell's diary does not mention them talking about it.'

When Popov got the news on 7 December 1941 Pearl Harbor had been attacked with the loss of nearly 2500 lives, he realised to his horror the Americans had done nothing with his information.

'Involuntarily, I shook my head till my brain felt as though it were coming unstuck. The bulletins simply were not believable. The Japanese had scored a surprise attack on Pearl Harbor. How, I asked myself, how? We knew they were coming. We knew how they were going to come. Exactly like at Taranto.[5] And that's how they came, combined torpedo and dive-bomber attacks, exactly as employed by Admiral [Andrew] Cunningham against the Italians. Except that the Japanese planes hardly should have got off the deck.

'More news. The battleships *West Virginia* and *California* had been sunk at their moorings. At their moorings, I moaned. They couldn't have been at their moorings. They had to be steaming to attack the Japanese fleet. Then it was the *Arizona*. Blown up. Every other battleship and unit of the fleet heavily damaged. This was Orson Welles, I thought, remembering his famous scare broadcast. I couldn't credit what I was hearing. Somewhere, somehow, there had to be an explanation. In one and a half hours the mastery of the Pacific had passed from American to Japanese hands. I had the right information to forestall the attack. I had travelled thousands of miles to deliver the information, which would certainly have shortened the war by a year or more. And American red tape had stopped the information going through.'

Popov writes of his anguish about 'the hundreds of thousands, perhaps millions, who died needlessly as a result of the mishandling of the information I brought to America concerning the impending Japanese attack'.

Had Ellis sabotaged Duško Popov and failed to stop Pearl Harbor through his own lack of remonstration with J. Edgar Hoover? This was the hedged view of Chapman Pincher in *Too Secret Too Long*, who surmises the Australian undermined Popov before the Serbian double agent's meeting with the FBI chief.

'Ellis's relations with the FBI might repay critical study by historians because he could, possibly, have been responsible for Hoover's decision to ignore a clear warning from Popov about the forthcoming attack on Pearl Harbor. Ellis might have given a bad report on Popov to Hoover, who became aggressively unpleasant to the agent and disinclined to believe anything he said. On the other hand, if Ellis had still been assisting the German intelligence authorities he would have told them what he knew about the Double Cross operation and there is no evidence that they learned anything about it.'[6]

Possibly. To be fair to Pincher, however, he could have been on to something if Ellis had been compromised by Japanese intelligence because of his connection to their agent, Vladimir von Petrov. Britain wanted the United States to join the war effort and Japan wanted to goad the United States into war. Had Ellis been blackmailed not only into being a German and Russian mole but also an agent of Japan? It's another tantalising albeit unanswerable question, but highly unlikely.

Yet even if it were true, it doesn't explain why others in the FBI – Lanham and Connelley – and Stephenson himself, who had been consulted on Popov's questionnaire by Ellis, couldn't have pressed Hoover to reconsider Popov's warnings. Stephenson could also have attempted via his own channels to warn President Roosevelt or Prime Minister Churchill that BSC and the FBI had intelligence in its possession that at least warranted a phone conversation between the two leaders of the free world.

In his CBC interview Ellis spoke of Jimmy Roosevelt delivering Popov's warning about Pearl Harbor to his father, but Ellis, then in his late 70s, was likely prevented from saying what he really knew of America's complicity in its shocking intelligence failure by Britain's Official Secrets Act – a point Loftis makes in his book.[7]

'I never did get an answer to the enigma of Pearl Harbor,' said Popov. 'Over the years, I have studied the question, tried to draw conclusions, heard all sorts of speculation and conjectures. There have been official inquiries and courts-martial, but nowhere have I ever read or heard mention of the documented evidence I brought to the United States of the Japanese plans to attack Pearl Harbor.'

Says Loftis: 'Hoover told no one, not FDR, not [commander-in-chief of the United States Pacific Fleet] Admiral [Husband E.] Kimmel, not naval intelligence. The [FBI] director kept the information classified his entire life. There were eight investigations into the Pearl Harbor disaster. Not one mentions Popov's questionnaire. Not one called him or Dick Ellis to testify. Worse, Hoover actively hid the information from FDR.'[8]

Popov himself also poured his scorn on Hoover, whom he called an 'irrational, ranting man . . . the person responsible for the disaster of Pearl Harbor'.

He may have been right. It certainly wasn't Dick Ellis, who in time Hoover came to actively mistrust, according to Raymond J. Batvinis in his book *Hoover's Secret War Against Axis Spies: FBI Counterespionage During World War II.*

'Charles Ellis had repeatedly disparaged the FBI and then lied when he was called on it,' he writes, which prompted Hoover to insist 'the FBI would have no further dealings with Ellis', thus precipitating Ellis's departure from BSC.

In *The Two Bills: Mission Accomplished*, Ellis makes no mention of Duško Popov or Jimmy Roosevelt and writes of Pearl Harbor that 'naval and military commanders took no emergency defence measures against a possible attack on the naval base, so that the Japanese air attack came as a complete surprise'.

Though the Australian would concede the events of that terrible day would help Britain's aims of bringing the United States into the war.

'The tragic losses of men and ships occasioned by the attack, while temporarily weakening the US Navy in the Pacific and opening the way for Japanese naval action against the Philippines and Pacific island bases, shocked the American public into a sense of reality . . . the attack on Pearl Harbor unified the nation.'

CHAPTER 14

LITTLE WINDOW

'Eminent positions are like the summits of rocks; only eagles
and reptiles can get there.'
– SUZANNE CURCHOD

O N THE LAST DAY OF 1941 DICK ELLIS was in Washington DC for
a conference between the US State Department, British government, FBI, BSC and the Royal Canadian Mounted Police (RCMP).
America was reeling from the attack on Pearl Harbor and the smell of
blood was in the air.

The agenda of United States Assistant Secretary of State Adolf
Berle, who was helming the meeting, was to 'coordinate plans for
handling security and intelligence in the western hemisphere' and 'the
cessation of BSC's independent activities within US territory'. In other
words, BSC was over. The knives were also out for Ellis, who was
settled in New York at the Hotel Weylin; he later resided at an address
at East 56th Street. His teenage son, Olik, furnished with a British
passport, was working as a clerk at BSC.

Prior to the Japanese attack, Ellis, under the codename HOWARD
(a character who features in *A Man Called Intrepid*), had been busy
running domestic intelligence assets such as Donald Chase Downes to get
America into the war, tapping into suspicions that isolationalist groups
such as the America First Committee (AFC) were fronts for National
Socialism and fascism. In essence, Ellis, the supposed Nazi agent, was
running an anti-Nazi 'political warfare' campaign on American soil.

Ellis told Downes, 'Our primary directive from the PM [Winston Churchill] is that American participation in the war is the most important single objective for Britain. It is the only way, he feels, to victory over Nazism . . . if we can pin a Nazi contact or Nazi money on the isolationists, they will lose many of their followers. It might be the deciding factor in America's entry into the war, if the American public knew the truth.'

'Downes was eager to be recruited,' wrote Robin W. Winks in *Cloak and Gown,* 'and when [they] met . . . at a chophouse looking out on the skating rink at Rockefeller Plaza, he agreed to spy on his fellow Americans to see whether Nazi money was supporting isolationist groups . . . thus, Downes, an American citizen, in contravention of any number of American laws, became a spy for British intelligence.'[1]

But after Pearl Harbor, the AFC disbanded.

Wrote H. Montgomery Hyde in *Secret Intelligence Agent*: 'It was clear from the outset that Berle's principal target was BSC, whose activities he plainly resented' while President Franklin D. Roosevelt's aide and future OSS liaison Ernest Cuneo believed 'the State and Justice Departments wanted BSC closed down in general and the departure of Colonel Ellis in particular. The cause of their animus was pure, but not simple. It was bureaucratic opposition to the establishment of the new OSS.'

Stevenson in *Intrepid's Last Case*: 'Ellis instructed the fledgling OSS on techniques of communications, in which he was the foremost expert . . . the very lifeline of any intelligence system . . . when OSS desperately needed instructors, Stephenson summoned Britain's best: Major General Colin Gubbins of SOE [Special Operations Executive, a British-formed espionage and sabotage unit operating in occupied Europe under the purview of the Ministry of Economic Warfare], whose mission was armed action behind enemy lines . . . and from the other branch, SIS, one of its commanding officers, Dick Ellis.'[2]

The tireless Ellis, flitting between the United States and Egypt, where he worked as an adviser 'for the purpose of intelligence liaison with the Americans' to Richard 'Dick' Casey (Lord Casey), British Minister of State in the Middle East and later governor-general of Australia,[3] had, according to Anthony Cave Brown, become indispensable to OSS chief

William Donovan, codename Q, and his nascent American intelligence agency. This relationship lasted at least until the end of 1942.

'Throughout the Pearl Harbor period and until the beginning of 1943, except for a brief mission to Cairo in the spring of 1942, Ellis was at the centre of Donovan's affairs. He had an office close to "Q's", and he consulted and assisted in all phases of the development of Donovan's organisations – its financing, both overt and covert; its selection of secret agents and their training; the establishment of Donovan's worldwide communications systems; the briefing of agents going out on secret missions; [and] the establishment of Donovan's special operations and counterespionage services. [Ellis] was responsible for such matters as the provision of a cover and documentation department; the development of secret inks and special weapons; and providing advice and assistance in the formation of Donovan's overseas bases. Also, he was consulted on the nature of Donovan's contacts with the enemy services.'[4]

Ellis was also meeting with President Roosevelt himself, according to Churchill biographer David Irving: 'Stephenson's deputy, the SIS career officer Colonel Charles H. Ellis, was sitting with Hoover and Donovan, and reporting regularly to the President.'[5] Thomas F. Troy likened Ellis's stature in Washington DC intelligence circles as subordinate only to Stephenson and Donovan: 'Next to [them, Ellis] was perhaps the person most intimately involved in the events of 1940–41.' The role required delicate diplomacy, not least because it meant dealing with the stubborn, paranoid Hoover, who plainly resented the wideranging remit on American soil given to the Canadian businessman Stephenson and his Australian-born deputy, Ellis.

Guy Liddell wrote in his diary on 27 April 1942 that 'I had a long talk with Dick Ellis . . . apparently BSC very nearly closed down a few months ago. Certain isolationists or anti-British elements both in the government and in the Senate had got together and drafted a Registration Bill which would have forced BSC to submit all their papers, personnel, etc, to examination by the police. This was due to several causes. J. Edgar Hoover was annoyed because Bill Stephenson had been dealing with Donovan. The senators were annoyed because certain friends of Stephenson's had got to know about the German

Charles Howard 'Dick' Ellis and his older brother, William Stanley Ellis, Brisbane, 1899. The two boys lost their mother, Lillian, the previous year. Their father, William, died in 1920.

National Library of Australia

A postcard 'Charlie' (CENTRE), as he called himself, sent to his sister, Maisie, Melbourne, 1913.

National Library of Australia

Ellis (LEFT) with his classical ensemble, Melbourne, 1913. *National Library of Australia*

Private Ellis, London, 1915. He entered the 'theatre of war' on the Western Front in 1916. *National Library of Australia*

Ellis with fellow soldiers on the SS *Mutlah*, Red Sea, on his way to India, 1918. Ellis appears to be top left. *National Library of Australia*

Isaak Brodsky's 'The Execution of the Twenty-Six Baku Commissars', painted in 1925, which was reputed to feature Ellis as one of the British soldiers in the painting. This is highly doubtful. *Wikimedia Commons*

The Stalin-era Soviet memorial to the murdered commissars in Baku, Azerbaijan, demolished in 2009. *Wikimedia Commons*

Captain Ellis in uniform, London, 1919.
National Library of Australia

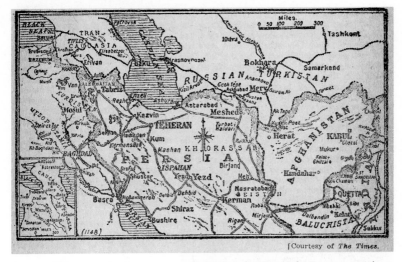

A map of Transcaspia that accompanied Ellis's 1920 *Stead's Review* article on Central Asia. *Stead's Review*

Ellis's defaced student portrait, Oxford University, 1921. The notation in Russian reads 'Anarchist'. *National Library of Australia*

Ellis, location and date unknown, though the lamppost in the background appears to be French, suggesting it is Paris, 1921. *National Library of Australia*

Ellis in Constantinople, 1922.
National Library of Australia

Ellis's ID photo for the British Chamber of Commerce, Vienna, 1927. On the evidence of this image, he'd aged rapidly. *National Library of Australia*

Dick Ellis (RIGHT) on his way to a friend's wedding, London, 1933. One of the two other men is Stanley Ellis. *National Library of Australia*

British registration cards from 1934 for Paul Hardt (Theodore Maly) and his wife, Lydia Hardt. Maly is one of the Soviet agents who recruited the Cambridge Five of British traitors, including Kim Philby. Lydia was allegedly in a relationship with one of Ellis's top sources, the quadruple agent (for Nazi Germany, Soviet Union, Great Britain and Japan) Vladimir von Petrov. *The National Archives*

A photograph printed in the *Saturday Evening Post* on 22 April 1939 showing Joseph Stalin at the May Day Parade in Moscow, 1937. *ACME*

ramifications of American chemicals, General Motors, Standard Oil, etc, and Adolf Birle [sic], an Under-Secretary of State for the State Department, had taken the view that BSC were going far beyond their charter for liaising with the appropriate departments of the government.

'A copy of the draft of the bill was shown by Stephenson to the embassy in Washington DC and they took the view that it was only directed against organisations under enemy control or influence. Stephenson did not accept this view and told Dick Ellis to go and see Birle in the State Department. Birle was extremely unpleasant, accused BSC of having 3000 agents in America and bumping people off in Baltimore. He said that this could not be tolerated and that BSC would come within the terms of the Registration Bill. Ellis pointed out to him that BSC had been set up by the Presidential decree and had been working in close cooperation with Hoover since their inception. If therefore he would not accept Ellis's statement that the allegations were categorically untrue he could refer the matter to Mr Hoover for investigation. Ellis then went on to point out that BSC were doing a considerable amount of work for the War Department and Navy Department and that as facilities had been accorded to these people to work on British territory, the British government might have to consider whether these activities could continue if BSC were virtually closed down.

'Ellis then went to Donovan who wrote a letter to the President. The latter decided to veto the bill. Birle, Francis Biddle (the Attorney-General), and Hoover got together and redrafted the bill in a slightly less noxious form. BSC then went to Quinn Tamm of the FBI who told [Ellis] that a meeting was to be held between Biddle, Birle, Hoover, the War Department and the Navy Department and suggested that Stephenson should be present. After listening to Biddle and Birle who both thought BSC should be reduced to the position of a liaison section with the appropriate government departments, he said that these conditions entirely met with his approval since that was in fact what they had been doing since the beginning of the war. He referred to Mr Hoover for verification and pointed out that he had rendered no less than 3900 reports to the FBI. Since however the authorities had decided to proceed with the bill he proposed to close down his organisation forthwith and to have no further relations with them.

'The meeting broke up in confusion. Next day Hoover came down to see Stephenson. Stephenson told Hoover exactly what he thought of him. He said that he had been a party to an intrigue for some considerable time and that had there been any real objection to any of Stephenson's activities it would have been quite simple for Hoover to ring him up and ask him to discuss the position. This he had not done. Stephenson therefore did not propose to have any further dealings with him. Hoover then tried to get Stephenson to agree to pass all his information through the FBI. Stephenson again refused. Eventually Hoover went away rather apologetically and undertook to smooth matters out which he did. The situation is now much better and Hoover has told his subordinates to co-operate wholeheartedly with BSC.'

As Ellis recalled in his CBC interview before his death: 'BSC was the only [organisation] in existence until [the] CIA came into existence after the war which represented all aspects of [a special operations, security and intelligence] operation . . . [BSC] laid the groundwork of [the CIA].'

How much sway Ellis had with Roosevelt (who died aged just 63 in 1945) in the setting up of the COI/OSS, and later the CIA, is a source of conjecture. There are suggestions that Director of Naval Intelligence Admiral John Henry Godfrey and Godfrey's aide Ian Fleming had more influence. This caused Ellis and Stephenson some annoyance in later years, especially with the publication of Donald McLachlan's 1968 book *Room 39: Naval Intelligence in Action 1939–45*. Godfrey and Fleming were considered to be 'would-be usurpers' of Stephenson's and Ellis's rightful credit.[6]

After setting up an OSS training centre in the Maryland area, Ellis was involved in the founding of Camp X, a 'secret-service training centre' on Lake Ontario – at Whitby near Oshawa outside Toronto – for the 'full-scale adoption by the OSS of British training methods'. Ellis described it himself as a 'combined intelligence and "special operations" training school' that called for 'a highly specialised type of training in which unarmed combat, the use of explosives, sabotage methods, radio communication and all the subtleties of infiltration and guerrilla operations were combined with the utilisation of newly developed technical devices'. FBI agents and resistance-movement fighters from foreign nations also received instruction at Camp X.

Today the location is called Intrepid Park. It was also where a Rockex or Telekrypton cipher machine developed by BSC's Benjamin deForest 'Pat' Bayly, Camp X's head, was installed and used to encipher and decipher MI6 traffic between London and New York.

Writes Richard J. Aldrich in *Intelligence and the War Against Japan: Britain, America and the Politics of Secret Service*, the idea of Camp X 'was not only to accelerate OSS, it was also "to impress the Americans". Many of the seconded British "professional" training staff had in fact been recruited from civilian life only months before, as Britain scrambled to mobilise.'

As Ellis said: 'SOE provided expert officers for training people, and the recruitment of French, Yugoslavs, Poles, Belgians and others was undertaken with the knowledge and assistance of the Canadian parties ... when Donovan's organisation came into being and expanded into what has subsequently become OSS, all his officers and the great number of his personal personnel were trained at Oshawa.'

Canada offered a number of advantages to BSC, SOE and OSS. It was where Ellis was spending most of his time – travel records of the war period indicate Ellis was regularly shuttling between New York, Ottawa, Toronto and Montrèal – and this is mentioned in J. L. Granatstein's and David Stafford's book *Spy Wars: Espionage in Canada from Gouzenko to Glasnost*: 'Ellis was [a] frequent visitor to Ottawa. A professional SIS officer since the 1920s, Ellis ran the BSC's Intelligence Division. In 1944 he visited Ottawa to brief RCMP Commissioner Stuart Wood on British perceptions of the Soviet and communist threat.'

Wrote William Stevenson in *Intrepid's Last Case*: 'Canada's vast hinterland concealed experimental projects and in World War II was the free world's only source of certain raw materials needed to create an atom bomb.'

It was also an easy place to dispose of bodies.

'Because Camp X was so secure, any fate could befall an inmate without public notice. Dick Ellis would later testify that during the war just ended, "We sometimes 'lost' individual enemies of Britain we picked up in the United States and smuggled into Canada. Sometimes the FBI would reproach us, or Hoover would demand explanations, and I could only say, "Sorry, we seem to have 'lost' the chap." We had *disposed of the body under the protection of the Crown*, to use the SIS phrase.'

On 20 September 1944, Ellis arrived back in Liverpool, England, on the Holland-American Line MV *Delftdijk*. It was three months after D-Day, an extraordinary Allied military operation in which William Stephenson's BSC and William Donovan's OSS had played an important early role and turned the tide of the war.[7] Ellis's work in America was done. He was almost 50, with a 33-year-old wife, Barbara, their 10-year-old daughter, Ann, and a now-adult son, Olik, by another woman, but his second marriage was in trouble.

Within less than a year, Hitler would be dead and Nazi Germany would surrender, the Third Reich crushed. Hiroshima and Nagasaki were bombed by the Americans in August 1945 and shortly thereafter Japan would surrender. The following month, in a seismic intelligence event, a Soviet cipher clerk called Igor Gouzenko defected to the West, began telling it what he knew, and the first known mention was made of the mysterious and to this day unidentified (at least publicly)[8] mole ELLI inside the British secret service. But as he relaxed at luxury hotel Storr's Hall at Bowness-on-Windermere in the Lake District, Ellis could have been forgiven for being proud of how far he'd come from his straitened early life in Australia.

For his considerable service to the United States and record of achievement while in the country during World War II, in 1946 Ellis was awarded a CBE by King George VI and the American Legion of Merit in the Officer class (LOM – O) by President Harry S. Truman. This could explain why so little examination has been made of Ellis's years in America from 1940 to 1944: it would be too catastrophic for MI6 and the CIA to admit a suspected Nazi and/or Soviet mole had been given such responsibility inside the heart of American intelligence.

Ernest Cuneo was Ellis's biggest fan, stating that Ellis 'uncovered one of the great spies of all time, Harry Dexter White,'[9] then virtually in command of the US Treasury, compared with whom Philby was small fry' and 'amassed one of the most brilliant records in the long history of British intelligence'.

Wrote Cuneo: 'To believe that, throughout these years, Dickie Ellis was a Soviet mole is to believe that Sir William Stephenson himself was a pigeon for the Kremlin, for the two men were as close as a picture to its frame ... it was on February 18, 1948, that Sir William Stephenson, then out of service but on a special mission, forewarned the United States that Moscow would produce its first atomic bomb on or about September 27, 1949. The Russian bombs went off four weeks early (announced by Truman on September 24, 1949) – close enough for a cigar.

'When Sir William gave me this staggering information on February 18, 1948 – a year and a half in advance of the event – I asked him how good the source was. He answered, "Triple A, Triple 1." I asked the question which never should be asked: Exactly how do you know?

'"We have a little window," Sir William said. Moles were then called "little windows."

'Except to transmit this to US authorities, I have never before disclosed this. I do so now as some evidence in defence of the honour of Colonel Ellis. What Sir William knew, Dickie Ellis knew. Hence, if Dickie Ellis had been a KGB mole, he would have reported the British mole in the Kremlin to his true masters. He had not.'

What's far more likely than Ellis working for the enemy is the most obvious conclusion of them all: there simply isn't anything incriminating to find.

'Surprisingly enough, no British or American authorities or authors have ever even hinted at any evidence of treachery on Ellis's part in those New York years,' wrote Thomas F. Troy in *Wild Bill and Intrepid*, failing to mention Pincher's unfounded accusation against Ellis regarding Pearl Harbor. 'Nor has anyone speculated on the possible damage done by Ellis to SIS, COI, and OSS. Likewise, no trace of Ellis is found in Pavel and Anatoli Sudaplatov's [sic] account of Soviet espionage in the United States during the war years.'[10]

Apart from the Pincher smear, as far as his time in America is concerned, Ellis is completely clean. Though this hasn't stopped conspiracy theories swirling around him because of his association with Cedric Belfrage, a British film critic and journalist who moved to the United States in 1920 and edited a left-wing New York newspaper called the *National Guardian*.

Again, these smears originate from Pincher and in later years were taken up by Christopher Andrew. Belfrage visited the Soviet Union in 1936 and was apparently recruited by Ellis in BSC as an agent in 1941.[11] He was among 'at least 12 Soviet sympathisers inside BSC', according to Pincher, identified in the 1960s by the Fluency Committee's 'decipherment' of 'KGB messages transmitted from New York to Moscow'. These were made public in the 1990s as part of the VENONA decrypts.

'A few, like Cedric Belfrage ... were identified but most of them remain known only by the codenames used in the traffic. The Committee therefore concentrated on the possibility that Ellis was one of the unknown agents having, perhaps, been pressed into KGB service, through blackmail or money, after 1940.'

Wrote the Russian state-owned Sputnik News Service in 2015: 'It is unclear from the MI5 file whether Belfrage had already been a Soviet agent or was spotted and recruited after he joined BSC. However the file contains detailed accounts of the kind of services Belfrage rendered to Moscow ... Belfrage is known to have supplied [Jacob] Golos [a Soviet master spy in North America] ... with a report apparently emanating from Scotland Yard which was a treatise on espionage agents.'

But the redoubtable John Simkin was not persuaded of Belfrage's guilt, arguing, 'he had definitely passed secrets to the Soviets. However, as he explained in his own interview with the FBI in April 1947, he only passed information to the Soviet Union on behalf of BSC. Belfrage, like several intelligence officers, worked as a double agent in the war ... it was clear to me that this was clearly part of a British intelligence disinformation campaign ... the evidence indicates that he was a double agent working for British intelligence.'

In other words, tantamount to what Ellis is most likely to have done with Turkul, Zelensky and Von Petrov in the 1930s: feeding them low-value information, or chickenfeed, in exchange for hopefully useful information from the other side. Possibly even faked information with the intent of causing trouble for the recipient: a strategy of 'provocation' straight out of Ellis's secret-service playbook written for William Donovan.

Walter Schellenberg in his 1945 interrogation complained of Von Petrov's reports to Ernst Kaltenbrunner being 'quite unimportant, indeed frequently false or misleading' and Kaltenbrunner even coming 'to grief' in an 'unpleasant way' over one such report.[12] In his own interrogation, Kaltenbrunner complained of Von Petrov furnishing reports that had a 'definite pro-Russian, anti-British and anti-US tendency', that the Chilean White Russian was 'lazy' and possibly a Japanese and Russian agent.[13]

If Ellis was feeding information to Zelensky, knowing it was going to Von Petrov, and then going to senior Nazis in Paris, he'd have good reason to provoke or sabotage his ultimate target. Ellis could well have been a double agent but, in all likelihood, Ellis was a double agent working against a Nazi target with the *approval* of his controlling organisation: a very important distinction from a double agent who is *betraying* his controlling organisation.[14]

As Bill Macdonald mentions in his book *The True Intrepid*, Bill Ross-Smith was contacted by Ellis in the 1960s and asked whether he thought Belfrage was a spy. He was convinced Belfrage was innocent: 'As far as I was concerned [Belfrage] was simply a normal one of the old chaps' and the 'charge laid afterwards against Ellis . . . was quite ridiculous'. It was a view also shared by Ellis's own asset in the United States, Donald Downes, who thought the idea of Ellis being a triple agent for Nazi Germany and the Soviet Union 'quite mad'.

After all, Valentine Vivian had recruited Kim Philby into MI6 but he was never accused of being a Russian spy. Why was Ellis, a war hero for the Allies and pivotal figure in the creation of what became the CIA, treated differently?

CHAPTER 15

PHILBY'S BLANK

'Dick Ellis fell into the "liberals" category. He was not tied to
institutional rigidities. As an SIS chief in Asia, after 1946, he
saw "the power of the peasant" and glimpsed Mao's vision
of millions of human atoms making an explosion of their
own, shaking the world as much as nuclear bombs . . . Ellis
was not popular among those who still believed that the way
to deal with rebellious peasants was to beat sense into them.
He preferred "to fight subversives but negotiate with honest
patriots" who might have turned to communism in desperation.
His critics thought in terms of sledgehammers.'

– WILLIAM STEVENSON, *INTREPID'S LAST CASE* (1983)

AFTER THE END OF WORLD WAR II, DICK ELLIS, now 50, found
his services more in demand than ever. He was handpicked for
a number of important positions in MI6, including 'field officer in
charge of South-East Asia and the Far East' and later, more officially,
Chief Controller Pacific (Far East and the Americas), or CFEA.

Befitting his status, in April 1946 he visited Washington DC for
talks with General John Magruder of the Strategic Services Unit or
SSU, OSS's postwar successor organisation until the creation of the
CIA the following year. British Security Coordination, the organisation that had made Ellis's reputation, would be officially disbanded by
the middle of the year.

The flurry of activity made the Australian effectively one of the
most powerful intelligence agents in the world, with responsibility for

North and South America and those regional hotbeds of communism, East Asia and South-East Asia. In the words of Chapman Pincher in *Their Trade is Treachery*, Ellis thus 'became No. 3 in the entire secret service hierarchy, controlling its activities in about half the world' and was involved in a 16-nation group called Intermarium, Latin literally for 'between seas'. As described by Stephen Dorril in *MI6: Fifty Years of Special Operations*, it was 'a cordon sanitaire within central Europe' designed to 'liberate their territories from the Soviet Union' and 'hasten the overthrow of the USSR. Before the Second World War, the organisation received support and funding from MI6 and French Intelligence for its anticommunist operations.' An odd posting, then, for a purported Soviet double agent.

A real Soviet double agent, Kim Philby, reported to Moscow after the war that SIS in Asia had stations in 'Singapore, Batavia, Honor [sic],[1] Hong Kong, Nanking. SIS plans also to open stations in Shanghai, Tientsin, Bangkok, Seoul and Tokyo.' One month Ellis could be in Cairo, the next in Havana, the next in Canberra, the next in Miami or Washington DC. Part of his wide-ranging influence was heading Combined Intelligence Far East (CIFE) in Singapore, with much of the group's efforts concentrated on China,[2] and Ellis personally sent George Blake, later exposed as a Soviet mole, to Seoul.[3] Ellis also earned a place on an internal MI6 committee set up to restructure the organisation itself.

Wrote Martin Pearce in *Spymaster*: 'The committee needed to absorb the remnants of the Special Operations Executive and to decide whether to structure MI6 vertically, with sections organised from top to bottom on a country-by-country basis and reporting back to Broadway, or horizontally, with regionally based intelligence being shared across the organisation. Those favouring a horizontal reorganisation, led by Kim Philby, were more trenchant in their arguments, and won the day . . . the big challenge was dealing with the USSR when the official policy was not to have spies operating in the territory of wartime allies – at least insofar as they weren't allowed to have agents working in the Soviet Union from the British Embassy. They knew from the Gouzenko case in 1945 that the Soviets didn't take that approach, but the British sense of fair play (together with not wanting to stir up a conflict) meant other proposals needed to be considered . . . Eastern European émigrés based in friendly nations would be trained and dropped by parachute or other means, dressed in local clothing, into remote parts of the satellite states – Bulgaria, Romania, Czechoslovakia and their like – just over the borders, to become embedded in the local communities.'

Ellis's fellow deputy director, rising star Philby, was one of five people on the committee. The treacherous Philby, Soviet codename STANLEY, sent a report about Ellis to his Soviet masters on 6 July 1945, which is unusual if Ellis really had been a Soviet spy. After all, why would Philby need to report on Ellis if the Russians were already blackmailing him?

'Dick Ellis has been an SIS officer for 24 years,' Philby wrote. 'For many years he was responsible for intelligence production in Western Europe. He spent several years during the war as deputy to Sir William Stephenson (the US head of station), an assignment he was given as a result of the animosity between him and [Claude] Dansey. When the latter returned to the UK from Switzerland in 1940, he was made assistant chief with broad responsibilities for intelligence production in Western Europe, thus putting Ellis out of a job.[4]

'Ellis returned to the UK in 1944 and was appointed Controller Production [CPR]. His job included the use of legal and natural cover (journalists, businessmen, etc) for intelligence gathering. His role was regarded as extremely secret even within SIS. Ellis was appointed to the committee for his experience and his objectivity (he does not intend to leave SIS) . . . Ellis makes a sensible and balanced contribution.'[5]

Philby elaborated on Ellis's responsibilities.

'The [CPR] position is temporarily held by Ellis. The CPR is responsible for recruiting and working with agents in the UK. When such agents go abroad, they will not maintain contact with SIS's stations. They will be used solely as travelling agents and will be drawn from among businessmen, commercial travellers and others who have good reason to go abroad on business for a short period of time . . . Ellis recently reached retirement age. It is not known whether or not he will actually retire. His future is undetermined. He may be persuaded to stay. If so, he will probably give up the CFEA job and retain only the CPR responsibility.'[6]

In September 1947, the French were fighting Ho Chi Minh's Viet Minh. Ellis went to Asia to review SIS's operations and stations. Fresh out of London and headquartered at the Cathay Building in the steamy environs of Singapore, his crisp white shirts crumpled and soaked with sweat like he'd stepped into a Graham Greene novel, Ellis found the task at hand more difficult than anticipated. While in Singapore he would eventually form a friendship with Maurice Oldfield, a future head of MI6, who'd been sent east on his 'first overseas tour of duty' as deputy to MI6's head of station in Singapore, James Fulton.

Noted Keith Jeffery in MI6's official history: 'Ellis was generally disappointed with the lack of intelligence being produced in the region but attributed it to difficulties with accommodation and the degree to which officers were obliged to become involved in their cover duties, an unwelcome feature of the postwar operating environment.'

By 1949, aged 54, Ellis was still travelling frequently – shipping records indicate that in July that year he sailed with Ann, then 15, on RMS *Queen Elizabeth* of the Cunard-White Star Line from New York to Southampton. On travel documents, he variously gave his profession as 'diplomat' or 'government official'. For the previous two years, he had nominated a London address – 2 Down Street, W1 – but was based full-time in Hong Kong at 514 The Peak.

Jeffery: 'Faced with the closing down of SIS's intelligence assets in China and increasingly insistent demands for information from customer departments, Ellis went out to Hong Kong to assess the situation and came to the conclusion that there was no alternative but to exploit the existing liaison with the Nationalist Chinese.'

As Panagiotis Dimitrakis put it in *Secrets and Lies in Vietnam: Spies, Intelligence and Covert Operations in the Vietnam Wars*: 'MI6 had few secret sources in China, and had to rely on a fragile collaboration with the KMT [Kuomintang] regime's Bureau of Information and Statistics.'

Ellis relocated from Hong Kong to Singapore, where he remained until 1951.[7] His area of attention was the Federation of Malaya (Malaysia) and French Indochina (Vietnam).

'Washington had little interest in the first guerrilla wars launched in the Malay archipelago which, from 1945 to 1950, was viewed usually as a colony resisting a national movement for independence,' wrote William Stevenson in *Intrepid's Last Case*. 'Ellis was the first of his breed to be caught up in the new struggles inspired by Asian communism, using "national independence" as a front. He helped create Phoenix Park in Singapore as a base against terrorism[8] . . . Ellis became a specialist in antiterrorist operations long before terrorism became a household word in the West.'

The MI6 Asian operation was underfunded and under-resourced, but as Ellis had demonstrated in Berlin and Paris, he was adaptable. In November 1949, Jeffery wrote, Ellis 'reported a proposal "made by the Far East for raising funds through the sale of opium confiscated by the Customs authorities"'.

In other words, drug trafficking. Ellis advised against it on the grounds that 'time would have to be devoted to it at the expense of [CPR] work' and 'we might get involved with rogues and undesirable characters'. But his sense of morality did not preclude straight theft – of documents rather than money. Ellis was not averse to 'burgling Russian embassies and consulates' and had been involved in it himself with 'two embassies [having] been penetrated and highly satisfactory results obtained'. According to Martin Pearce, '[Ellis's] view found favour in some quarters [but] the fear in others was one of risks versus rewards: a bungled burglary could potentially cause a diplomatic incident far beyond the value of any intelligence retrieved and set back the gathering process exponentially'.

While engagement on this exotic new frontier would have been professionally stimulating for Ellis, his private life was another matter: his second marriage was over. Ellis and Barbara Mary Burgess-Smith had divorced in 1946 and she later moved to Canada, according to a letter in the Ernest Cuneo Papers. Being a secret intelligence agent was no way to keep a marriage going. It was by necessity a lonely occupation.

Asia had got under Ellis's skin, as he confided in Richard Casey in a letter of 6 February 1950: 'During the past two years I have been travelling in these parts and have spent a good deal of time in China,

Japan, Indonesia, Siam [Thailand] and [the Federation of] Malaya. It has been an interesting experience and I am not altogether looking forward to my return to a gloomy desk in London.'

*

After Asia, Ellis might have had a straightforward retirement and lived out the rest of his life on a full pension had it not been for the passing mention of a 'Captain Ellis' during the interrogation of Abwehr III F's Richard Protze in the Netherlands.

As previously noted, Protze's close friend Admiral Wilhelm Canaris had been executed in 1945 by the Nazis for his role in the famous Valkyrie plot against Adolf Hitler but in 1946 Protze, about to turn 70, was alive if not in good health and locked up at Fort Blauwkapel, a military prison outside Utrecht. In Canada, Igor Gouzenko, codename CORBY, had independently spoken of a Soviet mole inside British intelligence called ELLI. All that was known about ELLI from Gouzenko's interrogation was that there was something Russian in his or her background, that he or she had been in Britain in 1942–43, possibly as late as 1945, and could remove files from London that dealt with Russians.

As Kim Philby explained to Phillip Knightley for his book *Philby: KGB Masterspy*: 'Elli's identity will probably never be satisfactorily resolved. Elli appears in the Gouzenko telegram story and never before or since. I am not Elli – as far as I know. An officer or agent does not necessarily know his own codename.'

KNIGHTLEY: You must know something about the Gouzenko and the Elli business.

PHILBY: Certainly. The first information about Gouzenko and Elli came from [William] Stephenson . . . 'C' [Sir Stewart Menzies] called me in and asked my opinion about it. I said it was obviously very important and we treated it as such.[9]

But Philby also spoke to a gathering of Stasi agents in East Germany about how easy it was to remove files for his Russian contacts and cover up his handiwork: 'Every evening I left the office with a big briefcase full of reports which I had written myself, full of files taken out of the actual documents, out of the actual archives. I was to hand them to my Soviet contact in the evening; the next morning I would get the files back, the contents having been photographed, and take them back early in the morning and put the files back in their place. That I did regularly – year in, year out . . . my advice to you is to tell all your agents that they're never to confess. Just deny everything.'[10]

It's not a stretch to think Ellis – who, ironically, had compiled a report on the CORBY case and wrote about Gouzenko in *The Two Bills: Mission Accomplished*[11] – could have done the same thing. He obviously had had a Russian wife, spoke Russian, and during the war had made trips between Washington DC and London.[12] Chapman Pincher, who had done more than anyone else to demolish the reputation of Ellis after his death, ruled out the Australian as a candidate in *Too Secret Too Long*: 'Ellis seems to have been put forward as a candidate for "Elli" on the grounds that the names are so alike, but in 1942 and 1943 he was working in New York at British Security Coordination Headquarters and could not possibly fit the information detailed in Gouzenko's evidence.'

Nevertheless, Ellis was travelling to London in late 1941 and early 1942 – that is evidenced by Guy Liddell's diaries, where he talks of having lunch with Ellis 'at the club' – and would have used London as a transit point between travel from his work for BSC in the United States to his work for Richard Casey in Egypt.

I wrote to intelligence expert, historian and author Antony Percy to ask his opinion. The erudite, knowledgeable Percy has written an inordinate amount on ELLI yet has barely mentioned Ellis on his blog. Evidently, he presumed I thought Ellis was a traitor. He replied: 'I don't think [Ellis] is a serious candidate for ELLI, because of timing and place. [Ellis] was a thoroughly bad lot, I would agree. It is nevertheless important not to exclude anyone, knowing how much deception and misinformation went on.' In one blog from 2023, Percy called Ellis a 'scoundrel' and that the Ellis case 'has so many twists that it makes the head of the most patient sleuth spin'.[13] He's not kidding.

Another ELLI detective, William A. Tyrer, obtained a telegram dated 23 November 1945 written by Roger Hollis regarding Hollis's own personal meeting two days before with Gouzenko in Ottawa, which confirmed Gouzenko was told in 1943, 'ELLI was a member of [a] high-grade intelligence committee, that he worked in British counterintelligence' and that 'the number 5 [was mentioned] in connection with [the] committee'.

On 6 May 1952, Gouzenko made a further statement about ELLI to RCMP at the request of MI5's director of counterespionage Dick White: 'I was not told by somebody, but saw the telegram myself concerning this person. And then, as a second confirmation, I was told by Lieutenant Lubimov. With these two pieces of evidence there is not the slightest doubt in my mind that there was a Soviet agent inside MI5 during the period of 1942–43, and possibly later on ... the telegram dealt with the description of a contact through a *dubok* – a hiding place for small objects, etc. It was clear that the person mentioned (and it was stated, I remember) was "one of five of MI". It was evident that personal contact with the man from MI5 was avoided. The place of the *dubok* in that particular case was at some graveyard – in a split between stones of a certain tomb ...

'In a short exchange of words, Lubimov said: "This man has something Russian in his background." I understood that he learned this from previous telegrams ... the words "something Russian" could be understood in different ways: A) The man himself (White Russian of noble origin, etc.) or his relatives (wife, father, mother etc) came from Russia or are Russian. B) He could be 100 per cent English but was in Russia (before the revolution of 1917 or during the 1919–21 civil war, or later on official duties, or as a tourist). C) Or, less probable, he has some friends of Russian origin. D) And, to stretch the words, he could have attended some Russian courses (language, history, etc).'[14]

So whoever ELLI was, he was possibly working in Britain in 1945. Ellis joined an MI6 not MI5 committee in June 1945. He had been in Britain for short durations during the war. It's highly unlikely Ellis was ELLI – it seems inconceivable that an intelligence service would come up with the codename ELLI when his real name was Ellis, though Richard Deacon has pointed out in his book *The Greatest Treason* that letters in Soviet codenames are sometimes taken from real names[15] – but the 1942–43 timeline mentioned by Gouzenko perhaps could be treated with some latitude.[16]

Either way, back in 1946 Major John Gwyer of MI5 was exploring whether there was any connection between 'Captain Ellis' or ELLIS and the shapeshifting ELLI after interviewing Protze, as evidenced by a letter/cable of 27 May that year to Philby.

'Dear Philby . . . you will see that our original surmise [sic] that this might be connected in some way with CORBY's ELLI is unfounded. We were led into this error by the fact that an earlier version of the extract omitted from the third paragraph the operative words "who had been put into position by Berlin". These words seem to me to make clear that Captain ELLIS, though he may have supposed that he was in touch with the Russian Intelligence Service, was in fact only in contact with the Abwehr. I think you will agree that this is a mistake into which ELLI would not have fallen.

'Nevertheless, PROTZE's information appears worth investigation for its own sake. We are causing a number of further questions to be put to him, so as to determine the approximate date at which this incident took place and the names of the various Abwehr officials apart from PROTZE who were concerned.

'As soon as we have received some answer to this, it may be possible to identify ELLIS and to discover what was the source of his information about the English Secret Service. In the meantime there is little that can be done unless you are in a position to suggest out of your head who ELLIS is likely to have been.'

Philby, bizarrely, could not or *chose* not to do this. Gwyer attached a one-page precis of what was known about ELLIS from MI5's Major D. I. Vesey.

```
EXTRACT FROM PROTZE's "HOME-WORK"
BELGIUM

In Belgium a Kriegs Organization was established.
A  Counter-Espionage  Officer  was  not  necessary
because  the  Abwehr  Stellen  in  the  Reich  on  the
```

other side of the Belgian frontier, as well as in Belgium, could carry out the work.

From the Abwehr Stellen in the Reich, Russian contacts which had been discovered in Belgium were followed up.

A man posing as an Englishman who called himself Captain ELLIS was in contact with two Russians who had been put into position by Berlin. ELLIS handed over extensive information about the organization of the English Secret Service, and several reports about the English armaments industry. Later enquiries proved that Ellis was a Russian who was only using the name ELLIS.

His reports were only partly believed. The meetings with ELLIS took place in Brussels. His reports were typed in English.

How long this contact was carried on is not known to the writer. He only had passing sight of the reports.

B.1.
24.5.46
D. I. Vesey

Major Vesey attached a series of comprehensive follow-up questions for Protze to get further details on the Ellis matter. But on 24 June 1946, the Intelligence Bureau in Bad Oeynhausen, Germany, informed London that Protze 'has been too ill for some time to be questioned' and that it was hoped to obtain answers 'in another three weeks' to a month's time'.

It was then that Philby, Soviet spy and covert chronicler of Ellis's intelligence career, famously responded that he didn't know anyone called Ellis. Evidently he had a complete blank. Odd internal MI6 machinations were happening around Protze, including an instruction that Protze 'cannot be interrogated except by our representative'.

By the end of the year, the interrogation of Protze had been called off altogether, with the blessing of Philby's superior, Roger Hollis, because the old Nazi was 'suffering dropsy at the time of his capture' and it was 'necessary to send him home'.

Wrote MI5's Joan Paine to Philby on 18 November 1946: 'Dear Mr Philby . . . you will remember that last May you discussed with Mr. Hollis the case of a certain "ELLIS", described by PROTZE . . . owing to PROTZE's illness, it was found impossible to continue his interrogation at the time.'

On 23 November, Philby responded to Paine: 'We much regret the delay in giving you the information required. With regard to the penetration of our Service, PROTZE stated that an individual named ELLIS supplied them with information on the London Office; this was our organisation. PROTZE always discounted this information as it was so complicated that it was likely not to be correct – he personally believed that the set-up was quite simple – other Abwehr Sections were impressed (before 1938). As it turned out later, this ELLIS was shown to be (a) a White Russian and not an Englishman, and (b) a fraud and a forger.

'PROTZE stated that ELLIS was in contact with two other White Russian officers, PETROV and NIEPOROSCHNE, who also went to Brussels.'

Those two men were personally known to Aleksei Zelensky, Ellis's former brother-in-law.

'Frl. [Fräulein] SKRODZKI [Protze's wife] added that ELLIS lived in Brussels and that he gave information on the British Intelligence Service, not on personalities and departments, which she stated PROTZE always considered to be nonsense, but which apparently impressed ROHLEDER and BAMLER.'

Ellis is not known to have ever lived in Brussels but by the description given in Protze's report it is clearly him: Protze was in Berlin when Ellis was trading information with Aleksei Zelensky and Vladimir von Petrov; Ellis spoke fluent Russian so could be mistaken as a Russian national; he had expertise in the armaments industry; he intimately knew the internal machinations of MI6; and the 'White Russians' he was supposedly in contact with were known to Zelensky.

The two Nazis in question were also significant figures. Rudolf Bamler, head of section III (counterespionage) of the Abwehr,[17] and Joachim Rohleder, who had aspired to be a writer but took over Abwehr III F from Protze in 1938. By Christmas 1944 he was given a Wehrmacht command. Bamler later attained the rank of general and fought in Norway and on the Eastern Front. So why was this line of investigation buried?

'The [Protze] case was finally cleared up after the capture of the VRINTON [sic] papers which contained warnings that ELLIS was a White Russian and a swindler.'[18]

Hardly convincing. Four days later, MI6 had shut down the Protze interrogation on the basis of Philby's response.[19]

Lamented Joan Paine: 'I understand that it is very doubtful whether PROTZE will ever regain sufficient strength to permit his subjection to further interrogation.'

Philby wrote again to Paine on 24 January 1947 that Protze and his new wife, who was also his former Stelle P secretary and his niece, were in such poor health that 'their physical condition and the conditions under which they have to be contacted exclude the possibility of thorough questioning.'

*

Philby's sudden amnesia about Ellis has been taken by Ellis's detractors as a sign that Philby was covering the tracks of a fellow Soviet mole. Granted, it was rather odd, and isn't easily explained. But it's also odd that the interrogation of Protze was called off simply on the basis of his poor health – unless British intelligence wanted it shut down for other reasons.

Even Chapman Pincher expressed puzzlement in *Too Secret Too Long*: 'Philby's action in covering up the evidence against Ellis seemed strange because the Russians were keen to bring retribution to anyone who had assisted the Nazis and Philby would, undoubtedly, have consulted his Soviet controller about the case.'

But Pincher (or rather his feeder, Peter Wright) had it all worked out.

'The Fluency Committee put forward a possible explanation. As it was certain by then that [Vladimir] Von Petrov had been primarily a GRU [Soviet] agent, Moscow would have known about Ellis's espionage activities for the Germans. It seemed likely that Von Petrov would have been required to recruit Ellis for Soviet intelligence, using the blackmail threat if necessary. Whether this had happened or not the Fluency Committee regarded it as inconceivable that once Philby had alerted the KGB to Ellis's position, the Russians would have failed to try to exploit it. The need to find out everything possible about Ellis's activities was therefore greatly increased and the Committee had to move beyond examining the record of a man who might have spied for Germany before and during the early part of the war.'[20]

Pincher is at it again: tweaking the story to fit his anti-Ellis agenda. *It seemed likely. Whether this had happened or not. Inconceivable.* As usual, no evidence of anything. Alternatively, a most reasonable explanation for Philby's forgetfulness, for want of a better word, was that Protze had probably revealed too much about British intelligence double-agent operations against the Nazis – using anti-Hitler elements within the German Army – before the war, and these were done with the express authority of MI6 head Stewart Menzies, who was in the position from 1939 to 1952, replacing Hugh Sinclair, who died in 1939. (Menzies had been deputy head to Sinclair from 1929.) The man in charge of completing this secret mission was Ellis. In regards to Ellis and Menzies, Philby had on his MI6 hat, not his GRU/KGB one.

Stephen Dorril, I believe, gets it right in his book *MI6: Fifty Years of Special Operations*: 'There is a suspicion that [Ellis] was later made a scapegoat in order to hide a more disturbing fact, namely that he had been trading information with the Germans on the orders of Menzies . . . until the end of 1938, MI6 believed that Hitler's ambitions lay in the East, and that he was "devoting special attention to the eastward drive, to securing control of the exploitable riches of the south, and possibly more, of Russia". Such intelligence was met with indifference by Prime Minister Neville Chamberlain, who told the Cabinet that a Russo-German conflict over Ukraine was no concern of Britain.

'Some of the intelligence that reached the Cabinet may have originated with Ellis, who knew that Admiral Wilhelm Canaris, chief of the Abwehr, had secret plans to use the White Russians in operations in Ukraine and southern Russia. Canaris was cooperating with many of the same organisations as those sponsored by the British, and there is evidence that on occasion they worked in concert. The Abwehr had apparently collaborated with the British in central Europe and the Balkans in counterintelligence operations against "communist agents who had begun to flood into Western Europe to provoke revolutions in support of the Kremlin". Anthony Cave Brown's suggestion that Canaris's eventual takeover of the émigré organisations was undertaken with MI6's knowledge and encouragement is probably correct.[21] In the meantime, MI6 was still engaged in plans to thwart Soviet expansionist claims and to deny the Germans access to oil for its war machine.'

In other words, MI6 knew exactly what Ellis was doing all along and Protze had let the cat out of the bag. Captain Ellis's activities in Europe were supposed to remain secret. It was not for anyone else to know, including MI5, and that was why Philby asked that no further action be taken – *not* to cover up another Soviet mole. What Ellis was doing was risky and perhaps foolhardy but well intended and certainly not traitorous with evil intent. This would explain why there was so much resistance in MI6 to MI5's later investigation of Ellis. Even Protze appeared to have realised he'd said too much.

Writes John Bryden in *Fighting to Lose*: 'Protze disclosed that a Captain Ellis had handed over "extensive information about the organisation of the English Secret Services". It appears to have been a slip because he then said Ellis was a Russian and the information was only partly believed. Protze probably played a part in the Abwehr's secret peace overtures to Stevens and Best in 1939 that led to the Venlo incident. It was in his territory.'

CHAPTER 16

THE CLOUDS ARE PARTING

'A mass murderer can take a score of lives, but in a nuclear age
the traitor can endanger the lives of millions.'
– CHAPMAN PINCHER, *THEIR TRADE IS TREACHERY* (1981)

IN OCTOBER 1947, AFTER NEARLY 30 YEARS in the Northern
Hemisphere as an intelligence agent, Dick Ellis returned to Australia to 'lobby . . . for the creation of an Australian base for SIS "special operations" in the Far East'.

Writes David Horner of Ellis in *The Spy Catchers*, the Australian Security Intelligence Organisation's official history, 'When he visited Australia in October–November 1947 he saw [then Liberal Party President Richard 'Dick'] Casey several times. During this visit Ellis also met [the Australian Army's director of military intelligence Charles] Spry.'

By March 1949, ASIO, Australia's version of MI5, had been founded and the following year plans for the Australian Secret Intelligence Service (ASIS), Australia's version of MI6 and CIA, were afoot. Ellis was sent to Canberra from Singapore by Stewart Menzies to liaise as a 'special adviser' with the Australian government and, like he had done with COI/OSS/CIA in the United States, launch the country's first foreign-intelligence service.

'In August 1949, the head of the Defence Department, Sir Frederick Shedden, asked Sir Stewart Menzies . . . if he would make someone available to visit Australia to discuss setting up a Special Operations organisation,' wrote Brian Toohey and William Pinwill.[1]

'Menzies agreed, and arrangements were made for a senior SIS officer, Colonel Dick Ellis, to visit in March–April 1950 . . . by the time of the visit, Alfred Brookes (later to become the founder of ASIS), who had been sent to London to be attached to Britain's Secret Intelligence Service, laying the foundations for an Australian equivalent, had firmly hitched his star to the [now] Minister for National Development, Dick Casey, and countered the Defence Department's plans for a Special Operations organisation by resurrecting his earlier proposal for a Secret Intelligence service [sic] that he had unsuccessfully put to [then Labor minister for external affairs H. V. 'Doc'] Evatt before the change of Government in 1949. Casey snapped it up and successfully bypassed the military alternatives.'

As a teenager, Ellis had sometimes struggled to get enough to eat on the Dunlop family's farms in Warragul and Murrumbeena. In Melbourne he'd filled inkwells at Stott & Hoare's. Now, in his mid-50s, he was advising politicians in Canberra about how to run a secret intelligence organisation.

Toohey and Pinwill continued: 'The cooperative Ellis went on to act as the channel for communication between Casey, the Cabinet subcommittee and the SIS. Soon after his arrival in Australia, Ellis had discussions with the Defence Committee – the body at the pinnacle of the Defence Department tree – where he indicated that he was happy to discuss the subject of Secret Intelligence as well as Special Operations. The committee, however, decided not to pursue the opportunity to discuss SI, and the Defence Department head, Sir Frederick Shedden, informed his Minister, Phillip McBride, accordingly on May 15, 1950.

'It was then that Casey intervened to take the issue beyond the Defence arena. The Minister for National Development was deeply concerned about the communist threat in Australia's region, and especially the emergency in the then British colony of Malaya . . . the following week he arranged a Cabinet-level meeting with Ellis that overturned the Shedden victory. The ministers present were (Prime Minister Robert) Menzies, Arthur Fadden (Treasury), Dick Casey, Percy Spender (External Affairs) and Phillip McBride. Also present were Allen S. Brown (Secretary of the Prime Minister's Department), Shedden, Brookes and a young man who was reluctantly thrust into the limelight in the last days of the Whitlam Government, Bill Robertson. The committee, meeting on May 24, 1950, formally "decided to establish a Secret Intelligence service".'

Brookes, later head of ASIS, remembered Ellis fondly according to the late Bruce Bennett, who interviewed Brookes before he died.

'He remembered Ellis "very well, of course" but had no view on the allegations about him. A "dear little man", his wife chipped in, "loved his food", especially Vichyssoise in a dinner they had shared in New York.'

In 1951, though still based in Singapore, Ellis was also spending time in London. On 23 April that year 26-year-old Olik, living in England as a civil servant, sailed on the MV *Telemachus* (Blue Funnel Line) for Singapore. In May, Guy Burgess and Donald Maclean disappeared into Russia. In July, Philby – suspected to be the 'Third Man' who'd tipped them off after Maclean (Soviet codename: HOMER) was detected in VENONA decrypts – resigned from MI6. Ellis fell under suspicion, too; though, according to Pincher in *Their Trade is Treachery*, 'not much could be learned about [Ellis's] activities in New York or in the posts he held soon after the war in the Far East and South-East Asia. So the inquiries were concentrated on his behaviour after he had returned to London.'

Wrote Pincher in *Too Secret Too Long*: 'Until 1951 there had been no suspicion concerning Ellis's loyalty . . . but evidence of his treachery then emerged by accident, as it so often does in intelligence affairs. MI5 officers who were convinced that Philby had betrayed their case against Maclean began to examine old documents for clues, including statements made by [Walter] Krivitsky.'

By 1952, with the fallout from the VENONA decrypts at its peak and ASIS established, head of counterintelligence and soon-to-be director-general of MI5 Dick White reopened the investigation into ELLI and a second statement was obtained from Igor Gouzenko.

In March 1953, Joseph Stalin died and a new round of purges was taking place in Moscow. That month, Vladimir von Petrov left Switzerland via Genoa bound for Santiago, Chile; two days later Ellis arrived in Southampton after a long sea voyage on the MS *Willem Ruys* from Jakarta via Singapore, Belawan in Sumatra, Colombo and Port

Said.[2] Ellis stayed in London for the best part of a year, living in Earls Court, was awarded a Companion of the Most Distinguished Order of St Michael and St George (CMG) and Territorial Efficiency Decoration (TD)[3] and prematurely retired from MI6, aged 58, claiming heart trouble. Thereafter the first MI5 investigation into Ellis was dropped.

'After being told in 1953 that Ellis had decided to retire, spontaneously and at his own request, White agreed to shelve the case. In short, at the top level of both MI5 and MI6 there was agreement that the Ellis scandal should be covered up for ever [sic] "in the national interest",' wrote Pincher in *Too Secret Too Long*. 'In pursuance of this cover-up the American FBI was told nothing officially of the strong suspicions against Ellis though they should have been because of Ellis's service in the U.S. from 1940 to 1944.'[4]

Then on 24 September 1953, Ellis departed England on the RMS *Strathaird* (P&O) for Melbourne with 19-year-old Ann in tow. He'd accepted a two-year contract with ASIO and would act 'as a link between the Australian Secret Intelligence Service . . . and London following his retirement from MI6'.

Pincher wouldn't have a bar of any health problems: 'Ellis's sudden departure for Australia on the grounds of nonexistent heart trouble in 1953 immediately appeared to have an explanation. Ellis knew, from his position in MI6, that the MI5 inquiries into Philby were gathering momentum and he may have feared that he would come under suspicion or he may even have been warned to get out of the country by a Soviet controller, who had been tipped off by a pro-Soviet source inside MI5. Once in Australia, Ellis would be safe from prosecution or interrogation because a suspected spy cannot be extradited for offences under the Official Secrets Act.'

*

As Ann Salwey remembered of her father: 'When we came out in 1953, he was so proud showing me around. His home, his school, his father's grave.'

But Ellis had barely unpacked his bags when he had a sudden change of heart, purportedly related to the impending defection of the Soviet Union's *rezident* in Canberra, Vladimir Petrov, who was similarly named but wholly unrelated to the double, triple and quadruple agent Vladimir von Petrov. Petrov had been appointed to his post by NKVD head and later First Deputy Premier Lavrentiy Beria, who'd been shot in the head following a coup by Nikita Khrushchev, and Petrov feared a similar fate in the event he was recalled to Moscow.

'On 24 November 1953 ... [Australia's director-general of security, the head of ASIO, Charles] Spry told Alfred Brookes, the director of ASIS, that Petrov was considering defecting. Among those present was Dick Ellis,' wrote David Horner in *The Spy Catchers*. Whereupon Ellis 'paid the deposit on the fare for the passenger ship *Otranto* on 26 November'. It was due to depart on 6 January 1954.

Pincher theorised that Ellis had heard Petrov's name and mistaken it for Von Petrov,[5] a view also shared by Spry and Peter Wright, and his pulling up stumps in Australia 'supported the suspicion that Ellis had been a KGB agent'. Wright in *Spycatcher*: 'I have always assumed that he thought that Petrov who was about to defect was the same Von Petrov with whom he had been involved in the 1920s, and who must have known the secret of his treachery.'

Ellis duly left Australia on 6 January and three days later, 9 January, came the first indication in ASIO records of a date of Petrov's intended defection: the month of April.[6] On 11 February Ellis arrived in London on the RMS *Otranto* (Orient Steam Navigation Company Ltd) from Sydney via Melbourne, Adelaide, Fremantle, Colombo, Aden, Port Said, Naples, Marseille and Gibraltar: it was a hell of a long trip.

Because of his departure date before 9 January, writes Richard Hall in *A Spy's Revenge*, 'there is no way that Ellis could have taken the April date back to England for the Russians', which is correct. However, David Horner in *The Spy Catchers* says Ellis on his return to London tried to warn Kim Philby of Petrov's defection, citing information being shared between ASIO and MI5 in 1967 as part of the EMERTON investigation.

'Ellis arrived in London ... a few days later he wrote to Kim Philby, who had resigned from MI6 but was still living in London, seeking a meeting ... although MI5 had firm evidence that Ellis tried to meet with Philby in February–March 1954, it could not prove that they actually met.'

Fearing certain death should he return to the Soviet Union, Petrov did defect in April, on the 3rd, but he gave no information to the Australians about Ellis or Philby, and didn't tell his wife, Evdokia Petrova, of his plans to defect. On 11 April Soviet henchmen left Rome for Australia – months after Ellis's supposed warning to Philby – and on 15 April the guards, Valery Karpinsky and Fedor Zharkov, arrived in Sydney, where on the 19th they bundled Evdokia onto a plane. When it refuelled in Darwin, she was rescued by ASIO officials, on the grounds that Karpinsky and Zharkov were illegally carrying weapons, and offered asylum.

'Spry and his officers knew nothing of the accusations against Ellis at the time of Petrov's defection,' writes Horner in *The Spy Catchers*. 'In retirement, however, Spry recalled that following the defection Ellis had offered to take the material provided by Petrov to London; while Spry did not suspect Ellis's loyalty, he personally did not trust him and declined the offer. This account cannot be right, because at the time Ellis departed from Australia on 6 January 1954, Petrov had not defected, and hence there were no documents to carry.'[7]

This is true and should be a major concern to anyone who seriously thinks Ellis went back to London early to warn Philby, a narrative that is found in dozens of books such as *Spy Book: The Encyclopedia of Espionage* by Norman Polmar and Thomas B. Allen: 'Ellis immediately contacted Philby, apparently telling him of Petrov's impending defection.' According to Peter Wright in *Spycatcher*, Ellis was 'specifically warned against doing so'.

To recap: Ellis left Australia in January, arrived in England in February and apparently warned Philby in March that Petrov was defecting in April. If the matter was so urgent, why would he take so long to warn Philby? In fact, the more the Petrov–Ellis–Philby story is told, the looser the facts become. The late Australian journalist Evan Whitton claimed Ellis left Australia in March. In *Too Secret Too Long*, Pincher says Ellis arrived in England in March, 'taking with him the motor car he had bought on his arrival in Australia – further evidence that he had intended to remain there'. In *A Spy Among Friends* Ben Macintyre gets the date of the defection wrong by four months – August 1954 not April – but correctly says 'Philby heard of Petrov's defection' and wasn't warned of it.

H. Montgomery Hyde in *Secret Intelligence Agent* says Ellis post retirement 'paid a short visit to his native Australia, where he was in touch with the Australian intelligence authorities, who, in exchange for information about the suspected English spy Philby, briefed him on the activities of Vladimir Petrov, the KGB chief in the Soviet Embassy in Canberra.'

William Stevenson in *Intrepid's Last Case* goes so far as to say Philby 'framed' Ellis. His reasoning was Philby could 'play on inter-departmental feuds' to ensnare Ellis and 'it would serve Moscow's purpose to label as one of their super-moles a man Philby professed not to know when they had offices in the same SIS building on Broadway in London'. Stevenson suggests that Philby deliberately 'made himself a suspect to divert attention away from other Russian moles' and that performing 'a similar operation, with similar aims, on Ellis' would be easily done.

According to the Ellis naysayers, Philby alerted Moscow, which duly dispatched the nearest Slav goons to kidnap the Petrovs. *Right*. If that were so, they wouldn't have taken *months* to get to Australia and they would have nabbed both the Petrovs, not just Mrs Petrov.

More sober minds have seen right through the malarkey. Harry G. Gelber: 'As against that, if Ellis really had been a Soviet agent, Moscow would have known quite early about Petrov's dealings with the Australian security [sic] and would hardly have allowed him to run free.' Donald Cameron Watt: 'The allegations linking Ellis's arrival in Australia and return to Britain have already been shown to have been impossible to reconcile with the timing of Petrov's defection.'

Two very different takes to the one told by Pincher in *Their Trade is Treachery*. The old conspiracy nut trod a fine line in airing contradictory theories almost simultaneously.

'[Ellis's decision] . . . to retire and return to Australia because of heart trouble . . . had not seemed unusual at the time, but his later behaviour strongly suggested that his "heart trouble" was an excuse for getting himself abroad, where, even in a British dominion, he could not have been extradited for offences under the Official Secrets Act.'

By his second attack tome on Ellis, *Too Secret Too Long*, Britain was suddenly a safer place.

'Ellis broke his contract saying that he had decided to return to England to remarry . . . Australia would have been a more dangerous place to be in than Britain, from which defection to the Soviet Union, if it became necessary, would be much easier. Further, by signing his contract with ASIS, Ellis had put himself under Australian law.'

Which was it going to be?

Ellis did remarry: in a Kensington registry office on 24 August 1954, to Alexandra Wood, a 48-year-old retired schoolteacher and widow (according to H. Montgomery Hyde in *Secret Intelligence Agent*). They took up residence at 'Meriden', 28 Freeman Avenue, Hampden Park, in the seaside town of Eastbourne, East Sussex.

Pincher again in *Too Secret Too Long*: 'To keep the inquiries as secret as possible, the investigators always referred to Ellis as "Emerton" in documents and in conversations.[8] But, as Philby's old colleagues were still refusing to believe that he was a spy and remained in touch with him, one of them who was in the know might have gossiped to him about the suspicion surrounding Ellis. Philby might then have alerted Ellis, for they were friends, and within a short time Ellis was to do a similar service for Philby.'

This is all according to Pincher, who has no evidence of anything. *Might have. Might then have.* All guesswork. What entitles him to write, 'Ellis was to do a similar service for Philby'? *Nothing.* It appears that Pincher, in order to move more units of his books, was quite happy to sell a dead man down the river.

More Pincher: 'After the customary farewell parties, Ellis emigrated back to Australia in late 1953. There, though he was supposed to be too ill to do further intelligence work, he quickly signed a two-year contract to work for the Australian Secret Intelligence Service, the counterpart of the British organisation from which he had just retired. Shortly after doing that, and in line of duty, he called on Sir Charles Spry, the director-general of the Australian Security Intelligence Organisation, the counterpart of MI5. Spry told him, in good faith, that his agency was in touch with an important KGB officer based in the Russian embassy in Canberra and that there were high hopes that he would defect. The man's name was Vladimir Petrov.'

*

The only problem with all this utter blather from Pincher was Ellis had left Australia *before* ASIO knew Petrov was definitely defecting in April 1954. Saying there were 'high hopes' Petrov might defect apparently was enough for Ellis to get on a very slow boat – really, if it were *that* urgent, the man would take a plane, even if he hated flying – back to England, a voyage of six weeks.

It's beyond ridiculous. The apparent excuse given by Ellis was that he was about to get married. But when MI5 made inquiries with the unknown woman he'd named as his bride to be, it was news to her – she was already married – and Ellis then compounded this mistake by producing the name of another unknown married woman, who similarly knew nothing about it.

Writes Robert Manne in *The Petrov Affair*: 'One of the most telling pieces of evidence against [Ellis being a Russian spy] were the two false alibis (concerning women he claimed to have intended to marry) he provided in explanation of his hasty return to Britain from Australia following the defection of Petrov.'

As Pincher explains in *Their Trade is Treachery*: '[Ellis] said that he had returned to marry a girl and, under pressure, gave her name. Inquiries soon showed that she had already been happily married at the time and, though she had met Ellis, had never had any intention of marrying him. Ellis then pleaded that his memory must have been at fault and gave the name of another girl. This, too, proved to be a false trail.'[9]

Or had Ellis, as Pincher hypothesises, left Australia suddenly – just nine days after he started his two-year contract – because he genuinely thought he was going to be exposed by Vladimir von Petrov, who was now living in Chile, not Vladimir Petrov in sleepy Canberra? A tenuous and implausible explanation at best.

Charles Spry was hardly a reliable narrator either, given he said his meeting with Ellis took place *after* Petrov's defection and not before: a difference of about four months. Spry told the *Sunday Telegraph* in London that his own account demolished Pincher's claims in *Their Trade is Treachery* and *Too Secret Too Long* that Philby had forewarning of the Petrov defection and that 'Petrov might blow his [Philby's] cover'.

'Such a serious error calls into question the accuracy of other parts of Pincher's books. If, after all, he can be so wrong on a demonstrable point of fact, a fact he could easily have checked with me and a fact on which he seems to place such weight, one has to wonder what weight to place on his speculations which cannot be objectively established.'

As stated already, Ellis left Australia well *before* the Petrov defection. It is established by shipping records: Ellis departed the country in January and arrived in England in February. Spry, Pincher and Australian writer Robert Manne all got it wrong.

Wrote Manne, it was 'Spry's distinct memory that it was in the week *following* the Petrov defection that Ellis arrived in ASIO's office (with the head of ASIS, Alfred Brookes, in tow) with an offer to assume responsibility for the interrogation of Petrov. On the grounds that there was to be an open Royal Commission and that, at the time, ASIS's existence had not even been revealed to the Australian public, Spry politely declined the Ellis–ASIS takeover bid.[10] Only now did Ellis, according to [Spry], depart antipodean shores.

'Dick Ellis sailed to Britain via Genoa. Almost at once upon his return . . . Ellis arranged to meet his old colleague from MI6, Kim Philby, at Philby's London club – the Travellers [sic: it was the Athenaeum] . . . after his conversation with Ellis, Philby (whose telephone was being tapped) called his current mistress with the news "the clouds are parting" . . . it seems likely at least, as Pincher surmises, that Dick Ellis was "the ingenious route" through which contact between Philby and Moscow Centre had been reestablished.'

Pincher in *Too Secret Too Long*: '[Ellis] is on record in documents as having briefed both the MI5 and MI6 leadership on the Petrov operation. In return, and probably because he made inquiries about it, Ellis was briefed on the state of the Philby case by Maurice Oldfield, an old friend in MI6. Oldfield put this briefing on record together with his instruction to Ellis that he should not see or speak with Philby, who had been out of MI6 for three years. In fact, Ellis was found to have taken immediate steps to contact Philby, leaving a note on Travellers Club paper for him at the nearby Athenaeum, which Philby still used. Philby did not pick up the message for more than a week but then telephoned Ellis to fix an appointment. This is known because Philby was under telephone surveillance but, as he was not being watched, it is not known what transpired when the two met for lunch. What is known is that on that same afternoon Philby telephoned his current girlfriend and told her that he had received some good news over lunch. He then added, "The clouds are parting."'

For the record, the relevant chapter in Philby's autobiography *My Silent War* is called 'The Clouds Part'. There is no text about clouds parting in the book.

Philby writes: 'Several times during this period, I revived the idea of escape . . . finally, an event occurred which put it right out of my head. I received, through the most ingenious of routes, a message from my Soviet friends, conjuring me to be of good cheer and presaging an early resumption of relations [with Moscow] . . . it was therefore with refreshed spirit that I watched the next storm gather. It began with the defection of Petrov in Australia.'

Pincher once more in *Too Secret Too Long:* 'Confirmation that Philby had advance information about the Petrov defection eventually came from [Anthony] Blunt in his [1964] confessions. The Fluency Committee therefore inferred that Ellis had not only warned Philby about the coming defection, which could incriminate them both, but also put him back in touch with the Russians.'

Apparently, according to Antony Percy, no written confession by Blunt exists.[11] Nor does one by Ellis – or it hasn't been released by MI6, and if it did, would it stand up to rigorous scrutiny?

*

All this amounts to a flimsy circumstantial case at best: Ellis leaves Australia following one mention of Petrov *considering* defecting, takes the slowest boat he can – not a plane – doesn't meet Philby (or there's no proof he did), doesn't marry the woman he said he would, Philby makes some curious remark about clouds, and the two Soviet heavies who are summarily dispatched to Australia can't even manage to get Evdokia Petrova back to Moscow.

It was enough for the Australian media to let Ellis twist slowly in the wind. According to a 1998 editorial without a byline in the *Canberra Times*,[12] 'Ellis's affable charm . . . enabled him to dupe people at the highest level' and the very foundation of Western security was in ruin.

'[There's a] possibility that Australia's three main intelligence gathering and counterespionage arms were compromised from the outset by Ellis, who had a hand in the setting up of each . . . the result was probably that the entire Western intelligence effort against the Soviet Union at the outbreak of the Cold War was similarly compromised. Although it was never proved conclusively that he spied for the Russians, probably after being blackmailed for his Nazi connections – and he always denied it – the strong likelihood is that he did, and with disastrous consequences.'

'Ellis . . . was held in the highest trust by Australians – notably the Liberal external affairs minister, Richard Casey (later governor-general) and the director-general of the Australian Security Intelligence Organisation, Sir Charles Spry – and was a key adviser in the formation, at the urging of the British and Americans, of both ASIO and the Australian Secret Intelligence Service.

'However, an interview with the late Brigadier Sir Frederick Chilton, then deputy secretary of the Department of Defence and a key player in the Petrov investigation, suggests that Ellis was also instrumental in the most secret area of Australian intelligence, the Defence Signals Branch – DSB (later renamed Defence Signals Directorate).

'Interviewed by a departmental researcher in 1992, shortly before his death, Sir Frederick gave the first indication that Ellis (whose name, curiously, was deleted from the transcript, as was that of the former head of MI5, Sir Roger Hollis, also a suspected mole) was also linked with DSB, although Chilton said he could not be certain.

'He was certain, however, about Ellis's links with ASIS, which he joined on a contract when it was set up, but left after only two months. "He'd been associated with the British Signal Intelligence Service [Government Code and Cypher School or GC&CS, renamed Government Communications Headquarters or GCHQ in 1946] and . . . he was sort of in a shadowy relationship which we thought was sponsored by the British . . . with Defence Signals."'[13]

According to Ball and Horner in *Breaking the Codes*, on account of Chilton's testimony, 'the three major arms of Australia's espionage and counterespionage effort – ASIO, ASIS, and DSD [Defence Signals Directorate] – were compromised from the outset given that they were established with the hands-on help of suspected Soviet "moles" . . . Ellis also appears briefly in the Venona saga as, at one stage, he was even on the verge of being sent out to Australia to advise on the Ultra wartime decrypts. (Ellis was in Australia in 1947–48 on unspecified MI6 business, during which he met [Frederick] Shedden at least once; his mere presence is a matter of suspicion.)'[14]

But the unflappable Richard Hall, like Gelber and Watt, wasn't buying it. He comprehensively destroyed the Petrov–Ellis–Philby fantasy in *A Spy's Revenge*. As Hall pointed out, just because Ellis 'didn't marry the woman he said he would . . . doesn't prove anything'. He 'could have invented an excuse so as not to hurt his new friends in Australia' after things didn't go to plan in Australia or he simply didn't like being back in a country he'd been so desperate to leave back in 1914. After decades living in England, Ellis was far more British in his ways and attitudes than he was Australian, though in a letter to Richard Casey he admitted, 'I often feel the nostalgic pull of Australia.'[15]

If Ellis knew he was under suspicion as a Russian spy, and undoubtedly he knew *very well* at this point, given what had happened with Burgess, Maclean and Philby, why offer up the name of his real romantic partner knowing she, too, would be immediately surveilled? Hall emphasises in his book that Ellis left Australia well before the date of Petrov's defection was known to Australian authorities.

Hall also took aim at Toohey and Pinwill in a *Sydney Morning Herald* review of their book, *Oyster: The Story of the Australian Secret Intelligence Service*. Bruce Bennett had remarked that the Toohey–Pinwill book suggested 'Ellis was the conduit through whom the Soviet KGB "reactivated their most valuable asset", Kim Philby'.

'The authors have unfortunately gone along with the story that a certain Dick Ellis, an Australian expatriate, who had served for many years with the British SIS and who had a lot to do with the foundation of ASIS, was a Nazi spy and then a long-time Soviet mole,' wrote Hall. 'The prime advocates of this theory are Peter Wright and his loony MI5 right-wing clique together with their mouthpiece, the journalist Chapman Pincher. For Toohey and Pinwill to depend upon this *galère* is as bizarre as Noam Chomsky embracing Lyndon Baines Johnson.'

Ellis was now a marked man, according to Norman Polmar and Thomas B. Allen: 'He was placed under surveillance by the Special Branch of Scotland Yard, including telephone taps, to prevent him from trying to defect.'

Which would have been prudent, if Ellis had actually had any reason to do so.

CHAPTER 17

CRYING TOWEL

'It was the Ellis case which really earned me the undying enmity
of the MI6 old guard, an enmity which I wore as a mark of
achievement. The Ellis case caused friction between MI5 and
MI6 for almost as long as the Philby case.'
– Peter Wright, *Spycatcher* (1987)

In 1955 Kim Philby was 'sacked by a reluctant MI6' because of
the Third Man scandal, though his dismissal from the service was
kept secret. He was later wrongly cleared in the British Parliament by
Foreign Secretary Harold Macmillan and Philby went off to Lebanon
to work as a foreign correspondent and resume his spy work for MI6
until his ultimate defection in 1963. Philby apparently 'confessed to a
colleague before vanishing into the Soviet Union. Someone had warned
him that the game was up – and Ellis's accusers said it was Ellis.'

Meanwhile, as a strike against the conspiratorial theory of
Chapman Pincher that Dick Ellis had left Australia early because it
would be easier to defect from Britain than from Down Under, Ellis
returned to his homeland within less than 12 months of the Petrov
defection, in March 1955 travelling with Alexandra Wood on the
RMS *Oronsay* (Orient Line) to Melbourne from London via the Suez
Canal, Fremantle and Adelaide.

Ellis gave his address as 23 Bruce Street, Toorak, and after returning to London for unknown business at the beginning of 1956, he flew
all the way from London to Sydney on VH-EAD *Southern Dawn*,

a Lockheed Super Constellation registered to Qantas Empire Airways. The flight took about 54 hours, via Rome, Cairo, Karachi, Calcutta, Singapore and Darwin, rather than the usual six-week journey by ship. (This was Qantas's 'Express Service'.)

Ellis put his stay as 'indefinite' on his arrival card, perhaps because he was in the process of helping put together the journal *Hemisphere*, 'An Asian-Australian Magazine' according to its subtitle, which had its first issue in March 1957.[1] All this shuttling between Britain and Australia was hardly the modus operandi of a man who was looking over his shoulder, expecting to be arrested by agents of MI5 or ASIO. That year, 1957, he'd depart Australia for English shores again, this time by sea on the QSMV *Dominion Monarch* from Melbourne to London via Wellington.

His writing career – on hiatus since the 1920s – was revived: Ellis not only worked for *Hemisphere* but contributed articles to the *Central Asian Review*[2] and *Soviet Affairs*. He was also commissioned in 1961 by William Stephenson to author an account of Stephenson's time at BSC. The resulting manuscript was the offputtingly titled *Anglo-American Collaboration in Intelligence and Security: Notes for Documentation*.

'Stephenson thought that Ellis could write a valuable history of "our" war, as well as greatly improve Ellis's financial position,' wrote Thomas F. Troy in *Wild Bill and Intrepid*. 'Stephenson offered Ellis all royalties and an advance and promised to "order 1000 copies himself", a promise that Ellis thought "was simply Bill trying to do me a good turn". Stephenson said he had the "necessary basic documents" and Ellis need not worry about the Official Secrets Acts [sic] because "it is all a fairly old story".'

But even with all these incentives Ellis turned in a plodding turkey.

'While I then described the entire manuscript as "useful", I also noted that its "usefulness would have been enhanced a hundredfold had I been able to query Colonel Ellis on the data he left out",' according to Troy. 'In fact, the draft, really boring, had hit many bumps. Since Ellis cited only secondary and published sources, the draft was short on names, operations, and controversies. There was no revelation of secrets, daring adventures, personal clashes, bureaucratic bungling, or sexual escapades. No one's ox was gored. There was only high praise for all the British and American intelligence and security services and their harmonious collaboration in the common cause. No wonder that Hyde told Ellis, when he read some early chapters, that it "read too much like an office history".'

In fact, Ellis's manuscript underwhelmed Stephenson so much that another writer and fellow former BSC agent, Ellis's good friend H. Montgomery Hyde, author of *Secret Intelligence Agent*, took over. The book was wholly subsumed along with BSC's unpublished official history into Hyde's moderately successful 1962 release *The Quiet Canadian* and a slighted Ellis was barely compensated for his time and research.[3]

Apart from a cursory acknowledgment from Hyde, Ellis gets about one line in the entire book, which must have been a bitter pill to swallow. He wrote to Richard Casey on 25 July that year: 'I have written a book . . . it has been cleared by the FO [Foreign Office]. The book will be known as *The Quiet Canadian*. I can't publish under my own name, so I have called in as collaborator Montgomery Hyde . . . the book will appear (in October) under his name.'

Stephenson's withering rebuke of his deputy's literary talents stung the Australian deeply, though Ellis did his best to mask his disappointment.

'Bill's criticism, as far as I can make out (he has said little in his letters) is that I have pulled my punches too much, my style is too dry, and I do not bring the story to life sufficiently to make a saleable book,' wrote Ellis to Hyde. 'I seemed to be too inhibited by former association with a certain "Firm" to let myself go . . . [Stephenson] considers that after 20 years we can let our hair down about SO [Special Operations], PWE [Political Warfare Executive], Security Executive[4] and other ops in the Carib[bean], SA [South America] and elsewhere, without restraint. (I'm not so sure, but that may be – as he thinks – because I spent 32 years keeping my mouth shut!)'

Hyde was in full agreement, and said so to Stephenson: 'I told [Ellis] that I frankly thought his story read too much like an office report. He quite agreed.'

But where Ellis, perhaps to save face, was telling friends he'd collaborated with Hyde but couldn't publicise his involvement for security reasons, Hyde rejected Ellis's proposal because 'I never think that (with rare exceptions) books written in double harness work out well. At the same time I have no doubt that [Ellis] has put in some useful spadework, and in view of this I hope he can be taken care of in some mutually satisfactory way, as I should not like him to feel sore or that his efforts have not been appreciated.'

But this did not happen. Remarked Troy: 'Ellis certainly thought there was an understanding on reimbursement, but he would soon be complaining about Stephenson's failure to pay up, even to answer his letters.' This might have had something to do with the blowback *The Quiet Canadian* was getting from MI6 in London, which, according to Timothy J. Naftali, saw Ellis 'reprimanded . . . by MI6. He lost his position with the Intelligence Research Board, a division of MI6.'[5] Losing any of his meagre income would have been catastrophic for Ellis. Hyde felt so bad for Ellis, he threw him a couple of hundred pounds.[6]

Writes Thomas E. Mahl in *Desperate Deception*: 'Unknown to historians or journalists of the time, this stunning book leaked roughly 35 per cent of the very secret after-action report "BSC Account". Passages deemed too sensitive were changed or removed from the American version, *Room 3603*.'[7]

Worse, according to Mary S. Lovell in her biography of American spy Betty Pack, *Cast No Shadow*, it was all Ellis's doing. Ellis 'engineered the book past the scrutiny of MI6's security officer' for the British and American editions (the latter with a foreword by Ian Fleming) and '[he] subsequently lost his job at MI6, almost certainly as a result of the publication of Hyde's books . . . the entire community of former BSC operatives were amazed that Hyde had been able to obtain permission to write this book and it had, indeed, come about in a surprising manner given the security which then existed and still exists now . . . according to letters from Ellis to Hyde in the CCC [Churchill College, Cambridge], it is obvious that a misunderstanding had occurred. MI6 approved Ellis's early (abandoned) manuscript, not Montgomery Hyde's much fuller account.'[8]

Ellis explained away his mistake in the foreword to *A Man Called Intrepid*: 'In 1962, I was working on a study of Soviet imperialism when a special watchdog committee of the Ministry of Defence and the Foreign Office in London discussed the wisdom of a partial leak. This took the form of a book, *The Quiet Canadian* . . . I was able to demonstrate that I had been given instructions by "higher authority" to disclose certain matters. These matters were, of course, a carefully limited disclosure of BSC's "secret" role.

'In no way did it reveal the full extent of the organisation's prime purposes or most sensitive activities . . . I can now disclose that the reason for the break in the silence about BSC in 1962 was the escape to the Soviet Union of Kim Philby . . . we knew that Philby took with him the knowledge of BSC's existence, but we also knew that he was not aware of the full and far-reaching purpose of Intrepid's organisation. Thus just enough of the truth was revealed for publication to blunt the effect of any disclosures that Philby or his supporters might reveal.'

The problem with Ellis's explanation in *A Man Called Intrepid*, of course, was that Philby defected in 1963 not 1962.[9] It doesn't wash. According to Timothy J. Naftali, Ellis had simply 'misunderstood what was expected of him' and had underestimated the strength of Stephenson's rampant ego and lust for publicity: 'Stephenson was not going to pay for a faithful bureaucratic history. Ellis refused, for example, to accept his former boss's claim that he had initiated the intelligence liaison between Washington and London, a link which Ellis, a career British intelligence officer, knew to have predated Stephenson's arrival in New York in 1940. Stephenson had no patience with this quibbling. He wanted a bestselling biography of himself.'[10]

That Stephenson got with *The Quiet Canadian*. Meanwhile, in 1963, the year of the Profumo Affair[11] and the year Philby defected to Moscow, Ellis published his second book, *The Transcaspian Episode, 1918–1919*, a characteristically dry, impersonal account of his experiences in Central Asia and the Malleson mission. Barely anyone bought it but Russian reviewers devoured it. In the words of Brian Pearce, the Russia expert and historian, it was widely lambasted for being 'anti-Soviet'. Which is important, because Chapman Pincher admitted to Pearce that he never actually read it but 'thumbed through a copy'.[12]

A stunning admission for someone whose agenda was to convince the world Ellis was a secret Soviet spy.

Ellis followed it up in 1965 with a similarly anti-Soviet pamphlet titled *The Expansion of Russia*: 'Soviet Russia has reasserted Russian power over the outlying regions of the old Empire, and dominates Eastern Europe by force; she is now consolidating that power in Central Asia by large-scale settlement of Russians so as to remove any possibility of resistance or protest by her subject people, while proclaiming to the outside world her condemnation of colonialism, or "imperialist aggression" and the suppression of natural rights. In the absence of any voice from the suppressed peoples of the Red Empire, or any sustained effort to enlighten the young generation of Asia and Africa about the real nature of the Soviet state, Soviet propaganda succeeds through default, and a lie becomes truth for millions.'

*

Money issues, as had always been the case, were a concern in Ellis's life post retirement but he remained a proud man. During an exchange of letters with Hyde in 1960 and 1961, Ellis talks a lot of Stephenson putting him up in New York at the Beekman Tower hotel on First Avenue and East 49th Street, everything paid for by Stephenson, but being prepared to pay his own way. Money was so tight for Ellis he even went back to working for MI6.

'I have been called back to HO on a full-time basis in connexion with the reorganisation following recent incidents and some expansion due to the impending Berlin crisis, and troubles in Africa, Mid-East and elsewhere.'

Since arriving back in London from Australia he'd also been doing office work, culling or weeding 'unnecessary Registry files' for MI6. Pincher says this started in 1954 and went on until at least 1956.[13] Stevenson puts the date of this weeding as around 1963, the same year Philby defected. It apparently ended 1 March 1964.[14]

'After he had hurriedly returned to Britain his old firm, MI6, helped him to live on his pension by taking him back on the payroll, part time,' writes Chapman Pincher in *Too Secret Too Long*.

The ramifications of which didn't bear even thinking about, as he argued in *Their Trade is Treachery*: 'If [Ellis] was still an active spy or keen to cover up past evidence of his own operations and those of his pro-Soviet colleagues, the damage he may have caused in destroying leads to KGB activities is incalculable. Fortunately, there were documents concerning himself and Philby that did not come his way.'[15]

But Ellis's defenders saw it differently. Stevenson: 'Clearly, Ellis had extraordinary freedom. He was being left alone with super-secret files, entrusted with the task of "arranging" them for future historians.' Bill Ross-Smith described it as an 'ultra-sensitive job' while H. Montgomery Hyde said 'this work was highly confidential and it is inconceivable that he should have been entrusted with it if he were officially regarded as being, or as having been, a traitor to his country. It was nothing less than going through the SIS files and weeding out those which he did not consider worth preserving.'

Alternatively, in the wake of Philby's defection, someone higher up the food chain had asked him to purge them and cover up their own malfeasance: 'Ellis was recruited by SIS's Colin Gubbins to purge British intelligence files, presumably of any other embarrassing evidence. As we shall see, there was quite a bit to be put into the shredder.'

Railed Pincher: 'I saw a handwritten letter from him to a friend in which [Ellis] had boasted of *inserting* documents into some MI6 files.'[16]

But, on the balance of all the evidence, Ellis slipping notes into the files was not, as Pincher infers, a way of covering his tracks. More likely, as Stevenson said, it was a way of helping future MI6 historians get their facts right about the BSC effort in World War II. Ellis was a thorough researcher by his very nature, which is demonstrated in his two books. Were some embarrassing documents removed? Quite possibly. But again, the more likely explanation is Ellis was simply being fastidious because he had better knowledge of the intelligence contained in the files. It all comes down to perspective, bias and judgement. Why would a man under suspicion of being a double agent since 1946 be allowed anywhere near MI6 files in the same year Kim Philby went behind the Iron Curtain? It's completely implausible.

*

Perhaps the strongest indication that Ellis was hard up after being shunted aside for Hyde was that he took out 'a loan during his retirement' – from MI6 – for an unknown amount. This raises the obvious question: Why would an intelligence service investigating one of their officers on suspicion of pocketing cash from the Nazis – because he'd borrowed money from his own brother-in-law, which he hadn't paid back – then turn around while the officer was being actively investigated and give him a loan? It doesn't make sense.

Ellis had a pressing problem, though: how to bring in some money of his own. So he went back to his abandoned BSC manuscript from the early 1960s, *Anglo-American Collaboration in Intelligence and Security: Notes for Documentation*, and resuscitated it as 1972's *The Two Bills: Mission Accomplished*, a sort of twin biography of William Stephenson and William Donovan, with a foreword by SOE boss Major General Colin Gubbins.[17] All this at a time when rumours about Ellis's alleged involvement with the Germans and Russians had become common knowledge in intelligence circles.

But this second attempt was also scuppered, and out of its demise William Stevenson went on in 1976 to write the mega-bestselling *A Man Called Intrepid*, in which Ellis gets a solitary nod in the main text (apart from the mentions of his BSC codename, HOWARD). He'd had his pension suspended for his alleged double agentry. He'd stopped lunching at the Travellers to save money. He was in debt to MI6. Had he lived beyond 1975, it would have been another blow for Ellis to witness *A Man Called Intrepid*'s international sales, especially when he composed the foreword and two other writers (Montgomery Hyde and Stevenson) had essentially cannibalised much of his work.[18]

As Stephenson's biographer Bill Macdonald writes perspicaciously in *The True Intrepid*, 'Each time he attempted to publicise the war work of William Stephenson, it didn't add to his job security. Ironically, if Ellis's imposed unemployment was meant as a punishment for selling out to the "enemy", it seemed to make him more dependent monetarily on others. Ellis went to Stephenson for financial assistance, and when Ellis died he owed Stephenson a large amount of money.'[19]

In a 2 March 1973 letter from Stevenson in Toronto to Stephenson in Bermuda, Stevenson refers to Ellis's unpublished book as the 'Dick Ellis opus' and comments that 'Dick must feel awfully cut up about it'. In another letter of 3 April 1973, he talks of his 'gratitude and of being honoured, or whatever the correct phrasing is in a case like this, that you should think me competent to take on where Dick left off. It was always my hope that Dick would find the right publisher. It is no reflection on his work that he has not.'[20]

But nearly a year later, on 2 March 1974, Stevenson wrote to Stephenson: 'I was amused to hear you'd bailed him out. Isn't he getting a little long in the tooth for that sort of thing?' On 31 July 1974, he complains of Ellis pestering him with letters 'and his harping on not hearing from me'. On 11 August 1974, he writes: 'He sounds rather low', 'I'll have to work out some arrangement whereby he might profit from AMCI' and 'he seems to be having more trouble with his eyes . . . it must be awfully frustrating', which suggests Ellis's vision was deteriorating badly.

Timothy J. Naftali uncharitably calls Ellis a 'failed biographer'. Troy was also unkind about this difficult period in Ellis's life – accusing him of having 'used Hyde as a crying towel' – and (somewhat rightly) belittling his literary flair: 'Ellis . . . in Stephenson historiography is a pathetic figure but who is much worse if he were guilty of that alleged Nazi–Soviet service. Still he did play a role in Stephenson's alleged "plan aimed at widespread public recognition". Ellis's aborted biographies of Stephenson and his Transcaspian history, workmanlike though the last is, demonstrated his inability to write a "sensational" and "bestselling" book about anything.

'Moreover, his fear of offending MI6 inhibited him from venturing into sensitive areas . . . in his first manuscript, he never dared tell any decoding secrets, much less mention Ultra. He fudged the Churchill angle, but made it clear that Stephenson insisted on and received a wide-ranging brief. He never mentioned the Heydrich assassination. In his second effort he forthrightly said Churchill sent his "close friend" Stephenson to New York and again said nothing about Ultra or Heydrich. Neither effort, however, ever saw daylight.'[21]

In Troy's estimation, the manuscript for *The Two Bills: Mission Accomplished* was a profound disappointment: 'In coverage, detail, and style it was not much better than his earlier venture . . . at one point Bantam Books had apparently agreed to publish it in paperback but then wanted it first published elsewhere in hardcover. To this end, as well as in the review and revision of the manuscript, Ellis sought help from Sir William and such friends as Hyde, the writer Roald Dahl, aviation writer Arch Whitehouse, Bill [William] Stevenson, and, yes, this writer.

'I was asked to write the foreword,[22] was sent the manuscript, but went no further because Ellis had meanwhile run into so many problems that he once again exhausted the patience of Sir William, ultimately the decision maker in producing Stephenson books. Fearing that Ellis's "faulty sparkplug" and "fiddling delays" might hold up Stevenson's TV show,[23] Sir William reached agreement with Stevenson and Ellis in March 1973 that Ellis would once again play second fiddle, this time to Stevenson, who would take over *The Two Bills*.'

CHAPTER 18

NAILING ELLIS

'Peter Wright is again shown to be a highly unreliable
chronicler. His accounts are historically and psychologically
inauthentic.'
– Antony Percy, 'What Gouzenko said about ELLI',
COLDSPUR.COM (31 July 2021)

PETER WRIGHT BEGAN HIS INVESTIGATION INTO DICK ELLIS as
part of the joint MI5–MI6 Fluency Committee (later replaced with
a unit called 'K7') into Soviet penetration in Britain's secret service.
This proceeded in tandem with the ongoing EMERTON investigation
into Ellis, steered by former Bonn and Bern MI6 station head William
Steedman.[1]

Wright said he was looking for 'definite clues' linking Ellis to the
Soviets. Curious thing a definite clue; sort of like an open marriage.
What is it exactly and how do you define it in terms everyone agrees
on? A clue is always simply a clue but, in Wright's case, a clue was just
another word for his confirmation bias. He wanted Ellis's blood on
his hands.

Wright's idea of 'definite' was reading the autobiography of Ignace
Reiss's widow, Elsa (Elisabeth) Poretsky (writing as Elisabeth K.
Poretski) in French, *Les Nôtres: Vie et Mort d'un Agent Soviétique*,
whereupon, as he writes in *Spycatcher*, he 'seized on an extraordinary
statement which had not appeared in the English edition. Elisabeth
Poretsky said that in the late 1920s Ludwik [Reiss] had an agent high

up in British intelligence.' So Wright 'travelled to Paris in 1966 to see Mrs Poretsky' and 'produced a spread of 20 photographs from my briefcase. Some were dummy photographs, others were of known colleagues of her husband, and one was of Ellis, dating from the mid-1920s. She picked out all those she ought to have known, and Ellis as well. "I do not know this man's name," she told me, "but I am sure he is familiar."'

Only problem is Mrs Poretsky's book, which Wright had also apparently read in English, was first published in French in 1969 and the English edition, *Our Own People: A Memoir of 'Ignace Reiss' and His Friends*, the same year in Britain and the United States. So why would Wright be going to see Mrs Poretsky in 1966, *three years* before its publication?

Wright then magically went to Amsterdam by bus from Paris to meet Bernie (Bernardha), the widow of a Dutch architect, artist and erstwhile Soviet agent of Ignace Reiss called Henri 'Han' Pieck. The Dutchman had a connection to Kim Philby's 1930s spymaster Theodore Maly (aka Paul Hardt, the dead husband of Vladimir von Petrov's lover, Lydia Hardt) and also Robert Vansittart, who from the Foreign Office had run Ellis as an operative before the war.[2] He writes of Bernie: 'She too picked out Ellis's photograph but refused to say why.' And then Wright had an MI6 officer, Stephen de Mowbray, visit Christiane, the widow of executed GRU spy Richard Sorge, in a seminary outside New York.

'She recalled . . . a meeting on a street corner in London. She and Rickie [Sorge] had gone together to meet this agent, but he had told her to stand well back and cover him in case there was trouble . . . she had seen him, but not well. [The officer] showed her the photographs. "This man looks familiar," she said, "but I could not be certain, after over 40 years." It was Ellis's photograph.'

So Ellis looked familiar to three women who were once married to Soviet agents who aren't known to have had *any* contact with Ellis. There was no reference to Ellis in F. W. Deakin's and G. R. Storry's 1966 book *The Case of Richard Sorge*, only a passing mention of Sorge's British mission, where 'he arrived in the spring of 1929 and stayed about ten weeks'.[3]

Yet that was enough for Wright and the paranoid, witch-hunting Fluency Committee, which then hauled the retired septuagenarian Ellis into a gruelling interrogation over eight days with Wright and Wright's German- and Russian-speaking colleague, Major Theodore Xenophon Henry 'Bunny' Pantcheff.

He was an MI6 officer, former vice-consul in Munich, and erstwhile translator of Alexander Pushkin who in 1981 would write a book of his own, *Alderney: Fortress Island*, under the name T. X. H. Pantcheff.[4] Ellis was placed under surveillance; he had his office bugged and home telephone tapped.[5] They had every right to do so because Ellis 'was in receipt of an MI6 pension'. But Wright must have gone back in time because the Ellis interrogation happened sometime between 1965 and 1966.[6] West, Wright and Pincher had a field day describing what happened next.

'Ellis was summoned to an interview and he was challenged about the kind of information he might have given his former brother-in-law,' wrote Nigel West in *MI6*. 'The investigator told Ellis that the Abwehr officer who had bought [Aleksei] Zelensky's information was willing to fly to London to identify "Captain Ellis".' Initially, Ellis denied the charge, claimed West, but on returning to SIS headquarters the next day for a second interrogation, '[Ellis] admitted to selling the SIS order of battle to the Abwehr. When pressed about whether or not the Soviets had subsequently taken advantage of this lapse, Ellis insisted that he had never had any contact with the Russians. He also denied any further contact with the Abwehr after he had left Paris for the last time.'

The investigators still harboured doubts as to the completeness of Ellis's confession,[7] but it did, West observed, clear up one of the remaining mysteries of the war: 'Best and Stevens had indeed confirmed the details of SIS's internal structure to the Germans, but most of the information had already been in their possession for some considerable time. This, then, was the explanation for some of the outdated material included in the *Informationsheft Grossbritannien*.'

Pincher writes in *Traitors* that 'the interrogation was gradually made more hostile . . . Ellis continued to profess his innocence with a stream of lies', and in *Their Trade is Treachery*: '[Ellis] was confronted with the report of the German officer who named him as a spy. His response was that it must be a forgery. He insisted that he had never heard of the secret telephone link between Ribbentrop and Hitler. Though severely shaken when shown his name at the top of the Post Office list, he said that he could not recall any involvement.' The interrogators threatened to bring the German officer over and confront Ellis with his evidence,[8] and ended the session by giving Ellis 24 hours to ponder the consequences if that came to pass. 'The following day, Ellis, who was kept under surveillance against his possible defection, arrived with a document that was an abject confession of his guilt in spying for Germany up to 1940.'

Wright in *Spycatcher*: 'Ellis denied everything for several days. He blustered and blamed the whole thing on jealous colleagues. But as we produced the evidence, the Abwehr officer's report, and the indoctrination list for the telephone tap, he began to wilt . . . after lunch on the Friday he returned to the interrogation room in the basement of the old War Office, known as Room 055, with a typed sheet of paper.' Wright described this as 'a confession of sorts', adding that Ellis said he had 'got into trouble during the early years in MI6 . . . Ellis's confession was carefully shaded at the edges to hide precisely what intelligence he had given, and where it had gone, so, under interrogation, we asked him to clarify it. He admitted passing over detailed order-of-battle plans for British intelligence, as well as betraying the Hitler–Von Ribbentrop telephone link, even though he knew this material was being passed by Von Petrov to the Germans . . . we asked Ellis when he last had contact with the Russian emigre's [sic]. He admitted that it was in December 1939, after the outbreak of war.'

Pincher: 'Ellis explained that he had run into debt because his British pay was too low and had borrowed from Zilenski [sic], who then started pressurising [sic] him for information to sell to the Germans and Russians. He claimed that, at first, the information he handed over was trivial, but Zilenski, urged on by his Soviet contact, then threatened to expose him to his secret service chiefs unless he provided more valuable material.'

Ellis, said Pincher, informed his interrogators he'd needed the money to pay for medical treatment for his wife.

'So he had taken the easy way out, becoming more and more deeply compromised. Under further questioning, he admitted handing over detailed charts of the organisation of British intelligence before the war, knowing that they would go both to Germany and to Russia. This had been the source of much of the information that the Abwehr used during its interrogations following the Venlo kidnappings.'

Pincher asserted that Ellis had 'betrayed the British intelligence achievement in tapping the Hitler–Ribbentrop telephone link', fully aware that this information would end up being relayed to the Nazis.

'He also admitted making use after the war began of a brother secret service officer to deliver secrets, unwittingly, in an envelope delivered to an agent, whom he knew to be working for the Germans, and to bring back a package containing money.'

Pincher also claimed that Ellis, aware that his interrogators had nothing on him during his time at BSC, denied having continued to spy for Nazi Germany while in the United States and Canada.

'Nevertheless, his confession constituted unquestionably the worst case of British espionage to the Germans both before and during the war. When told that he had committed treason in war and could have justifiably been hanged, he broke down and pleaded physical frailty against any further cross-examination, but the interrogators were determined to continue their probing on the following day.'

According to Pincher, Ellis 'continued to deny any secret dealings with the Russians' and insisted that the Petrov affair hadn't been the cause of his sudden dash to Britain from Australia. 'He denied that he had met Philby on his return from Australia, which was known to be a lie, or that the secret service had warned him not to contact his former colleague.'

Pincher claimed that Ellis's interrogators were concerned that he 'might collapse under the strain' of any further questioning.

'It was decided that, as a last throw, Ellis should be offered immunity, after the Attorney General had been consulted, if he would confess his treacherous activities with Russia and name his contacts. He refused to believe that immunity would really be granted and held to his position regarding any Russian espionage after 1940.'

But Wright was undeterred. As Pincher described it, Ellis 'resolutely denied' being a double agent for the Russians yet Wright pressed Ellis on the all-important Soviet connection.

'We wanted to know about his involvement with the Soviets, we said. For a moment he wavered in front of us, then he fought back. "Never!" he shouted, "Never with the Communists . . ." The next day we took him through the odd chain of events – his trip to Australia, and his rapid return to Britain, and the coincidence of Petrov's defection. But he denied everything, even when he was caught out in repeated lying about his actions until he retired. Not even an authorised offer of immunity could make him change his mind. But I have little doubt of Ellis's involvement with the Russians.'

Even Pincher admits, 'There was no firm evidence against him, nor were there any witnesses.'

But what did it matter? An accusation was enough. Ellis 'was broken'.[9]

*

Wright and Pantcheff wrote up their report, which 'was endorsed without reservation by [MI6 director of counterintelligence and security] Christopher Phillpotts, and submitted to [head of MI6] Dick White and his deputy, Maurice Oldfield' who 'at first . . . doubted the veracity of Ellis's confession, until eventually Bunny Pancheff [sic] played the crucial exchanges to him. But even though we had uncovered a traitor of major proportions, I sometimes felt as if it were I who was being blamed. Oldfield despised the climate of fear engendered by Phillpotts's vetting purges, and campaigned hard to change Dick's mind. The fact that Ellis had confessed seemed to weigh hardly at all on his thinking. As far as he was concerned, it was all a long time ago, and best forgotten.'

Oldfield's biographer Martin Pearce notes: 'Maurice was aggrieved at what he described as Phillpotts's "Gestapo methods" in extracting what was in his view a dubious confession from his friend, and subjected his rival to a reprimand.'

Not that any dubiousness dissuaded Pincher from plunging the knife into Ellis's twitching corpse.

'Through Zilenski [sic], the Centre in Moscow [sic] knew that Ellis had supplied secrets for money, and it was considered inconceivable that it could resist applying pressure when he was in such a sensitive post, both in New York and later when he returned to the secret service proper,' he wrote in *Their Trade is Treachery*. 'It was concluded that it would never be possible to make a detailed assessment of the damage he had done, but if, as seemed likely, his treachery had covered something like 30 years, it would have put Philby's in the shade . . .

'Further independent confirmation of Ellis's treachery [came] from former colleagues of his and from an international authority on intelligence and defence affairs who prefers not to be named[10] . . . the secret was so closely held that Ellis's relatives and intimate friends never heard of it and still find it hard to believe . . . the two wives with whom Philby spent most of his adult life had no inkling that he was a spy. Neither did the family or friends of Colonel Ellis, John Cairncross or Anthony Blunt, save for those who were helping them.'

Considered inconceivable. As seemed likely. Pincher was up to his usual supposition but worse, now he was gaslighting Ellis's 'relatives and intimate friends', who, perish the thought, perhaps didn't believe it; not because it was so hard to get their heads around but because it wasn't true.

Like Wright, Pincher didn't know Ellis, nor did the three widows he'd spoken to who'd apparently convinced him to haul Ellis in for an interrogation. One of Ellis's staunchest defenders, Bill Ross-Smith, *did* know Ellis. In a letter to the *Sydney Morning Herald* of 2 February 1983, he maintained Ellis had never been on the radar of a molehunt. He even said no interrogation of Ellis had taken place, on the basis of Ellis having been so trusted as to be tasked with weeding top-secret files at MI6. He claimed Australia's former external affairs minister Percy Spender agreed with him.

But today, in spy books found in bookshops and libraries all around the world, the narrative sticks. You'll find it in books such as *Unholy Trinity*: 'Only a handful of people in British intelligence were told Ellis's secret, and they decided that it was so shocking that neither the FBI nor the CIA should know.'

*

When I emailed Monika Stevenson in 2022, she took the conspiratorial view on Dick Ellis and his fate. Her line of thinking was similar to William Stephenson's, who'd told an Australian journalist, Peter Game, in 1983 that it would have been 'child's play' for Kim Philby or another unknown Soviet mole to set up Ellis.

'You probably know,' she wrote to me, 'that the charge of double agent against Colonel Ellis originated at a time when the infamous Soviet spy Kim Philby set in place directives received from his Soviet bosses. Because of Philby's high rank in SIS he had virtual carte blanche to carefully construct false messages, which were then leaked to the British communications system in order to deceive the decision-making elite and the public.

'From there, through a network of other Soviet spies – some of whom Philby himself had put in place – and others who were part of the larger web of double agents put in place by the Soviet Union, disinformation was also leaked to the US, Canada and many European countries.'

One of the 'most important' of these disinformation leaks, she claimed, was about Ellis.

'Philby was finally exposed and fled to the Soviet Union; the night before he had promised [Nicholas] Elliott, a former head of MI6, that he would turn himself in voluntarily the next morning. (I was there when my late husband interviewed Elliott, who was the person assigned to escort Philby back to London [from Beirut in Lebanon] to turn himself in and be debriefed.)'

As Mrs Stevenson observed, Philby lived out his days in the Soviet Union as a hero but British, American and other Western intelligence services didn't know how many other Soviet moles had successfully infiltrated their ranks.

'I [was] part of conversations my husband had about this with Sir William Stephenson and others who were directly involved in tracking down other double agents who had been set in place under Philby's tenure. No one in that world had ever seen an alleged confession by Colonel Ellis.'

What her late husband wrote in *Intrepid's Last Case* is a fair assessment: 'There seem to have been two groups, nominally in fierce conflict with each other, who for different reasons wanted to nail Ellis. First, the Soviets . . . the other group, in head-on collision with Moscow, was Western counterintelligence. At some point, as Ellis had told me before he died in 1975, he did fall foul of a British security investigation. By 1981 alleged details of such investigations had made newspaper headlines. Stories of Soviet double agents threatened public trust, caused confusion within the security services, and seriously damaged relations between agencies. One faction was scoring off another faction within the Atlantic alliance's intelligence groups. Ellis could be seen as a convenient scapegoat.'

But I'm not sure Soviet interest in Ellis was as strong as the Stevensons make it out to be. Their talk of disinformation from Moscow about Ellis seems a stretch (as well as convenient); it's reminiscent of how accusations of 'fake news' are made today in response to public-relations crises or incidents of poor behaviour by politicians or public officials.

Ellis was a historically important agent for the United Kingdom and a colossus of spycraft in the United States, Europe, Australia and Asia but he was at his core a man who didn't seek publicity, who stayed in the background and was quite happy to let others take all the glory. He was a loyal deputy in war and in intelligence. He didn't set himself up as a prime target to be knocked off.

Both in his actions and words Ellis was an avowed opponent of the Soviet state whose personal misfortune, according to Phillip Knightley, was to have his case 'resurrected to show the extent of Soviet penetration of Britain'. A dubious circumstantial case has been made that he worked for the Soviets, both before and after the war. This, however, has never been proven. Ellis never made an outright confession that he supplied information to the Soviet Union; he categorically denied it. He was a loyalist to King and Country who passed himself off as an Englishman, who was simultaneously repelled and seduced by the British class system, and had been that way all his life.

He was a survivor of impoverished circumstances in Australia who'd picked himself up from being on the bones of his arse and made something of his life – but he had scruples. The most logical explanation for any 'confession', if such a confession was made and exists, is loyalty to his superiors. Ellis was probably protecting his superiors, likely Stewart Menzies, after the latter's gambit against the Nazis *using the Nazis* was exposed and Ellis fell on his sword. Better to take the fall than have the entire MI6 leadership go down with you.

'[Ellis] may have been down, but he was not out,' wrote Thomas F. Troy in *Wild Bill and Intrepid*. 'He had suffered that hostile inter-rogation in the mid-sixties, been practically convicted of treason, and probably suffered a diminution of his pension. He had not been hanged, however, as he had been assured would have been the case in wartime. Rather the government allowed him, for whatever practical reasons – a simple cover-up or weak evidence, perhaps – to live out his life under his private dark cloud. Had he lived long enough – he died in 1975 – to experience the revelations by Pincher and Wright, that cloud would have become a public cloudburst.'

*

In a 1983 *New York Times* review of *The Last Hero: Wild Bill Donovan* (which briefly mentions Ellis's work with William Donovan and the COI/OSS) by Anthony Cave Brown,[11] American journalist and author Edward Jay Epstein wrote: 'Colonel Ellis remained an eminence grise in the OSS throughout most of the war. But the real importance of Colonel Ellis emerged only in 1965, long after Donovan had died and his microfilmed files had gathered dust in his executor's office. Under gruelling interrogation by a team of British intelligence investigators, Colonel Ellis broke down and confessed that before World War II began, he had been recruited as a double agent by the Germans and then blackmailed into service by the Soviet Union.'

This was a blatant falsehood and misrepresentation, perhaps fed to Epstein by the CIA's counterintelligence chief from 1954 to '74, James Jesus Angleton, who was notoriously paranoid about widespread Soviet penetration after his trusted friend, Kim Philby, defected in 1963. Ellis, unlike Philby, never confessed to spying for the Russians.

'Thus the man who really organised American secret intelligence was a German–Soviet mole. Situated at the core of the OSS, he was in a perfect position to expose and compromise every secret agent, operation and modus operandi of the agency. (Indeed, in 1963 Ellis even wrote a history of the wartime Anglo-American intelligence collaboration that was based on secret intelligence documents) . . . the British Government suppressed any mention of the Ellis betrayal until 1981, possibly to avoid damaging its intelligence relationships with the United States.'[12]

Cave Brown himself was appalled by the review, telling *Interview* magazine in 1983: 'I have responded to a statement in *The New York Times* by Edward J. Epstein that Col. Charles H. Ellis, who was the senior British liaison officer between General Menges [sic][13] in London and General Donovan in Washington, was, in fact, a Soviet agent. I mean, that story is just such patent balls that I've written a letter – a rather mild letter – to *The New York Times* regretting the fact that Mr Epstein, in an otherwise excellent review, found it necessary to betray the memory of a distinguished British officer.'[14]

Throw enough mud, though, and some of it has to stick.

CHAPTER 19

AMONG THE DRIPPING SHRUBS

'It is not known how many KGB agents Ellis and Philby were
able to foist on the Australian intelligence service.'
– EVAN WHITTON, *SYDNEY MORNING HERALD*, 27 JANUARY 1983

MI6 HEAD STEWART MENZIES, an old Etonian and veteran of the
Western Front in World War I who retired in 1952 and died in
1968, encouraged Dick Ellis to keep up his connections with Anton
Turkul before World War II, and presumably Vladimir von Petrov.

Menzies sent Ellis to New York to deputise for William Stephenson
at BSC and represent MI6 in the United States in dealings with J. Edgar
Hoover and Franklin D. Roosevelt. Postwar, he made Ellis one of
the most powerful men in MI6, with purview over North and South
America and Asia. He dispatched Ellis to Australia to help found
ASIO. And in the early 1960s, circa 1961–62, a couple of years prior
to Ellis's immense distress and bother with the Fluency Committee,
he allegedly recommended Ellis[1] for the International Documentary
Centre, or Interdoc, a joint Dutch–French–German intelligence
organisation backed by MI6 that 'specialised in distributing accurate
versions of communist-inspired news reports' but 'depended largely
on West German subsidies'.

Interdoc historian Giles Scott-Smith says the group's 'central focus
was to increase the level of understanding of communist doctrine
and practice by stimulating and making available well-researched
information on the policies and realities of the Soviet bloc' and Ellis

'remained Interdoc's "desk officer" in the UK until retiring due to ill-health in 1969'.

The anti-communist Interdoc was not the natural home for a covert Soviet spy. These were all decisions reflecting Menzies's supreme confidence in Ellis or, at the very least, rewarding him for his fealty, discretion and loyalty. If Ellis really had taken the fall for his superiors, Menzies's continued faith in Ellis was a sure sign that the man had been owed something.

According to Chapman Pincher, who snidely remarked in *Too Secret Too Long* that despite Ellis's 'alleged frailty . . . he was fit enough to have found himself a job' with Interdoc, an anonymous security official had told him after Ellis's death 'how he had been approached by an officer from MI6 because he was believed to have recommended Ellis for a retirement post in Interdoc . . . the person was as surprised as any of Ellis's friends and relatives to be told that the colonel had confessed to spying for Germany and had then almost certainly switched his espionage activities to the Soviet interest under blackmail pressure'.

*

Ellis duly joined Interdoc, attending one of French intelligence officer Antoine Bonnemaison's *colloques* (conferences) 'in the picturesque setting of Mont Saint-Michel, in the late spring of 1962'. He then headed up a British branch called Interdoc UK with offices (for a time) in Norfolk Street, London, and served the organisation until about 1967, when he relinquished the position for health reasons. However, he continued in a limited capacity up till 1971, staying 'in the background as part of the network, continuing with translation work and information gathering as health permitted, and was even asked by the CIA to write "a confidential history of the early days of OSS"'. He also continued his writing, contributing articles on the Soviet Union to anti-communist pamphlets published by Interdoc and various anthologies.

'The controversy surrounding Ellis does not seem to have affected in any way his involvement with Interdoc,' writes Scott-Smith. 'Ellis wrote the following candid note to [Dutch intelligence officer and

Interdoc director Cees] van den Heuvel at the end of 1967: "I told [MI6] that I would stand no more nonsense about myself and demanded that they put their cards on the table or shut up. I have been told that 'no action is contemplated'; they regret having embarrassed me (and others) but in view of the seriousness of the Philby and Blake cases (there is more to come!) they have to examine every possibility, however remote.'"

Van den Heuvel, responding to the publication of *Spycatcher* in 1987, defended his former colleague: 'He perhaps went too far in his attempts to exchange information, which has therefore given a false impression. He was a remarkably active man. I have personally never doubted his loyalty.'

But according to Scott-Smith, quoting from Ellis, 'doubts about Ellis's past had not gone away easily, and during the transition of MI6 leadership from Dick White to John Rennie in 1967 Ellis was once again the target of an investigation "in which inquiries were made regarding me of your people, and in [the] US and among other former colleagues, which might have done me a great deal of harm".'[2]

Clearly this was a reference to the ongoing Fluency and EMERTON investigations that now encompassed the United States, Canada, the United Kingdom and Australia – four of the so-called 'Five Eyes' – and was making Ellis's life hell. Indeed, Ellis threatened to sue Charles Spry, the head of ASIO from 1950–70, if the accusations against him were leaked, writing to Spry on 11 November 1967, 'If it is brought to my knowledge that any statement that is injurious to me, or which reflects on my integrity as a member of the service, is made to any outside person or is repeated outside the immediate circle of inquiry, I shall immediately institute proceedings for slander.'[3]

'I found Ellis to be a fascinating character,' Scott-Smith told me from The Hague, where he is dean at Leiden University College. 'It seemed to me that he was being protected by the service from the inquisitions of Wright, et al. At the same time, it looked like he was given things to do of lesser importance for the service, such as Interdoc, which the Brits never took seriously.'

*

In 1969, after his quick trip to Bermuda to meet William Stephenson at Camden House on Camden North Road, Paget, Bermuda, and an impromptu meeting with Dick Ellis at the local waterfront hotel at Pitts Bay, The Princess,[4] Thomas F. Troy agreed to meet Ellis again in England. But then he got an unexpected phone call.

'[The] planned meeting in London ... had been thoroughly co-ordinated with all CIA's baronies, including counterintelligence under the redoubtable James Jesus ("Jim") Angleton. Hence, on the eve of my departure I was surprised by a telephone call from Angleton's deputy, Raymond Rocca. His message? "We've been asked on the highest authority to tell you: 'Don't see Ellis.'" Of course, I began to expostulate: "Whaddya mean 'Don't see Ellis?' It's all been laid on. He knows I'm coming." Then another voice came on the line: "This is Jim Angleton. Do you need higher authority?" That was the time when CIA often seemed to have no higher authority. "No," was my prompt, and proper, response. "And," he continued, "don't tell the chief of station [in London]." Yes, sir. That was Angleton, running operations about which others knew nothing. With Ellis awaiting me, I had a problem.'

Angleton, the CIA's 'gaunt, conspiratorial' chief of counterintelligence, had been wholly duped by Kim Philby and spent the rest of his life existentially wounded for not having detected him when he had the chance.[5] After Philby's defection Angleton, who got his start in William Donovan's and Dick Ellis's COI/OSS, was convinced 'that the CIA was penetrated by a high-level "mole" – a view echoed in Britain, of course, by the receptive Peter Wright', possibly by as many as half a dozen moles, but 'joint investigations by the FBI and the CIA on the lines of Wright's British Fluency Committee found evidence of none'.

In this climate of fear and suspicion, Angleton was even investigated by the CIA himself (the author Anthony Cave Brown suspected he could have been a mole and said so publicly). Angleton was known to feed journalists information on agents he suspected of being Soviet operatives.[6] Just like Wright had done with Chapman Pincher. Angleton even had contact with Pincher himself.[7]

Much of Angleton's own information came from KGB major Anatoli Golitsyn, who defected to the United States in 1961, was personally interviewed by Angleton, and whose claims of wide-scale Soviet penetration and 'vast KGB deception' of Western security services, shared with the British and which formed the impetus for Wright's Fluency Committee investigation that ensnared Ellis and others, proved to be largely exaggerated, suspect and unreliable.

But, critically, Golitsyn found willing believers in Angleton and Wright.[8] The pair in turn found a willing believer in Pincher. Angleton eventually was sacked in 1974 and died in 1987. The fact that he was warning Troy to stay away from Ellis in 1969 means British attempts to hide the Ellis case from the FBI and CIA had not succeeded and were common knowledge within intelligence circles. It's likely Angleton was driving a lot of the campaign against Ellis.

'Compounding the problem was Stephenson, whom I saw on the way over but to whom I did not reveal my predicament,' continued Troy. 'Ever helpful, but despite my demurrer, he cabled Ellis my ETA. Hence in London I immediately found his invitation for lunch the next day. Weaselling out of that – leaving regrets at his club – was not difficult, but a later message set another luncheon five days hence. Meanwhile, I had skirted Angleton's ban enough to send a Mayday message to my friend Walter Pforzheimer in headquarters. That obviously produced some scurrying around, because the station chief, Bronson Tweedy, called me in: "What are you doing about Ellis?" My response was short: "Nothing." His rejoinder, dutifully echoing Angleton, was shorter: "Don't." When I started to explain the ridiculous situation, he cut me off. "He'll understand." Understand what?

'Before answering that question, let me dispose of the second luncheon. Because Ellis was then moving out of London, we had no direct communication. I could only leave another "regrets only" message at his club and then, like a fugitive from justice, clear out of my hotel from 8:00 a.m. to 10:00 p.m. lest he come looking for me. Which he did. And he left a package – a long note and 193 typescript pages of a projected book [*Anglo-American Collaboration in Intelligence and Security: Notes for Documentation*] about Stephenson and BSC . . . the Ellis case, for which the word "fuss" is inadequate, is too complex to try to synthesise here. Suffice it to say that by 1966 it had become a very contentious issue within MI5 and MI6 and led to what the experts call a "hostile" interrogation of Ellis . . . one must wonder what seismic secrets, such as Ellis's actual confession, are locked up in British and American intelligence vaults.'[9]

*

By 1970, Ellis was being frozen out of all his old professional and social networks. He had to give up his club membership at the Travellers in Pall Mall for the cheaper Royal Automobile Club, and his wife, Alexandra, who'd been in poor health for some time, died.[10] Ellis had 'a dicky heart' himself. Even worse, he'd had to stop playing music, his first love, because 'arthritis in his hands compelled him to give up playing'.

In *Intrepid's Last Case* William Stevenson described Ellis's appearance as 'dressed like a man of modest means who had known better times: dark suit carefully pressed and brushed, striped shirt a little frayed at the cuffs, shoes highly polished'.

The only bright spot during this awful period for Ellis was winning the Sir Percy Sykes Memorial Medal from the Royal Society for Asian Affairs, which is awarded 'to distinguished travellers and writers deemed to have increased man's knowledge of and stimulated interest in Asia'. Ellis was honoured 'in recognition of his work on Transcaspia and adjacent regions'. He also wrote a piece called 'Soviet Imperialism' for the anthology *'We Will Bury You': Studies in Left-Wing Subversion Today*, which contained the same anti-Russian venom he'd displayed 50 years earlier. In it he compared the Soviet state to a 'form of government harnessed . . . to an ideology that is a combination of reactionary Russian obscurantism and messianic fanaticism with 19th-century Marxist economics'.

That March, he flew Qantas from London to Australia for a 15-day holiday and stayed at the Hotel Metropole, Sydney, Hotel Canberra, Canberra, and Federal Hotel, Melbourne. Over the next couple of years, he'd revisit Australia and be placed under surveillance by ASIO. It is an obvious irony that Ellis, against whom no real evidence of treason was ever produced by the authorities, would be tracked and surveilled in the country of his birth by the very spy agencies he personally set up in Canberra.

'It was not until March 1971 that ASIO again became involved,' wrote John Blaxland in *The Protest Years*. 'Information arose that new evidence pointed to Ellis having been an RIS [Russian Intelligence Service] agent as early as 1929, even before he was a German agent. According to [ASIO head Peter] Barbour's note for record, a former foreign officer expressed the conviction that Ellis was a more important spy than Philby, and certainly of great significance for Australian intelligence services because of his Australian associations. ASIO was urged to collaborate with ASIS, both for internal security and for the Organisation's [sic] professional status in the eyes of allies. Barbour, and Bill Robertson, who was then Director of ASIS, agreed to look at this and any future similar cases. At another meeting in January 1972, ASIO was told that Ellis's leak to the Germans of the interception of communications between Joachim von Ribbentrop . . . and Hitler was "high treason and [Ellis] should have been hanged for this particular act of treachery".'[11]

In 1972 MI5's Patrick Stewart, a member of the Fluency Committee, flew to Canada to meet Igor Gouzenko, the man who'd first named the mysterious Soviet mole ELLI back in 1946. According to Gouzenko biographer Amy Knight in *How the Cold War Began: The Igor Gouzenko Affair and the Hunt for Soviet Spies*, when he saw the reports written by the BSC and RCMP about his case, 'Gouzenko went into a fury and threw the papers across the room. He claimed that he had not said what was written in the BSC report, that someone had falsified his statements. As for the notes of the RCMP interview . . . Gouzenko said they had been forged . . . he convinced himself that it was a cover-up and that Elli worked for MI5. Later, when he realised that the MI5 officer who had interviewed him in 1945 was Roger Hollis, and that Hollis was suspected of being a mole, Gouzenko became certain that Hollis had deliberately misrepresented his statements to hide the fact that he was Elli.'

Hollis, who would later become the prime suspect for ELLI in Chapman Pincher's *Their Trade is Treachery*, died aged 67 in 1973. *Time* magazine called him 'a civil servant so umbrous that his name was never publicly mentioned'. Early that year, on 25 January, Ellis, then 77, had married his fourth wife, Joyce Hatten (née Steeples), 44, at a registry office in Eastbourne.[12] Their age difference was a staggering 33 years. In November 1973 Ellis and Joyce left for Australia via South Africa on the SS *Australis*, arriving in Sydney on 19 December and staying at a friend's apartment, 4/313A Edgecliff Road in Woollahra.

ASIO agents tailed Ellis for months, monitoring his entering and leaving the 'Gainsborough' apartment building, covertly taking photographs of him walking down the street, following him as he caught the Route 388 public bus into the city (where they managed to lose Ellis as he walked on foot and entered the Koala Motor Inn shopping arcade on the corner of Oxford, Riley and Pelican Streets – comically inept surveillance work), and reading his private mail, including a letter from H. Montgomery Hyde sent from Funchal, Madeira, Portugal. Warned a secret ASIO minute paper on 17 January 1974: 'Extreme care is to be exercised in any surveillance operation against Ellis.'

They really needn't have bothered: it was humdrum stuff and they were amateurish at their jobs at best. Ellis was clearly an old man going about mundane personal business, not a Soviet super-mole on a top-secret mission in his homeland; though amusingly – judging by ASIO photographs of his surveillance – he *did* dress impeccably, much like Alec Guinness's George Smiley in the BBC adaptation of John le Carré's *Tinker Tailor Soldier Spy*. An ASIO agent monitoring Ellis wrote in a 4 February 1974 surveillance report: 'Ellis did not appear interested in the possibility of surveillance. He appeared neatly dressed in a light khaki coat and dark trousers, collar and tie.'

The Ellises eventually departed Sydney for London via Panama on the SS *Britanis*. It was the last time the boy from Annandale would see Australia. According to Ann Salwey, her father knew the end was near: 'The idea of him defecting is ludicrous. He visited Australia months before his death because he wanted to see it all again. He cried because it had changed.'

Blaxland: 'When ASIO was advised of Ellis's impending visit to Australia in December 1973, ASIO and ASIS agreed that there was no evidence that Ellis had worked for the Russians, but that they would continue to follow the case. When Ellis arrived in Sydney, ASIO placed him under "spasmodic surveillance", but this produced nothing of

Double agent Duško Popov, who warned the FBI's J. Edgar Hoover of the impending Japanese attack on Pearl Harbor when Ellis was in the room with the two men. Ellis says that the warning was then relayed to President Franklin D. Roosevelt through Roosevelt's son, Jimmy. *Wikimedia Commons*

FBI chief J. Edgar Hoover. *Wikimedia Commons*

Double agent Folkert Arie van Koutrik, one of the possible sources of British intelligence leaks to the Nazis that have been blamed on Ellis. *The National Archives*

Abwehr chief Admiral Wilhelm Canaris. How much did he and his Nazi friends, including Abwehr III F counterespionage chief Richard Protze, secretly collaborate with Ellis and MI6? *Wikimedia Commons*

SD chief Walter Schellenberg, who ran Vladimir von Petrov as an agent. *Wikimedia Commons*

Lieutenant Colonel Ellis's ID card in Egypt, 1942. *Imperial War Museum*

BSC chief William Stephenson, the man known around the world as 'Intrepid'. Ellis was Stephenson's deputy in New York during World War II. *Photographer unknown*

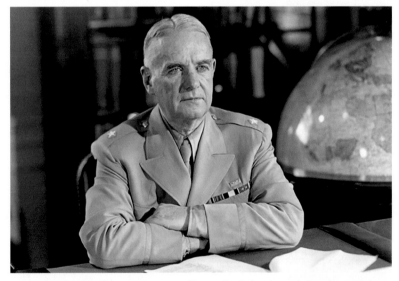

COI/OSS chief William Donovan. Ellis worked closely with Donovan and provided the blueprint for the American wartime secret-service organisation that morphed into the CIA. *Wikimedia Commons*

Kim Philby's memo to Major John Gwyer in 1946 during the Richard Protze interrogation, telling Gwyer he doesn't know who the 'Captain Ellis' mentioned by Protze could be. Philby and Ellis were on an MI6 reorganisation committee together in 1945. *The National Archives*

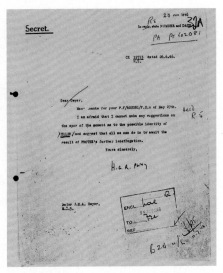

Ellis's 1946 Legion of Merit citation from President Harry S. Truman. *National Library of Australia*

The 1956 Chilean interrogation report of Vladimir von Petrov in Santiago, with the curious annotation '? ELLIS'. *The National Archives*

A still of Ellis being interviewed in the unreleased Canadian TV documentary about William Stephenson, 1973. It is the only known film or audio recording of Ellis. *CBC/YouTube*

ASIO surveillance photographs of Ellis in Sydney, 1974, the year before his death. *NAA/ASIO*

The campaign to expose Ellis in the 1980s was led by former MI5 intelligence officer Peter Wright, who was the unnamed source for Chapman Pincher's books *Their Trade is Treachery* (1981) and *Too Secret Too Long* (1984) and then followed up with his own book, *Spycatcher* (1987). Wright was a member of the Fluency Committee, which investigated Ellis in the 1960s. *Bulletin*

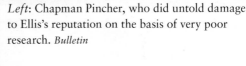

Left: Chapman Pincher, who did untold damage to Ellis's reputation on the basis of very poor research. *Bulletin*

Below: Espionage author Nigel West, an enthusiastic subscriber to the idea that Ellis worked for the Nazis. *Antonin Cermak/Fairfax Media via Getty Images*

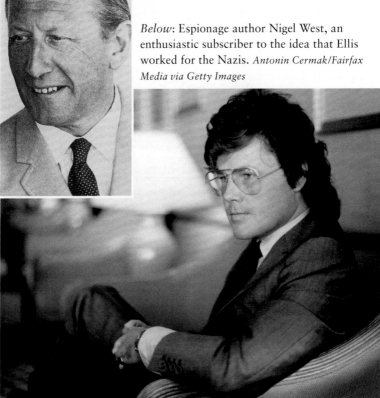

CIA counterintelligence chief James Jesus Angleton, who was betrayed by Kim Philby and became convinced that Ellis was also a traitor. *Bettmann/Getty Images*

MI6 chief Stewart Menzies, a close ally of Ellis during the Australian's intelligence career. Did he instruct Ellis to play spy games with Nazis before World War II and did Ellis cover for him? *Bentley Archive/Popperfoto via Getty Images*

MI6 chief Maurice Oldfield, who worked with Ellis in Singapore in the 1950s, sent birthday wishes to Ellis just before Ellis died in 1975: 'My dear Dick, a very happy eightieth birthday from all of us [at MI6].' *Hulton-Deutsch Collection/CORBIS/ Corbis via Getty Images*

Left: Phillip Knightley, biographer of Kim Philby and espionage author, attempted to get a film made about Ellis's life. *Ross Anthony Willis/Fairfax Media via Getty Images*

Above: Anthony Cave Brown, biographer of Stewart Menzies and Kim Philby, who considered the idea of Ellis being a Soviet spy 'such patent balls' and wrote a letter to the *New York Times* to salvage the reputation of 'a distinguished British officer'. *Charles Del Vecchio/Washington Post via Getty Images*

Above: William Stevenson, author of *A Man Called Intrepid* (1976) and *Intrepid's Last Case* (1983), who came to Ellis's defence in print but was saying different things privately. *Reg Innell/Toronto Star via Getty Images*

Right: H. Montgomery Hyde, (IN HAT) author of *The Quiet Canadian* (1962) and *Secret Intelligence Agent* (1982), initially a staunch Ellis defender, also had his doubts about Ellis and eventually expressed them publicly: 'People can and do lead double lives without their friends having any idea of their seamy side.' *Evening Standard/ Hulton Archive/Getty Images*

CHARLES HOWARD ELLIS   **KIM PHILBY**

When Ellis was named as a traitor by Chapman Pincher in *Their Trade is Treachery*, his image went around the world but Ellis was so shadowy and unknown many picture editors had no useful images of him. This crude, altered image from his time in Ashkhabad, taken from Ellis's book *The Transcaspian Episode* (1963), was published in the *Australian* on 27 February 1982 alongside a photo of Kim Philby. *Australian*

Philby, whose intelligence career for the United Kingdom and ultimate defection to the Soviet Union was inextricably linked to Ellis's downfall. *Laski Diffusion/Getty Images*

interest.[13] Ellis left Australia on 11 April 1974 . . . in the end, however, there was never any evidence that Ellis had acted improperly while in Australia. Whether he had done so while working elsewhere is another matter.'

And still not proven. In July 1974, with Hollis dead less than a year, Lord Trend (Burke St John Trend), former Secretary to the Cabinet, was asked by Prime Minister Harold Wilson to lead an inquiry into the findings of the Fluency Committee and could find no irrefragable evidence of Soviet penetration from Hollis, his deputy Graham Mitchell, Dick Ellis or anyone else. His report has never been released.

*

On 10 February 1975 MI6 director-general Maurice Oldfield wrote to Ellis for his 80th birthday. This suggested that Oldfield, like one of his predecessors in the top job, the late Stewart Menzies, regarded the Australian highly, even amid all the clouds of suspicion: 'My dear Dick, a very happy eightieth birthday from all of us [at MI6] – and from me in particular . . . by all means pursue the Interdoc invitation. There is no objection on our part, if you want to take it up . . . Yours ever, Maurice.'[14] As his biographer Martin Pearce writes, 'Whatever the truth about Ellis's treachery, Oldfield remained loyal to the man and they stayed in regular contact until Ellis died in 1975.'

Oldfield finished up at MI6 in 1978. Much has been made of the report that Oldfield shortly before his death made an admission to Chapman Pincher regarding Ellis's guilt. In a letter to the *Sydney Morning Herald* in 1983, Pincher claimed: 'I discussed the Ellis case with Sir Maurice Oldfield on the latter's deathbed. He had forgiven him because he was a very forgiving man.'[15]

But this apparently didn't happen, according to another Oldfield biographer, Richard Deacon, the pen name of Donald McCormick.

'In the weeks in hospital immediately preceding his death Sir Maurice was in no condition to indulge in much more than small talk and exchange jokes,' Deacon writes in *'C': A Biography of Sir Maurice Oldfield, Head of MI6*. 'Any lengthy discussion would soon exhaust him. To make an admission that Ellis was guilty then or [on] another occasion would not only have been totally out of character, but a breach of the Official Secrets Act. For the investigation of Ellis had been a secret inquiry and, as a result of this, no charges had been brought against him. The matter was closed . . . the [suggestion Ellis spied for the Russians] can be dismissed totally, as it was in his investigation.

'As to the allegations of Ellis having acted as a German agent . . . he had to play the role of a double agent on occasions, thereby building up contacts inside the German ranks. This proved of enormous value when he was operating inside the United States in World War II . . . [Ellis] never betrayed [double agent Duško] Popov to the Nazis.'

MI6 officer Anthony Cavendish also made this statement to Deacon on 17 May 1984: 'Any connections Dick Ellis had with the Abwehr were simply part of his duties in working for British intelligence.' Cavendish personally arranged the 'first meeting' between Pincher and Oldfield at the latter's bedside before Oldfield's death and was adamant Oldfield, despite Pincher's public claims to the contrary, did not for a minute believe that Ellis was guilty of sinister acts. Oldfield, he said, 'did not take this [meeting with Pincher] as an opportunity to confirm Dick Ellis's treachery, *in which he did not believe*' (Deacon's emphasis) and Cavendish himself was 'distressed to learn that Mr Pincher is in the process of developing further allegations against Ellis'.

It contradicts Pincher's somewhat pathetic claim that 'most' of Ellis's friends 'have finally been convinced by the evidence . . . Nicholas Elliott, who knew about Ellis's guilt,[16] admonished Oldfield – the latter perhaps appreciating the delicacy of his own secret homosexuality'. What Oldfield's sexual preferences had to do with anything is puzzling.

Cavendish would have none of it: 'Pincher claims he was responsible for exposing Dick Ellis as a traitor and for initiating the claim that [Roger] Hollis was a Russian spy. I knew both these gentlemen and no proof has ever been produced that Ellis was a traitor. The same is true of Hollis.'[17]

*

On Saturday, 5 July 1975, a colony of seagulls massed in the sky over Eastbourne Pier. Just 300 metres away, a broke, half-blind

Dick Ellis died in his flat at Gannett House, 6 Hartington Place, near Eastbourne's shingly beach. It was 17,000 kilometres from his birthplace of Annandale, but even that considerable distance gave no sense of just how far Ellis had travelled and how much he'd achieved over the course of a truly extraordinary life. He was 80 years old. Nigel West writes in *The Faber Book of Espionage* that Ellis passed away 'without telling even his family of his disgrace'.

At his funeral, 'a number of senior officers' were in attendance. 'They were secret service men from MI6, there to honour their friend and colleague, and to comfort his son, Peter, and daughter, Ann.' As described in *Intrepid's Last Case*, Maurice Oldfield 'trod softly behind the procession of mourners to the open grave in the burial grounds dark under the damp elms and stood back beside a gravedigger among the dripping shrubs . . . inside his wooden box, forever laid, Ellis was lowered into the ground . . . a shovel turned. The first clod of earth dropped upon the coffin with a thud.'[18]

Oldfield would pass away in 1981, aged 65. After Ellis's funeral, he invited Ellis's daughter, Ann, to his home in London. He gave her his card and said, 'If you need help, call me.'

CHAPTER 20

A BREAK IN THE SILENCE

'Treachery to one's country, especially in the interests of a savage regime with which war was then inevitable, is the one crime to which forgiveness should not extend.'
– CHAPMAN PINCHER, *DAILY TELEGRAPH*, LONDON, 22 APRIL 1983

IN 1976 *A MAN CALLED INTREPID* BY WILLIAM STEVENSON, a book that began as an aborted manuscript by Dick Ellis and was subsequently offered to H. Montgomery Hyde, who turned it down,[1] was released with a posthumous foreword by Ellis, titled 'A Break in the Silence'.

> From New York, while the United States was at peace and at war, Britain ran the most intricate integrated intelligence and secret-operations organisation in history. Could such activity be kept secret?

It carried the rider: '[Ellis] convinced [Winston] Churchill at the end of World War II to pay a veiled but public tribute to INTREPID'S BSC teams in these words: "We may feel sure that nothing of which we have any knowledge or record has ever been done by mortal men which surpasses the splendour and daring of their feats of arms."'

Chapman Pincher called it 'brass nerve' from 'an old man living, apparently, in honourable retirement in Eastbourne in Sussex' and sheer 'impudence . . . to write a "historical note" extolling the virtues of secrecy'. But Timothy J. Naftali, who interviewed H. Montgomery Hyde before Hyde's death, said 'there is reason to doubt that Ellis wrote the foreword attributed to him. Hyde believed that Ellis had not been in any shape to write it.' Either way, Olik, Ellis's son, made an attempt to get money from William Stevenson over its inclusion in the book and Stevenson had apparently 'taken care of' the matter.[2]

By March 1981, with the release of Pincher's *Their Trade is Treachery* – which publisher Sidgwick & Jackson had paid a then-record advance to the author, believed to be £70,000 (about £320,000 today, or US$370,000) – Ellis's name was mud in the United Kingdom, the United States, Canada and Australia. Incendiary extracts of the book appeared in London's *Daily Mail*. Sydney's *The Australian* would later also carry extensive extracts from the book under damning headlines such as 'The hunt for the Australian spy', 'A chain of incriminating lies' and 'Apologia confirms Ellis as a traitor'.

Pincher, 'Britain's foremost authority on espionage', according to his employers, had travelled from his home in the village of Kintbury, Berkshire, to spend nearly two weeks in Cygnet, Tasmania, interviewing Peter Wright for the book.

'Wright's home proved to be a wooden shack made from two apple-pickers' huts set in a former apple orchard, and I could see how, remote from the exciting life that he had formerly led, he had stewed there in the sticks on a miserable pension, while sitting on information that he knew to be eminently saleable. For nine days, I listened in wonder and made copious notes, while he poured out the MI5's [sic] most sacred secrets.'

When he got back to Kintbury, Pincher 'wrote the book rapidly, checking facts with other sources when I could, hopefully, without arousing suspicion. I finished the book in less than four months.'

The haste showed in his poor research. Nevertheless, Pincher duly went to town on Ellis, who along with John Cairncross (who confessed to espionage in 1964) he called 'major new spies', introducing to the *Mail*'s readers a story 'which has been so carefully concealed for political purposes that even former Secret Servicemen will be astonished by what I have to tell.'

The Washington Post reported:

Allegations in Britain's current spy scandal have made headlines in London all week, as the *Daily Mail* has been serializing a book by its defense specialist, Chapman Pincher.

The latest allegation, published today in London, is that Britain's third-ranked spy at the end of World War II, Charles Howard Ellis, cooperated with Nazi Germany and the Soviet Union for 30 years . . . according to news service reports of the *Daily Mail* articles, Pincher charged that Ellis made an "abject confession" in 1965 of spying for Germany up to 1940, and admitted to handing over detailed charts of British intelligence, knowing they would go both to Germany and the Soviet Union.

According to The Associated Press, the *Daily Mail* said Ellis did not admit to spying for Germany after 1940 or for the Soviets following the war, but said his interrogators believed he acted as an agent for the Nazis before and during the war and later for the Soviet Union.

Ellis, a former Oxford University student born in Australia, allegedly was recruited for the Nazis by a relative and later decided to work for the Soviets purely for the money, the newspaper said.[3]

It was as bad as it could get for the family of Ellis, though not everyone was sold on Pincher's theory that the boy from Annandale, MI6's longest serving agent, had been a Nazi and Soviet super-mole for the better part of three decades. Pincher's journalistic professionalism also came into question. Was it acceptable for the former chief defence correspondent of the *Daily Express* and Beaverbrook Newspapers to be in the habit of using 'confidential information' or

'FBI document[s]' as sources in his footnotes? Pincher's slackness was a harbinger of the sloppy journalism that would become the norm in the internet age, when research and due diligence would become a secondary consideration to publishing as quickly as possible. The fact is an unsubstantiated smear is still an unsubstantiated smear when a journalist is 'protecting' a source.

'Without proof, this is McCarthyism at its worst.'
– Ernest Cuneo, 'Of moles and men', 1981

'Utter nonsense.'
– William Stephenson, *Daily Telegraph*, 27 March 1981

'Turgid tripe . . . how soon will Pincher or his colleagues tell us that Sir Winston Churchill, Sir William Stephenson and General Donovan of the OSS spent weekends at Berchtesgaden playing crokinole with Adolf, while Eva served English muffins and American hot dogs?'
– Elizabeth L. Wood, *Globe and Mail*, 11 April 1981

'[Ellis] never betrayed the slightest hint that his sympathies and actions were other than altogether loyal to the British cause and the service which he served devotedly for 30 years.'
– H. Montgomery Hyde, *Times*, 27 April 1981

'Unpardonable short of being in possession of irrefragable evidence.'
– Giles Playfair, *Times*, London, 1 May 1981[4]

'The evidence presented against Ellis is much less convincing [than Pincher's case against Hollis], although some of his behaviour was peculiar, even for an intelligence operator.'
– Alan Renouf, *Sydney Morning Herald*, 2 May 1981

On 26 March 1981, the same day Pincher's extract about Ellis appeared in the *Daily Mail*, Prime Minister Margaret Thatcher defended Roger Hollis in a 'hushed' House of Commons but failed to do the same for Ellis, neither confirming nor denying his guilt, or even mentioning him by name.

Writes Nigel West in *The Faber Book of Espionage*, Thatcher's 'reluctance to vilify him had given his few remaining supporters, Hyde and Stephenson among them, the vain hope that the accusations had been false'. The next day, after the Pincher allegations in *Their Trade is Treachery* were raised in the Canadian Parliament, Igor Gouzenko gave a TV interview in which he alleged evidence in the ELLI case had been suppressed. Gouzenko died in 1982.

'The extent of penetration was thoroughly investigated after the defection of Burgess and Maclean, as, indeed, the author of the book makes clear,' Thatcher told the Commons. 'The book contains no information of security significance that is new to the security authorities, and some of the material is inaccurate or distorted. All the cases and individuals referred to have been the subject of long and thorough investigation.

'The investigations into the possibilities of past penetration have inevitably extended widely. They have covered not only those suspected of being guilty but all those who could conceivably fit the often inconclusive leads available. The fact that somebody has been the subject of investigation does not necessarily, or even generally, mean that he has been positively suspected. Many people have had to be investigated simply in order to eliminate them from the inquiry . . . I do not propose to comment on the allegations and insinuations in the book. Nor can I say which allegations are unsubstantiated or untrue – as some certainly are – since by doing so I should be implicitly indicating those that were suspected of having a degree of substance.'

The Ellis family privately implored Thatcher to make a public statement clearing the Australian but she refused.[5] Instead, the British Prime Minister wrote a letter on 10 April 1981 to Ellis's daughter, Ann Salwey, who was then living in Norwich, England: 'I am very sorry for the distress that you are suffering on account of the reference to your father in Chapman Pincher's book and I deplore as strongly as you do his attacks on the memories of those who are no longer living and cannot defend themselves . . . I cannot make an exception in one case without being pressed to make it in others as well and that, I fear, would do more harm than good.'[6]

On 6 May 1981, Salwey told historian Brian Pearce that she'd written 'to Mrs Thatcher asking to be told the truth – no matter what it might be – but it is not in the national interest to be told. Is it in the national interest to have Chapman Pincher's kind of revelations passing for historical, honourable facts? Heaven help us all.'

She confided: 'The past few weeks have been a nightmare and very isolating' and 'so many people have been hurt by the book, which contributes nothing to the greater wellbeing of the country'. The 'whole business', she wrote, was 'disgusting'. She also complained that 'a few old friends and colleagues of my father's have written to *The Times* but have produced nothing but official silence or further self-righteous and unpleasant letters from Chapman Pincher who does not have to produce evidence nor the names of those who gave him information'.[7]

Pincher himself gloated, '[Thatcher] and her advisers were looking for ways of discrediting my book. She was unable to do so' and explained the Prime Minister's silence on Ellis thus: 'The Prime Minister had been advised to avoid the Ellis case because the details were so accurate that confirmation of it would have made it difficult for her parliamentary statement to cast any doubt on my sources concerning the case of Sir Roger Hollis.'[8]

Nigel West, author of *A Matter of Trust: MI5 1945–72*, chimed in: 'The fact that the pre-war MI6 "order of battle" was betrayed to the Germans is beyond dispute. I have in my possession a number of Abwehr documents which faithfully describe MI6's internal structure and I have published a selection in my history of the security service. Confirmation that Ellis was the original source of this material can only come from the Prime Minister, who has already declined to comment.'

Pincher would write to the editors of the *Sydney Morning Herald* to say thanks for a positive review of *Their Trade is Treachery* in its Sunday edition, the *Sun-Herald*.

'Several of my acquaintances who had never breathed a word about Dick Ellis's treachery have volunteered such remarks as "It's high time that traitor was exposed. He spied for the Abwehr"[9] . . . you will find a great deal of other confirmatory evidence in the paperback to be published next year (Bantam Books of USA). It is virtually a rewrite as so much has flowed in.'[10]

He'd write to historian and staunch Ellis defender Brian Pearce in a letter: 'First you may be absolutely certain that the story of the investigation into Ellis and his subsequent confession of spying for Germany is accurate. I think you will agree that the wealth of detail which could only have come from official sources is convincing in itself. Mrs Thatcher, of course, made no effort to deny it because she could not.[11]

'Former friends of Ellis have claimed that he was innocent but that is just the vanity factor – no friend of mine could have been a spy! It happened with Philby, Maclean, and the rest, including Hollis . . . there is no evidence that Ellis was ever an ideological spy. He spied for the Germans purely for money – as he admitted – and if he spied for Russia was probably blackmailed into doing so for small reward.'

If he spied. Was probably blackmailed. Pincher went on to become 'not only the most famous journalist in Britain but also a very wealthy man'. Everyone had made money out of Dick Ellis's remarkable life and storied career except for Ellis. Disgusted, his daughter, Ann, returned his CBE and CMG to Whitehall and emigrated to the United States.[12]

'I didn't see any point in hanging on to honours when my father's honour had been taken from him without any hope of redress,' she said.

His son, Olik, also refused to accept the charges against his father and was in possession of 'many photos and letters that will support the fact that my father was completely honourable'.

*

In Canberra, just days after Thatcher's speech in the House of Commons, Australian Prime Minister Malcolm Fraser was fielding questions from the Opposition's deputy leader Lionel Bowen regarding Ellis. He'd been informed in a 20 March 1981 letter by ASIO director-general of security Justice Edward Woodward that Ellis was 'believed, on good authority, to have worked for the Russians' and 'this view is in fact accepted by the United Kingdom Services'.

BOWEN: 'My question, which is directed to the Prime Minister, relates to a matter raised today by my leader . . . is the Prime Minister in a position to advise the House whether the Australian Government was informed of British doubts about, and the interrogation of, British agents Hollis and Ellis? If the Government was informed, what action was taken to vet Australian officials?'

FRASER: 'These matters occurred very many years ago. I have already made it plain that since that time we have had our own royal commission. Mr Ellis was involved some 25 to 30 years ago. Obviously I would have no personal knowledge of the details of what occurred 25 or 30 years ago . . . I think that honourable gentlemen opposite are really going on a far-fetched fishing operation, especially since our own royal commission examined all Australia's security agencies much more recently than when these events occurred. The royal commission has reported and we have acted upon that report. As the honourable gentleman knows, there is full consultation with the Leader of the Opposition.'

Labor Party leader Bill Hayden followed up on the Ellis matter in Parliament on 8 April 1981. Fraser replied: 'The suggestion in one newspaper article that there was a mole somewhere in the higher echelons of the Australian Public Service and that the Central Intelligence Agency or the United States government had known of that but had not told Australia of it was too absurd to contemplate.

'If there had been any knowledge of that kind within the ranks of the United States I have no doubt that Australia would have been told . . . there is no evidence that Australian security has been prejudiced in any way as a result of relationships between ASIS and MI6. For the honourable gentleman to claim that in recent days there is a possibility of Australia's security being prejudiced because of that relationship is so much humbug.'

The following year, on 27 April 1982, Labor Senator Tony Mulvihill raised the subject of Ellis in the Senate: 'My question, which is directed to Liberal Senator [Peter] Durack . . . I put it to the Attorney-General, in light of the precedent whereby a Senate committee investigated the Australian Security Intelligence Organisation within a certain ambit: Will he consider such a committee following up the Chapman Pincher allegations about whether Mr Ellis was a mole in the Australian security apparatus?'

DURACK: 'I think the question of whether there should be parliamentary scrutiny of intelligence organisations, particularly ASIO, has been debated considerably in this chamber in recent years. The Government has taken the view that it is not appropriate that a parliamentary committee be established to oversee the operations of ASIO.'

On 17 August 1982, the Ellis affair was brought up on notice by Labor Senator Robert Ray, who asked of Prime Minister Fraser:

(1) When was the Government officially informed that two senior members of the British intelligence community, Sir Roger Hollis, closely associated with the foundation of the Australian Security Intelligence Organisation, and Mr Dick Ellis, an Australian closely associated with the foundation of the Australian Security Intelligence Service, were seriously suspected of being long-term Soviet agents?

(2) Does the Prime Minister intend to make a public statement on this matter, as Mrs Thatcher has done in Great Britain, in order to reassure the public that our intelligence community has not been 'white-anted'?

(3) Have there been internal investigations in Australia following the revelations in Great Britain; if so, does the Government intend to make the results of such investigations public; if not, why not?

Fraser replied:

(1), (2) and (3) There is nothing I would wish to add to my answers to questions without notice on this matter on 31 March and 8 April 1981 (House of Representatives Hansard, pages 1085 to 1087 and 1432).

*

Across the Pacific, in the *New York Times*, Edward J. Epstein trashed Ellis's legacy in his 16 January 1983 review of Anthony Cave Brown's 1982 book *The Last Hero*. At the same time an FBI investigation of Ellis was reputedly underway, though likely nothing more than a continuation of the quixotic molehunt that had been going nowhere since the early 1950s.

'Inquiries are now in progress in the United States concerning Ellis's activities there while working under Sir William Stephenson,' wrote Chapman Pincher that February. 'Meanwhile, FBI documents in my possession show that American counterintelligence was actively interested in Ellis as early as 1953. Essential parts of these documents were blacked out at the request of British intelligence when they were released under the US Freedom of Information Act in July 1981 – three months after the appearance of my book.'

Pincher was really making much of nothing. The 'FBI documents' were found by me in Pincher's hitherto uncopied research notes on

Ellis held by King's College, London. An undated letter from the FBI states: 'The files of this office contain no information concerning . . . DICKIE ELLIS, who . . . is well known to the Director', but that 'the Director would probably be interested in hearing that . . . ELLIS . . . has almost lost his eyesight.' Pincher has scribbled: 'It is, of course, rubbish that E has lost his eyesight!'[13]

On 26 April 1983, in Washington DC, Larry McDonald (Georgia) raised Ellis in the House of Representatives.

'Mr Speaker, it has recently been revealed that Col. Dick Ellis, now deceased, as an MI6 officer spied for the Germans as well as the Soviets. This would be simply of passing interest, except for the fact that Dick Ellis was one of the British advisers who came to the United States after World War II to assist in setting up our Central Intelligence Agency. Coming on top of the revelation that Anthony Blunt, a renowned Briton, had been a Soviet mole, [this] creates convulsions in intelligence circles.'[14]

Meanwhile, according to Ernest Cuneo, the revelations or accusations about Ellis, Hollis and Co. 'caused deep repercussions in the United States, particularly among the veterans of the Office of Strategic Services'. The penetration by Philby, Maclean and Burgess had 'caused Great Britain and the United States immeasurable damage, to say nothing of the loss of many, many lives . . . the charges against Col. Ellis, if true, could mean that the communications of the OSS were vulnerable and possibly compromised from birth.'

Even Ellis's old friends were privately starting to have doubts. A 'terribly shocked' H. Montgomery Hyde had defended Ellis in *Secret Intelligence Agent*, released in 1982, but even before the book came out he had, according to Pincher, 'changed his view about Ellis' and 'will alter his new book accordingly'.

By 1983 Hyde went public with his concerns: 'I felt obliged to defend him. I asked Stephenson if Ellis was a spy, and he said, no, he wasn't, but I'm beginning to have doubts now.'

In a letter to London's *Daily Telegraph* on 15 April 1983 he back-pedalled a bit: 'To the best of my knowledge he was no traitor.' But in a letter to Pincher on 15 August 1984, he switched again: 'I have been looking through the portion of Ellis's unpublished memoirs which I have . . . Alexander Zelensky is described as "one of Lilia's relatives" and not as her brother . . . Little Bill's [Stephenson's] principal concern is that Ellis did not get up to any dirty tricks after he joined him in New York in 1940, and he appears satisfied from what you have written that there is no evidence that he did . . . PS It is odd that Ellis makes no reference to Lilia in *Who's Who*, although he mentions his subsequent three wives.'

By February 1985, in a *Books and Bookmen* review of Pincher's book *Too Secret Too Long*, Hyde had comprehensively betrayed his friend: 'I refused to believe Pincher's charges [in *Their Trade is Treachery*] but now they are repeated in such circumstantial detail I must admit that I am now inclined to accept the assertion that Ellis "confessed" in 1966, particularly since this has been confirmed to me personally by Nicholas Elliott, the MI6 official who obtained Philby's confession . . . people can and do lead double lives without their friends having any idea of their seamy side.'

Richard Hall elegantly summed up what was at stake in the Ellis affair: 'The Sydney suburb of Annandale has no particular claim to fame. It has a number of interesting surviving 19th-century houses and Sir Henry Parkes died there. Can it now claim the distinction of being the birthplace of the most accomplished spy against the British ever, a man who in 30 years of working for both Nazi Germany and Soviet Russia, delivered the secrets of Britain's MI6 and could be said to have out-Philbied Philby?'

*

In the Intrepid camp, there was at least a united front publicly but there were some ructions behind the scenes. In September 1981, William Stevenson, according to a note from Chapman Pincher, was 'now convinced that Ellis was a spy'. The following month, he wrote to Pincher and reported William Stephenson 'tacitly acknowledges problems about Ellis but can't yet bring himself to go back, publicly, on his loyalty'. Stephenson even telephoned Pincher himself and 'agreed that he could be wrong about Ellis'. This is significant given the 1983 publication date of their sequel to *A Man Called Intrepid*.

In an attempt to defend Ellis's memory from an onslaught of press attacks (or, more likely, absolve Stephenson of any blame for this grave embarrassment), the two Canadians teamed up again for the 'engrossing but rather muddled' *Intrepid's Last Case*. To his immense credit, Stevenson made a spirited case that 'Dick Ellis was framed' but critics largely savaged the book.

David Stafford in the *Globe and Mail* called *Intrepid's Last Case* a 'sorry volume, which is even less substantial than its predecessor . . . virtually no evidence is produced by this volume to prove anything, one way or the other; it is best placed on the shelf along with spy fiction.'

He rightly raised the issue of Stephenson's ego: 'Imagine [Stephenson's] consternation when, during the claims and counter-claims that erupted three years ago about Soviet penetration of MI5, Ellis was named as a long-time Soviet (and also German) agent. Had Intrepid, superspy, been duped? Had the author failed to unearth a terrible secret within the bosom of the enterprise itself?'

Walter Arnold in the *Wall Street Journal* called it a 'confusing book . . . a maddeningly ill-organised work in which the whole is less than the sum of its too-many parts . . . aside from its constant digres-sions into far-from-new subjects, the book has a dangerous secondary agenda, which is to clear . . . Ellis.

'It is understandable and even honourable for the author to attempt this, but he cannot possibly establish adequate critical objectivity here. For what it's worth, I find his "refutation" of the charges against Col. Ellis full of special pleading, inconsistent and plain unconvinc-ing. In contrast, I find London journalist Chapman Pincher's account of Col. Ellis's career, in his book *Their Trade is Treachery*, logically compelling and morally convincing.'

David Kahn in the *Washington Post*: '[The book's] real purpose is to acquit one of Stephenson's deputies of charges that he was "ELLI" . . . and thus clear Stephenson of the taint of either having been unaware of this or having permitted it . . . the lack of substantia-tion of Stevenson's argument renders his book unacceptable as history. And any remaining credibility is eroded by the continual dribble of errors and exaggerations.

'Both [*Intrepid*] books are dangerous in their poisoning of the wells of history – the one of World War II, the other of the Cold War.

They should be shunned for their errors. In the end, however, they are to be thought of as expressing not logical concerns, but psychological ones: egotism in the first instance, fear of conspiracy in the second. Their true subject is not intelligence. It is megalomania and paranoia.'

James Bamford in the *New York Times*: 'The primary purpose of *Intrepid's Last Case* is to clear the late Col. Charles H. Ellis, Intrepid's wartime aide, of recent allegations that he had been a mole for both Germany and the Soviet Union. The charge is all the more significant in the light of the major role Ellis played in helping to create America's OSS, the predecessor of the Central Intelligence Agency, during World War II . . . poor Ellis. The result of their search is a tedious sermon on Soviet disinformation which, Mr Stevenson concludes, has been responsible for everything from the expulsion of valuable "creative eccentrics" from Western intelligence organisations to the 1981 allegations that the CIA Director William J. Casey was involved in questionable business and financial activities. It is with little surprise, therefore, that Mr Stevenson sees Soviet disinformation – and even the British mole Kim Philby who defected to the Soviet Union – behind the allegations against Ellis . . . the issues involving Colonel Ellis are important ones, but Mr Stevenson and his patron are not the ones to deal with them.'

Reg Whitaker in the *Citizen* (Ottawa): 'Purportedly non-fiction, [*Intrepid's Last Case*] goes right over the line into Robert Ludlum-land . . . Stephenson/Stevenson have constructed a vast and fanciful edifice of speculation . . . [it] claims to vindicate Ellis, mainly it seems on the grounds that anyone who was an old buddy of Sir William was obviously all right . . . the entire book is a rather pointless tale of an old gentleman batting at unseen threads with his cane.'

*

In 1983 a chastened and possibly now senile Stephenson was still defending Ellis: 'About half the security people I talked to are convinced he was [a traitor], and the other half think he wasn't. I've concluded he was maligned deliberately to take the heat off other people.'

He was especially angry with the Australian government.

'Dick Ellis was not a traitor or a mole, or a double or a triple agent – just a patriot doing his proper job. He was a man of integrity and dedication. I knew a lot of Australians and I can tell you that Dick was a damn good one – absolutely first rate. You can be proud of him. Your prime minister should demand from London either a taped or a written and signed confession. If one or the other is not forthcoming, your PM should publicly exonerate Ellis as a victim of KGB disinformation. A confession has never been produced. I know Dick Ellis's voice; I know his handwriting. If a confession exists – which I doubt – I could tell whether it was genuine . . . Dick was the best man MI6 had.'

But by 1984, he wasn't so sure. H. Montgomery Hyde wrote to Chapman Pincher on 25 May that year that 'Little Bill [Stephenson] . . . is coming around to the idea that Dick Ellis did make a confession but he wishes to be satisfied that Ellis was not in communication with the Germans after the formation of the British BSC'. Stephenson even cabled Pincher directly and 'said that if he can be satisfied that there is no hard evidence that Ellis spied while in BSC then that is an end of his interest in the matter'.

But Stephenson would comprehensively knife Roger Hollis in 1987: '[Hollis] was a double agent. What happened was that Guy Liddell, who was by far the best man in MI5, told me Hollis was not to be trusted because of his "anti-Americanism". I took it as meaning there was something far more sinister about Hollis than his merely being anti-American. As I later discovered, Hollis was already working for the Soviets at that time.'

Reported United Press International: 'Stephenson said he later prevented Hollis from coming in contact with Igor Gouzenko, a file clerk at the Soviet Embassy in Ottawa who defected to the Canadians in 1945 and revealed that communist agents had penetrated MI5.

'"I had him sent back across the Atlantic on the same US Air Force bomber he had arrived on," Stephenson said. "Hollis is one case where Peter Wright's criticisms are justified. He was a bad egg if ever there was one."'

Hollis's turning up to meet with Gouzenko *was* described in *Intrepid's Last Case*.[15] Yet rather oddly, in this book published just four years before, Stevenson described Hollis and the accusations against him as 'the exasperating mystery of Roger Hollis' and the charges against him as 'unsubstantiated'. If Stephenson knew Hollis was a double agent all along, why did he and Stevenson describe it as an 'exasperating mystery' and 'unsubstantiated' and not defend Pincher's work back in 1981 when *Their Trade is Treachery* had already come out and accused Hollis of being a spy?

Why did he not take Thatcher to task for defending Hollis but not defending Ellis? It does raise the bizarre scenario that Stephenson was a Soviet mole himself. He hired Ellis. He informed Philby about Gouzenko. He turned away Hollis from Gouzenko. If Ellis could have been a Soviet spy, why couldn't Stephenson, Ellis's boss, have been one himself? The proposition, of course, is patently absurd but stranger things have happened in the world of international espionage, and innocent men and their families have suffered as a result.

Stephenson, the 'Quiet Canadian', the 'Man Called Intrepid', died in 1989, aged 92.

*

And then, finally and somewhat shabbily, there was the *Spycatcher* saga. After pocketing a payment of £5000 for passing secrets to Chapman Pincher for *Their Trade is Treachery*, a financially destitute and physically ailing Peter Wright, unable to publish his book owing to an injunction in the United Kingdom, had to survive a protracted court case in Australia when the British government tried to prevent its publication there.[16]

Famously, the government ended up losing and, as documented in *Official Secrets: The Use and Abuse of the Act* by David Hooper, the solicitor of Wright's London publishers, it was forced to admit in court to Wright's Sydney-based lawyer (and future Australian prime minister), Malcolm Turnbull,[17] that 'for the purposes of [the legal] proceedings only, all the allegations in Wright's manuscript . . . were true'.

But this does not mean the passages about Ellis were necessarily true. All it meant was that the government did not want to go through the process of having to tell the judge, the late Justice Phillip Powell, what parts of Wright's manuscript on individual pages were true by answering under oath what are called 'interrogatories'.

Explains Hooper: '[The government] would be asked specifically if an allegation of misconduct made by Wright on a particular page was true or false. The government believed that it could fight this case without indicating which parts of the book were true or showing what real detriment it would suffer if Wright's book were published. The government seems to have been under the impression that no Australian judge would order it to answer such questions. Only after two days of the hearing in August 1986 did the government realise that this was exactly what Mr Justice Powell had in mind.'

It was easier just to make a blanket admission.

'This admission was a mistake . . . it made it very much more difficult for the British government to argue that it was contrary to the Australian public interest to read about the criminal activities which it had now admitted. These included admitting that Sir Roger Hollis, who had helped set up ASIO (the Australian MI5) was a Soviet spy and indeed that the man who assisted setting up ASIS (their MI6), Dickie Ellis, was also a spy.'

Guy Burgess's biographer and London literary agent Andrew Lownie reviewed Hooper's book for the *Times*: 'It is easy to dismiss the book for it is obviously hurriedly assembled and is full of errors of fact and interpretation; it is badly structured, full of grammatical errors and poorly indexed.[18]

'While much attention in the press has been devoted to the question of whether or not Sir Roger Hollis was a Soviet agent, few commentators have noticed the far more important revelations made about Charles "Dickie" Ellis, an MI6 officer who admitted passing information to the Germans during the Second World War and who is generally assumed to have worked also for the Russians.'

But who cared if the content of *Spycatcher* was true or not? The penniless Wright got what he'd really wanted all along: money. That he is considered by MI5 historian Christopher Andrew as one of 'the most damaging conspiracy theorists in the history of the Security Service' who from the early 1960s 'began to descend into his conspiratorial wilderness of mirrors' is largely lost on the general public. He's mostly just remembered as the old guy who'd turn up to court in the funny Australian hat whose case ensured that practically everyone in Australia – and many people around the world – suddenly knew Malcolm Turnbull's name.

Thanks to the sensational outcome of the court case in Australia, the book sold millions of copies and made a lot of people stinking rich. As the late CIA historian Cleveland C. Cram noted in an internal review of the book for the CIA: 'It was banned in Britain but the incredible circus trial in Australia prevented its being banned there. The result, however, was to send sales of this otherwise ordinary book skyrocketing to bestseller levels all around the world and overnight made Wright a multimillionaire.'

EPILOGUE

THE ELLIS IDENTITY

'Most of his brother officers, American and British, including
the writer, scorn the idea of "Dickie" Ellis being a mole.
However, in this vale of tears, anything is possible.'
– ERNEST CUNEO, 'OF MOLES AND MEN', 1981

So, IN THE END, WHO WAS CHARLES HOWARD 'DICK' ELLIS? Was
an innocent man 'framed', as William Stevenson alleged? Or was
Ellis a traitor as bad as they come, as Chapman Pincher kept muttering to his dying breath?

Ellis had his supporters:

'I'm quite convinced that Dick Ellis, whom President Harry Truman made an officer of the Legion
of Merit after the war, was Simon Pure.'
- Kiki Olson, *Philadelphia Inquirer*, 12 February
1984

'Friendly and unassuming, he was a man of proven
loyalty and outstanding integrity of character.'
- H. Montgomery Hyde, *Secret Intelligence Agent*
(1982)

'A sturdy, genial Australian-born survivor of the intelligence wars from Paris to the Soviet border.'
- Burton Hursh, *The Old Boys: The American Elite and the Origins of the CIA* (1992)

'The only professional, the long-term professional, in the business.'
- Benjamin deForest 'Pat' Bayly in Bill Macdonald, *The True Intrepid* (1998)

'He was a very pleasant, affable bloke. I liked him and he had some great stories about his service in various parts of the world but whether he was a shadowy spy I haven't a clue, but I certainly had no indication that he wasn't other than he was.'
- Frederick Chilton, *Canberra Times*, 6 September 1998

'Ellis, a good friend of mine, was and is considered one of the best British intelligence and counterintelligence officers by Intrepid, Sir William Stephenson . . . I worked with Ellis after the war and know what an outstanding officer he was. God bless him. For the sake of his two daughters [sic], his friends and veterans all over the world, these false allegations should be corrected.'
- Carl Armfelt, *Hamilton Spectator*, 18 March 2000[1]

And he had his detractors:

'[A] self-confessed traitor.'
- Nigel West, *Molehunt* (1987)

'[Ellis] slid down the slippery slope of treachery in support of alien creeds, until he was committing treason to a degree which could have sent him to the gallows.'
– Chapman Pincher, *Australian*, 26 April 1982

'MI6 controller for half the world . . . [Ellis] was saved from the gallows because MI6 found it too embarrassing to admit that one of its top operatives was a Nazi spy.'
– Evan Whitton, *Sydney Morning Herald*, 26 January 1983

'Did the NKVD use its knowledge of Ellis's spying for the Germans to blackmail him into serving the NKVD while at the BSC? That appears likely. In summary, one can conclude that there was indirect penetration of OSS through the BSC and that joint operations, personnel names, cover assignments, training techniques, and plans were made known to Soviet intelligence. The complete OSS picture could only come, however, from moles inside OSS and related government agencies.'
– Hayden Peake, 'Soviet espionage and the Office of Strategic Services', 1992

And there, it appears, ne'er the twain shall meet. But more pertinently, why should we care? Why do real-life spy stories continue to grip the public imagination? Is it what Pulitzer Prize–winning author Arthur Schlesinger Jr called 'the melodrama of spy and counterspy'?

Whatever the answers, Ellis's life story is worth more than just a lousy Wikipedia article and a grainy black-and-white photo in Google Images. Granted, it is difficult to create a clear picture from such scant biographical resources. Without the cooperation of a willing descendant, we know next to nothing about his family or personal life beyond what is available in archives and is now documented in this book.

Ellis's son, Olik, so angered by the way his late father had been portrayed by Pincher and his cohorts, had hoped to get Ellis's *Two Bills: Mission Accomplished* manuscript in print 'if only to give the lie to all the accusations made against him by Pincher et al' but chose not to pursue it too much 'so as to avoid raising another spate of public correspondence by those authors who have caused nothing but pain to my sister and me, not to mention others who knew my father whose loyalty to the Western cause was unfailing'. But as the historian David Stafford remarked in a letter to Olik, Ellis, as he had done all his life, had resisted revealing anything about himself in print. It made *The Two Bills: Mission Accomplished* practically unpublishable.

'If [Ellis] had told his *own* story of his experience in BSC, it would have been quite a different matter. But he so carefully keeps himself out of [the manuscript] that there is very little, if anything, that is not already known.'

To our collective loss. A biographer of Reginald Teague-Jones, Ben Wright, remarked to me: 'My feeling, and it is one shared by other researchers, is that [Ellis's] story in the public record is most incomplete. Certainly, Ernest Cuneo remained his staunch defender to the end.'[2]

Cuneo, it should be said, revealed in a 1983 interview that Ellis had even left his daughter, Ann, temporarily in his care when Ellis left the United States at the end of 1944.

'What the hell! If the guy was doing me and my country in, would he leave her in my custody? This business grieves me because I think he did a hell of a lot for his country and mine.'

Indeed, the more human elements of Ellis's story remain frustratingly unknown, but whatever he did or didn't do with or for the Nazis, I don't think any man's life or contribution can be judged on the basis of one possible moral mistake, especially on the eve of or in time of war. We weren't there when he was playing spy games with Vladimir von Petrov, Anton Turkul and Richard Protze and nor were Nigel West, Peter Wright and Chapman Pincher. As William Stevenson wrote in *Intrepid's Last Case*: 'The only game Ellis had admitted to playing was the Great Game against the Russian bear.'

Ellis was certainly no Philby: a calculating, deliberate traitor. We are all complex, nuanced human beings living in a complex, nuanced world. The jigsaw puzzle of Ellis's life still has missing pieces. His biography can only be told in scattered fragments. But that, arguably, is also the mark of a great spy, a man whose job description was to exist in the shadows. Ann Salwey says her father left very little behind. Perhaps that was intentional.

For two years, I spent every day trying to work out who Dick Ellis was and still don't have all the answers. The mystery remains. But I know this: Ellis's was one of the more historic Australian stories and as an Australian who made an inestimable personal contribution in two world wars, made it to the near-top of MI6, and was critically involved in the founding of ASIS and COI/OSS, what would ultimately become the CIA, the boy from Annandale rightly deserves to be thought of in the same company as Australians Hubert Wilkins, Wilfred Burchett, Elizabeth Kata, Peter Allen and Neil Davis: a self-styled, self-made 'internationalist' who – through his own drive, independence and talent – made his mark on the world and quietly achieved his own form of greatness. He did so without any fanfare or publicity. That the Ellis story has remained untold for so long is an indictment of us for neglecting history, not a reflection of Ellis's candidacy for biography.

*

One of Ellis's biggest supporters, somewhat of an unsung hero in this whole saga, was Australian businessman Bill Ross-Smith, who'd been recruited by Ellis at BSC. He never stopped writing letters defending Ellis's honour and reputation and got up Chapman Pincher's nose so much that Pincher complained Ross-Smith's remarks were 'professionally damaging and many people had noticed them ... it gives me no pleasure to attack dead people'. Ross-Smith's battery of attacks on Pincher was so relentless and sustained, William Stephenson apparently requested H. Montgomery Hyde 'to get Ross-Smith to lay off'.

Hyde wrote that Ross-Smith was 'a most remarkable ... genial and vivacious' man who'd started a ships' observers spying organisation under Ellis and Stephenson at BSC.[3]

'Bill Ross-Smith's great achievement was to recruit and operate the activities of several hundred secret agents on neutral ships trading between America, north and south, and other parts of the world, including Spain, Portugal and Japan . . . in 1942, after Pearl Harbor, the ships' observers organisation was handed over to US Naval Intelligence.'

Ellis wrote in *The Two Bills: Mission Accomplished* that the scheme was 'in operation in practically all ships sailing between North American ports, Europe and Africa' and provided 'invaluable information concerning smuggling, enemy courier service, the movements of enemy agents, and attempts to evade censorship of mail and documents'.

In the 1980s, Ross-Smith stoutly defended Ellis in newspapers from Britain to Australia from his homes in McMahons Point, Sydney, and Midhurst, Sussex, calling accusations against his old SIS colleague a 'travesty of the truth . . . an unwarranted attack impugning the honour and integrity of a defenceless dead man'. On Ultra: 'If Ellis had been working for Germany, he would, undoubtedly, have apprised Berlin that their Enigma codes were being broken and that Popov was really a British agent.'

Nigel West, never far away from the controversy, responded by saying that Ellis didn't know of these things until after the war started: 'The incident [of Ellis selling secrets to the Nazis] predated Ellis's knowledge of both ULTRA and TRICYCLE . . . Ellis steadfastly denied any repetition [of his gaffe] . . . [Ellis] insisted he had not been a long-term source for either the Abwehr or the Russians.'

Ellis didn't confess to being a *short-term* source for the Russians either, so it was arguably disingenuous of West, the so-called experts' expert,[4] to write such a thing. He deserves a mention in this book's denouement, given his output of espionage books and his apparent commitment over his career (particularly in the absence of Pincher and Wright) to dismantling Ellis.[5]

In 1983 West stated, 'From my careful investigations I am satisfied that at one time Ellis was a German spy' and 'there was never any suggestion that Ellis passed information to the Germans other than the time he was in Paris'. As for suspicions Ellis was a Soviet spy, he said in 1984, 'There is only minimal, circumstantial evidence to support the contention that Ellis was ever a Soviet agent.' Yet there in *A Matter of Trust: MI5 1945–72*, published in 1982, he went right out and made an emphatic, unambiguous link between Ellis and the Soviet Union: 'As a German linguist, Ellis had been one of the MI6 officers assigned to translating the [Hitler–Von Ribbentrop] transcriptions. Might he have betrayed it to the Russians, who in turn had told their ally, Nazi Germany?' West might have dressed it up as legitimate speculation but it left a lasting smear on Ellis's reputation when there is no evidence of Ellis spying for the Soviet Union – minimal, circumstantial or otherwise.

Meanwhile, Chapman Pincher would issue another feeble and false justification of his wilful demolition of Ellis: 'Is it not odd that none of those [high-ranking officers of the secret services] who were serving at the time of Ellis's abject confession to having spied for the Abwehr and knew the facts has defended him?'

In the letters pages of all the major newspapers, Ross-Smith wouldn't let either West or Pincher off the hook. He claimed both had engaged in 'character assassination' and failed to produce 'one iota of evidence or one witness to support their charges'; that if Ellis's alleged Nazi collaboration had been known by 1945, 'why would he have been appointed chief of SIS for Far East and Asia' and 'be seconded to assist setting up the Australian SIS'. It's a fair question.

According to Ross-Smith, Ellis did not live in Paris before the war: 'Ellis worked in England for the years preceding the war and had no untoward financial problems and no expensive tastes or hobbies.' He said Pincher's claiming Philby was a 'pal' of Ellis's was 'beneath contempt . . . he was no pal of Philby and scarcely knew him'.[6]

An obviously ruffled Pincher retorted: 'Mr Ross-Smith's challenge that I must produce secret documents and tape-recordings out of MI5's registry is ludicrous. It will be 50 years before they are released, if they ever are. I think, however, that we shall have to wait even longer before any official who knows the facts of the case will deny them . . . Mr Ross-Smith is behaving like friends of Maclean and Philby before their guilt became undeniable. Incidentally, no secret documents relating to their activities have yet been published and they are never likely to be. As with the Ellis files they are far too embarrassing to the departments which the spies penetrated.'

Yet, as we have seen, Pincher's statement about the Ellis files appears to be baseless. The official historian of MI6, the late Keith Jeffery, is the only historian, journalist or biographer who has had access to them and he could find nothing to suggest Ellis had betrayed anyone. Indeed, every serious charge against Ellis made by Wright, West and Pincher – selling secrets to Vladimir von Petrov, the leaking of the Hitler–Von Ribbentrop phone taps, the Venlo Incident, 'The Black Book', spying for the Soviet Union – finds zero support in Jeffery's monumental book. Why would Jeffery have any reason to omit such things if Ellis was indisputably guilty? Enough time, a half century, has passed since Ellis's death for MI6 to own up to any mistakes, if indeed mistakes were made. The British public could have handled the exposure of another traitor.

West had only this to say in response to Ross-Smith's understandable rage: 'Mr Ross-Smith implied in the letter that my information was at fault but when Sir Michael Havers, the Attorney-General, applied for an injunction in the High Court last October to prevent publication of my book [*A Matter of Trust: MI5 1945–72*], he swore an affidavit that its contents, including the account of the Ellis affair, contained hitherto unpublished classified information.'

As I see it, that's hardly a defence for everything he'd written about Ellis.

*

Donald Cameron Watt's 1988 review of the 'implausible' and 'inconsistent' *Spycatcher* in *Political Quarterly* stands for all time as one of the best demolitions of the case against Ellis mounted by West, Wright, Pincher and others since the Australian's death in 1975.

'The best that can be said of it is that, if no German evidence were available, if every piece of oral evidence recollected at distances of 30 years from the event was assumed to be unquestionably reliable, then this is the kind of reconstruction that an ignorant, simplificatory but conspiratorially inclined mind might advance as though it were reality.

'However, there is no shadow of evidence that any German intelligence agency after the kidnapping of Best and Stevens in November 1939 enjoyed any reliable intelligence out of the UK, let alone out of MI6 or BSC, and not even the most boastful and self-inflating of German agents to publish their memoirs have ever claimed this. There is however a good deal of evidence to show (to put it no more strongly) that before 1939 MI6 stations operating against Germany, in Vienna, Prague and The Hague were German targets, and that the Hague station had been "penetrated" by the Abwehr from 1936 onwards. This would in itself provide a perfectly adequate explanation for Best's and Stevens's experience. They were so completely taken in by the SS, who sold them a story of a military conspiracy against Hitler, and a lure to bring them to the point of kidnapping, that they were in no state to resist interrogation.[7] As for the tap on the German Embassy phone, evidence in the diaries of Sir Alexander Cadogan, then Permanent Under Secretary in the Foreign Office, suggests first, that this was an MI5, not an MI6 ploy, and that it was still in operation in 1939 . . .[8]

'It is of course possible . . . that Ellis may have fed his White Russian contacts in Paris with information of a kind in the hope of using them both as a means of finding out what the Abwehr were interested in, and of creating a degree of confidence which could then be turned to advantage. It is equally possible, given the well-known paucity of resources put at MI6's disposal in the 1930s, that he attempted to better his situation by some kind of illegal financial dealings (as some believe). But the identifications, such as they are, to which [Peter] Wright appeals, are worthless; and the rest is contrary to the historical evidence of the Abwehr's knowledge of, and activities against, MI6.'

I can only agree. Ellis, the man, deserved none of it. Chapman Pincher includes an odd undated note in his papers: 'Part of the tapes of Ellis's confession were eventually played to Sir William Stephenson. He was devastated.' But, typical for Pincher, there is no source for this statement and in the margin on the piece of paper he has scrawled: 'Now doubtful.' Like so much of Pincher's work. Eminent historian and former military intelligence officer M. R. D. Foot's professional opinion of Pincher speaks volumes: 'My view on the man would be sulphuric. The stuff he produced on the intelligence services was almost totally inaccurate.'

The issue of whether Ellis's confession exists (I suspect it does, in some form; perhaps more of an inconclusive interview than a full-blown admission of guilt) obscures what is really the core issue: the whole circumstantial case against Ellis is so doubtful that he deserves the *benefit* of that doubt. He was another victim of the Cold War, when hysteria and fear overtook sense and reason, when paranoid intelligence agencies on both sides of the Atlantic were utterly convinced there were other Philbys to be uncovered, so long as they looked *somewhere* in that wilderness of mirrors. Anything could be made to look treacherous if there was sufficient motive to look for it.

Any confession from Ellis, signed or otherwise, is practically worthless without substantial evidence to back it up. Again, there is no evidence – period – he ever worked for the Soviet Union. Just because he knew Vladimir von Petrov was in contact with the Soviets does not make that charge stick. In the event Ellis was involved with the Nazis, we don't know who he might have been protecting; what his intentions might have been; whether he was engaged in an MI6-approved disinformation campaign; what amount of money was allegedly involved and who collected it on his behalf; how he fitted in with Stewart Menzies's pre–World War II chess game with Admiral Wilhelm Canaris; and what precisely his answers to his interrogators were. There is no transcript, just Peter Wright's account (as relayed under his own name in *Spycatcher* and preceded by Pincher's telling of the story in *Their Trade is Treachery* and *Too Secret Too Long*).

I have attempted to explain on the basis of actual available evidence what I believe Ellis was doing and in my view it wasn't sinister. The telling of his entire life story shows he was a man of integrity, committed to Britain, the United States and Australia as a soldier, colonel and intelligence officer, and a man who earned the confidence of spymasters such as Stewart Menzies, William Donovan, William Stephenson and Maurice Oldfield and national leaders such as Winston Churchill and Franklin D. Roosevelt. In the final analysis, when it comes to Ellis's purported confession, Wright has been shown to be a completely unreliable witness. MI6's official historian, Keith Jeffery, took a far more favourable view of Ellis – and, critically, he'd actually *seen* Ellis's MI6 file, an item not accessible to biographers, espionage writers or other historians.

So, without irrefutable proof of treason and judged on the breadth of his career, Ellis should be remembered not as a traitor but as one of the great intelligence officers of the 20th century whose character, loyalty, doggedness, reliability and vision marked him out as someone truly significant. James Cotton was correct to call him a 'rare talent'. Ellis was a titan of our own age in his own right, not merely William Stephenson's, William Donovan's or anyone else's deputy.

As William Stevenson recalled fondly of Ellis in his book *The Bormann Brotherhood*: 'Ellis still kept, even in his seventies, the impish sense of humour that distinguishes good intelligence agents. (As he himself has said: "They're no good if they think they should make a career in intelligence, to begin with.") He was recalling the atmosphere in Hitler's Berlin when he was working there. He came home one night and sensed a subtle change in the manner of his landlady. "My husband," she declared with a new hauteur, "is a block master."'

Ellis was likely referring to a *blockleiter* (block warden), a lower rung position in the Nazi Party denoting a supervisor of a city block or neighbourhood who acts as a sort of community-liaison officer and propagandist between local residents and the party.[9] They had their own uniforms.

'Her man could hold his head up now, for he had been admitted to the outer circle of the secret circles around the *Führer*. He had entered into the "popular togetherness" of *Volksgemeinschaft*.'

The word literally means 'folk community'. It was an early German term enthusiastically embraced by the Nazis to promote national unity, solidarity, common purpose, and a classless society.[10]

'As he told this anecdote, Ellis slipped into German. He was an inoffensive little Australian, mild and benign of manner, unfailingly courteous to waiters, with no time for pretension. Suddenly, as he gave this imitation of his German landlady, his back stiffened, his blue eyes flashed, and the guttural German accents rolled out across the somnolent club lounge. It was not a conscious imitation. He was simply quoting from the original. The effect around us was electric. Heads snapped back. One of the hovering waiters scuttled over to see what disaster had fallen. I caught a glimpse of what *Volksgemeinschaft* really meant.'

Recalled Ellis's daughter, Ann: 'He might have been short, but he was bright, full of enthusiasm, energetic, very talkative on every subject under the sun. He also wept easily about his experiences in the trenches in France, about Mozart, about Dickens and Shakespeare, whom he quoted at length – and, believe it or not, Australia. He loved it.'

Dick Ellis, a good man, could look in the mirror and be happy with what he saw.

ACRONYMS

AFC	America First Committee
AMCI	*A Man Called Intrepid*
ASIO	Australian Security Intelligence Organisation
ASIS	Australian Secret Intelligence Service
BISS	Business Industrial Secret Service
BSC	British Security Coordination
CBC	Canadian Broadcasting Corporation
CBE	Commander of the Most Excellent Order of the British Empire
CCC	Churchill College, Cambridge
CE	Counterespionage (*see also* **Section V** in Glossary section)
CFEA	Chief Controller Pacific (Far East and the Americas)
CIA	Central Intelligence Agency
CIC	Counter Intelligence Corps
CIFE	Combined Intelligence Far East
CMG	Companion of the Most Distinguished Order of St Michael and St George
CPR	Controller Production
COI	Office of the Coordinator of Information
DCI	Director of Central Intelligence (Director of CIA)
DNI	Director of Naval Intelligence
DSB	Defence Signals Branch (Australia, later renamed Defence Signals Directorate, or DSD)
DSO	Defence Security Officer
FBI	Federal Bureau of Investigation

FDR	Franklin Delano Roosevelt
FO	Foreign Office
FOI	Freedom of Information
FOIA	Freedom of Information Act
FOIPA	Freedom of Information/Privacy Act
GC&CS	Government Code and Cypher School, later renamed Government Communications Headquarters, or GCHQ
G2	United States Army Military Intelligence
GRU	*Glavnoye Razvedyvatelnoye Upravleniye* (Soviet Military Intelligence Department, USSR); also known as Fourth Department
HMAT	His Majesty's Australian Transport
HO	Head Office
HOS	Head of Station
IMT	International Mining Trust
IS	Intelligence Service
JIC	Joint Intelligence Committee
KGB	*Komitet Gosudarstvennoy Bezopasnosti* (Committee for State Security, USSR)
KMT	Kuomintang (Chinese Nationalist Party)
KPD	*Kommunistische Partei Deutschlands* (Communist Party of Germany)
KV 2	Personal files released by MI5 at National Archives, Kew
LOM	Legion of Merit
MI5	British Security Service (Military Intelligence, Section 5)
MIS	Military Intelligence Service
MI6	*See* SIS
MP	Member of Parliament
NAA	National Archives of Australia
NFA	No Further Action
NKVD	*Narodnyi Kommissariat Vnutrennikh Del* (People's Commissariat for Internal Affairs, USSR); successor of OGPU and predecessor of the KGB
NLA	National Library of Australia
NTS	*Narodnyi Trudovoy Soyuz* (National Labour Council)

OGPU	*Obyedinyonnoye Gosudarstvennoye Politicheskoye Upravleniye* (Joint State Political Directorate, USSR)
OBE	Officer of the Most Excellent Order of the British Empire
ONI	Office of Naval Intelligence
OSS	Office of Strategic Services
PCO	Passport Control Officer
PWE	Political Warfare Executive
QSMV	Quadruple Screw Motor Vessel
RAF	Royal Air Force
RCMP	Royal Canadian Mounted Police
RMS	Royal Mail Ship
ROVS	Russian All-Military Union
RSAA	Royal Society for Asian Affairs
RSHA	*Reichssicherheitshauptamt* (Reich Security Main Office, Nazi Germany)
RW	Report writer
SD	*Sicherheitsdienst des Reichsführers-SS* (security service or intelligence division of SS, Nazi Germany)
SI	Secret Intelligence
SIS	British Secret Intelligence Service (Military Intelligence, Section 6)
SIS	Special Intelligence Service (FBI)
SO	Special Operations
SOE	Special Operations Executive
SS	*Schutzstaffel* (paramilitary organisation, Nazi Germany)
SS	Screw steamer or steam ship
SS	Secret Service
SSU	Strategic Services Unit
STS	Special Training School
TD	Territorial Efficiency Decoration
TNA	The National Archives
USS	United States Ship
USSR	Union of Soviet Socialist Republics (Soviet Union)

GLOSSARY

5 MI5

6 MI6

Abwehr Military intelligence service of Nazi Germany; shortened form of *Abwehr im Oberkommando der Wehrmacht* (Defence Office of the Armed Forces High Command)

Abwehroffizier Abwehr officer

Abwehr III F Counterespionage unit of Abwehr III, the Abwehr's counterintelligence department

Agent Spy who collects intelligence for his or her controller

Allies Military coalition of the United States, the United Kingdom, Soviet Union and China

Amt *Amtsgruppe*: government office group or department in Nazi Germany

Amt IV Gestapo department in the RSHA

Amt IV E4 Counterespionage Scandinavia; department of Gestapo dedicated to counterespionage in Scandinavia

Amt VI Foreign political intelligence department of SD; part of RSHA

Anschluss Union of Germany and Austria

Axis Military coalition of Nazi Germany, Fascist Italy and Imperial Japan

Baku Project Aborted British plan to bomb Soviet Union oil facilities in Azerbaijan

Bletchley Park The estate where the ULTRA codebreaks were made

Blitzkrieg Lightning war; the 1940–41 German aerial bombing campaign against Britain was colloquially known as 'The Blitz'

Blockleiter Block warden

Bolsheviks Leninist communist group that seized power in Russia in 1918

Brigadeführer Brigade leader, or major general

Broadway 54 Broadway, or Broadway Buildings, in London; headquarters of MI6 1924–64

C British codename for both Stewart Menzies and Maurice Oldfield; also abbreviation of CSS (Chief of the Secret Service), or director-general of MI6

Cambridge Five Group of British traitors and spies for the Soviet Union: Kim Philby, Anthony Blunt, Guy Burgess, Donald Maclean and John Cairncross. A sixth spy/traitor, Wilfrid Mann, was outed by Guy Burgess biographer Andrew Lownie in 2015, though Mann, who died in 2001, denied he was ever part of the spy ring

Camp X BSC, COI/OSS and SOE training centre for secret-service agents

Century House Headquarters of MI6 1964–94

Chickenfeed Intelligence jargon for information of little or no value

Cipher Encrypted, or coded, secret message

Cold War Nuclear standoff between United States and Soviet Union after World War II

Colloque Conference

Comintern Executive committee of Soviet-controlled Communist International, an organisation created in 1919 to promote global communism and revolution

Commissar Political officer of the Soviet Communist Party overseeing a military unit

Commission Term for a formal document of appointment to a senior military rank in the British Army (a 'commissioned officer'), signed by the monarch

Controller Spy who relays intelligence from agents to headquarters

CORBY Canadian codename for Igor Gouzenko

Counterespionage Form of counterintelligence; denotes penetration of a rival intelligence service by an agent

Counterintelligence Information-gathering and/or activities designed to counteract threats from foreign intelligence agencies

Cover Agent's assumed identity or role while undertaking covert intelligence activity

Dead drop Prearranged, concealed, discreet location for passing information to an intelligence service or agent

Debrief Interview with cooperative source who volunteers intelligence information

Decrypt Decode encrypted or coded messages; render in everyday language

Disinformation False information designed to deceive or sabotage activities of rival intelligence services or agents. In Russian, *dezinformatsiya*

Double agent Agent who betrays intelligence service of one country to secretly work for the intelligence service of another country while remaining employed by both

Double Cross British counterespionage and disinformation operation to dupe Nazi Germany during World War II

Dubok Hiding place for drop-offs or dead drops; dead-letter box

ELLI Unidentified Soviet mole inside British intelligence

EMERTON British/American codename for Dick Ellis when he was being investigated for Soviet collaboration

Enigma Nazi Germany cipher machine: against the odds it was decrypted or decoded by British intelligence at Bletchley Park. *See also* **ULTRA**

Farsi The Persian language

The Firm (Old Firm) *See* **SIS** in Acronyms section

Five Eyes Intelligence alliance of United Kingdom, United States, Australia, New Zealand and Canada

Fluency Committee Joint MI5–MI6 team assembled to investigate Soviet penetration. *See also* **K7** in Acronyms section

Foreign Office British government department for foreign affairs; oversees MI6

Fourth Department *See* **GRU** in Acronyms section

Führer Leader of Nazi Germany (Adolf Hitler)

Generaloberst Colonel general

Gestapo Shortened form of *Geheime Staatspolizei* (secret state police) of Nazi Germany; absorbed into RSHA in 1939 as Amt IV

Great Britain The island containing England, Scotland and Wales. Also known as Britain; *Grossbritannien* (German)

Great Game Territorial contest between the British and Russian empires over control of Afghanistan and Central Asia, chiefly in the 19th century

Gruppenführer Lieutenant general

Home Office British government department for security, immigration, and law and order

HOWARD British codename for Dick Ellis while at BSC

Jahnke Büro A freelance spy agency working for the Nazis, run by Kurt Jahnke

Illegal Spy operating in a country not working under official or diplomatic cover

Informationsheft G. B. 'Information Brochure Great Britain', the SS handbook for the invasion of Britain

Inner Line Counterintelligence unit of **ROVS**

Intelligence Corps British Army intelligence unit

Interdoc International Documentary Centre

Intermarium 16-nation anti–Soviet Union organisation

Iron Curtain Boundary between Western Europe and Soviet Union and Soviet-aligned European states

Kapitän zur see Naval captain

King's Messenger Official courier of the Foreign Office who handles delivery of secret documents to embassies

Kriegsmarine Navy of Nazi Germany

Kriegs Organisation German intelligence in the Netherlands

K7 Successor of Fluency Committee

Little window Mole

Luftwaffe Air force of Nazi Germany

Marinenachrichtendienst German Naval Intelligence Service

Marri A tribe in northeastern Baluchistan

Mensheviks Non-Leninist socialist opposition group to Bolsheviks

Microdot Miniaturised text or photographs that can be seen only with microscope

MI5 British security service (domestic matters)

MI6 British secret service (foreign matters)

Mole Double agent or triple agent

Moscow Centre Russia-based controllers of Soviet double agents in the West; essentially KGB headquarters

Nazi Member of National Socialist German Workers' Party

Oberführer Senior leader, or brigadier general

Obergruppenführer Senior group leader, or general

Official Secrets Act British legislation prohibiting the release or publication of state secrets on national security matters

Order of battle Structure of intelligence organisation; also the formation and command structure of a military force before battle

Q British codename for William Donovan

Red Army Bolshevik army during Russian Civil War

Reds Slang for communists

Reich Realm, or empire

Reichsführer-SS Reich leader of the SS; title used by Heinrich Himmler

Reichsleiter Reich leader; title used by both Adolf Hitler and Martin Bormann

Reichsminister Minister of the realm

Rezidentura Soviet intelligence station headed by a *rezident* (senior intelligence officer)

Rote Kapelle Red Orchestra: Soviet spy network inside Western Europe

Scotland Yard Headquarters of police in London

Section V or MI6(V) MI6's counterespionage department

Sigint Signals intelligence

SMERSH NKVD assassination squad

Sonderfahndungsliste G. B. 'Special Wanted List Great Britain'; dubbed 'The Black Book'

Soviet Russian communist term for council

Soviet Union Union of Soviet Socialist Republics (USSR)

Special Branch Branch of Scotland Yard dealing with security and terrorism

Staff grade Military term for a commissioned officer under a commanding officer

STANLEY Soviet codename for Kim Philby

Stasi State security service of East Germany after World War II

Station MI6 headquarters in a foreign country

Stelle P Abwehr counterintelligence unit in the Netherlands

Sturmbannführer Major

Third section Russian secret police

T100 German codename for Vladimir von Petrov

TRICYCLE British codename for Duško Popov

Triple agent Agent who simultaneously works for the intelligence services of three rival countries without any of those intelligence services being aware of the agent's duplicity

22000 Organisation Intelligence network set up by Dick Ellis in Europe before World War II

ULTRA (or Ultra) The decrypting or decoding operation of the Enigma cipher machine by British military intelligence at Bletchley Park

United Kingdom Great Britain and Northern Ireland

Urdu National language of Pakistan

VENONA (or Venona) Joint US–British cryptographic mission to decrypt or decode Soviet cables

Volksgemeinschaft National community, or people's community

Waffen-SS Military wing of the SS, an elite fighting group

War Office British government department for administration of the army; replaced by Ministry of Defence in 1964

Wehrmacht Unified armed forces of Nazi Germany

White Army Anti-Bolshevik army during Russian Civil War

Whitehall Government offices in London

Z Organisation Intelligence network in Europe set up by SIS prior to World II, focused on Germany and Italy

GAZETTEER

A

Albert Town in the Somme, France

Annandale Suburb in Sydney, Australia, birthplace of Dick Ellis

Ashkhabad (also known as Askhabad, now Ashgabat) Capital city of Transcaspia

B

Bad Oeynhausen Town in North Rhine-Westphalia, Germany

Bairam Ali (now Baýramaly) City in Transcaspia

Baku Capital city of Azerbaijan

Balochistan (also known as Baluchistan) Province in Pakistan, once part of British India

Batum (now Batumi) City in Georgia

Black Sea Sea lying between Europe and Asia, surrounded by Ukraine, Bulgaria, Turkey, Russia, Georgia and Romania

C

Caspian Sea World's largest inland sea, surrounded by Azerbaijan, Iran, Kazakhstan and Turkmenistan

Caucasus (also known as Caucasia) Region between Caspian Sea and Black Sea, comprising Armenia, Georgia, southern Russia and Azerbaijan. *See also* **South Caucasus**

Central Asia Region comprising modern-day Uzbekistan, Turkmenistan, Azerbaijan, Kazakhstan, Kyrgyzstan, Tajikistan and Afghanistan

Constantinople (now Istanbul) City in Turkey (now Türkiye)

E

Eastbourne Seaside town in East Sussex, England, deathplace of Dick Ellis

Enzeli (now Bandar-e Anzali) City in Persia (now Iran)

H

The Hague City in the Netherlands

K

Krasnovodsk (now Türkmenbaşy) City in Transcaspia

M

Merv (now Mary) Historical city in Transcaspia (now Turkmenistan), site of Merv Oasis

Meshed (now Mashhad) City in Persia (now Iran)

N

Nasik (now Nashik) City in Maharashtra, India

O

Oshawa City in Ontario, Canada, site of Camp X

P

Pamirs (Pamir Mountains) Mountain range in Pakistan, China, Tajikistan, Kyrgyzstan and Afghanistan

Pearl Harbor Site of US naval base in Oahu, Hawaii

Persia (now Iran) Country in West Asia

Q

Quetta City in Pakistan and capital of Balochistan, once part of British India

R

Russian Turkestan Western part of Turkestan (with Afghan, or Southern, Turkestan); absorbed into the Russian Empire in the 19th century

S

Samarkand City in Uzbekistan

Seistan (now Sistan) Region spanning parts of eastern Persia (now Iran) and southern Afghanistan

Sevastopol City in Crimea

Somme (the Somme) Department in northern France named after the river Somme

South Caucasus (also known as Transcaucasia) Region between the Black Sea and Caspian Sea

Sudetenland German name for a historical part of Czechoslovakia largely populated by ethnic Germans

T

Tashkent Capital city of Uzbekistan

Tehran Capital city of Persia (now Iran)

Tiflis (now Tbilisi) Capital city of Georgia

Transcaspia (now Turkmenistan) Historical region of the Russian Empire east of the Caspian Sea

Transcaucasia *See* **South Caucasus**

Turkestan Historical region in Central Asia which today consists of the republics of Kazakhstan, Kyrgyzstan, Tajikistan, Turkmenistan and Uzbekistan. *See also* **Russian Turkestan**

U

Utrecht City in the Netherlands

V

Venlo City in the Netherlands on the Dutch-German border; location of the Venlo Incident

Y

Yekaterinodar (now Krasnodar) City in southern Russia

Ypres Town in West Flanders, Belgium

KEY EVENTS

1895 Charles Howard 'Dick' Ellis born in Annandale, Sydney, Australia

1898 Ellis's mother, Lillian, dies

1909 Ellis gets his first job – at Stott & Hoare's Business College, Melbourne

1911–14 Ellis completes high school at Carnegie State School in Malvern, Victoria; plays with various orchestras in Melbourne; attends night classes at Melbourne University; sails for England

1915–18 Ellis enlists as a British soldier in the Great War; fights on the Western Front, including at the First Battle of the Somme; serves in Italy, Egypt and India; Russian Revolution; Ellis joins Malleson mission in Persia and Transcaspia; 26 Commissars massacre

1919 Ellis awarded OBE; joins Foreign Office as liaison officer and King's Messenger; applies to study at Oxford University; on military duty in Afghanistan, southern Russia, and the Caucasus

1920 Ellis's father, William, dies

1921–23 Ellis enrols at Oxford but abandons studies; joins SIS (later MI6) and is sent to Paris and Constantinople; marries Lilia 'Elizabeth' Zelensky in Turkey; goes to Berlin as acting vice-consul; works under MI6 Berlin station chief Frank Foley on 'Soviet target'

1924 Ellis and Zelensky have a son, Olik – or 'Peter' – in Berlin

1926–27 Ellis goes undercover for MI6 as a journalist, mainly in Vienna and Geneva

1928 Ellis publishes his first book, *The Origin, Structure and Working of the League of Nations*

1931 Ellis divorces Zelensky

1933 Ellis marries Barbara Mary Burgess-Smith

1934 Ellis and Burgess-Smith have a daughter, Ann

1937 Walter Krivitsky defects to the West after the assassination of Ignace Reiss

1938 Ellis involved in phone taps of the German Embassy in London; starts 22000 Organisation

1939 Venlo Incident; Germany invades Poland; United Kingdom and France declare war on Germany

1940 Krivitsky debriefed by MI5 officer Jane Archer in London and mentions an unnamed British source for Nazi double agent Vladimir von Petrov; Baku Project; Winston Churchill becomes UK prime minister; British Security Coordination established; Ellis arrives in New York as His Britannic Majesty's Consul and deputy to William Stephenson at BSC; Battle of Britain

1941 Krivitsky murdered/suicides in Washington DC; Germany invades Soviet Union; William Donovan made head of COI/OSS, with Ellis as his main adviser; Atlantic Conference; Pearl Harbor bombed by Japan; United States declares war on Japan; Germany declares war on United States

1942 Ellis sets up COI/OSS training centre in Maryland and Camp X in Ontario; Soviet cipher clerk Igor Gouzenko first hears the codename ELLI; Ellis briefly stationed in Egypt

1943 Ellis wraps up work with COI/OSS

1944 D-Day landings; Ellis leaves New York

1945 Adolf Hitler suicides and Germany surrenders; Hiroshima and Nagasaki bombed and Japan surrenders; Igor Gouzenko defects to Canada; Nazi Walter Schellenberg interrogated

1946 Major John Gwyer telegrams Kim Philby about ELLI; Ellis and Burgess-Smith divorce; Ellis awarded CBE and LOM; Nazi Richard Protze interrogated

1947 CIA established; Ellis made MI6 Chief Controller Pacific (Far East and the Americas) and based in Asia; Ellis visits Australia

1949 ASIO established

1951 Guy Burgess and Donald Maclean defect to Soviet Union; Philby and Ellis suspected of spying for Russians

1952 ASIS established; Joseph Stalin dies; MI5 head Dick White reopens investigation into ELLI; Von Petrov leaves Europe for Chile

1953 Ellis retires from MI6 and takes up ASIO role in Australia; awarded CMG and TD

1954 Ellis leaves Australia for England; Vladimir Petrov defects to Australia; Ellis marries Alexandra Wood

1955 Philby is cleared of being the 'Third Man' by Harold McMillan in British Parliament

1956 Ellis awarded Commemorative Medal of the Battles of the Somme

1959 Donovan dies

1962 H. Montgomery Hyde's *The Quiet Canadian* is released

1963 Philby defects to Soviet Union and Ellis is investigated; Ellis publishes his second book, *The Transcaspian Episode, 1918–1919*

1964 Anthony Blunt interrogated

1965 Ellis interrogated

1970 Wood dies; Ellis is awarded Sir Percy Sykes Memorial Medal by the Royal Society for Asian Affairs

1973 Ellis marries Joyce Hatten; Ellis and Joyce visit Australia together

1974 Ellis and Joyce leave Australia; Lord Trend heads secret inquiry into Fluency Committee findings; Lilia Zelensky dies

1975 Ellis dies in Eastbourne, England

1976 William Stevenson's *A Man Called Intrepid* is released

1979 Blunt is exposed as a double agent by Margaret Thatcher

1981 Chapman Pincher's *Their Trade is Treachery* is released – in the book Pincher alleges the late Roger Hollis and Ellis were double agents; Thatcher defends Hollis in British Parliament but does not do the same for Ellis

1982 Gouzenko dies; Nigel West's *A Matter of Trust: MI5 1945–72* and Hyde's *Secret Intelligence Agent* are released

1983 Stevenson's *Intrepid's Last Case* is released

1987 Peter Wright wins court case in Australia to publish
     Spycatcher
1988 Philby dies
1989 Stephenson and Hyde die
1995 Wright dies
2012 Olik Ellis dies
2013 Stevenson dies
2014 Pincher dies
2023 *The Eagle in the Mirror* is released

DRAMATIS PERSONAE

A

James Jesus Angleton CIA chief of counterintelligence 1954–74. Died in 1987

Jane Archer MI5 officer and debriefer of Walter Krivitsky. Died in 1982

B

Benjamin deForest 'Pat' Bayly Canadian BSC agent and head of Camp X. Friend and defender of Ellis. Died in 1994

Cedric Belfrage British BSC agent. Journalist and film critic. Died in 1990

Adolf Berle United States Assistant Secretary of State. Died in 1971

Sigismund Payne Best One of the two British intelligence agents involved in the Venlo Incident. Died in 1978

George Blake British intelligence agent and traitor. Died in 2020

Anthony Blunt British intelligence agent and traitor. Died in 1983

Alfred Deakin Brookes Head of ASIS 1952–57. Died in 2005

Isaak Brodsky Russian painter of 'The Execution of the Twenty-Six Baku Commissars'. Died in 1939

David K. E. Bruce Head of OSS in Europe. Later United States ambassador to France, Germany and the United Kingdom. Trainee, friend and defender of Ellis. Died in 1977

John Bryden Canadian historian and author

Guy Burgess British intelligence agent and traitor. Died in 1963

Barbara Mary Burgess-Smith Second wife of Ellis. Year of death unknown

C

John Cairncross British intelligence agent and traitor. Died in 1995

Wilhelm Canaris Nazi. Head of the Abwehr. Plotter against Hitler. Executed by the Nazis in 1945

Richard 'Dick' Casey (Lord Casey, or Baron Casey) British Minister of State in Egypt and later Governor-General of Australia. Died in 1976

William Casey Director of CIA 1981–87. Died in 1987

Anthony Cave Brown British journalist and author. Defender of Ellis. Died in 2006

Anthony Cavendish British intelligence agent. Defender of Ellis. Died in 2013

Frederick Chilton Deputy secretary of Australia's Department of Defence. Defender of Ellis. Died in 2007

Winston Churchill Prime Minister of the United Kingdom 1940–45 and 1951–55. Died in 1965

Earl Connelley FBI assistant director. Died in 1957

John Costello British author. Died in 1995

Ernest Cuneo Presidential aide and OSS liaison to Franklin D. Roosevelt. Friend and defender of Ellis. Died in 1988

D

Roald Dahl BSC agent. Author. Friend of Ellis. Died in 1990

William J. 'Wild Bill' Donovan Head of COI/OSS 1941–45. Died in 1959

Donald Downes American BSC agent. Author. Died in 1983

E

Nicholas Elliott British intelligence agent. Died in 1994

Charles Howard 'Dick' Ellis Australian-born British intelligence agent. Died in 1975

Lillian Mary Ellis Mother of Ellis. Died in 1898

Olik Cyril 'Peter' Ellis Son of Ellis. Died in 2012

William Edward Ellis Father of Ellis. Died in 1920

Alfred Brotherston Emden Principal of St Edmund Hall, Oxford University. Died in 1979

F

Ian Fleming BSC agent. Author of James Bond novels. Died in 1964

Frank Foley Head of Berlin station for MI6. Died in 1958

Percy E. Foxworth Head of FBI's Special Intelligence Service. Killed in a plane crash in 1943

G

Igor Gouzenko Soviet cipher clerk and defector. Died in 1982

Colin Gubbins Head of Special Operations Executive 1940–46. Friend of Ellis. Died in 1976

H

Richard Hall Australian journalist and author. Defender of Ellis. Died in 2003

Joyce Hatten (née Steeples) Ellis's fourth wife

Reinhard Heydrich Nazi. Head of the *Reichssicherheitshauptamt* (RSHA). Assassinated by Czech resistance operatives in 1942

Heinrich Himmler Nazi. *Reichsführer-SS*. Died by suicide in 1945

Adolf Hitler *Der Führer*. Leader of Nazi Germany 1933–45. Died by suicide in 1945

Roger Hollis Head of MI5 1956–65. Alleged double agent. Died in 1973

Leslie Howard British actor. Killed by the *Luftwaffe* in 1943

Harford (H.) Montgomery Hyde Irish BSC agent. Author of *The Quiet Canadian* and *Secret Intelligence Agent*. Friend and defender of Ellis but turned on him after Ellis's death. Died in 1989

J

Keith Jeffery Northern Irish author and historian. Died in 2016

K

Ernst Kaltenbrunner Nazi. Head of the RSHA after Heydrich's assassination by Czech resistance operatives. Sentenced to death at the Nuremberg trials. Executed in 1946

Phillip Knightley Australian author. Died in 2016

Helmuth Knochen Nazi. *Sturmbannführer*. Died in 2003

Walter Krivitsky Soviet intelligence agent and defector. Assassinated in 1941

L

Guy Liddell Counterespionage chief and later deputy head of MI5. Died in 1958

M

Donald Maclean British intelligence agent and traitor. Died in 1983

Theodore Maly (aka Paul Hardt) Hungarian-born Soviet intelligence agent. Presumed to have died in 1938

Stewart Menzies Head of MI6 1939–52. Friend of Ellis. Died in 1968

Taline Ter Minassian French academic. Biographer of Reginald Teague-Jones

Heinrich Müller Nazi. *Gruppenführer*. Presumed to have died in 1945

N

Aleksandr Nelidov White Russian double agent. Died by suicide in 1942

O

Maurice Oldfield Head of MI6 1973–78. Friend of Ellis. Died in 1981

P

Major Theodore 'Bunny' Pantcheff British intelligence agent and interrogator of Ellis. Died in 1989

Brian Pearce Russia historian. Correspondent with Chapman Pincher, Reginald Teague-Jones and Ann Salwey. Died in 2008

Vladimir Petrov Soviet *rezident* in Australia who defected in 1954. Died in 1991

Vladimir von Petrov Chilean-born Soviet and Nazi double agent. Year of death unknown

Harold Adrian Russell 'Kim' Philby British intelligence agent and traitor. Died in 1988

Chapman Pincher (Harry Chapman Pincher) British journalist and author. Died in 1973

Duško (Dusko) Popov Serbian-born Nazi and British double agent. Died in 1981

Traugott Andreas 'Richard' Protze Nazi. Head of the Abwehr III F. Year of death unknown

R

Ignace Reiss Soviet intelligence agent. Assassinated in 1937

Joachim von Ribbentrop Nazi. Ambassador to the United Kingdom and later Minister of Foreign Affairs. Sentenced to death at the Nuremberg trials. Executed in 1946

Franklin D. Roosevelt President of the United States 1933–45. Died in 1945

Alban M. (A. M.) 'Bill' Ross-Smith Australian BSC agent. Friend and defender of Ellis. Died in 1993

S

Ann Veronica Salwey Daughter of Ellis

Walter Schellenberg Nazi. Chief of SD. Sentenced to six years' imprisonment after the Nuremberg trials and released early in 1951. Died in 1952

Frederick Shedden Head of Australia's Department of Defence. Died in 1971

Hugh Sinclair Head of MI6 1923–39. Died in 1939

Charles Spry Head of ASIO 1950–70. Died in 1994

Joseph Stalin Dictator of Soviet Union 1924–53. Died in 1953

William Steedman British intelligence agent. Investigator of Ellis. Year of death unknown

William Stephenson Canadian fighter pilot, businessman and head of BSC. Friend and defender of Ellis. Died in 1989

Richard Henry Stevens British intelligence agent involved in the Venlo Incident alongside Sigismund Payne Best. Died in 1967

William Stevenson British-Canadian fighter pilot. Author of *A Man Called Intrepid* and *Intrepid's Last Case*. Died in 2013

T

Reginald Teague-Jones (aka Ronald Sinclair) British 'political representative'. Intelligence agent in Transcaspia. Friend of Ellis. Died in 1988

Margaret Thatcher Prime Minister of the United Kingdom 1979–90. Died in 2013

Thomas F. Troy CIA historian and author. Died in 2008

Harry S. Truman President of the United States 1945–53. Died in 1972

Anton Vasilyevich Turkul White Russian general. Soviet and Nazi double agent. Died in 1957

Malcolm Turnbull Lawyer for Peter Wright. Prime Minister of Australia 2015–18

V

Robert Vansittart, 1st Baron Vansittart British diplomat. Permanent Under-Secretary of State for Foreign Affairs. Died in 1957

Valentine Vivian Deputy head of MI6. Died in 1969

W

Donald Cameron Watt British historian. Defender of Ellis. Died in 2014

Nigel West Pen name of Rupert William Simon Allason. British author of dozens of secret-intelligence books

Dick White Head of MI5 1953–56 and head of MI6 1956–68. Died in 1993

Alexandra Wood Ellis's third wife. Died in 1970

Peter Wright MI5 intelligence officer. Member of Fluency Committee. Interrogator of Ellis. Author of *Spycatcher*. Died in 1995

Z

Aleksei (Alexander) Zelensky Ellis's Ukrainian brother-in-law and reputed Soviet agent. Died in 1987

Lilia (Elizabeth) Zelensky Ellis's Ukrainian first wife. Mother of Olik Ellis. Died in 1974

HONOURS RECEIVED BY
CHARLES HOWARD 'DICK' ELLIS

1919 Officer of the Most Excellent Order of the British Empire (OBE)
1932–37, 1957–60 Fellow, Royal Geographical Society
1946 Commander of the Most Excellent Order of the British Empire (CBE)
1946 Legion of Merit (LOM)
1953 Companion of the Most Distinguished Order of St Michael and St George (CMG)
1953 Territorial Efficiency Decoration (TD)
1956 Commemorative Medal of the Battles of the Somme (Médaille Commémorative des Batailles de la Somme)
1970 Sir Percy Sykes Memorial Medal, Royal Society for Asian Affairs

WRITTEN WORKS BY
CHARLES HOWARD 'DICK' ELLIS

Books

War and Politics in Central Asia (unknown publisher, 1920)

The Origin, Structure and Working of the League of Nations (G. Allen & Unwin, London, 1928)

The Transcaspian Episode, 1918–1919 (Hutchinson, London, 1963; published in the United States as *The British 'Intervention' in Transcaspia*)

Articles/Papers

'The British in Central Asia' (*Stead's Review*, Melbourne, 24 July 1920)

'Central Asian History, 1917–1924' (*Central Asian Review*, London, 1958)

'The Revolt in Transcaspia, 1918–1919' (*Central Asian Review*, London, 1959)

'Operations in Transcaspia, 1918–1919 and the 26 Commissars Case' (*Soviet Affairs: Number Two*, London, 1959)

'Anglo-Indian Troops in Persia, 1914–1920' (*Central Asian Review*, London, 1959)

'The History of Soviet Central Asia: Soviet Views on Falsification' (*Central Asian Review*, London, 1961)

'Central Asian History, 1917–19: Recent Soviet Works' (*Central Asian Review*, London, 1961)

'Foreign Prisoners of War in Turkestan, 1917–18' (*Central Asian Review*, London, 1961)

Pamphlets

Mozart and the Orchestra (unknown publisher, 1921)

The Expansion of Russia (Ilmgau Verlag, Pfaffenhofen, 1965)

The New Left in Britain: The Origin, Development and Impact of the New Left, with a Comment on its Failure to Contribute to a Solution of the Problems of To-day [sic] (Common Cause Publications, London, 1968)

Anthologies (as Contributor)

The New Left in the United States of America, Britain, the Federal Republic of Germany (International Documentation and Information Centre, The Hague, 1969)

'*We Will Bury You': Studies in Left-Wing Subversion Today* (Tom Stacey Ltd, London, 1970)

Unpublished Manuscripts

*Anglo-American Collaboration in Intelligence and Security: Notes for
     Documentation* (1963)

The Two Bills: Mission Accomplished aka *Mission Accomplished: The Story of
     the 'Two Bills' and their Partnership in Wartime Intelligence and Clandestine
     Operations* (1972)

QUOTES

Page numbers have not been included for book quotes as different editions (mass-market paperbacks, updated editions, transatlantic editions, translations, reprints, e-books in various formats, Google Books, etc) invariably have different pagination, making specific page references largely redundant. A good student of espionage should be able to find these quotes in their original volumes. – JF

Author's Note   TWIST SLOWLY IN THE WIND
'Britain's number-three spy at the end of World War II' *Washington Star*, 26 March 1981 'The most intriguing figure who has crossed the often surprising landscape of Australian intelligence' Toohey and Pinwill, *Sydney Morning Herald*, 22 July 1989 'One of the most shadowy figures of all' Ball and Horner, *Breaking the Codes*, 1998 'Gained a reputation as tough, ruthless and brilliant. In World War II he was a big shot in intelligence' Sulzberger, *The Last of the Giants*, 1970 'The Grand Old Man of British espionage . . . the oldest living professional agent' Stevenson, *Intrepid's Last Case*, 1983 'Short (5'5" in his prime), slightly rounded, white-haired, proper person' Troy, *Wild Bill and Intrepid*, 1996 'Widely believed to have been both a Nazi and a Soviet agent' *ibid*. 'The most blatant cover-up' Pincher, *Daily Mail*, 2 November 1981 'Broke down after interrogation in 1965 . . . this would have been a capital offence in wartime' *ibid*. 'Inferred [sic] during his 1964 confession . . . link between [Kim] Philby and Ellis' Costello, *Mask of Treachery*, 1988 'It's amusing to see the security services spinning round like mad dogs chewing their own tails' Blunt in Atkins, *Daily Telegraph*, 4 May 1984 'The most remarkable spy in the history of espionage . . . the most successful penetration agent ever . . . professionally, as a spy, he is in a class all by himself' Knightley, *Philby: KGB Masterspy*, 1988 'A spy for both Hitler and Stalin' Charles Spry in McAdam, *Bulletin*, 27 November 1984 'Sold vast quantities of information to the Germans' Hudson, *Daily Mail*, 23 February 2000 'Nail Ellis' Stevenson, *Intrepid's Last Case*, 1983 'The powerful protections of the Nazi agent, Charles Howard Ellis' Higham and Moseley, *Cary Grant: The Lonely Heart*, 1989 'Because all the channels were open to Nazi sympathisers' Brian, *Fair Game*, 1994 'Grotesque myth . . . one of the most ludicrous works ever to be written . . . on such a subject' Trevor-Roper, *Sunday Telegraph*, 19 February 1989 'Egregious publication' Trevor-Roper, *New York Review of Books*, 13 May 1976 'Among the bombed ruins of the Houses of Parliament' Stevenson, *A Man Called Intrepid*, 1976 'Dark figure' *ibid*. 'One of the very few you could be quite certain about' Tendler, *Times*, 27 March 1981 'Could have, should have, moved up to the number-two, or even the number-one, spot in MI6' Stephenson as paraphrased in Troy, *Wild Bill and Intrepid*, 1996 'I knew everything about him' Jones, *Sydney Morning Herald*, 28 March 1981 'Major stroke' Troy, *Wild Bill and Intrepid*, 1996 'An invalid by 1964' *ibid*. 'He

shuffles about, tires easily, is slightly forgetful, but is still alert and coherent, remains active in the conduct of his affairs, and retains an interest in world affairs' Troy, 'Report on interviews with Sir William S. Stephenson in Paget, Bermuda', 13 March 1969 'Obvious physical disabilities . . . his left eye seemed half-closed, and the right corner of his mouth was slightly contorted, especially when he spoke' Troy, *Wild Bill and Intrepid*, 1996 'Signed nothing, avoided all written commitments. That was the mark of a good agent . . . left himself unprotected by memos' Stevenson, *Intrepid's Last Case*, 1983 'KGB character assassination' Stevenson, *Intrepid's Last Case*, 1983 'Neutralise enemies of the Soviet Union by sowing seeds of mistrust and discord among members of the intelligence or counterintelligence services' *ibid*. 'Pure disinformation by the KGB' Hyde, *Secret Intelligence Agent*, 1982 'I would have known about it . . . should be produced instead of relying on hearsay' *ibid*. 'Ellis is dead; any papers . . . though she states that she has none' Winks, *Cloak and Gown*, 1987 'Ever-fluid landscape where fact and illusion merge' Angleton as quoted from an internal CIA memo in Morley, theintercept.com, 1 January 2018 'A former member of MI6 and a close friend of the [Ellis] family said . . . Mr Ellis himself had told him of his interrogation. No mention was made of any confession' Tendler, *Times*, 30 March 1981 'If the charge against Ellis is true . . . it would mean that the OSS, and to some extent its successor, the CIA, in effect was a branch of the Soviet KGB' Mahl, *Desperate Deception*, 1999 'The security and intelligence authorities decided that a court case . . . save among the very few of his former MI6 colleagues who knew the truth about him' Pincher, *Traitors*, 1987 'The British government has certainly allowed Ellis, who died in 1975, to twist slowly in the wind. The United States, an interested – possibly an injured – party, has likewise said nothing' Troy, *Wild Bill and Intrepid*, 1996

Chapter 1   THE PURGE

'A most refreshing sense of humour which made being in his company always a most enjoyable and rewarding experience' Hyde, *Times*, London, 21 July 1975 'Greatly liked and trusted in his day' Foster, *Sun-Herald*, 21 June 1981 'Old friend and comrade' Krivitsky, *In Stalin's Secret Service*, 1939 'Chief of the Soviet Military Intelligence in Western Europe' *ibid*. 'Worked for years in our secret service abroad' *ibid*. 'Had been deeply shocked by the purge of the Old Bolsheviks and the "treason trials" and was already determined to break away from Moscow . . . the leading generals of the Red Army were bound for the firing squad' *ibid*. 'Up to now I have followed you . . . the day of judgment is nearer, much nearer, than the gentlemen in the Kremlin think' *ibid*. 'Reiss was a thorough idealist who had enlisted heart and soul in the cause of communism and world revolution . . . to some remote corner where he could be forgotten' *ibid*. 'Doubtless intended' Conquest, *The Great Terror*, 1968 'He went out with her to dine in a restaurant near Chamblandes to discuss the whole situation . . . there were five bullets in his head and seven in his body' Krivitsky, *In Stalin's Secret Service*, 1939 'I realised that my lifelong service to the Soviet government was ended . . . I had lived by that oath; but to take an active hand in these wholesale murders was beyond my powers' *ibid*. 'If they ever try to prove I took my own life, don't believe it' no byline, *New York Times*, 11 February 1941 'Knowledge was on an altogether different scale' William J. West, *Spymaster*, 1990 'Behind the guarded doors of Leconfield House, Peter Wright was behaving like a Witchfinder-General' Leigh, *The Wilson Plot*, 1988 'Was a double agent working both for the German Abwehr and the Russians' Watt, *Political Quarterly*, April 1988 'That he betrayed to the Germans the MI5 tap on the German Embassy telephone to Berlin' *ibid*. 'That he continued to work for the Abwehr when he was posted to Washington in December 1939' *ibid*. 'That Ellis "betrayed" the entire MI6 organisation in Western Europe to the Abwehr' *ibid*. 'That Ellis was a Soviet mole in the pre-war years' *ibid*. 'The more one reads Wright's account, the sorrier one becomes for the unfortunate Ellis. One is even left to doubt whether Ellis's interrogation ever took place (though I am assured by persons who claim to have spoken with the interrogating officer that it did), or that he could have admitted one tenth of these accusations' *ibid*.

Chapter 2   THE TOILS OF CHILDHOOD

'Lifelong anti-communist' Knightley, *The Second Oldest Profession*, 1986 'Originally came from the Welsh border country, probably Monmouthshire' Ellis, 'My early life (the Ellis family)', undated 'The Boer War was in progress . . . the little school on Cataract Hill must have been a good one as I was reading long before we left Tasmania' *ibid*. 'Fashion artist and designer of clothes' *ibid*. 'The loss of three wives, in such circumstances, would have shaken any man . . . particularly at a time when his affairs were not going well' *ibid*. 'Although father must have been hard put to cope with us, he gave us a good deal of attention . . . to break away from the rut that we found ourselves in as a result of the neglect and lack of opportunity from which we suffered' *ibid*. 'Curious teacher' *ibid*. 'Descended in the academic scale through drink' *ibid*. 'Often failed to appear' *ibid*. 'Had his good side. If he spotted a child with intelligence, he gave that child some attention . . . I learned masses of poetry and prose at his behest' *ibid*. 'And acquired an image of London from his novels that was one of the determining factors in my decision to go there as soon as I could escape from the toils of childhood' *ibid*. 'The Russo-Japanese war was raging, causing scares of possible raids by Russian battleships on Australian ports . . . and from the sale of bones and bottles to itinerant "rag and bone" men' *ibid*. 'Messenger boy and "ink boy"' *ibid*. 'Keeping ink wells [sic] full and ringing the bell between classes' *ibid*. 'Permission to attend classes in shorthand, English, bookkeeping and typing' *ibid*. 'Made new contacts and mixed with a less bucolic class of people' *ibid*. 'I gained a good deal of practical knowledge to enable me to earn my living as a clerk, but there were many gaps in my education, and in more ways than one, I was innocent and ill-equipped for life' *ibid*. 'Robust health' *ibid*. 'We had a brief glimpse of Maisie as she passed through London, a shy little girl of eight or nine. She had not met her father, and it was clear that she knew little or nothing of him or of us' *ibid*. 'Worked in the office, ran messages and delivered books' *ibid*. 'Also played from time to time in dance bands' *ibid*. 'Torn between the desire to be a professional musician or a writer' *ibid*. 'Small scholarship' *ibid*. 'Generosity of one of the lecturers' *ibid*. 'The possibility of taking a course at one of the English universities, provided a small sum of money could be found to cover the cost of the journey and sojourn in England' *ibid*. 'Limited outlook of suburbia and the dull country towns' *ibid*. 'I decided that the time had come to make a break with my existing environment, and take full advantage of the opportunity now offered to strike out on a new path' *ibid*.

Chapter 3   FRONT TO FRONTIER

'Too delicate' no byline, *Sunday Times*, 14 December 1919 'After special treatment his health improved so much' *ibid*. 'He had fought in Egypt and France. He was a survivor of the slaughter of the Second Battle of the Somme. Some 400,000 British soldiers in 40 days were sacrificed to Field Marshall [sic] Sir Douglas Haig's folly' Cuneo, 'Of moles and men', 1981 'Devoting as much time as possible to finding my way about London and visiting all the sights which were already familiar to me from books and pictures . . . I quickly made the acquaintance of the theatres (cheap gallery seats) the Albert Hall and the Queens Hall, and the parks and gardens' Ellis, 'My early life (the Ellis family)', undated 'Missed being sent to Gallipoli owing to [a] bout of influenza' Olik Ellis, 'Charles Howard Ellis' timeline, 1994 'Line [northeast] of Albert' *ibid*. 'He was wounded while on a raid' *ibid*. 'Came out of [the] line and [was] sent on [a] refresher course' *ibid*. 'Back in [the] line near Ypres' *ibid*. 'Where he was badly wounded' *ibid*. 'Received his first pip – a subaltern' *ibid*. 'Mountain warfare course' *ibid*. 'Great tract of country north of Persia and Afghanistan, stretching in the North towards Russia proper, and bounded on the East and West by the Pamirs and the Caspian Sea' Ellis, *Stead's Review*, 24 July 1920 'After the Russo-Japanese war, which obliged Russia to change her foreign policy entirely . . . in the first two a garrison of nearly 10,000 troops was stationed, and great military depots created' *ibid*. 'A small guard of Indian cavalry' Ellis, *The Transcaspian Episode*, 1918–1919, 1963 'The savage murder of responsible officials of Soviet power in Baku by the British imperialists . . . savages' Stalin, *Izvestiya*, 23 April 1919 'Unhappy incident' Hyde, *Secret Intelligence Agent*, 1982

Chapter 4   STALIN AND THE KING'S MESSENGER

'Raised to epic rank by a voluminous and unanimous Soviet historiography' Ter Minassian, *Asian Affairs*, 14 February 2014 'It must be taken as proven that our Baku comrades . . . devoid of all moral integrity need to resort to murder by night' Stalin, *Izvestiya*, 23 April 1919 'Direct practical organiser' Hopkirk (introduction) in Teague-Jones, *The Spy Who Disappeared*, 1990 'Teague-Jones, cast as the central figure in the inquiry . . . the 26 Commissars, an affair which had been exclusively Russian from the outset' Ter Minassian, *op. cit.* 'He almost certainly could have stopped the executions if he had insisted' Beevor, *Russia: Revolution and Civil War 1917–1921*, 2022 'The British authorities, including myself, had no part whatever [sic] in or connected with the tragedy of the 26 . . . on the contrary, they made every possible effort to avert it' Letter, Teague-Jones to Pearce, 20 November 1979 'Was a matter of anxiety . . . he lived long enough to also witness the decline of the British empire' Ter Minassian, *op. cit.* 'Ellis . . . was perhaps an even worse traitor [than Philby], making Philby look like a rank amateur. Yet Jeffery, who says that he was allowed to look at Ellis's file, concludes that he was guilty of nothing more than indiscretion and a poor choice of White Russian friends in Paris before the war' West, *International Journal of Intelligence and CounterIntelligence*, 14 September 2011

Chapter 5   A STRANGER IN A STRANGE LAND

'I obtained passage on the very first available steamer which was due to arrive in England in early September' Letter, Ellis to Brotherston Emden, 8 September 1920 'Innumerable delays' *ibid*. 'A somewhat war-scarred and not particularly bright student of Slav languages' Letter, Ellis to Brotherston Emden, 13 March 1937 'The holy grail of British archives' Jeffery, Lowy Institute, October 2011 'C. H. Ellis has been absent in Constantinople on Intelligence Service under the Foreign Office' *St Edmund Hall Magazine*, December 1922 'Long vacation' Olik Ellis, 'Charles Howard Ellis' timeline, 1994 'French courses at [the] Sorbonne' *ibid*. 'Received [a] call from [the] War Office from one Col. Shakespeare who offered [Ellis] reinstate-ment [to rank of captain] on active list for a two-year term of service in [the] Black Sea area' *ibid*. 'I hoped to be able to return to Oxford for a few days . . . I shall be able to return to England before going to Constantinople' Letter, Ellis to Brotherston Emden, 3 November 1921 'Should be within six or eight months' *ibid*. 'When I come back to the Hall, it will be very different to me from when I came up a year ago – a stranger in a strange land and a pretty sick stranger at that!' *ibid*. 'Caucasus and Trans-Caspia' Letter, Vivian to Burnham, 8 October 1920 'Local Russian Intelli-gence, Southern Russia, etc' *ibid*. 'Between them they control Russian, Caucausian, Trans-Caspian and Central Asiatic sources of information' *ibid*. 'Pan-Islamic' *ibid*.

'Muhammadan relations with Bolshevism, etc' *ibid*. 'Egypt and the Arab-speaking countries' *ibid*. 'Any regular officer found suitable to all parties concerned' *ibid*. 'Sometime press correspondent for [the] League of Nations secretariat' Ethridge and Kopala, *Contemporary Authors*, 1965 '[Captain D. O. 'Charles'] Seymour had sent [Ellis] to Geneva, where he was attached to the League of Nations in order to target Comintern [Communist International] agents in Europe' West and Tsarev, *TRIPLEX*, 2009 'I went from Constantinople to Berlin in order to replace Captain Ellis . . . for which he relied exclusively on the evidence of the German police. Ellis had established connections' *ibid*.

Chapter 6   THE LEAGUE OF GENTLEMEN
'Journalist in Geneva' Burns, *International Journal of Ethics*, January 1929 'Has been in close and continuous contact with the Secretariat and has attended all the chief League meetings' *ibid*. 'An important book, not merely because it is the only adequate record of the working of the League system, but also because it includes criticism of the moral practices and theories on which war and peace depend' *ibid*. 'This book is undoubtedly the nearest approach to a perfect text book [sic] for the more serious student that has been produced . . . undoubtedly the fullest account of the origin, composition and working of that body that has ever appeared in print' no byline, *Saturday Review*, 20 October 1928 'It is such a mine of useful information that the present reviewer is tempted to recommend it to the exclusion of all others on the subject of international relations' Advertisement by George Allen & Unwin in C. Delisle Burns, *Democracy: Its Defects and Advantages*, 1929 'Important publication . . . well documented, the nature of the subject has obliged the author to rely for much of his matter upon observation and personal contacts, and this method adds vividness to his narrative' no byline, *The Economist, Weekly Commercial Times, Banker's Gazette and Railway Monitor*, 29 September 1928 'Exhaustive . . . Mr Howard-Ellis [sic] is a dispassionate and discerning critic, a profound believer in the League in theory, and a convinced admirer of the League in practice, but at the same time fully conscious of its weaknesses, and always alive to the dangers besetting it' no byline, *The Economist, Weekly Commercial Times, Banker's Gazette and Railway Monitor*, 3 November 1928 'Defective' Bewes, *Journal of the Royal Institute of International Affairs*, January 1929 'Good work . . . it is unfortunately necessary to draw attention to the tendency of the author to make depreciatory and often insulting remarks about public men and institutions, which certainly cheapens his book . . . still, I shall retain the volume in my library, and expect to consult it' *ibid*. 'A small man, slender, wiry, blond, keen-eyed and fine-boned . . . graceful movement of his hands' Cuneo, 'Of moles and men', 1981 'Maverick ways . . . the very model of eccentric creativity essential to any successful intelligence service' Stevenson, *Intrepid's Last Case*, 1983 'Worked alone in the field, dealing with agents from both sides [Nazi and Soviet] and reporting back to London' *ibid*. 'To reorganise the SIS network in the Far East' Andrew, *Intelligence and National Security*, 1989 'They're very good at duchessing you, the British Establishment . . . you've entered the magic circle, and after that you're frightened to say something that shows you don't belong inside the circle' Ellis in Stevenson, *Intrepid's Last Case*, 1983 'Never lived or worked in Paris from 1921 to 1940' Ross-Smith, *Daily Telegraph*, 9 May 1984 'The time has now come to consider the education of my own boy . . . a small prep school at Winchester' Letter, Ellis to Brotherston Emden, 13 March 1937 'He came late to English schooling and even to the language . . . he knows French and Russian well' *ibid*. 'Shortcomings' *ibid*. 'Mainly the knowledge of facts – he is quite erudite on continental affairs, but somewhat hazy about English kings and the exact geographical situation of say, Manchester' *ibid*. 'Using the cover of a journalist' Knightley film pitch, undated 'His assignment was to try to expose those members

of White Russians ... Ellis had managed to establish a spy link that led right to Hitler' *ibid*. 'Espionage network' *ibid*. 'Included that of a newspaper correspondent in Europe. Ellis cultivated both White Russian and German contacts' Stevenson, *Spymistress*, 2007 'Hard up' Hyde in Pincher note in the Chapman Pincher Papers, 24 October 1981 'The Germans would know anyway' Knightley film pitch, *op. cit*. 'Now the trap snapped shut' *ibid*.

Chapter 7   THE SPY FROM SANTIAGO

'No record whatsoever', 'The records of the Chilean Ministry of Foreign Affairs contain no information on the grant of a Chilean passport', 'There is therefore a strong presumption that PETROV is not a Chilean and that the passports were forged', 'Enemigo de Heydrich', '? ELLIS', 'Petrov admitted having visited Brussels in 1932/33 but he denied having bought any documents dealing with the British Secret Service from any Englishman in Brussels, and having sold such a document to the German counterintelligence ... [Von Petrov] denied having worked for the Germans and Russians', 'Zelenky [sic] was a great friend of Neporozny [sic] ... I do not know if a relation of his married an Englishman', 'Dancing master', '30 years ago', 'Swiss Jewess' All from Waldemar von Petrow files KV 2/3858, KV 2/3859 'After schooling led a quiet adult life as an industrial chemist in Paris, with no intelligence or political background' Ross-Smith, *Daily Telegraph*, London, 26 May 1984 'PETROFF, who is now furnished with a South American passport, is the son of a Czarist general who migrated to Japan ... is the only possible exchange mart' 'Interrogation Report No. 7 on Carl Marcus', undated, Carl Marcus file KV 2/964 'JAHNKE's principal agent in Western Europe and ... his main task was the penetration of French government circles ... the daughter of the diamond king, to establish contacts in British circles' 'Report on Interview with DICTIONARY on 21st July 1950', Carl Marcus file KV 2/965 'We believe [Von Petrov] to be married to, or at any rate living with the wife of Paul HARDT and both PETROV and his wife undoubtedly have information of very considerable counter-espionage interest' Waldemar von Petrow files KV 2/3858, KV 2/3859 'In the company of PETROFF in Germany before the war ... it seems likely that Lydia FASSNACHT may be identical with Lydia HARDT' Carl Marcus file KV 2/964 'Terrific snob' Cave Brown, C-SPAN, 1994 'All of exactly the same social grouping and age' *ibid*.

Chapter 8   THE GENERAL

'One of Ellis's key agents' Dorril, *MI6: Fifty Years of Special Operations*, 2000 'Had turned NTS into the most deadly weapon of Soviet espionage ... British intelligence had sold a communist net to the gullible Americans' Aarons and Loftus, *Unholy Trinity*, 1991 'One of his most trusted contacts' Albanese, 'In search of a lesser evil: anti-Soviet nationalism and the Cold War', August 2015 'Secured the support of Stewart Menzies, the chief of SIS' *ibid*. 'Ellis claimed that it was Menzies who ordered him to keep up Turkul's Nazi contacts in the first place' Aarons and Loftus, *Unholy Trinity*, 1991

Chapter 9   A DANGEROUS GAME

'The addresses of the operation, the safe houses, the floors on which each section worked, and the names of the heads and deputy heads of each section' Whitton, *Sydney Morning Herald*, 16 March 1985 'The exact hierarchical structure of the organisation and who occupied what post – knowledge that intelligence organisations prize because it helps them to identify their exact rivals but which, over the whole intelligence spectrum, is only of minor importance' Knightley, *The Second Oldest Profession*, 1986 'There was no official [MI6] liaison with [the Abwehr] in the late 1930s' Pincher note in the Chapman Pincher Papers, undated 'Made the point again and again in private conversation that "without aid from our friends inside the German Abwehr, we shouldn't have won the war quite so soon"' Deacon, 'C': A Biography of Sir Maurice Oldfield, Head of MI6, 1985 'Menzies was contemplating a dialogue with Canaris or those close to him with a view to ousting Hitler' Popov, Spy/Counterspy, 1974 'Today people are more careful, but in those days you didn't get a signed chit telling you to go ahead. After World War II there was a frightful tangle – everybody had been playing double agent, and German spies tried to prove their anti-communism through false accusations' Stephenson in Game, Herald, 22 October 1983 'A double-crossing lot of bastards who would sell intelligence to whoever would pay them' Pincher, Too Secret Too Long, 1984 'Only at the highest levels of the Secret Service would the truth be known and Ellis would have to depend on his chiefs to protect him if ever MI5 became suspicious of him' Knightley film pitch, op. cit. 'Secret Security Division of the Post Office' Hyde, Secret Intelligence Agent, 1982 'His own espionage service' Bryden, Fighting to Lose, 2014 'Operated within the main SIS establishment' Jeffery, MI6, 2010 'Its primary tasks were the penetration of Germany and Italy . . . agents were recruited mostly from the business, journalistic and academic world' ibid. 'Had created his own private clandestine industrial intelligence organisation, the services of which he offered to the British government' ibid. 'Traced the records of the prewar operation to tap the Hitler–Von Ribbentrop link. The officer in charge of processing the product was Ellis' Wright, Spycatcher, 1987 'Almost up to the outbreak of the war' Pincher, Their Trade is Treachery, 1981 'A list of the six translators of German who had been involved' Pincher, Too Secret Too Long, 1984 'The top name on the list was that of Captain C. H. Ellis' ibid. 'Suddenly abandoned the telephone link for no known reason' Pincher, Their Trade is Treachery, 1981 'Recorded that this Captain Ellis had warned the Germans, before the war, that the British were listening in' Pincher, Too Secret Too Long, 1984 'Senior secret service officers . . . denied that Ellis had ever been involved in the operation and insisted that there was no way he could possibly have known about it' Pincher, Their Trade is Treachery, 1981 'Satisfied that Ellis had been a spy for Germany, at least until the British were driven out of Europe in 1940' ibid. 'Decided to investigate the possibility that he had continued to spy for the Nazis afterward or had been recruited by the Russians' ibid. 'A more likely explanation is that Ribbentrop left London to become Reich Foreign Minister in March 1938 and the [telephone] link was no longer required' Hyde, Secret Intelligence Agent, 1982

Chapter 10   THE VENLO MYTH

'I met him about the end of '38 when I was engaged on some research work on German rearmament, and he was introduced to me by a Member of Parliament, Sir Ralph Glyn' 'A Man Called Intrepid: Sir William Stephenson', Canadian Broadcasting Corporation documentary, 1973 'Was engaged in a similar kind of activity in Scandinavia and Germany' ibid. 'Stephenson's cover story was that he had to go to Sweden on business. He had commercial interests there. The secondary cover, for intelligence types who needed to know his movements, was that he would destroy the source and the supply lines of iron ore which Germany's steel industries depended upon' Stevenson, A Man Called Intrepid, 1976 '[Stephenson] had been providing a great deal of information on German rearmament to Mr Churchill at that time he was not in office . . . that was the beginning, I think, of my official connection to him' 'A Man Called Intrepid: Sir William Stephenson', op. cit. 'All being done through his personal relationship with people like Mr Churchill, and Lord Leathers and others . . . I introduced him to my own channels, to heads of intelligence. And that led to his being asked if he was going to America . . . if he would do what he could to reestablish a link between security authorities here and the FBI' ibid. 'A brief spell in cable censorship' West, Historical Dictionary of British Intelligence, 2005

Chapter 11 THE BLACK BOOK

'After Dunkirk there was . . . a strong wave of pessimism regarding British chances of survival, much of which derived from official appraisal of logistic and other objective factors, but also from the defeatist attitude on the part of certain diplomatic representatives in London and Paris. We were, not unnaturally, disturbed by the extent and the comparatively unhindered scope of Axis intelligence and sabotage potential in the western hemisphere' Ellis, note to Whitney Shepardson, undated 'Old friend' 'A Man Called Intrepid: Sir William Stephenson', *op. cit.* 'Personal representative' Stevenson, *A Man Called Intrepid*, 1976 and Stevenson foreword to Hyde, *Secret Intelligence Agent*, 1982 'Unique special-intelligence organisation which I created and financed in the US to the extent of $3,000,000 and which operated throughout World War II, with headquarters in Rockefeller Center, New York' Stephenson foreword to Hyde, *Secret Intelligence Agent*, 1982 '[Stephenson] was Churchill's secret intelligence ambassador to President Roosevelt, who, no thanks to [United States ambassador] Joseph Kennedy in London, supported Churchill's view of Hitler even when Churchill himself was in the wilderness' Le Carré, *New York Times*, 29 February 1976 'Spread subversion and sabotage' Stevenson, *Intrepid's Last Case*, 1983 'Who knew where Stalin's physical weaknesses were to be found along the borders, starting from the first mission to Baku' *ibid.* 'Simply beyond British resources' *ibid.* 'Have leaked the Baku Project . . . to frighten Stalin into reducing aid to the Nazis. Such a leak could be made to seem sinister if there should be no paperwork proving official sanction' *ibid.* '[His] services [were] demanded from SIS as a *sine qua non* for his own acceptance of the PCO [Passport Control Officer] post' Troy, 'The Coordinator of Information and British Intelligence', 1974 'The most intricate integrated intelligence and secret-operations organisation in history' Ellis introduction to Stevenson, *A Man Called Intrepid*, 1976 'World War I combat hero and self-made Wall Street millionaire lawyer' Talbot, *The Devil's Chessboard*, 2015 'Quiet and urbane' Ellis, *The Two Bills: Mission Accomplished*, 1972 'Forceful' *ibid.* 'OSS's tutor and mentor' Waller, Britain's World War II intelligence network', 1999 'BSC inspired COI (later OSS) and Bill [Stephenson] talked Donovan into starting it' Letter, Ellis to Hyde, 17 August 1961

Chapter 12 OUR MAN IN NEW YORK

'Ran the organisation' Mahl, *Desperate Deception*, 1999 'To Washington to open a sub-station to facilitate daily liaison with Donovan, who reciprocated by sending [future Director of Central Intelligence, DCI] Allen Welsh Dulles to liaise with BSC in the Rockefeller Center' Aldrich, *Intelligence and the War Against Japan*, 2000 'Was the tradecraft expert, the organisation man, the one who furnished Bill Donovan with charts and memoranda on running an intelligence organisation' Troy, *Wild Bill and Intrepid*, 1996 'It's simply not true; [Fleming] had nothing to do with it' 'A Man Called Intrepid: Sir William Stephenson', *op. cit.* 'Gave no formal lectures but had many talks with individual officers of COI on work "in the field", the handling of agents, methods of reporting, etc . . . I spent some months in Washington in close liaison with D [Donovan] and members of his staff, and during this time was frequently called upon to advise on this or that "I" [intelligence] problem . . . I had frequent contact with D, both in his office and at his home in Washington' Ellis, note to Whitney Shepardson, undated 'It might explain why many OSS operations unravelled without apparent reason' Powers, *Intelligence Wars: American Secret History from Hitler to al-Qaeda*, 2002 'An associate of the MI6 cabal of Philby, Burgess and Maclean' De Toledano, *Insight on the News*, 15 April 2003 'OSS was set up for "Wild Bill" Donovan by Dickie Ellis, an MI6 official and member of the Philby gang, and the CIA was organised on a scheme by Philby himself' De Toledano, *Insight on the News*, 26 March 2001 'Without whose assistance . . .

American intelligence could not have gotten off the ground in World War II' Hursh, *The Old Boys*, 1992 'Remarkable, unpublicised individual' Bruce foreword to Hyde, *The Quiet Canadian*, 1962 'Helping him set up COI's Secret Intelligence branch' Lankford, *The Last American Aristocrat*, 1996 'The really active head of the intelligence section in [William] Donovan's [OSS] group is [Ellis] . . . in other words, [Stephenson's] assistant in the British intelligence [sic] is running Donovan's intelligence service' Mahl, *Desperate Deception*, 1999 'Intense personal ambition . . . bad strategist: crystallises opposition and underrates political enemies. Indiscreet. Inclination to flashy work' Ellis in McLachlan–Beesly Papers (Donald McLachlan and Patrick Beesly) at Churchill College, Cambridge, quoted in MacPherson, *American Intelligence in War-Time London*, 2003 'He was apt to call one at unusual hours to discuss organisation problems, projects or simply to exchange ideas. He liked one to argue with him, to submit ideas and schemes, to criticise and to comment freely. One had to be cautious in suggesting schemes, as he was apt to seize upon them at once and start the wheels rolling without sufficient preparation or study' Ellis, note to Whitney Shepardson, undated 'One of the most violent and prolonged interdepartmental battles in modern Washington history, as all the established intelligence departments in Washington closed rank and opposed both man and concept' Cave Brown, 'C': *The Secret Life of Sir Stewart Graham Menzies, Spymaster to Winston Churchill*, 1987 'All the senior representatives of the British secret services in the United States' *ibid*. 'Stephenson, [Rex] Benson, David Bowes-Lyon (brother of Queen Elizabeth and chief of the Political Warfare Executive), Colonel Ellis, and Professor J. W. Wheeler-Bennett of the New York office of PWE [Political Warfare Executive]. It was a war council the purpose of which was to establish a US secret service with Donovan as its chief' *ibid*. 'Was a major starting point of convoys heading across the Atlantic. Canadian intelligence on the identification and movement of known or suspected spies, saboteurs, and couriers, and disaffected workers, sailors, cargo handlers, and others was essential to the establishment of a pool of intelligence without which the security job could not be done' Troy, 'The Coordinator of Information and British Intelligence', Spring 1974 'In and out of Halifax' Ellis, *The Two Bills: Mission Accomplished*, 1972 'Had become a central point of enemy espionage' *ibid*. 'The largest state-sponsored influence campaign ever run on American soil' Hemming, *Our Man in New York*, 2019 'To do what he could of course to bring the United States in the war' 'A Man Called Intrepid: Sir William Stephenson', *op. cit*. 'On a mission for Churchill . . . to arouse the sentiment in the United States in favour of joining the Allies' *ibid*. '[Stephenson's] greatest achievement was through [Bill] Donovan, starting a very widespread campaign throughout the United States, through the press and by radio, drawing American attention to the dangers of a Nazi victory; the effects it would have on the United States' *ibid*. 'The charge that BSC endeavoured to involve the US in war was absurd. The President knew we would be forced to stop Hitler long before the British realised it . . . a "pilot" program was started in 1938 under Louis Johnson, Under Secretary of War, and 250 millions [sic] diverted from [Secretary of Commerce Harry] Hopkins's and [Secretary of the Interior Harold] Ickes's domestic programs to refitting of Army bases' Cuneo, 'Of moles and men', 1981 'The US commander-in-chief was deploying American sailors in the hope that they would be attacked, so that he could have a better chance of taking the country to war' Hemming, *op. cit*. 'As early as March 1941' *ibid*. 'Counterespionage measures before Pearl Harbor' Tendler, *Times*, 27 March 1981 'US case officer' Haufler, *The Spies Who Never Were*, 2006 'The whole thing doesn't make sense' Macdonald, *The True Intrepid*, 1998 'Swears, he did to me' *ibid*. 'He swears that they knew therefore of the oncoming attack' *ibid*. '[Stephenson] was convinced from the information that was reaching him that this attack was imminent, and through Jimmy Roosevelt, President Roosevelt's son, he passed this information to the President. Now whether the President at that time had other information which corroborated this ... it's impossible to say' 'A Man Called Intrepid: Sir William Stephenson', *op. cit.*

Chapter 13   A SLEDGEHAMMER IN SEARCH OF AN ANVIL

'Some useful lessons in counterespionage techniques as well as passing on important domestic security intelligence which they could not otherwise have obtained' Hyde, *Secret Intelligence Agent*, 1982 'In Popov's briefcase was a treasure trove worthy of an international spy' Loftis, *Into the Lion's Mouth*, 2016 'A German questionnaire with an English translation' *ibid.* 'A vial of white crystals for making secret ink' *ibid.* 'Forty per cent of [the document] pertains to investigation of Pearl Harbor's defences' Loftis press release, '75 years after "the date which will live in infamy", declassified files reveal FBI director Hoover was warned of the Pearl Harbor attack in August 1941, new book shows', 16 November 2016 'Naval and military commanders took no emergency defence measures against a possible attack on the naval base, so that the Japanese air attack came as a complete surprise' Ellis, *The Two Bills: Mission Accomplished*, 1972 'The tragic losses of men and ships occasioned by the attack, while temporarily weakening the US Navy in the Pacific and opening the way for Japanese naval action against the Philippines and Pacific island bases, shocked the American public into a sense of reality ... the attack on Pearl Harbor unified the nation' *ibid.*

Chapter 14   LITTLE WINDOW

'Coordinate plans for handling security and intelligence in the western hemisphere' Hyde, *Secret Intelligence Agent*, 1982 'The cessation of BSC's independent activities within US territory' *ibid.* 'Our primary directive from the PM [Winston Churchill] is that American participation in the war is the most important single objective for Britain. It is the only way, he feels, to victory over Nazism' Ellis in Downes, *The Scarlet Thread*, 1959 'It was clear from the outset that [Adolf] Berle's principal target was BSC, whose activities he plainly resented' Hyde, *Secret Intelligence Agent*, 1982 'The State and Justice Departments wanted BSC closed down in general and the departure of Col. Ellis in particular. The cause of their animus was pure, but not simple. It was bureaucratic opposition to the establishment of the new OSS' Cuneo, 'Of moles and men', 1981 'For the purpose of intelligence liaison with the Americans' Entry for 24 April 1942, *The Guy Liddell Diaries: MI5's Director of Counter-Espionage in World War II, Volume I: 1939–42*, 2005 'Next to [them, Ellis] was perhaps the person most intimately involved in the events of 1940–41' Troy, 'Report on interviews with Sir William S. Stephenson in Paget, Bermuda', 1969 'Throughout the Pearl Harbor period and until the beginning of 1943, except for a brief mission to Cairo in the spring of 1942, Ellis was at the centre of Donovan's affairs ... he was consulted on the nature of Donovan's contacts with the enemy services' Cave Brown, '*C*': *The Secret Life of Sir Stewart Graham Menzies, Spymaster to Winston Churchill*, 1987 'Stephenson's deputy, the SIS career officer Colonel Charles H. Ellis, was sitting with Hoover and Donovan, and reporting regularly to the President' Irving, *Churchill's War*, 1988 'BSC was the only [organisation] in existence until [the] CIA came into existence after the war which represented all aspects of [a special operations, security and intelligence] operation ... [BSC] laid the groundwork of [the CIA]' 'A Man Called Intrepid: Sir William Stephenson', *op. cit.* 'Secret-service training centre' Aldrich, *Intelligence and the War Against Japan*, 2000 'Full-scale adoption by the OSS of British training methods' Stafford, *Camp X: Canada's School for Secret Agents 1941–45*, 1986 'Combined intelligence and "special operations" training school' Ellis, *The Two Bills: Mission Accomplished*, 1972 'A highly specialised type of training in which unarmed combat, the use of explosives, sabotage methods, radio communication and all the subtleties of infiltration and guerrilla operations were combined with the utilisation of newly developed technical devices' *ibid*. 'Because Camp X was so secure, any fate could befall an inmate without public notice . . . I could only say, "Sorry, we seem to have 'lost' the chap." We had disposed of the body under the protection of the Crown, to use the SIS phrase' Ellis in Stevenson, *Intrepid's Last Case*, 1983 'Uncovered one of the great spies of all time, Harry Dexter White, then virtually in command of the US Treasury, compared with whom Philby was small fry' Cuneo in Stevenson, *Intrepid's Last Case*, 1983 'Amassed one of the most brilliant records in the long history of British intelligence' Cuneo, 'Of moles and men', 1981 'To believe that, throughout these years, Dickie Ellis was a Soviet mole . . . he would have reported the British mole in the Kremlin to his true masters. He had not' Cuneo, 'Britain's mentor of the OSS: Was he a "mole" for the KGB?', 4 October 1981 'At least 12 Soviet sympathisers inside BSC' Pincher, *Too Secret Too Long*, 1984 'Decipherment' *ibid*. 'KGB messages transmitted from New York to Moscow' *ibid*. 'A few, like Cedric Belfrage . . . were identified but most of them remain known only by the codenames used in the traffic. The Committee therefore concentrated on the possibility that Ellis was one of the unknown agents having, perhaps, been pressed into KGB service, through blackmail or money, after 1940' *ibid*. 'It is unclear from the MI5 file whether Belfrage had already been a Soviet agent or was spotted and recruited after he joined BSC. However the file contains detailed accounts of the kind of services Belfrage rendered to Moscow . . . Belfrage is known to have supplied [Jacob] Golos [a Soviet master spy in North America] . . . with a report apparently emanating from Scotland Yard which was a treatise on espionage agents' Sputnik News Service, 'The Cambridge Six: MI5 confirms the name of another top Soviet spy', 20 August 2015 'As far as I was concerned [Belfrage] was simply a normal one of the old chaps' Macdonald, *The True Intrepid*, 1998 'He had definitely passed secrets to the Soviets . . . the evidence indicates that he was a double agent working for British intelligence' Simkin, 'The problems of appearing in a BBC documentary', spartacus-educational.com, 17 September 2015 'Charge laid afterwards against Ellis . . . was quite ridiculous' *ibid*. 'Quite mad' Winks, *Cloak and Gown*, 1987

Chapter 15 PHILBY'S BLANK

'Field officer in charge of South-East Asia and the Far East' Hyde, *Secret Intelligence Agent*, 1982 'Singapore, Batavia, Honor [sic], Hong Kong, Nanking. SIS plans also to open stations in Shanghai, Tientsin, Bangkok, Seoul and Tokyo' Philby, 'The Structure of SIS' in West and Tsarev, *TRIPLEX*, 2009 All Protze quotes KV 2/1740, KV 2/1741

Chapter 16 THE CLOUDS ARE PARTING

'Lobby . . . for the creation of an Australian base for SIS "special operations" in the Far East' Andrew, 'The evolution of Australian intelligence', 1988 'Special adviser' Toohey, *National Times*, 15–21 March 1981 'He remembered Ellis "very well, of course" but had no view on the allegations about him. A "dear little man", his wife chipped in, "loved his food", especially Vichyssoise in a dinner they had shared in New York' Bennett, 'In the shadows', 2006 'Ellis's sudden departure for Australia on the grounds of nonexistent heart trouble in 1953 immediately appeared to have an explanation . . . a suspected spy cannot be extradited for offences under the Official Secrets Act' Pincher, *Too Secret Too Long*, 1984 'When we came out in 1953, he was so proud showing me around. His home, his school, his father's grave' Ann Salwey in Game, *Herald*, 22 October 1983 'As a link between the Australian Secret Intelligence Service . . . and London following his retirement from MI6' West, *A Matter of Trust: MI5 1945–72*, 1982 'Supported the suspicion that Ellis had been a

KGB agent' Pincher, *Too Secret Too Long*, 1984 'As against that, if Ellis really had been a Soviet agent, Moscow would have known quite early about Petrov's dealings with the Australian security [sic] and would hardly have allowed him to run free' Gelber, 'The hunt for spies: another inside story', April 1989 'The allegations linking Ellis's arrival in Australia and return to Britain have already been shown to have been impossible to reconcile with the timing of Petrov's defection' Watt, 'Fall-out [sic] from treachery: Peter Wright and the *Spycatcher* case', April 1988 'Petrov might blow his [Philby's] cover' McAdam, *Sunday Telegraph*, 14 December 1986 'Such a serious error calls into question the accuracy of other parts of Pincher's books. If, after all, he can be so wrong on a demonstrable point of fact, a fact he could easily have checked with me and a fact on which he seems to place such weight, one has to wonder what weight to place on his speculations which cannot be objectively established' *ibid*. 'Ellis was the conduit through whom the Soviet KGB "reactivated their most valuable asset", Kim Philby' Bennett, 'In the shadows', 2006 'The authors have unfortunately gone along with the story that a certain Dick Ellis, an Australian expatriate, who had served for many years with the British SIS and who had a lot to do with the foundation of ASIS, was a Nazi spy and then a long-time Soviet mole. The prime advocates of this theory are Peter Wright and his loony MI5 right-wing clique together with their mouthpiece, the journalist Chapman Pincher. For Toohey and Pinwill to depend upon this *galère* is as bizarre as Noam Chomsky embracing Lyndon Baines Johnson' Hall, *Sydney Morning Herald*, Sydney, 29 July 1989 'He was placed under surveillance by the Special Branch of Scotland Yard, including telephone taps, to prevent him from trying to defect' Polmar and Allen, *Spy Book: The Encyclopedia of Espionage*, 1997

Chapter 17   CRYING TOWEL

'Sacked by a reluctant MI6' Wright, *Spycatcher*, 1987 'Confessed to a colleague before vanishing into the Soviet Union. Someone had warned him that the game was up – and Ellis's accusers said it was Ellis' Stevenson, *Intrepid's Last Case*, 1983 'Bill's criticism, as far as I can make out (he has said little in his letters) is that I have pulled my punches too much, my style is too dry, and I do not bring the story to life sufficiently to make a saleable book. I seemed to be too inhibited by former association with a certain "Firm" to let myself go . . . [Stephenson] considers that after 20 years we can let our hair down about SO [Special Operations], PWE [Political Warfare Executive], Security Executive and other ops in the Carib[bean], SA [South America] and elsewhere, without restraint. (I'm not so sure, but that may be – as he thinks – because I spent 32 years keeping my mouth shut!)' Letter, Ellis to Hyde, 10 December 1960 'I told [Ellis] that I frankly thought his story read too much like an office report. He quite agreed . . . I never think that (with rare exceptions) books written in double harness work out well. At the same time I have no doubt that [Ellis] has put in some useful spadework, and in view of this I hope he can be taken care of in some mutually satisfactory way, as I should not like him to feel sore or that his efforts have not been appreciated' Letter, Hyde to Stephenson, 4 December 1960 'Ellis certainly thought there was an understanding on reimbursement, but he would soon be complaining about Stephenson's failure to pay up, even to answer his letters' Troy, *Wild Bill and Intrepid*, 1996 'Misunderstood what was expected of him' Naftali, 'Intrepid's last deception: documenting the career of Sir William Stephenson', 1994 'Stephenson was not going to pay for a faithful bureaucratic history. Ellis refused, for example, to accept his former boss's claim that he had initiated the intelligence liaison between Washington and London, a link which Ellis, a career British intelligence officer, knew to have predated Stephenson's arrival in New York in 1940. Stephenson had no patience with this quibbling. He wanted a bestselling biography of himself' *ibid*. 'Anti-Soviet' Pearce in Pincher note in Chapman Pincher Papers, undated 'I have been called back to HO on a full-time basis in connexion with the reorganisation following recent incidents and some expansion due to the impending Berlin crisis, and troubles in Africa, Mid-East and elsewhere' Letter, Ellis to Hyde, 20 July 1961 'Unnecessary Registry files' West, *MI6*, 1983 'Clearly, Ellis had extraordinary freedom. He was being left alone with super-secret files, entrusted with the task of "arranging" them for future historians' Stevenson, *Intrepid's Last Case*, 1983 'Ultra-sensitive job' Ross-Smith, *Daily Telegraph*, 2 May 1983 'This work was highly confidential and it is inconceivable that he should have been entrusted with it if he were officially regarded as being, or as having been, a traitor to his country. It was nothing less than going through the SIS files and weeding out those which he did not consider worth preserving' Hyde, *Secret Intelligence Agent*, 1982 'Ellis was recruited by SIS's Colin Gubbins to purge British intelligence files, presumably of any other embarrassing evidence. As we shall see, there was quite a bit to be put into the shredder' Aarons and Loftus, *Unholy Trinity*, 1991 'I saw a handwritten letter from him to a friend in which [Ellis] had boasted of inserting documents into some MI6 files' Pincher, *Daily Mail*, 11 November 1981 'A loan during his retirement' Tendler, *Times*, 30 March 1981 'Failed biographer' Naftali, *op. cit.* 'Used Hyde as a crying towel' Troy, *Wild Bill and Intrepid*, 1996 'Ellis . . . in Stephenson historiography is a pathetic figure but who is much worse if he were guilty of that alleged Nazi–Soviet service . . . in his second effort he forthrightly said Churchill sent his "close friend" Stephenson to New York and again said nothing about Ultra or Heydrich. Neither effort, however, ever saw daylight' *ibid.* 'Each time he attempted to publicise the war work of William Stephenson, it didn't add to his job security. Ironically, if Ellis's imposed unemployment was meant as a punishment for selling out to the "enemy", it seemed to make him more dependent monetarily on others. Ellis went to Stephenson for financial assistance, and when Ellis died he owed Stephenson a large amount of money' Macdonald, *The True Intrepid*, 1998 'In coverage, detail, and style it was not much better than his earlier venture . . . Sir William reached agreement with Stevenson and Ellis in March 1973 that Ellis would once again play second fiddle, this time to Stevenson, who would take over *The Two Bills*' Troy, *Wild Bill and Intrepid*, 1996

Chapter 18 NAILING ELLIS

'She too picked out Ellis's photograph but refused to say why' Wright, *Spycatcher*, 1987 'She recalled . . . a meeting on a street corner in London. She and Rickie [Sorge] had gone together to meet this agent, but he had told her to stand well back and cover him in case there was trouble . . . she had seen him, but not well. [The officer] showed her the photographs. "This man looks familiar," she said, "but I could not be certain, after over 40 years." It was Ellis's photograph' *ibid.* 'Was in receipt of an MI6 pension' Pincher, *Their Trade is Treachery*, 1981 'Ellis explained that he had run into debt because his British pay was too low and had borrowed from Zilenski [sic], who then started pressurising [sic] him for information to sell to the Germans and Russians . . . he refused to believe that immunity would really be granted and held to his position regarding any Russian espionage after 1940' *ibid.* 'Resolutely denied' Pincher, *Traitors*, 1987 'We wanted to know about his involvement with the Soviets, we said . . . I have little doubt of Ellis's involvement with the Russians' Wright, *Spycatcher*, 1987 'There was no firm evidence against him, nor were there any witnesses' Pincher, *Traitors*, 1987 'Was broken' *ibid.* 'Was endorsed without reservation by [MI6 director of counterintelligence and security] Christopher Phillpotts, and submitted to [head of MI6] Dick White and his deputy, Maurice Oldfield' Wright, *Spycatcher*, 1987 'At first . . . doubted the veracity of Ellis's confession, until eventually Bunny Pancheff [sic] played the crucial exchanges to him . . . the fact that Ellis had confessed seemed to weigh hardly at all on his thinking. As far as he was concerned, it was all a long time ago, and best forgotten' *ibid*. 'Maurice was aggrieved at what he described as Phillpotts's "Gestapo methods" in extracting what was in his view a dubious confession from his friend, and subjected his rival to a reprimand' Pearce, *Spymaster*, 2016 'Child's play' Stephenson in Game, *Herald*, 22 October 1983 'Resurrected to show the extent of Soviet penetration of Britain' Knightley, *The Second Oldest Profession*, 1986

Chapter 19   AMONG THE DRIPPING SHRUBS

'Central focus was to increase the level of understanding of communist doctrine and practice by stimulating and making available well-researched information on the policies and realities of the Soviet bloc' Scott-Smith, 'Confronting peaceful co-existence: psychological warfare and the role of Interdoc, 1963–72', 2007 'Remained Interdoc's "desk officer" in the UK until retiring due to ill-health in 1969' *ibid*. 'Specialised in distributing accurate versions of communist-inspired news reports' Stevenson, *Intrepid's Last Case*, 1983 'Depended largely on West German subsidies' Crozier, *Free Agent*, 1993 'How he had been approached by an officer from MI6 because he was believed to have recommended Ellis for a retirement post in Interdoc . . . the person was as surprised as any of Ellis's friends and relatives to be told that the Colonel had confessed to spying for Germany and had then almost certainly switched his espionage activities to the Soviet interest under blackmail pressure' Pincher, *Times*, 6 May 1981 'In the picturesque setting of Mont Saint-Michel, in the late spring of 1962' Crozier, *Free Agent*, 1993 'In the background as part of the network, continuing with translation work and information gathering as health permitted, and was even asked by the CIA to write "a confidential history of the early days of OSS"' Scott-Smith, *Western Anti-Communism and the Interdoc Network*, 2011 'Gaunt, conspiratorial' Leigh, *The Wilson Plot*, 1988 'That the CIA was penetrated by a high-level "mole" – a view echoed in Britain, of course, by the receptive Peter Wright' *ibid*. 'Joint investigations by the FBI and the CIA on the lines of Wright's British Fluency Committee, found evidence of none' *ibid*. 'Vast KGB deception' Andrew, *The Defence of the Realm*, 2009 'A dicky heart' Stevenson, *Intrepid's Last Case*, 1983 'Arthritis in his hands compelled him to give up playing' Obituary by the *Times*, 16 July 1975 'A civil servant so umbrous that his name was never publicly mentioned' no byline, *Time*, 6 April 1981 'The idea of him defecting is ludicrous. He visited Australia months before his death because he wanted to see it all again. He cried because it had changed' Ann Salwey in Game, *Herald*, 22 October 1983 'First meeting' Cavendish, *Daily Telegraph*, 3 May 1984 'Did not take this [meeting with Pincher] as an opportunity to confirm Dick Ellis's treachery, in which he did not believe' *ibid*. 'Distressed to learn that Mr Pincher is in the process of developing further allegations against Ellis' *ibid*. 'Most' Pincher, *Traitors*, 1987 'Have finally been convinced by the evidence . . . Nicholas Elliott, who knew about Ellis's guilt, admonished Oldfield – the latter perhaps appreciating the delicacy of his own secret homosexuality' *ibid*. 'Pincher claims he was responsible for exposing Dick Ellis as a traitor and for initiating the claim that [Roger] Hollis was a Russian spy. I knew both these gentlemen and no proof has ever been produced that Ellis was a traitor. The same is true of Hollis' Cavendish, *Sunday Times*, 17 May 1987 'A number of senior officers' Ann Salwey in Tendler, *Times*, 30 March 1981 'They were secret service men from MI6, there to honour their friend and colleague, and to comfort his son, Peter, and daughter, Ann' Game, *Herald*, 22 October 1983 'If you need help, call me' *ibid*.

Chapter 20   A BREAK IN THE SILENCE

'There is reason to doubt that Ellis wrote the foreword attributed to him. Hyde believed that Ellis had not been in any shape to write it' Naftali, *op. cit*. 'Brass nerve'

Pincher, *Their Trade is Treachery*, 1981 'An old man living, apparently, in honourable retirement in Eastbourne in Sussex' *ibid.* 'Impudence . . . to write a "historical note" extolling the virtues of secrecy' Pincher, *Traitors*, 1987 'Wright's home proved to be a wooden shack made from two apple-pickers' huts set in a former apple orchard, and I could see how, remote from the exciting life that he had formerly led, he had stewed there in the sticks on a miserable pension, while sitting on information that he knew to be eminently saleable. For nine days, I listened in wonder and made copious notes, while he poured out the MI5's [sic] most sacred secrets' Pincher, '*Their Trade is Treachery*: a retrospective', 2013 'Wrote the book rapidly, checking facts with other sources when I could, hopefully, without arousing suspicion. I finished the book in less than four months' *ibid.* 'Major new spies' *ibid.* 'Which has been so carefully concealed for political purposes that even former Secret Servicemen will be astonished by what I have to tell' Pincher, *Daily Mail*, 26 March 1981 'Hushed' Associated Press, *Globe and Mail*, 27 March 1981 'I am very sorry for the distress that you are suffering on account of the reference to your father in Chapman Pincher's book and I deplore as strongly as you do his attacks on the memories of those who are no longer living and cannot defend themselves . . . I cannot make an exception in one case without being pressed to make it in others as well and that, I fear, would do more harm than good' Hyde, *Secret Intelligence Agent*, 1982 '[Thatcher] and her advisers were looking for ways of discrediting my book. She was unable to do so' Contained in McDonald, 'Treason of British spy has serious effects on American intelligence', House of Representatives, 26 April 1983 'The Prime Minister had been advised to avoid the Ellis case because the details were so accurate that confirmation of it would have made it difficult for her parliamentary statement to cast any doubt on my sources concerning the case of Sir Roger Hollis' Pincher, *Too Secret Too Long*, 1984 'The fact that the pre-war MI6 "order of battle" was betrayed to the Germans is beyond dispute. I have in my possession a number of Abwehr documents which faithfully describe MI6's internal structure and I have published a selection in my history of the security service. Confirmation that Ellis was the original source of this material can only come from the Prime Minister, who has already declined to comment' McDonald, *op. cit.* 'Not only the most famous journalist in Britain but also a very wealthy man' Cram, 'A review of counterintelligence literature 1975–1992', 1992 'I didn't see any point in hanging on to honours when my father's honour had been taken from him without any hope of redress' Ann Salwey in Game, *Herald*, 22 October 1983 'Many photos and letters that will support the fact that my father was completely honourable' Hughes, *Far Eastern Economic Review*, 17 November 1983 'Believed, on good authority, to have worked for the Russians' Blaxland and Crawley, *The Secret Cold War*, 2018 'This view is in fact accepted by the United Kingdom Services' *ibid.* 'Inquiries are now in progress in the United States concerning Ellis's activities there while working under Sir William Stephenson. Meanwhile, FBI documents in my possession show that American counterintelligence was actively interested in Ellis as early as 1953. Essential parts of these documents were blacked out at the request of British intelligence when they were released under the US Freedom of Information Act in July 1981 – three months after the appearance of my book' Pincher, *Sydney Morning Herald*, 10 February 1983 'Caused deep repercussions in the United States, particularly among the veterans of the Office of Strategic Services' Cuneo, 'Of moles and men', 1981 'Caused Great Britain and the United States immeasurable damage, to say nothing of the loss of many, many lives . . . the charges against Col. Ellis, if true, could mean that the communications of the OSS were vulnerable and possibly compromised from birth' *ibid.* 'Terribly shocked' Letter, Hyde to Pincher, 26 March 1981 'Changed his view about Ellis' Pincher, note in Chapman Pincher Papers, 24 October 1981 'Will alter his new book accordingly' *ibid.* 'I felt obliged to defend him. I asked Stephenson if

Ellis was a spy, and he said, no, he wasn't, but I'm beginning to have doubts now' no byline, *Sydney Morning Herald*, Sydney, 15 February 1983 'The Sydney suburb of Annandale has no particular claim to fame. It has a number of interesting surviving 19th-century houses and Sir Henry Parkes died there. Can it now claim the distinction of being the birthplace of the most accomplished spy against the British ever, a man who in 30 years of working for both Nazi Germany and Soviet Russia, delivered the secrets of Britain's MI6 and could be said to have out-Philbied Philby?' Hall, *Sydney Morning Herald*, 5 February 1983 'Now convinced that Ellis was a spy' Pincher, note in Chapman Pincher Papers, 22 September 1981 'Tacitly acknowledges problems about Ellis but can't yet bring himself to go back, publicly, on his loyalty' Letter, Stevenson to Pincher, 15 October 1981 'Agreed that he could be wrong about Ellis' Pincher, note in Chapman Pincher Papers, 26 December 1981 'Engrossing but rather muddled' Atkins, *Daily Telegraph*, 4 May 1984 'Sorry volume, which is even less substantial than its predecessor . . . virtually no evidence is produced by this volume to prove anything, one way or the other; it is best placed on the shelf along with spy fiction' Stafford, *Globe and Mail*, 26 November 1983 'Imagine [Stevenson's] consternation when, during the claims and counter-claims that erupted three years ago about Soviet penetration of MI5, Ellis was named as a long-time Soviet (and also German) agent. Had Intrepid, superspy, been duped? Had the author failed to unearth a terrible secret within the bosom of the enterprise itself?' *ibid.* 'It is understandable and even honourable for the author to attempt this, but he cannot possibly establish adequate critical objectivity here. For what it's worth, I find his "refutation" of the charges against Col. Ellis full of special pleading, inconsistent and plain unconvincing. In contrast, I find London journalist Chapman Pincher's account of Col. Ellis's career, in his book *Their Trade is Treachery*, logically compelling and morally convincing' Arnold, *Wall Street Journal*, 25 January 1984 '[The book's] real purpose is to acquit one of Stephenson's deputies of charges that he was "ELLI" . . . they are to be thought of as expressing not logical concerns, but psychological ones: egotism in the first instance, fear of conspiracy in the second. Their true subject is not intelligence. It is megalomania and paranoia' Kahn, *Washington Post*, 5 February 1984 'The primary purpose of *Intrepid's Last Case* is to clear the late Col. Charles H. Ellis, Intrepid's wartime aide, of recent allegations that he had been a mole for both Germany and the Soviet Union . . . the issues involving Colonel Ellis are important ones, but Mr Stevenson and his patron are not the ones to deal with them' Bamford, *New York Times*, 22 January 1984 'About half the security people I talked to are convinced he was [a traitor], and the other half think he wasn't. I've concluded he was maligned deliberately to take the heat off other people' Stephenson in French, *Globe and Mail*, 6 September 1983 'Dick Ellis was not a traitor or a mole, or a double or a triple agent – just a patriot doing his proper job. He was a man of integrity and dedication. I knew a lot of Australians and I can tell you that Dick was a damn good one – absolutely first rate. You can be proud of him. Your prime minister should demand from London either a taped or a written and signed confession. If one or the other is not forthcoming, your PM should publicly exonerate Ellis as a victim of KGB disinformation. A confession has never been produced. I know Dick Ellis's voice; I know his handwriting. If a confession exists – which I doubt – I could tell whether it was genuine . . . Dick was the best man MI6 had' Stephenson in Game, *Herald*, 22 October 1983 'Little Bill [Stephenson] . . . is coming around to the idea that Dick Ellis did make a confession but he wishes to be satisfied that Ellis was not in communication with the Germans after the formation of the British BSC' Letter, Hyde to Pincher, 25 May 1984 'Said that if he can be satisfied that there is no hard evidence that Ellis spied while in BSC then that is an end of his interest in the matter' Letter, Pincher to Hyde, 15 June 1984 '[Hollis] was a double agent. What happened was that Guy Liddell, who was by far the best man in MI5, told me Hollis was not to be trusted because of his "anti-Americanism". I took it as meaning there was something far more sinister about Hollis than his merely being anti-American. As I later discovered, Hollis was already working for the Soviets at that time' Hodgson, United Press International, 27 July 1987 'Stephenson said he later prevented Hollis from coming in contact with Igor Gouzenko, a file clerk at the Soviet Embassy in Ottawa who defected to the Canadians in 1945 and revealed that communist agents had penetrated MI5. "I had him sent back across the Atlantic on the same US Air Force bomber he had arrived on. Hollis is one case where Peter Wright's criticisms are justified. He was a bad egg if ever there was one"' ibid. 'It is easy to dismiss the book for it is obviously hurriedly assembled and is full of errors of fact and interpretation; it is badly structured, full of grammatical errors and poorly indexed . . . while much attention in the press has been devoted to the question of whether or not Sir Roger Hollis was a Soviet agent, few commentators have noticed the far more important revelations made about Charles "Dickie" Ellis, an MI6 officer who admitted passing information to the Germans during the Second World War and who is generally assumed to have worked also for the Russians' Lownie, Times, 25 July 1987 'The most damaging conspiracy theorists in the history of the Security Service' Andrew, The Defence of the Realm, 2009 'Began to descend into his conspiratorial wilderness of mirrors' ibid. 'It was banned in Britain but the incredible circus trial in Australia prevented its being banned there. The result, however, was to send sales of this otherwise ordinary book skyrocketing to bestseller levels all around the world and overnight made Wright a multimillionaire' Cram, 'A review of counterintelligence literature 1975–1992', 1992

Epilogue   THE ELLIS IDENTITY
'The melodrama of spy and counterspy' Schlesinger Jr, Wall Street Journal, 31 March 1987 'If only to give the lie to all the accusations made against him by Pincher et al' Letter, Olik Ellis to Stafford, 21 August 1988 'So as to avoid raising another spate of public correspondence by those authors who have caused nothing but pain to my sister and me, not to mention others who knew my father whose loyalty to the Western cause was unfailing' ibid. 'If [Ellis] had told his *own* story of his experience in BSC, it would have been quite a different matter. But he so carefully keeps himself out of [the manuscript] that there is very little, if anything, that is not already known' Letter, Stafford to Olik Ellis, 19 September 1988 'What the hell! If the guy was doing me and my country in, would he leave her in my custody? This business grieves me because I think he did a hell of a lot for his country and mine' Cuneo in Game, Herald, 22 October 1983 'Professionally damaging and many people had noticed them . . . it gives me no pleasure to attack dead people' Letter, Pincher to Hyde, 18 May 1984 'To get Ross-Smith to lay off' Letter, Hyde to Pincher, 17 May 1984 'Bill Ross-Smith's great achievement was to recruit and operate the activities of several hundred secret agents on neutral ships trading between America, north and south, and other parts of the world, including Spain, Portugal and Japan . . . in 1942, after Pearl Harbor, the ships' observers organisation was handed over to US Naval Intelligence' Hyde, Secret Intelligence Agent, 1982 'Travesty of the truth . . . an unwarranted attack impugning the honour and integrity of a defenceless dead man' Ross-Smith, Sydney Morning Herald, 2 February 1983 'If Ellis had been working for Germany, he would, undoubtedly, have apprised Berlin that their Enigma codes were being broken and that Popov was really a British agent' Ross-Smith, Sydney Morning Herald, 21 February 1983 'The incident [of Ellis selling secrets to the Nazis] predated Ellis's knowledge of both ULTRA and TRICYCLE . . . Ellis steadfastly denied any repetition [of his gaffe] . . . [Ellis] insisted he had not been a long-term source for either the Abwehr or the Russians' West, Daily Telegraph, 13 April 1983 'From my careful investigations I am satisfied that at one time Ellis was a German

spy' West in Rais, *Daily Telegraph*, 13 April 1983 'There was never any suggestion that Ellis passed information to the Germans other than the time he was in Paris' *ibid*. 'There is only minimal, circumstantial evidence to support the contention that Ellis was ever a Soviet agent' West, *Daily Telegraph*, 4 May 1984 'Is it not odd that none of those [high-ranking officers of the secret services] who were serving at the time of Ellis's abject confession to having spied for the Abwehr and knew the facts has defended him?' Pincher, *Daily Telegraph*, 17 May 1984 'Character assassination' Ross-Smith, *Daily Telegraph*, 2 May 1983 'One iota of evidence or one witness to support their charges' *ibid*. 'Why would he have been appointed chief of SIS for Far East and Asia' *ibid*. 'Be seconded to assist setting up the Australian SIS' *ibid*. 'Ellis worked in England for the years preceding the war and had no untoward financial problems and no expensive tastes or hobbies' *ibid*. 'Pal' *ibid*. 'Beneath contempt . . . he was no pal of Philby and scarcely knew him' *ibid*. 'Ellis entrusted with secrets' *ibid*. 'Mr Ross-Smith's challenge that I must produce secret documents and tape-recordings out of MI5's registry is ludicrous . . . as with the Ellis files they are far too embarrassing to the departments which the spies penetrated' McDonald, *op. cit.* 'Mr Ross-Smith implied in the letter that my information was at fault but when Sir Michael Havers, the Attorney-General, applied for an injunction in the High Court last October to prevent publication of my book [*A Matter of Trust: MI5 1945–72*], he swore an affidavit that its contents, including the account of the Ellis affair, contained hitherto unpublished classified information' *ibid*. 'My view on the man would be sulphuric. The stuff he produced on the intelligence services was almost totally inaccurate' Foot, *Telegraph*, 6 August 2014 'He might have been short, but he was bright, full of enthusiasm, energetic, very talkative on every subject under the sun. He also wept easily about his experiences in the trenches in France, about Mozart, about Dickens and Shakespeare, whom he quoted at length – and, believe it or not, Australia. He loved it' Ann Salwey in Game, *Herald*, 22 October 1983

BIBLIOGRAPHY

Researching *The Eagle in the Mirror* was just like Thomas F. Troy had said: a sentence here, a paragraph there. It was an exceedingly difficult and time-consuming exercise. Readers are welcome to point out any errors or omissions by contacting me through my official website or my Facebook, Twitter, LinkedIn and Instagram accounts. Similarly, if you know anything about Charles Howard 'Dick' Ellis and his family that I don't know, or there's something I've overlooked, please get in touch. –JF

Archives/Libraries/Historical Societies
Australia
Caulfield Grammar School, Melbourne
Glen Eira Historical Society, Melbourne
Inner West Council, Sydney
National Archives of Australia, Canberra
National Library of Australia, Canberra
State Library of New South Wales, Sydney

Canada
Dr. John Archer Library, University of Regina, Regina
Library and Archives Canada, Ottawa
McPherson Library, University of Victoria, Victoria

India
National Archives of India, New Delhi

Thailand
Neilson Hays Library, Bangkok

United Kingdom
Churchill Archives Centre, Cambridge
Imperial War Museum, London
King's College, London
National Archives, London
National Library of Scotland, Edinburgh
Royal Geographical Society, London
Royal Society for Asian Affairs, Haileybury
St Edmund Hall Archive, Oxford

United States
Central Intelligence Agency, Washington DC
Federal Bureau of Investigation, Washington DC
Franklin D. Roosevelt Presidential Library & Museum, Hyde Park (NY)
National Archives and Records Administration, College Park (MD)

Books/Manuscripts/Monographs/Pamphlets

A Bigger Picture, Malcolm Turnbull, Hardie Grant Books, Melbourne, 2020

A Death in Washington: Walter G. Krivitsky and the Stalin Terror, Gary Kern, Enigma Books, New York, 2004

Alexander Orlov: The FBI's KGB General, Edward Gazur, Carroll & Graf, New York, 2002

A Man Called Intrepid: The Secret War, The Authentic Account of the Most Significant Secret Diplomacy and Decisive Intelligence Operations of World War II, William Stevenson, Harcourt Brace Jovanovich, New York, 1976

American Intelligence in War-Time London: The Story of the OSS, Nelson MacPherson, Frank Cass Publishers, London, 2003

A Matter of Trust: MI5 1945–72, Nigel West, Weidenfeld & Nicolson, London, 1982 (published in the United States as *The Circus: MI5 Operations 1945–1972*)

An Impeccable Spy: Richard Sorge, Stalin's Master Agent, Owen Matthews, Bloomsbury Publishing, London, 2019

The Art of Betrayal: Life and Death in the British Secret Service, Gordon Corera, Weidenfeld & Nicolson, London, 2011

A Spy's Revenge, Richard V. Hall, Penguin Books Australia, Melbourne, 1987

A Spy Among Friends: Kim Philby and the Great Betrayal, Ben Macintyre, Bloomsbury Publishing, London, 2014

At Her Majesty's Secret Service: The Chiefs of Britain's Intelligence Agency, MI6, Nigel West, Greenhill Books, London, 2006

Australia's First Spies: The Remarkable Story of Australia's Intelligence Operations, 1901–45, John Fahey, Allen & Unwin, Sydney, 2018

A Web of Deception: The Spycatcher Affair, Chapman Pincher, Sidgwick & Jackson, London, 1987

The Bedbug: Klop Ustinov, Britain's Most Ingenious Spy, Peter Day, Biteback Publishing, London, 2015 (original title *Klop: Britain's Most Ingenious Secret Agent*)

Beyond the Frontiers: The Biography of Colonel F. M. Bailey, Explorer and Special Agent, Arthur Swinson (Sir Fitzroy Maclean, preface), Hutchinson, 1971

The Bormann Brotherhood, William Stevenson, Harcourt Brace Jovanovich, New York, 1973

Breaking the Codes: Australia's KGB Network, 1944–1950, Desmond Ball and David Horner, Allen & Unwin, Sydney, 1998

British Intelligence in the Second World War: Its Influence on Strategy and Operations, Vols 1 & 2, F. H Hinsley with E. E. Thomas, C. F. G. Ransom and R. C. Knight, Her Majesty's Stationery Office, London, 1979

British Security Coordination: The Secret History of British Intelligence in the Americas, 1940–45, British Security Coordination (with an introduction by Nigel West), St Ermin's Press, London, 1998

'C': *A Biography of Sir Maurice Oldfield, Head of MI6*, Richard Deacon, Macdonald, London, 1985

'C': *The Secret Life of Sir Stewart Graham Menzies, Spymaster to Winston Churchill*, Anthony Cave Brown, Macmillan, New York, 1987

Camp X: Canada's School for Secret Agents 1941–45, David Stafford, Lester & Orpen Dennys, Toronto, 1986

The Case of Richard Sorge, F. W. Deakin and G. R. Storry, Chatto & Windus, London, 1966

Cast No Shadow: The Life of the American Spy Who Changed the Course of World War II, Mary S. Lovell, Pantheon Books, New York, 1992

Churchill's War: The Struggle for Power, Vol. 1, David Irving, Hutchinson, London, 1988

CIA: The 'Honourable' Company, Brian Freemantle, Michael Joseph, London, 1983

Cloak and Gown: Scholars in the Secret War, 1939–1961, Robin W. Winks, William Morrow, New York, 1987

Contemporary Authors: A Bio-Bibliographical Guide to Current Authors and their Works, James M. Ethridge and Barbara Kopala (eds), Vols 13–14, Gale Research Company, Detroit (MI), 1965

Counterfeit Spies: Genuine or Bogus?, An Astonishing Investigation into Secret Agents of the Second World War, Nigel West, St Ermin's Press, London, 1998

Daring Missions of World War II, William B. Breuer, Wiley, New York, 2001

The Defence of the Realm: The Authorised History of MI5, Christopher Andrew, Penguin, London, 2009

Democracy: Its Defects and Advantages, C. Delisle Burns, George Allen & Unwin, London, 1929

Desperate Deception: British Covert Operations in the United States, 1939–44, Thomas E. Mahl, Potomac Books, Washington DC, 1999

The Devil's Chessboard: Allen Dulles, the CIA, and the Rise of America's Secret Government, David Talbot, HarperCollins, New York, 2015

The Diaries of Sir Alexander Cadogan (1938–45), David Dilks (ed.), Cassell & Company, London, 1971

Documents on British Foreign Policy 1919–1939, E. L. Woodward and Rohan Butler (eds), His Majesty's Stationery Office, London, 1949

Donovan and the CIA: A History of the Establishment of the Central Intelligence Agency, Thomas F. Troy, Central Intelligence Agency, Center for the Study of Intelligence, Washington DC, 1981

The Double-Cross System, J. C. Masterman, Yale University Press, New Haven (CT), 1972

Drozdovtsy v ognie: zhivye razskazy i materialy, A. V. Turkul, Svetlost, Belgrade (Serbia), 1937

Encyclopedia of Cold War Espionage, Spies and Secret Operations, Richard C. S. Trahair and Robert L. Miller, Enigma Books, New York, 2009

Encyclopedia of the Third Reich, Louis L. Snyder, Robert Hale, London, 1976

Espionage: An Encyclopedia of Spies and Secrets, Richard M. Bennett, Virgin Books, London, 2002

The Expansion of Russia, Charles Howard Ellis, Ilmgau Verlag, Pfaffenhofen an der Ilm (Germany), 1965

The Faber Book of Espionage, Nigel West (ed.), Faber & Faber, London, 1993

The Factory: The Official History of the Australian Signals Directorate, Vol. 1, John Fahey, Allen & Unwin, Sydney, 2023

Fair Game: What Biographers Don't Tell You, Denis Brian, Prometheus Books, New York, 1994

Fighting to Lose: How the German Secret Intelligence Service Helped the Allies Win the Second World War, John Bryden, Dundurn Press, Toronto, 2014

The First Fifty Years: Soviet Russia, 1917–67, Ian Grey, Coward-McCann, New York, 1967

Free Agent: The Unseen War 1941–1991, Brian Crozier, HarperCollins, New York, 1993

The Friends: Britain's Post-War Secret Intelligence Operations, Nigel West, Weidenfeld & Nicolson, London, 1988

The Game of the Foxes: The Untold Story of German Espionage in the United States and Great Britain During World War II, Ladislas Farago, Bantam Books, New York, 1971

Games of Intelligence: The Classified Conflict of International Espionage, Nigel West, Weidenfeld & Nicolson, London, 1989

The Ghost: The Secret Life of CIA Spymaster James Jesus Angleton, Jefferson Morley, St Martin's Press, New York, 2017

The Great Terror: Stalin's Purge of the Thirties, Robert Conquest, Macmillan, London, 1968

The Greatest Traitor: The Secret Lives of Agent George Blake, Roger Hermiston, Aurum, London, 2014

The Greatest Treason: The Bizarre Story of Hollis, Liddell and Mountbatten, Richard Deacon, Century, London, 1989

The Guy Liddell Diaries: MI5's Director of Counter-Espionage in World War II, Volume I: 1939–42, Nigel West (ed.), Routledge, Abingdon-on-Thames, 2005

Het Koninkrijk der Nederlanden in de Tweede Wereldoorlog, Deel 2: Neutral (The Kingdom of the Netherlands in World War II, Part 2: Neutral), Loe de Jong, Martinus Nijhoff, The Hague (The Netherlands), 1969

Historical Dictionary of British Intelligence, Nigel West, Scarecrow Press, Lanham (MD), 2005

Historical Dictionary of International Intelligence, Nigel West, Scarecrow Press, Lanham (MD), 2006

Hitler's Secret Service: Memoirs of Walter Schellenberg, Walter Schellenberg (Louis Hagen, translator), Pyramid Books, New York, 1958 (original title *The Labyrinth*)

Hitler's Spy Chief: The Wilhelm Canaris Mystery, Richard Bassett, Weidenfeld & Nicolson, London, 2005

Hoover's Secret War Against Axis Spies: FBI Counterespionage During World War II, Raymond J. Batvinis, University Press of Kansas, Lawrence (KS), 2014

How the Cold War Began: The Igor Gouzenko Affair and the Hunt for Soviet Spies, Amy Knight, Carroll & Graf, New York, 2005

The Ian Fleming Miscellany, Andrew Cook, History Press, Cheltenham (UK), 2015

In Stalin's Secret Service, W. G. Krivitsky, Enigma Books, New York, 2000 (first published in 1939, British title *I Was Stalin's Secret Agent*)

The Intelligence Game: The Illusions and Delusions of International Espionage, James Rusbridger, Bodley Head, London, 1989

Intelligence and the War Against Japan: Britain, America and the Politics of Secret Service, Richard J. Aldrich, Cambridge University Press, Cambridge, 2000

Intelligence Wars: American Secret History from Hitler to al-Qaeda, Thomas Powers, New York Review Books, New York, 2002

Into the Lion's Mouth: The True Story of Dusko Popov, World War II Spy, Patriot, and the Real-Life Inspiration for James Bond, Larry Loftis, Berkley Caliber, New York, 2016

Intrepid's Last Case, William Stevenson, Villard Books, New York, 1983

KGB: The Inside Story of its Foreign Operations from Lenin to Gorbachev, Christopher Andrew and Oleg Gordievsky, Hodder & Stoughton, London, 1990

Klaus Barbie: Butcher of Lyons, Tom Bower, Michael Joseph, London, 1984

The Last American Aristocrat: The Biography of David K. E. Bruce, 1898–1977, Nelson D. Lankford, Little, Brown, Boston, 1996

The Last of the Giants, C. L. Sulzberger, Macmillan, New York, 1970

The Last Hero: Wild Bill Donovan, Anthony Cave Brown, Times Books, New York, 1982

Martin Bormann: Nazi in Exile, Paul Manning, Lyle Stuart Inc, Secaucus (NJ), 1981

Mask of Treachery: Spies, Lies, Buggery & Betrayal, The First Documented Dossier on Anthony Blunt's Cambridge Spy Ring, John Costello, William Morrow, New York, 1988

MI5 MI6: Britain's Security and Secret Intelligence Services, R. G. Grant, Bison Books, London, 1989

MI6: British Secret Intelligence Service Operations, 1909–45, Nigel West, Weidenfeld & Nicolson, London, 1983

MI6: Fifty Years of Special Operations, Stephen Dorril, Fourth Estate, London, 2000

MI6: The History of the Secret Intelligence Service 1909–1949, Keith Jeffery, Bloomsbury Publishing, London, 2010

MI6 and the Machinery of Spying: Structure and Process in Britain's Secret Intelligence, Philip H. J. Davies, Routledge, Abingdon-on-Thames, 2004

Molehunt: The Full Story of the Soviet Spy in MI5, Nigel West, Weidenfeld & Nicolson, London, 1987

Most Secret Agent of Empire: Reginald Teague-Jones Master Spy of the Great Game, Taline Ter Minassian (translated by Tom Rees), Oxford University Press, New York, 2014

My Silent War, Kim Philby, Grove Press, New York, 1968

Need to Know: World War II and the Rise of American Intelligence, Nicholas Reynolds, Mariner Books, New York, 2022

Official and Confidential: The Secret Life of J. Edgar Hoover, Anthony Summers, G. P. Putnam's Sons, New York, 1993

Official Secrets: The Use and Abuse of the Act, David Hooper, Secker & Warburg, London, 1987

The Old Boys: The American Elite and the Origins of the CIA, Burton Hursh, Charles Scribner's Sons, New York, 1992

On Secret Service East of Constantinople: The Plot to Bring Down the British Empire, Peter Hopkirk, John Murray, London, 1994

Operation Sea Lion: How Britain Crushed the German War Machine's Dreams of Invasion in 1940, Leo McKinstry, John Murray, London, 2014

Operation Snow: How a Soviet Mole in FDR's White House Triggered Pearl Harbor, John Koster, Regnery History, Washington DC, 2012

The Origin, Structure and Working of the League of Nations, C. Howard-Ellis (Charles Howard Ellis), G. Allen & Unwin, London, 1928

OSS Against the Reich: The World War II Diaries of Colonel David K. E. Bruce, David K. E. Bruce (Nelson D. Lankford, ed.), Kent State University Press, Kent (OH), 1991

Our Man in New York: The British Plot to Bring America into the Second World War, Henry Hemming, Quercus, London 2019 (published in the United States as *Agents of Influence: A British Plot, a Canadian Spy, and the Secret Effort to Bring America into World War II*)

Past to Present: A Reporter's Story of War, Spies, People, and Politics, William Stevenson, Lyons Press, Guilford (CT), 2012

The Petrov Affair: Politics and Espionage, Robert Manne, Pergamon Press, Sydney, 1987

Philby: KGB Masterspy, Phillip Knightley, Andre Deutsch, London, 1988

Princess Merle: The Romantic Life of Merle Oberon, Charles Higham and Roy Moseley, Coward-McCann, New York, 1983

The Private Life of Kim Philby: The Moscow Years, Rufina Philby, Mikhail Lyubimov and Hayden Peake, St Ermin's Press, London, 1999

The Protest Years: The Official History of ASIO, 1963–1975, Vol. II, John Blaxland, Allen & Unwin, Sydney, 2015

The Quiet Canadian: The Secret Service Story of Sir William Stephenson, H. Montgomery Hyde, Hamish Hamilton, London, 1962 (published in the United States as *Room 3603: The Study of the British Intelligence Center in New York During World War II*)

Rendezvous with Destiny: How Franklin D. Roosevelt and Five Extraordinary Men Took America into the War and into the World, Michael Fullilove, Penguin Press, New York, 2013

Russia: Revolution and Civil War 1917–1921, Antony Beevor, Weidenfeld & Nicolson, London, 2022

The Scarlet Thread, Donald Downes, Hamilton and Co., Stafford (UK), 1959

The Second Oldest Profession: The Spy as Bureaucrat, Patriot, Fantasist and Whore, Phillip Knightley, Andre Deutsch, London, 1986

The Secret Cold War: The Official History of ASIO, 1976–1989, Vol. III, John Blaxland and Rhys Crawley, Allen & Unwin, 2018

The Secret History of the Five Eyes: The Untold Story of the International Spy Network, Richard Kerbaj, Blink Publishing, London, 2022

Secret Intelligence Agent, H. Montgomery Hyde, Constable, London, 1982

Secrets and Lies in Vietnam: Spies, Intelligence and Covert Operations in the Vietnam Wars, Panagiotis Dimitrakis, I. B. Tauris, London, 2016

The Secret War: Spies, Codes and Guerrillas 1939–45, Max Hastings, William Collins, London, 2015

Secret Servant: My Life with the KGB & the Soviet Elite, Ilya Dzhirkvelov, Touchstone, New York, 1987

The Secret War Against Hitler, William Casey, Simon & Schuster, New York, 1989

Shanghai on the Metro: Spies, Intrigue, and the French Between the Wars, Michael B. Miller, University of California Press, Berkeley, 1994

The Siren Years: A Canadian Diplomat Abroad, 1937–1945, Charles Ritchie, Macmillan of Canada, Toronto, 1974

SOE: The Special Operations Executive 1940–46, M. R. D. Foot, BBC Books, London, 1984

The Spies Who Never Were: The True Story of the Nazi Spies Who Were Actually Allied Double Agents, Hervie Haufler, New American Library, New York, 2006

Spy Book: The Encyclopedia of Espionage, Norman Polmar and Thomas B. Allen, Random House, New York, 1997

Spycatcher: The Candid Autobiography of a Senior Intelligence Officer, Peter Wright with Paul Greengrass, William Heinemann Australia, Melbourne, 1987

The Spy Catchers: The Official History of ASIO, 1949–1963, Vol. I, David Horner, Allen & Unwin, Sydney, 2015

The Spycatcher Trial, Malcolm Turnbull, William Heinemann, London, 1988

Spy/Counterspy, Dusko Popov, Grosset & Dunlap, New York, 1974

Spymaster: The Betrayal of MI5, William J. West, Wynwood Press, New York, 1990

Spymaster: The Life of Britain's Most Decorated Cold War Spy and Head of MI6, Sir Maurice Oldfield, Martin Pearce, Bantam Press, London, 2016

Spymaster: The Man Who Saved MI6, Helen Fry, Yale University Press, New Haven (CT), 2021

Spymistress: The True Story of the Greatest Female Secret Agent of World War II, William Stevenson, Arcade Publishing, New York, 2007

Spy Wars: Espionage and Canada from Gouzenko to Glasnost, J. L. Granatstein and David Stafford, Key Porter Books, Toronto, 1990

The Spy Who Disappeared: Diary of a Secret Mission to Russian Central Asia in 1918, Reginald Teague-Jones (introduction and epilogue by Peter Hopkirk), Victor Gollancz Ltd, London, 1990

Strolling About on the Roof of the World: The First Hundred Years of the Royal Society for Asian Affairs (Formerly Royal Central Asian Society), Hugh Leach with Susan Maria Farrington, RoutledgeCurzon, London, 2002

Their Trade is Treachery: The Full, Unexpurgated Truth About the Russian Penetration of the World's Secret Defences, Chapman Pincher, Sidgwick & Jackson, London, 1981 (updated edition published by Biteback Publishing, 2014)

The Third Reich's Intelligence Services: The Career of Walter Schellenberg, Katrin Paehler, Cambridge University Press, Cambridge, 2017

Too Secret Too Long: The Great Betrayal of Britain's Crucial Secrets and the Cover-Up, Chapman Pincher, Sidgwick & Jackson, London, 1984

Traitors and Spies: Espionage and Corruption in High Places in Australia, 1901–50, John Fahey, Allen & Unwin, Sydney, 2020

Traitors: The Labyrinths of Treason, Chapman Pincher, Sidgwick & Jackson, London, 1987

The Transcaspian Episode, 1918–1919, C. H. Ellis (Charles Howard Ellis), Hutchinson, London, 1963 (published in the United States as *The British 'Intervention' in Transcaspia*)

Treachery: Betrayals, Blunders, and Cover-ups: Six Decades of Espionage Against America and Great Britain, Chapman Pincher, Random House, New York, 2009

TRIPLEX: Secrets from the Cambridge Spies, Nigel West and Oleg Tsarev (eds), Yale University Press, New Haven (CT), 2009

The True Intrepid: Sir William Stephenson and the Unknown Agents, Bill Macdonald, Raincoast Books, Vancouver, 1998 (republished in 2001)

The Two Bills: Mission Accomplished (also titled *Mission Accomplished: The Story of the 'Two Bills' and their Partnership in Wartime Intelligence and Clandestine Operations*), Charles Howard Ellis, unpublished manuscript, 1972

Unholy Trinity: The Vatican, the Nazis, and the Swiss Banks, Mark Aarons and John Loftus, St Martin's Press, New York, 1991

Unreliable Witness: Espionage Myths of the Second World War, Nigel West, Weidenfeld & Nicolson, London, 1984

Western Anti-Communism and the Interdoc Network: Cold War Internationale, Giles Scott-Smith, Palgrave Macmillan, Basingstoke (UK), 2011

'We Will Bury You': Studies in Left-Wing Subversion Today, Brian Crozier (ed.), Tom Stacey Ltd, London, 1970

Who's Who in Literature: A Continuance of the Bibliographical Section of the Literary Year Book, Literary Year Books Press, Bootle (UK), 1933 and 1934

Wild Bill and Intrepid: Donovan, Stephenson, and the Origin of CIA, Thomas F. Troy, Yale University Press, New Haven (CT), 1996

The Wilson Plot: The Intelligence Services and the Discrediting of a Prime Minister, David Leigh, William Heinemann, London, 1988

Works, J. V. Stalin, Vols 1–13, Foreign Languages Publishing House, Moscow, 1952–55

Documents/Annuals/Magazines

'A Man Called Intrepid: Sir William Stephenson', transcript of Canadian Broadcasting Corporation documentary on Sir William Stephenson, Alf Norris (producer) and William Harcourt (executive producer), Ottawa, 1973

'Australian Imperial Force attestation paper of persons enlisted for service abroad', Captain C. H. Ellis, Middlesex Regiment, Australian Military Forces Headquarters, Melbourne, 22 May 1920

'Bill Hooper and secret service', F. A. C. (Frans) Kluiters, Netherlands Intelligence Studies Association, The Hague (The Netherlands), date unknown

'British Forces identification card issued to Lieutenant Colonel Charles Howard Ellis, GHQ Middle East, by the Permit Officer, British Forces Middle East', Imperial War Museum, London, 5 June 1942

'British patriot or Soviet spy? Clarifying a major Cold War mystery: an analysis of Chapman Pincher's indictment of Sir Roger Hollis', Paul Monk and John L. Wilhelm, Melbourne and Washington DC, 10 April 2015

'Charles Howard aka Dick Ellis', File No. E/16/94, ASIO, National Archives of Australia, Canberra, undated

'Charles Howard Ellis', World War I service record, WO 372/6/192406, National Archives, London, undated

'Citation for the Legion of Merit, Degree of Officer', official citation for Dick Ellis, Harry S. Truman, The White House, Washington DC, undated

'The Coordinator of Information and British Intelligence', Thomas F. Troy, Central Intelligence Agency, Washington DC, Vol. 18, Spring 1974

'Ellis, Charles H., Col. (British Army)', Office of Strategic Services file for Charles Howard Ellis, National Security Council, Central Intelligence Agency, Washington DC, 1947

'Facts concerning Ellis family history', handwritten and uncredited note in the Dick Ellis Papers, National Library of Australia, Canberra, undated

'Foreign Service list: January 31, 1944', Department of State, Publication 2079, United States Government Printing Office, Washington DC, 1944

'Meetings: Session 1957–1958', *The Geographical Journal*, Vol. CXXIV, No. 1, Royal Geographical Society, London, March 1958

'Meetings: Session 1932–1933', *The Geographical Journal,* Vol. LXXXI, No. 1, Royal Geographical Society, London, January 1933

'Military implications of hostilities with Russia in 1940', Report by the Chiefs of Staff Committee, War Cabinet, London, 8 March 1940

'My early life (the Ellis family)', typescript by Dick Ellis, Dick Ellis Papers, National Library of Australia, Canberra, undated

'Of moles and men', draft typescript by Ernest Cuneo, Ernest Cuneo Papers, Franklin D. Roosevelt Presidential Library, Washington DC, 1981 (later developed into 'Britain's mentor of the OSS: Was he a "mole" for the KGB?', syndicated by Independent News Alliance, Chicago, 4 October 1981)

'Opposition to the Nazis', typewritten article by Dick Ellis, Dick Ellis Papers, National Library of Australia, Canberra, undated

'Otto Rusche v. Herbert Brownell, Jr., 244 F.2d 782 (D.C. Cir. 1957)', United States Court of Appeals (District of Columbia Circuit), Washington DC, 1957

'Proposed citation', typewritten draft for Dick Ellis's Legion of Merit citation, WO 373/148/259, National Archives, London, undated

'Report on interviews with Sir William S. Stephenson in Paget, Bermuda', Thomas F. Troy, Central Intelligence Agency, Washington DC, 13 March 1969

'St Edmund Hall, Oxford, Form of Application for Admission' and accompanying untitled form, St Edmund Hall, Oxford University, Oxford, 1920

St Edmund Hall Magazine, St Edmund Hall, Oxford University, Holywell Press, Oxford, Vol. 1, No. 1, November 1920

St Edmund Hall Magazine, St Edmund Hall, Oxford University, Holywell Press, Oxford, Vol. 1, No. 2, December 1921

St Edmund Hall Magazine, St Edmund Hall, Oxford University, Holywell Press, Oxford, Vol. 1, No. 3, December 1922

St Edmund Hall Magazine, St Edmund Hall, Oxford University, Holywell Press, Oxford, Vol. 6, No. 1, December 1951

'Treason of British spy has serious effects on American intelligence', Hon. Larry McDonald (GA), House of Representatives, Washington DC, 26 April 1983

'Venona naval GRU US cables decrypted by the National Security Agency's Venona Project', transcribed by students of the Mercyhurst College Institute for Intelligence Studies, arranged by John Earl Haynes, Library of Congress, Washington DC, 2011

'Walter Krivitsky', File No. 100-11146, four-part file on Krivitsky, Federal Bureau of Investigation, United States Department of Justice, New York, 1941

Genealogical Databases

ancestry.com (Australia, Birth Index, 1788–1922; England & Wales, Civil Registration Death Index, 1916–2007; California, U.S., Arriving Passenger and Crew Lists, 1882–1959; England & Wales, Civil Registration Death Index, 1916–2007; England & Wales, Civil Registration Marriage Index, 1916–2005; Florida, U.S., Arriving and Departing Passenger and Crew Lists, 1898–1963; New York, U.S., Arriving Passenger and Crew Lists (including Castle Garden and Ellis Island), 1820–1957; UK and Ireland, Incoming Passenger Lists, 1878–1960; UK and Ireland, Outward Passenger Lists, 1890–1960; U.S., Border Crossings from Canada to U.S., 1895–1960; U.S., Border Crossings from Mexico to U.S., 1895–1964; U.S., Departing Passenger and Crew Lists, 1914–1966)

familysearch.org (World Miscellaneous Marriages, 1662–1945)

findmypast.com (Passenger Lists Leaving UK 1890–1960; Australia, Inward, Outward & Coastal Passenger Lists 1826–1972; Lives of the First World War 1914–1918; GRO Consular Marriages 1849–1965)

Hansard/Parliamentary Debates

Australia

House of Representatives, 31 March 1981, 8 April 1981

Senate, 27 April 1982, 17 August 1982

Canada

House of Commons, 26 March 1981

United Kingdom

House of Commons, 26 March 1981

House of Commons, 22 February 1994

United States

House of Representatives, 26 April 1983

Lectures

'Real spies and real secrets: the history of MI6', Keith Jeffery, Lowy Institute, Sydney, October 2011

Letters

Brian Pearce Private Archives (held by Taline Ter Minassian)

Dr G. M. Bayliss to Brian Pearce, 6 February 1978

David Morison to Brian Pearce, 18 May 1981

Chapman Pincher to Brian Pearce, 24 February 1982

Ann Salwey to Brian Pearce, 3 May 1976, 21 February 1978, 6 May 1981

Churchill Archives Centre, University of Cambridge, Cambridge
Dick Ellis to H. Montgomery Hyde, 5 November 1960, 10 December 1960, 26
    December 1960, 20 July 1961 and 17 August 1961
H. Montgomery Hyde to William Stephenson, 4 December 1960
William Stephenson to H. Montgomery Hyde, 7 October 1961

King's College, London
Stanislav A. Auský to Chapman Pincher, 2 December 1985
Antony D. Cliff to Chapman Pincher, 18 May 1984
H. Montgomery Hyde to Chapman Pincher, 26 March 1981, 17 May 1984, 25 May
    1984, 15 August 1984
Brian Pearce to Chapman Pincher, 19 February 1982, 1 March 1982
Chapman Pincher to H. Montgomery Hyde, 18 May 1984, 15 June 1984
William Stevenson to Chapman Pincher, 15 October 1981
Reginald Teague-Jones to Brian Pearce, 20 November 1979

National Archives of Australia, Canberra
Dick Ellis to Richard Casey, 6 February 1950, 25 July 1962

National Archives of India, Delhi
Major V. Vivian to Major C. W. Burnham, 8 October 1920

National Library of Australia, Canberra
Dick Ellis to May and June Henry, 20 March 1919 and 3 October 1919
Olik Ellis to Frank Cain, 8 July 1994

St Edmund Hall Archive, University of Oxford, Oxford
Dick Ellis to Alfred Brotherston Emden, 8 September 1920, 3 November 1921 and
    13 March 1937

University of Regina, Regina
Roald Dahl to William Stephenson, 21 February 1973
William Stevenson to William Stephenson, 2 March 1973, 3 April 1973, 2 March
    1974, 31 July 1974, 11 August 1974, 9 October 1975

University of Victoria, Victoria
Olik Ellis to Brian Stafford, 21 August 1988
Brian Stafford to Olik Ellis, 19 September 1988

Personal Files/Papers
Central Intelligence Agency
Walter Schellenberg

National Archives, London
Cedric Belfrage KV 2/4004
Paul Hardt KV 2/1008, KV 2/1009
Ernst Kaltenbrunner KV 2/270, KV 2/271
Helmuth Knochen KV 2/2745
Walter Krivitsky KV 2/805
Carl Marcus KV 2/964, KV 2/965
Dr Heinz Pannwitz KV 2/1971
Richard Protze KV 2/1740, KV 2/1741
Joachim Rohleder KV 2/2136

Ignace Reiss KV 2/1898
Walter Schellenberg KV 2/94, KV 2/95, KV 2/96, KV 2/97, KV 2/98, KV 2/99
Anton Turkul KV 2/1591, KV 2/1592
Folkert Arie van Koutrik KV 2/3643
Waldemar von Petrow KV 2/3858, KV 2/3859
Helmuth Wehr KV 2/2467, KV 2/2468

National Archives of India, Delhi
'Abolition appointment of the Special Intelligence Officer, Constantinople. Case of Messrs. Vivian and Miller', File No. 96, Part III, Serial Nos. 1–11, Home Department (Political), Government of India, Simla, 1922

Memos
'The German Intelligence Service and the war', Central Intelligence Agency, Washington DC, undated
'Memorandum for: Director of Training', Central Intelligence Agency, Washington DC, 10 November 1972
'A review of counterintelligence literature 1975–1992', Cleveland C. Cram, Central Intelligence Agency, Washington DC, 1992
'Working of a secret service organisation', Dick Ellis to William Donovan, Washington DC, undated (circa 1941)

Newspaper and Magazine Articles/Blog Posts/Letters to the Editor (Print and Online)
'A case for exoneration', A. M. Ross-Smith, *Daily Telegraph*, London, 11 April 1983
'A chemist in Paris', A. M. Ross-Smith, *Daily Telegraph*, London, 26 May 1984
'Accused MI6 officer's daughter makes plea to Mrs Thatcher', Stewart Tendler, *Times*, London, 30 March 1981
'Alleged British spy gave out disinformation', Carl Armfelt, *Hamilton Spectator*, Hamilton (Ontario), 18 March 2000
'Always a gentleman', Anthony Cavendish, *Daily Telegraph*, 3 May 1984
'A mole in MI5?', no byline, *Time*, New York, 6 April 1981
'The Annandale boy a traitor? Never', Richard Hall, *Sydney Morning Herald*, Sydney, 5 February 1983
'Another name crops up in spy scandal', Associated Press, *Washington Star*, Washington DC, 26 March 1981
'Anthony Cave Brown', John Weitz, *Interview*, New York, April 1983
'Apologia confirms Ellis as traitor', Chapman Pincher, *Australian*, 29 April 1982
'ASIS: Joke and dagger', Brian Toohey and William Pinwill, *Sydney Morning Herald*, Sydney, 22 July 1989
'The Australian connection', Chapman Pincher, *Australian*, Sydney, 26 April 1982
'Authors "certain" that MI6 officer spied for Nazis', Guy Rais, *Daily Telegraph*, London, 13 April 1983
'Baku commissars', H. Montgomery Hyde, *Times*, London, 18 October 1961
'Books received', no byline, *The Economist, Weekly Commercial Times, Banker's Gazette and Railway Monitor*, Vol. CVII, No. 4400, London, 29 September 1928
'British Cold War double agent Philby details life of betrayal in Stasi video', no byline, reuters.com, London, 4 April 2016
'The British in Central Asia', Captain C. H. Ellis (Charles Howard Ellis), *Stead's Review*, Melbourne, 24 July 1920
'British operative supports double agent charges', Timothy Hodgson, United Press International, Boca Raton (FL), 27 July 1987

'"Bunny" Pantcheff', no byline, *Daily Telegraph*, London, 29 November 1989

'The Cambridge Six: MI5 confirms the name of another top Soviet spy', Sputnik News Service, Moscow, 20 August 2015

'The case of the ongoing cover-up', extract from *Breaking the Codes: Australia's KGB Network 1944–1950* by Desmond Ball and David Horner, *Canberra Times*, Canberra, 5 September 1998

'Chapman Pincher – obituary: Chapman Pincher was a journalist who specialised in spy-hunting and enraged Harold Macmillan with his scoops about defence', M. R. D. Foot, *Telegraph*, London, 6 August 2014

'Col. Ellis: case for innocence', A. M. Ross-Smith, *Sydney Morning Herald*, Sydney, 21 February 1983

'Closing the books on Intrepid's cloak-and-dagger doings', Kiki Olson, *Philadelphia Inquirer*, Philadelphia, 12 February 1984

'Dead men may tell no lies: but spies' lives full of drama', R. T. Foster, *Sun-Herald*, Sydney, 21 June 1981

'Dick Ellis: now even a defender has doubts', no byline, *Sydney Morning Herald*, Sydney, 15 February 1983

'Did affable Aussie wreck Cold War for West?', Norman Abjorensen, *Sunday Canberra Times*, Canberra, 6 September 1998

'"Disinformation" planted on Col. Ellis', H. Montgomery Hyde, *Daily Telegraph*, London, 24 April 1984

'Down the mole hole', David Kahn, *Washington Post*, Washington DC, 5 February 1984

'Ellis charge "absolutely false"', Stewart Tendler, *Times*, London, 27 March 1981

'Ellis entrusted with secrets', A. M. Ross-Smith, *Daily Telegraph*, London, 2 May 1983

'Ellis's confession', Nigel West, *Daily Telegraph*, London, 13 April 1983

'Ellis's service to the Crown', H. Montgomery Hyde, *Daily Telegraph*, London, 15 April 1983

'England's spy in America', John le Carré, *New York Times*, New York, 29 February 1976

'Ex-British no. 3 spy called triple agent', no byline, *Los Angeles Times*, Los Angeles, 26 March 1981

'Fact: Dick Ellis did spy', Chapman Pincher, *Sydney Morning Herald*, Sydney, 10 February 1983

'The faking of Intrepid', Hugh Trevor-Roper, *Sunday Telegraph*, London, 19 February 1989

'FBI, CIA chickens come home to roost', Ralph de Toledano, *Insight on the News*, Vol. 19, No. 9, Washington DC, 15 April 2003

'Foreign affairs', no byline, *Saturday Review*, Vol. 146, No. 3808, London, 20 October 1928

'Fragmentary documents and a skewed picture of a hero', David Stafford, *Globe and Mail*, Toronto, 26 November 1983

'From office clerk to King's messenger: the romantic story of an Australian boy's progress – staff work in Russia', no byline, *Sunday Times*, Sydney, 14 December 1919

'"Gay" Edgar Hoover and other smears', Ralph de Toledano, *Insight on the News*, Vol. 17, No. 12, Washington DC, 26 March 2001

'Gen. Krivitsky found dead; suicide finding questioned', no byline, *New York Times*, New York, 11 February 1941

'Gross insult to SOE members', A. M. Ross-Smith, *Sydney Morning Herald*, Sydney, 11 May 1985

'The hoax of the Blunt confession (Part 1)', Antony Percy, coldspur.com, 31 January 2021

'Hope calls for "attack function"', Brian Toohey, *National Times*, Sydney, 15–21 March 1981

'How a spy was revealed', Chapman Pincher, *Daily Telegraph*, London, 13 April 1983

'How Carib Cement founder inspired James Bond', Klao Bell-Lewis, *Gleaner*, Kingston (Jamaica), 16 June 2019

'How Petrov case shows Wright is wrong', Anthony McAdam, *Sunday Telegraph*, London, 14 December 1986

'How to avoid another Wright fiasco', Andrew Lownie, *Times*, London, 25 July 1987

'In defence of Ellis', Elizabeth L. Wood, *Globe and Mail*, Toronto, 11 April 1981

'Inside Menzies's dirty tricks brigade', Richard Hall, *Sydney Morning Herald*, Sydney, 29 July 1989

'Intelligence and sometimes folly', Edward Jay Epstein, *New York Times*, New York, 16 January 1983

'The intelligence mystique', Arthur Schlesinger Jr, *Wall Street Journal*, New York, 31 March 1987

'Intrepidly into Ludlum-land', Reg Whitaker, *Citizen*, Ottawa, 19 November 1983

'"Intrepid" says Ellis was not a spy', Margaret Jones, *Sydney Morning Herald*, Sydney, 28 March 1981

'Last word on Ellis', Chapman Pincher, *Daily Telegraph*, London, 17 May 1984

'Little evidence on Ellis as Soviet agent', Nigel West, *Daily Telegraph*, London, 4 May 1984

'The MI5 chief who destroyed vital files', Chapman Pincher, *Daily Mail*, London, 11 November 1981

'MI6 eventually muddled through', Alex Sheppard, *Sydney Morning Herald*, Sydney, 7 January 1984

'More shocking than a shocker', no byline, *Daily Telegraph*, London, 1 December 1939

'Mr C. H. Ellis', H. Montgomery Hyde, *Times*, London, 21 July 1975

'Mr C. H. Ellis', no byline, *Times*, London, 16 July 1975

'Mrs Thatcher refuses to comment on man named as spy', Stewart Tendler, *Times*, London, 22 April 1981

'Nazi and Soviet double agent claim "utter nonsense"', Richard Beeston, *Daily Telegraph*, London, 27 March 1981

'Nazis put Britain's Scouts on hit list', York Membery, *Sunday Times*, London, 30 May 1999

'New evidence on a spy that never was', A. M. Ross-Smith, *Daily Telegraph*, London, 19 April 1984

'New evidence on Ellis', A. M. Ross-Smith, *Daily Telegraph*, London, 9 May 1984

'Newly published SS handbook gives blueprint for Nazi Britain', James Dalrymple, *Independent*, London, 3 March 2000

'"Nothing is ever what it seems"', Alan Renouf, *Sydney Morning Herald*, Sydney, 2 May 1981

'On Philby, Gouzenko, and ELLI', Antony Percy, coldspur.com, 31 March 2021

'On the trail of a mole', James Bamford, *New York Times*, New York, 22 January 1984

'Orwell in Paris: under surveillance', Darcy Moore, darcymoore.net, Kiama (Australia), 4 July 2021

'Oz spies abroad', Brian Toohey, *National Times*, Sydney, 15–21 March 1981

'Passengers by S.S. *Benalla*', no byline, *Argus*, Melbourne, 12 August 1920

'Patriot or spy?', William Stevenson, *Toronto Sun*, Toronto, 14 July 1981

'Philby: Hollis? I just don't know', Phillip Knightley, *Sunday Times*, London, 3 April 1988

'The problems of appearing in a BBC documentary', John Simkin, spartacus-educational.com, 17 September 2015

'Rare film emerges of double-agent Kim Philby speaking after defection', Bill Chappell, npr.org, Washington DC, 4 April 2016

'Revealed: Hitler's little black guide to the crushing of Britain', Christopher Hudson, *Daily Mail*, London, 23 February 2000

'Ronald Sinclair: carrying his true identity to the grave', Peter Hopkirk, *Times*, London, 25 November 1988

'Russian general protests French expulsion order', no byline, *New York Herald Tribune*, Paris, 26 April 1938

'Security risks', Chapman Pincher, *Times*, London, 8 April 1981

'Security risks', Chapman Pincher, *Times*, London, 6 May 1981

'Security risks', H. Montgomery Hyde, *Times*, London, 27 April 1981

'The shooting of the twenty-six Baku comrades by agents of British imperialism', Joseph Stalin, *Izvestiya*, Moscow, 23 April 1919

'Sir Robert Vansittart – the hidden ringleader of British intelligence', Virginia McClaughry, mikemcclaughry.wordpress.com, 8 March 2018

'Sir William Stephenson, man believed to be inspiration for James Bond, honoured with Manitoba lake', Kayla Rosen, CTV News Winnipeg, Winnipeg (Canada), 25 January 2022

'Sorry, but Dick Ellis did confess', Nigel West, *Sydney Morning Herald*, Sydney, 1 February 1983

'Spies stranger than fact', A Special Correspondent, *Canberra Times*, Canberra, 29 March 1981

'Spry lays an old spook to rest', Anthony McAdam, *Bulletin*, Sydney, 27 November 1984

'Spy book "sought to reform MI5"; Peter Wright memoirs case', Stephen Taylor, *Times*, London, 9 December 1986

'Spycatcher in court', no byline, *Sydney Morning Herald*, Sydney, 12 April 1987

'Spy-hunter on the trail of a master mole', Evan Whitton, *Sydney Morning Herald*, Sydney, 16 March 1985

'The spy "made" into a mole', Peter Game, *Herald*, Melbourne, 22 October 1983

'Spy revelations that are rocking Britain', Margaret Jones, *Sydney Morning Herald*, Sydney, 28 March 1981

'Spy story leaves readers out in the cold', Walter Arnold, *Wall Street Journal*, New York, 25 January 1984

'Spy was no double agent', A. M. Ross-Smith, *Sydney Morning Herald*, Sydney, 2 February 1983

'Superagent', Hugh Trevor-Roper, *New York Review of Books*, New York, 13 May 1976

'Telling tales of dead men', Anthony Cavendish, *Sunday Times*, London, 17 May 1987

'Thatcher denies Hollis was double agent', Associated Press, *Globe and Mail*, Toronto, 27 March 1981

'"There are traitors in our midst . . . "', Evan Whitton, *Sydney Morning Herald*, Sydney, 26 January 1983

'The theory and practice of the League', no byline, *The Economist, Weekly Commercial Times, Banker's Gazette and Railway Monitor*, Vol. CVII, No. 4445, London, 3 November 1928

'Trading in treachery', H. Montgomery Hyde, *Books and Bookmen*, London, February 1985

'Traitor's wife asks: Why didn't he share his secret with me?', Harry Longmuir, *Daily Mail*, 2 November 1981

'Treachery', Chapman Pincher, *Sydney Morning Herald*, Sydney, 30 August 1981

'Trouble and spies', Harold Atkins, *Daily Telegraph*, London, 4 May 1984
'Uncovered: yet another spy high in the Secret Service hierarchy', Chapman Pincher, *Daily Mail*, London, 26 March 1981
'Under cover [sic] for 22 years, and then in 1972 . . . ' Evan Whitton, *Sydney Morning Herald*, Sydney, 27 January 1983
'Unforgivable crime', Chapman Pincher, *Daily Telegraph*, London, 22 April 1983
Untitled column, Richard Hughes, *Far Eastern Economic Review*, Hong Kong, 17 November 1983
'Untold tales', Andrew Lycett, *Times*, London, 6 June 1996
'Washington writer cites role in unmasking British spy: writer says he unmasked spy', Joe Ritchie, *Washington Post*, Washington DC, 26 March 1981
'What Gouzenko said about ELLI', Antony Percy, coldspur.com, 31 July 2021
'Who framed Roger Hollis?', Antony Percy, coldspur.com, 31 May 2021
'Wilderness of mirrors', Jefferson Morley, theintercept.com, 1 January 2018
'Work for Russia went on after war', Chapman Pincher, *Daily Mail*, London, 2 November 1981
'Writers gamble on public to help support their cause', William French, *Globe and Mail*, Toronto, 6 September 1983
'Zinoviev letter was dirty trick by MI6', Richard Norton-Taylor, *Guardian*, London, 4 February 1999

Press Releases
'75 years after "the date which will live in infamy", declassified files reveal FBI director Hoover was warned of the Pearl Harbor attack in August 1941, new book shows', PRWeb Newswire, Vocus PRW Holdings LLC, Beltsville (MD), 16 November 2016

Research Papers/Dissertations/Journals
'A better history of the SIS', Nigel West, *International Journal of Intelligence and CounterIntelligence*, Vol. 25, No. 2, Routledge, Abingdon-on-Thames, 12 March 2012
'A skewed survey of the UK's intelligence history', Nigel West, *International Journal of Intelligence and CounterIntelligence*, Vol. 22, No. 4, Routledge, Abingdon-on-Thames, 3 September 2009
'Britain's Secret Intelligence Service in Asia during the Second World War', Richard J. Aldrich, *Modern Asian Studies*, Vol. 32, No. 1, Cambridge University Press, Cambridge, February 1998
'Britain's World War II intelligence network', John H. Waller, *International Journal of Intelligence and CounterIntelligence*, Vol. 12, No. 1, Routledge, Abingdon-on-Thames, 1999
'Confronting peaceful co-existence: psychological warfare and the role of Interdoc, 1963–72', Giles Scott-Smith, *Cold War History*, Routledge, Abingdon-on-Thames, 5 March 2007
'The construction of the League of Nations Secretariat: formative practices of autonomy and legitimacy in international organisations', K. Gram-Skjoldager and H. A. Ikonomou, *International History Review*, Routledge, Abingdon-on-Thames, 21 December 2017
'The evolution of Australian intelligence', Christopher Andrew, *Studies in Intelligence*, Central Intelligence Agency, Washington DC, Fall 1988
'Fall-out [sic] from treachery: Peter Wright and the *Spycatcher* case', Donald Cameron Watt, *Political Quarterly*, Vol. 59, No. 2, Wiley, London, April 1988
'The growth of the Australian intelligence community and the Anglo-American connection', Christopher Andrew, *Intelligence and National Security*, Vol. 4, No. 2, Frank Cass Publishers, London, 1989

'The hunt for spies: another inside story', Harry G. Gelber, *Intelligence and National Security*, Vol. 4, No. 2, Frank Cass Publishers, London, 1989

'In search of a lesser evil: anti-Soviet nationalism and the Cold War', dissertation by David C. S. Albanese, Northeastern University, Boston, August 2015

'In the shadows: the spy in Australian literary and cultural history', Bruce Bennett, *Antipodes*, Vol. 20, No. 1, American Association of Australasian Literary Studies, United States, June 2006

'Intrepid: myth and reality', David Stafford, *Journal of Contemporary History*, Vol. 22, SAGE, London, 1987

'Intrepid's last deception: documenting the career of Sir William Stephenson', Timothy J. Naftali, *Espionage: Past, Present, Future?*, Wesley K. Wark (ed.), Frank Cass Publishers, London, 1994

'Issues in British and American signals intelligence, 1919–1932', John Ferris, Center for Cryptologic History, Special Series, Vol. II, National Security Agency, Fort George G. Meade (MD), 2015

'*The Origin, Structure and Working of the League of Nations*' (review), Wyndham A. Bewes, *Journal of the Royal Institute of International Affairs*, Vol. III, No. 1, Royal Institute of International Affairs (Chatham House), London, January 1929

'*The Origin, Structure and Working of the League of Nations*' (review), C. Delisle Burns, *International Journal of Ethics*, Vol. XXXIX, No. 2, University of Chicago Press, Chicago, January 1929

'Questions, questions, questions: memories of Oberursel', Arnold M. Silver, *Intelligence and National Security*, Vol. 8, No. 2, Frank Cass Publishers, London, 1993

'REMINISCENCE: CIA's indebtedness to Bill Stephenson', Thomas F. Troy, *International Journal of Intelligence and CounterIntelligence*, Vol. 20, No. 4, Routledge, Abingdon-on-Thames, 14 August 2007

'Slightly less secret', Nigel West, *International Journal of Intelligence and CounterIntelligence*, Vol. 24, No. 4, Routledge, Abingdon-on-Thames, 14 September 2011

'Small states and big secrets: understanding Sigint cooperation between unequal powers during the Second World War', Eunan O'Halpin, *Intelligence and National Security*, Vol. 17, No. 3, Frank Cass Publishers, London, 2002

'Some fresh news about the 26 Commissars: Reginald Teague-Jones and the Transcaspian Episode', Taline Ter Minassian, *Asian Affairs*, Vol. 45, No. 1, Routledge, Abingdon-on-Thames, 14 February 2014

'Soviet espionage and the Office of Strategic Services', Hayden Peake, *America Unbound: World War II and the Making of a Superpower*, Palgrave Macmillan, New York, 1992

'*Their Trade is Treachery*: a retrospective', Chapman Pincher, *Intelligence Studies in Britain and the US: Historiography Since 1945*, Christopher R. Moran and Christopher J. Murphy (eds), Edinburgh University Press, Edinburgh, 2013

'"The standard work in English on the League" and its authorship: Charles Howard Ellis, an unlikely Australian internationalist', James Cotton, *History of European Ideas*, Routledge, Abingdon-on-Thames, 10 June 2016

'The unresolved mystery of ELLI', William A. Tyrer, *International Journal of Intelligence and CounterIntelligence*, Vol. 29, No. 4, Routledge, Abingdon-on-Thames, 13 June 2016

'Walter Schellenberg: SD chief', Kenneth Campbell, *American Intelligence Journal*, Winter 2007/2008, Vol. 25, No. 2, National Military Intelligence Foundation, Charlotte Court House (VA), 2007

Videos

Camp X, youtube.com, Victory Motion Pictures, Halifax (Canada), 2001

'Kim Philby: unseen footage of Soviet spy – BBC News', youtube.com, BBC News, London, 4 April 2016

Operation Overlord: OSS and the Battle for France, youtube.com, OSS Society, Falls Church (VA), 5 June 2020

'*Treason in the Blood*: the most remarkable double agent and spy case of the century', youtube.com, *Booknotes*, Cable-Satellite Public Affairs Network (C-SPAN), Washington DC, 1994

Websites/Blogs

abhilekh-patal.in
adastron.com
americanairmuseum.com
ancestry.com
aph.gov.au
api.parliament.uk
archive.org
asis.gov.au
billiongraves.com
caribcement.com
coldspur.com
darcymoore.net
familyhistory.bdm.nsw.gov.au
findagrave.com
findmypast.com
foia.cia.gov
forces-war-records.co.uk
govinfo.gov
legislation.gov.au
library.georgetown.edu

marxists.org
mikemcclaughry.wordpress.com
myheritage.com
nam.ac.uk
nisa-intelligence.nl
niod.nl
ossreborn.com
osssociety.org
parl.canadiana.ca
rsaa.org.uk
spartacus-educational.com
spylegends.com
tracesofwar.com
vault.fbi.gov
ukwhoswho.com
ushmm.org
wilsoncenter.org
winstonchurchill.org
worldcat.org
yumpu.com

ACKNOWLEDGEMENTS

Research is the backbone of any biography and takes an inordinate amount of time. A book of this historic sweep and technical difficulty would not be possible to write without the assistance and experience of skilled archivists and librarians.

Thank you to Kevin R. Thomas at Franklin D. Roosevelt Presidential Library & Museum in Hyde Park, New York; Jessica Collins, Chris Knowles and Madelin Evans at Churchill Archives Centre, University of Cambridge, Cambridge; Brendan Fenton at National Archives of Australia, Canberra; Rob Petre at St Edmund Hall, University of Oxford, Oxford; Alyssa Hyduk and Elizabeth Seitz at Dr. John Archer Library, University of Regina, Regina; Paul B. Brown at National Archives and Records Administration, College Park, Maryland; Michael Ryder and Dr Toby Parker at the Royal Society for Asian Affairs Library, Haileybury; Julie Carrington at the Royal Geographical Society (with the Institute of British Geographers), London; Oliver Snaith and Dr Toslima Khatun at King's College, London; John Frederick at University of Victoria, Victoria (British Columbia); and Carmel Andrew at Inner West Council, Sydney. I also visited the National Archives of Japan in Tokyo, the National Library of Vietnam in Hanoi, and other libraries and archives in South-East Asia. It was an amazing research adventure. My sincere appreciation to everyone who helped.

Also, profuse thanks to Taline Ter Minassian for her thorough investigation of the 26 Commissars massacre and granting me access to Brian Pearce's personal papers on Dick Ellis; to Giles Scott-Smith for his tremendously helpful research on Ellis and Interdoc; to Larry Loftis and John Bryden for their respective books mentioning Ellis's connection to Pearl Harbor; to Judith Gibson, Glen Eira Historical Society, Ray Toye, John Blaxland, Andrew Lownie, Ben Wright, Ron Drabkin and James Cotton for generously giving me some of their time; and to Andrew Harris and Melanie Bois for reading very early rough versions of the manuscript and helping me out with their constructive notes.

I acknowledge the following authors, all of them long dead: Peter Wright for *Spycatcher*; William Stevenson for *Intrepid's Last Case*; Chapman Pincher for *Their Trade is Treachery* and *Too Secret Too Long*; H. Montgomery Hyde for *Secret Intelligence Agent*; Keith Jeffery for *MI6*; and Thomas F. Troy for *Wild Bill and Intrepid*. Between them, these six men undoubtedly compiled the most useful (if not always accurate) accounts of Ellis's life and times before the writing of this book. They were valuable signposts on my journey into exploring the personality and character of the man and for picking up valuable clues.

To all my friends and readers who have helped me over the years by buying my books, lending them to friends, borrowing them from libraries, posting about them on social media and leaving reviews, I wouldn't still be involved in this book-writing caper were it not for your generosity and support. It's not an easy road being a writer but it's worth travelling when you get the chance to tackle neglected stories like Ellis's. To my family – thanks for being there when I've needed you.

Lastly, thanks to the backroom team at Penguin Random House Australia: senior editor Patrick Mangan was my reliable sounding board once again (this is our fourth book together); freelance editor Anne Reilly edited the manuscript with immense experience and unfailing precision; senior production controller Benjamin Fairclough carefully restored some old photographs of Ellis; freelance designer Luke Causby of Blue Cork produced another cracking cover; rights manager Sarah McDuling sold rights to North America and the United Kingdom prior to publication; senior publicist Connor Parissis handled publicity; former adult publishing director Justin Ractliffe greenlighted my original proposal while adult and audio publishing director Holly Toohey oversaw the book to publication; and my longtime non-fiction publisher Alison Urquhart championed *The Eagle in the Mirror* from the moment I first mentioned the idea for a book about Ellis in 2021. Authors need friends, believers and great publishers on their side. Alison is all of those things. A grateful nod, too, to my longtime publisher in Edinburgh, Campbell Brown at Black & White Publishing, for releasing the book in the United Kingdom, and to James Abbate at Kensington Publishing for bringing it out in the United States. Cheers to you both.

ENDNOTES

Author's Note   TWIST SLOWLY IN THE WIND

1   Both quotes are taken from Phillip Knightley's typewritten pitch for a proposed film
    on Dick Ellis, held in the Knightley collection at the National Library of Australia.

2   *ibid.*

3   The date of Ellis's interrogation has been variously described as happening in 1965
    or 1966, including by Chapman Pincher himself. It's even been printed as 1967,
    as seen in Nigel West's books *Unreliable Witness: Espionage Myths of the Second
    World War* (1984) and *Counterfeit Spies: Genuine or Bogus?, An Astonishing
    Investigation into Secret Agents of the Second World War* (1998). This would
    suggest there is some reasonable doubt over the particulars of the interrogation
    and that no one has seen a copy of Ellis's confession, including West, who had a
    letter published in the *Sydney Morning Herald* on 12 February 1983 in which he
    adamantly stressed it happened in 1965. It was first mentioned by him in *A Matter
    of Trust: MI5 1945–72* (1982). Another West book, *Historical Dictionary of
    International Intelligence* (2006), has it as 1966. Why the timing anomalies? All this
    suggests it's hearsay. Nigel West, incidentally, is the pen name of former MP Rupert
    Allason. West makes a point of upbraiding other writers for mistakes, so he should
    be held to the same standard.

4   See Chapman Pincher, 'Security risks', *Times*, 8 April 1981.

5   It appears this was a warning from Philby to Blunt, before Vladimir Petrov's famous
    defection to Australia in 1954, that the defection was about to take place and, in
    the words of West, Blunt 'should take extreme caution for a while'. But there is no
    evidence Ellis tipped off Philby. See West's *The Friends: Britain's Post-War Secret
    Intelligence Operations* (1988). No mention is made of Ellis in *My Five Cambridge
    Friends: Burgess, Maclean, Philby, Blunt and Cairncross* (1994), the autobiography
    of the Five's KGB controller, Yuri Modin. Nor is any mention made of Ellis in *The
    Philby Files: The Secret Life of Master Spy Kim Philby* (1994) by Genrikh Borovik,
    the account of Russian playwright Borovik's 500 pages of interview transcripts with
    Philby. Borovik also had access to Philby's KGB file. Neither is there anything in
    The Mitrokhin Archive: The KGB in Europe and the West (1999) by Christopher
    Andrew and Vasili Mitrokhin – 'an unprecedented treasure-trove of KGB material'
    from defector Mitrokhin.

6   Thatcher's exposure of Blunt came after the publication of Andrew Boyle's book
    The Climate of Treason: Five Who Spied for Russia (1979), in which Blunt, for legal
    reasons, was called 'Maurice'.

7   The Russian State Archive of Socio-Political History in Moscow wrote to me in
    November 2021 to say they had no records of Ellis in any of its collections.

8   Chapman Pincher in *Their Trade is Treachery* (1981) claimed Philby 'avoided
    making reference in his book to Ellis or to any Soviet spy who was then "unblown"'.

9　According to Chapman Pincher in *Too Secret Too Long* (1984), Ellis's alleged confession 'stated that the intelligence about the Soviet Union that he had produced had been gratefully received in London but headquarters had given him insufficient money to pay his agents. He had therefore started giving them trivial information about British affairs so that they could feed it to the Russians who paid them for it.'

10　The German title literally means 'special most wanted list Great Britain' but more in the sense it is an 'extra' or 'extraordinary' most wanted list.

11　Seven Britons were hanged for wartime collaboration: George Johnson Armstrong (1941), Jose Estella Key (1942), Duncan Scott-Ford (1942), Oswald John Job (1944), John Amery (1945), Theodore Schurch (1946) and William Joyce aka 'Lord Haw-Haw' (1946). Key was Gibraltarian, so technically a British subject.

12　See the section 'Written Works by Charles Howard "Dick" Ellis' in this book. Ellis has been translated into Persian and German.

13　Contrary to popular belief, INTREPID was not Stephenson's codename. Writes Nigel West in *Unreliable Witness* (1984): 'INTREPID was the actual cable address of British Security Coordination, an office located in the Rockefeller Center at 630 Fifth Avenue [sic]. It was registered as such with Western Union. Stephenson himself was assigned the code-number 48100, which indicated to SIS headquarters in London that telegrams bearing that figure had come from the SIS Head of Station in New York. All SIS Stations around the world identified themselves by an ingenious system of five-figure numbers. The first two digits indicated the country. The following two digits identified individual members of the Station staff. Thus 200 was invariably the Deputy Head of Station (in this case Dick Ellis) and 500 was the Section V representative. Agents run by these officers were always referred to in communications by the last two digits. If a message to London signed by 48900 mentioned a recent meeting with 48903 who was scheduled to sail to THIRTYSIXLAND, the meaning was instantly clear to those indoctrinated in the system. The system had come from Bill Ross-Smith, one of Stephenson's case officers. His agent 48903 would soon be visiting Sweden.'

14　Writes Nigel West in his introduction to *British Security Coordination* (1998): 'Closer examination of *A Man Called Intrepid* showed that it was largely a work of fiction, and was so categorised by the American publishers following overwhelming criticism, thereby ensuring that Sir William's reputation was irretrievably damaged, although he was in such poor physical and mental condition until his death on the last day of January 1989 that he never realised the extent of what had happened.'

15　'My dear Bill – we have matters to discuss. Pray come as you are, to the Beaver's, seven tonight. WC.' 'Beaver's' is a reference to Stornoway House, the home of Lord Beaverbrook (William Maxwell Aitken).

16　On 21 February 1978, Ellis's daughter, Ann Salwey (spelling her name as 'Salway'), wrote a letter to historian Brian Pearce saying she 'gave all my father's papers to the [Royal Society for] Asian Affairs people', 'my father left very little which he had not already disposed of – as you say to the Imperial War Museum' and 'he rarely mentioned anybody (professional discretion I suppose)'. It's unclear why Salwey misspelled her own name but in another letter to Pearce she had taken to concealing her real name with a torn scrap of paper stuck over the top. This would indicate she was worried about her privacy.

　　　According to Salwey, it was Ellis's wish that his papers be donated to the Royal Society for Asian Affairs. Dr G. M. Bayliss, keeper in the Department of Printed Books of the Imperial War Museum, had written to Pearce weeks earlier to say no trace of Ellis's papers, supposedly donated in October 1964 and missing since 1969, could be found. 'It seems probable that [the collection] may have been destroyed in a fire which gutted our reading room in October 1968,' he said.

17　This was typical of Stephenson, a rampant egotist who'd taken to talking of himself in the third person and wildly embellished his role in history, but in the end, he was, as I came to believe through my own investigation, right about Ellis.

18 H. Montgomery Hyde letter to *Daily Telegraph*, 24 April 1984.

19 As Monica Jensen-Stevenson she co-authored a book with her late husband, *Kiss the Boys Goodbye: How the United States Betrayed its Own POWs in Vietnam* (1990).

20 Ellis's obituary in the *Times* by Hyde mentions Olik as working 'in the Canadian Ministry of Defence in Ottawa'. See H. Montgomery Hyde, 'Mr C. H. Ellis', *Times*, London, 21 July 1975. James Cotton in his 2016 paper '"The standard work in English on the League" and its authorship: Charles Howard Ellis, an unlikely Australian internationalist' writes: 'Peter Ellis was a Russian linguist who, it is apparent from his correspondence with his father, worked for Canadian intelligence.' This is true. Olik lived in Ottawa and Toronto. His last known address in Ottawa was 191 McLeod Street.

21 However, she made them available to Hyde for *Secret Intelligence Agent* (1982).

22 Writes Cotton: '"Ann Veronica" was, of course, the central figure in one of Wells's later novels – her character based upon that of his then-mistress Amber Reeves (daughter of New Zealand politician and scholar, William Pember Reeves). Moreover, it can confidently be asserted that Ellis chose the name because of his personal association with Wells. One of Ann's studio photographs as a baby carries the inscription, "not by [signed] H.G. Wells".' Wells's *Ann Veronica* was published in 1909.

23 Cuneo in 'Britain's mentor of the OSS: Was he a "mole" for the KGB?' (4 October 1981): 'British intelligence has produced many brilliant men, but none so dazzling as Dickie Ellis . . . mentally, he was gigantic. His knowledge of history, particularly of the ancient cultures and Islam, was perhaps more encyclopaedic than that of his good friend H. G. Wells. He mastered not only all the major European languages, but Turkish, Urdu and Persian as well. He told me he could "think in Russian". He was an extraordinary pianist, and it was by his choice that he did not become a concert musician.' Stevenson in *Intrepid's Last Case* (1983): 'He became a friend of H. G. Wells, who was writing his classic [*The*] *Outline of History*. They both, like Stephenson, attended a weekly luncheon meeting of the creative eccentrics who would assist in irregular warfare if Hitler's Soviet-supported armies continued their aggressive course.' Other friends of Ellis included Stalin biographer Robert Conquest and Lieutenant Colonel Frederick Marshman Bailey, author of *Mission to Tashkent* (1946).

24 Moura Budberg, a lover of H. G. Wells, was a suspected double agent of the United Kingdom and the Soviet Union. She's the subject of the biography *A Very Dangerous Woman* by Deborah McDonald and Jeremy Dronfield (2015). Ellis is not mentioned in the book or in Claire Tomalin's *The Young H. G. Wells* (2021), however he is mentioned in relation to Budberg in Peter Day's *The Bedbug* (2015), a biography of Peter Ustinov's father, Jona 'Klop' von Ustinov: 'A telephone tap also revealed that [Budberg] was trying to contact Dick Ellis on behalf of a Russian friend, three months after [Guy] Burgess disappeared. He was identified as a Russian mole within MI6 by Peter Wright when he reinvestigated the Cambridge spy ring of [Anthony] Blunt, Burgess, [Kim] Philby, [Donald] Maclean and John Cairncross 20 years later.' This suggests there was indeed a connection between Budberg and Ellis.

25 A term commonly credited to the CIA's James Jesus Angleton in 1975, and claimed by him to be his invention, but actually found in T. S. Eliot's 'Gerontion' (1920). See Jefferson Morley, 'Wilderness of mirrors', theintercept.com, 1 January 2018.

26 Whether Ellis saw out his days on full pension is unclear. Nigel West can't seem to make up his mind. Writes West in *British Security Coordination* (1998): 'Ellis admitted the first offence [German collaboration], so forfeiting his SIS pension' but previously wrote, 'No action was taken against him, and the pension which he had received since his retirement in 1953 continued to be paid' in *Unreliable Witness* (1984). In *The Friends: Britain's Post-War Secret Intelligence Operations* (1988), he changes his tune again and says, 'Soon after his confrontation with the molehunters, Ellis . . . pleaded financial hardship to the CIA and, in recognition of his war service, which had already been rewarded with the American Legion of Merit, was granted

a small pension. At least one CIA officer regarded Ellis's behaviour as little short of blackmail.'

William Stevenson in *Intrepid's Last Case* (1983) says Ellis's 'pension [had] been reduced'. But David Hooper in *Official Secrets: The Use and Abuse of the Act* (1987) writes: 'Ellis . . . was able to keep his pension. This may be the price of living in a free society, but it contrasts strangely with the threats that are from time to time issued by MI5 to its former officers that they will lose their often paltry pensions if they fail to do what they are told. MI5 must be one of the few organisations in the world that finds it appropriate to begin letters to its former employees – when for example warning them in November 1982 not to speak to the author Nigel West – with the formula "Dear Pensioner".'

Chapman Pincher writes similarly in *Too Secret Too Long* (1984): 'A self-confessed spy can be deprived of his pension rights only if he is prosecuted and convicted. Ellis continued in honourable retirement on full pension . . . it has been established by a statement in the House of Lords that, as the law stands, public-service pensions cannot be withheld in the case of traitors and other serious offenders under the Official Secrets Act unless the individuals concerned have been convicted of the offences. In sum, the Ellis case speaks eloquently of the value of oversight in the interests of the efficiency of the secret services themselves.'

Chapter 1   THE PURGE

1   *Obyedinyonnoye Gosudarstvennoye Politicheskoye Upravleniye* (Joint State Political Directorate), the secret police and intelligence service of the Soviet Union from 1923 to 1934.

2   Philby described Krivitsky in his autobiography, *My Silent War* (1968), as 'the Red Army intelligence officer who defected to the West in 1937, only to kill himself a few years later in the United States – a disillusioned man'.

3   Writes Phillip Knightley in *Philby: KGB Masterspy* (1988): 'Krivitsky told [Archer] that the Russian intelligence service had a young Englishman working for it in Spain under cover [sic] as a journalist.' Philby writes about it in *My Silent War*: 'There was the nasty little sentence in Krivitsky's evidence that the Soviet secret service had sent a young English journalist to Spain during the Civil War. But there were no further identifying particulars, and many young men from Fleet Street had gone to Spain.'

4   Philby praises Archer in *My Silent War* as 'the ablest professional intelligence officer ever employed by MI5'. When they worked together at MI6, Philby feared being exposed by Archer himself and had her perform work where his chances of being exposed were reduced.

5   Krivitsky biographer Gary Kern writes in *A Death in Washington: Walter G. Krivitsky and the Stalin Terror* (2004): 'The [Krivitsky] file released in 2002 shows only an agent named Petroff, a White Russian working in the Japanese embassy in Berlin, whom Krivitsky suspected of padding his reports with published material . . . [Krivitsky's] chief interest remained Germany. Soon after arriving in The Hague, reviewing and reactivating the network that he had helped create some ten years before, he learned that one of his agents – possibly Vladimir von Petrov . . . had linked into secret negotiations between Lieutenant General Hiroshi Oshima, the Japanese military attaché in Berlin, and Baron Joachim von Ribbentrop, Hitler's special envoy. Krivitsky realised that this was a major operation and rushed back to Moscow to request special powers and additional forces to carry it through to the end. Thus empowered, he returned to The Hague, gave directions and secured lines of communication. By the end of the year he had enough information to confirm that the Japanese and Germans were preparing a secret military pact designed to coordinate their operations and to neutralise the Soviet Union. His reports were conveyed to Stalin.'

6   The British writer Owen Matthews mistakenly confuses Von Petrov for Soviet agent David Petrovsky in the book *An Impeccable Spy: Richard Sorge, Stalin's Master Agent* (2019).

7   Von Petrov 'served in Red Army intelligence but also spied for the Nazis'. See Miller, *Shanghai on the Metro* (1994).

8   When I requested Von Petrov's file from the National Archives, it had to be digitised and paid for, unlike most of the other personal files used in the research for this book, which were made free of charge during the COVID-19 pandemic. The cover description reads: 'Waldemar von PETROV, aliases PETROW, PETROFF, Dimitri PETROV, Frederick de PETROV, Otto von BOHL, etc: Russian, German, Chilean. A Czarist army officer before and during the First World War, PETROV worked for Japanese Intelligence from 1920 until at least 1939. By 1927 he was working also for the Germans, including later for the JAHNKE BURO, and in 1945 was acting as an emissary of HIMMLER in Switzerland.'

There is a curious mention of Von Petrov under another alias in Katrin Paehler's *The Third Reich's Intelligence Services: The Career of Walter Schellenberg* (2017): 'Nicolaus Alexejeff, known as T-100/2, was born in Moscow in 1895. His supervisor seems to have been T-100, identified by Schellenberg as a certain Rittmeister von Petrow, conceivably called Wladinir Feodorowitsch in Alexejeff's letters. Schellenberg indicated that T-100 visited Rome sometime in 1941 to meet an old V-man [a spy or informer], maybe Alexejeff. This man was later arrested by the Italian police, creating an overall unpleasant situation, as the Amt VI representative in Rome, Dr. Groebl, was also involved. Schellenberg fired Groebl.'

The name 'Rittmeister Petroff' is also mentioned in Von Petrov's file in KV 2/3858 – 'the head of a factory in the Friedrich Strasse [sic], BERLIN, for the manufacture of forged Soviet documents' – and quite at length in Walter Schellenberg's file in KV 2/99, where he is described as a 'high-grade professional intelligence agent' who had 'direct contact' with Reinhard Heydrich.

9   From page 24 of Archer's 29 March 1940 summary of Krivitsky in KV 2/805.

10 See KV 2/94, KV 2/95. Kaltenbrunner once had Adolf Eichmann work for him; Kaltenbrunner was captured in Austria in 1945. He was executed after the Nuremberg trials in 1946 and William Donovan prosecuted him. Schellenberg refers to Von Petrov (but not by name) in his memoirs published in 1958, *Hitler's Secret Service*: 'Jahnke [Büro] had excellent connections with Japan. One was a former Czarist Russian colonel, now a naturalised Chilean, who lived partly in Berlin and partly in Paris.' Von Petrov is mentioned extensively in the Kaltenbrunner files at the National Archives. See KV 2/270.

11 See KV 2/96, document dated 4 August 1945.

12 See KV 2/96, statement dated 21 July 1945.

13 'Intermediate Interrogation Report of Ernst Kaltenbrunner', Walter Schellenberg files, CIA.

14 See KV 2/270.

15 See KV 2/3858, KV 2/3859.

16 Writes William Stevenson in *Intrepid's Last Case* (1983): 'Then Gouzenko asked me: Was Dick Ellis married to a Russian? Did he serve inside Russia? Was he in Paris before the Hitler war? These questions arose from what Gouzenko had heard in Moscow about a Soviet agent in British service. The answers were all affirmative. Gouzenko said, "Then it's possible ELLI was Ellis."'

17 The name 'Captain Ellis' was said to have popped up again out of the mouths of other 'Abwehr officers', but in the various tomes that have been written about spies since World War II none of these officers have actually been given names. Schellenberg himself is said (chiefly in Nigel West's string of books) to have named a man inside British intelligence called 'Ellis' who was working for the Gestapo. Writes West in *Historical Dictionary of International Intelligence* (2006): 'The fact that SIS had first learned from Walter Schellenberg in 1945 that a man named Ellis had betrayed SIS but had failed to identify him for two decades was a major embarrassment for the organisation.' Von Petrov is mentioned in passing in the Schellenberg files (KV 2/99). Oddly, though, Document 236b, 'From Section V

re PETROW', dated 30 November 1945 in the same files, is mysteriously missing (KV 2/98). Could Ellis, who had access to the files in the 1960s, have removed it?

18 Antony Percy writes: 'A highly sedated Volkov (and his wife) had been abducted by the KGB for torture and execution in Moscow.' See 'On Philby, Gouzenko, and ELLI', coldspur.com, 31 March 2021.

19 See KV 2/1740, 26 June 1946.

20 See KV 2/1740, 29 May 1946.

21 Somewhat bizarrely, no mention of Ellis is made in Christopher Andrew's official biography of MI5, *The Defence of the Realm: The Authorised History of MI5* (2009). But this is not unusual. Australian writer Paul Monk noted in a shrewd review of the book for *Quadrant* ('Christopher Andrew and the strange case of Roger Hollis') that much was overlooked in the organisation's approved history. Ellis gets one mention in Nigel West's *MI5: British Security Service Operations, 1909–45* (1981).

22 It remains unclear who exactly this Abwehr officer is, though it is most likely Protze. In *Their Trade is Treachery*, Chapman Pincher refers only to 'an officer of the German secret service, the Abwehr' who had Von Petrov as a source. Von Petrov got his 'high-grade intelligence inside the British secret service'. He also mentions 'another captured German officer of the Abwehr' who 'confirmed the information and had been able to name Zilenski's [sic] British source as a certain Captain Ellis. Further, he had known that Ellis was an Australian and had a Russian wife.' Ellis allegedly had 'supplied documents showing the detailed organisation of the British secret service and information about secret operations'. Protze's file mentions a 'Captain Ellis' but makes no mention of Australia or Ellis's Russian wife. Protze's file does mention 'Captain Ellis' and Von Petrov.

Peter Wright, who supplied Pincher with his information and received money via Lord Victor Rothschild's Swiss bank account so his connection to Pincher could not be traced by the British government (Lord Rothschild himself was a suspected Soviet spy and got involved with Wright and Pincher in an effort to clear his name), reproduces essentially the same story in *Spycatcher*, saying he and his investigators 'found a series of debriefing reports of Abwehr officers taken at the end of the war. The Abwehr officers confirmed that Von Petrov was being run by them as their agent, although, of course, they did not know that he was also working for the Russians. Several mentioned that Von Petrov had a source in British intelligence who could obtain our order of battle, as well as details of vital operations, such as the tap on the secret telephone link between Hitler and his ambassador in London, Von Ribbentrop. One Abwehr officer even remembered the name of Von Petrov's source – it was a Captain Ellis, who was an Australian, a brilliant linguist, and who had a Russian wife.'

23 Nigel West quotes differently in *At Her Majesty's Secret Service: The Chiefs of Britain's Intelligence Agency, MI6* (2006): 'Who is this Ellis?'

24 Unsurprisingly, Pincher and Wright pretty much carry the same account of the Philby notation being in the unnamed Abwehr officer's report, though according to Nigel West the notation was in Dick Ellis's personal file, which is not available at the National Archives. Writes West in *A Matter of Trust: MI5 1945–72* (1982), with my italics added for emphasis: 'A senior MI6 officer with strong Russian connections, whose *personal file* was examined with particular care, was Dick Ellis. One curious, dismissive entry *on his file* had been made by another MI6 colleague concerning the post-war interrogation of an Abwehr officer . . . the officer who had been responsible for making the entry in the file had been Kim Philby.' But there is also another account. In John Costello's *Mask of Treachery* (1988) he says Wright had 'checked the still very secret file on people named by Krivitsky' and this, apparently, was where the notation by Philby was made: 'Philby had written in the margin on the file.'

25 As Paul Monk and John L. Wilhelm write in their 2015 paper 'British patriot or Soviet spy? Clarifying a major Cold War mystery': 'Archer, who was Hollis's immediate superior at that time, wrote up a detailed report based on her debriefing

of Krivitsky. Shortly after she completed the report, she was moved to totally different work. Hollis took over her job and with it custody of her report on Krivitsky. At almost exactly that time, the report was supplied to Moscow, well before it was supplied (in an edited form) to the FBI in Washington. We know that the edited version for Washington was prepared by Hollis and that it omitted a number of significant things. We don't know who supplied it to Moscow; only that Hollis was in the immediate vicinity and had direct custody of the document . . . the handling of the Krivitsky report is a very early and very telling pointer not simply to the confirmed existence of ELLI within MI5, but to ELLI's having been Hollis.' According to Antony Percy, it was not tape recorded. See 'What Gouzenko said about ELLI', coldspur.com, 31 July 2021.

26 Costello: 'It was the conclusion of Wright and the Fluency Committee, set up in 1964 by MI5 and MI6 to investigate Soviet penetration, that Ellis could well have been an undercover agent for 30 years; first with the GRU before the war and later, after Philby saw his file, blackmailed into spying for the KGB. The case is more astonishing because of (1) the apparent ease with which Philby was able to cut off any investigation into Ellis, and (2) the fact that Wright had obtained a partial confession from Ellis.' Gordon Corera in *The Art of Betrayal* (2011) says the Fluency Committee's '1967 report concluded there were 28 anomalies that could not be attributed to any spy who had yet been identified'.

Chapter 2 THE TOILS OF CHILDHOOD

1 Friedmann was the surname of Litzi's first husband, Karl, whom she had divorced when she met Philby. Her actual maiden name was Kohlman. In *A Spy Among Friends* (2014), Ben Macintyre refers to her as Kohlman, as did Yuri Modin in *My Five Cambridge Friends: Burgess, Maclean, Philby, Blunt and Cairncross* (1994). Litzi Friedmann is spelled 'Lizi Friedman' by Chapman Pincher in *Too Secret Too Long* (1984) while Philby's autobiography, *My Silent War* (1968), gives the spelling as 'Litzi Friedman'.

2 Ellis's birth is registered in 1895 with the New South Wales Registry of Births, Deaths & Marriages in the district of Leichhardt, New South Wales. The registration number is 1121.

3 Ellis may privately have been a proud Australian, but for James Cotton to argue in his 2016 paper that Ellis was 'pleased to be identified as an Australian' is arguable. It appears he spent much of his life pretending to be otherwise.

4 Sourced from Hyde, *Secret Intelligence Agent* and Ellis, 'My early life (the Ellis family)'. The latter piece of writing was likely part of a planned book by Ellis on his time in Melbourne. Ann Salwey told Melbourne's *Herald* on 22 October 1983: 'I have all the notes on a book he wanted to write about Melbourne from around 1900 to 1910 – all his early recollections.'

5 Various accounts have Ellis being a distant relation of William Webb Ellis of rugby fame, but this is likely apocryphal.

6 Carmel Andrew, the community history technician at Inner West Council, Sydney, uncovered an interesting document regarding Ellis's birthplace: 'In the 1895 *Annandale Rate Book* W. Ellis was recorded as an occupier or tenant living in the third house from the corner at 110 Annandale Street, Annandale, located between Collins and Reserve Streets.' The house at 110 Annandale Street still exists and a reconnaissance confirmed it is the same unidentified property pictured in the Dick Ellis Papers at the NLA. I actually came across the house by complete accident while driving with my daughter, and thought to myself, 'That looks like the house in the picture.' It can now be verified as the birthplace of Ellis.

7 Lillian Ellis is buried at Rookwood Cemetery, Sydney.

8 Hyde in *Secret Intelligence Agent* says Ellis was raised by his mother's grandparents in Christchurch until he went to school in Melbourne. This is not true according to Ellis's late son, Olik Ellis. In an 8 July 1994 letter to Frank Cain for Ellis's entry in the 1996 edition of the *Australian Dictionary of Biography*, Olik says his father was

taken to Brisbane and Launceston and returned to Melbourne in 1902–03. Maisie went to Christchurch. Oddly, there is both a birth and death notice at myheritage. com for Lillian M. Ellis in 1898, though this is likely a mix-up with her mother.

9   Ellis described his father as an 'artist' in his entry in *Contemporary Authors* (1965).

10 William Edward Ellis was born in 1829 and married his first wife, Ann Ball Cooper or Annie Ball (1831–84), in Sydney in 1851 when he was 22. Ellis's siblings/ half-siblings were Annie, Katie, Stanley and Maisie.

11 Rosstown is now called Carnegie. It was renamed in 1909.

12 Glen Eira Historical Society informed me: 'The school history contains a class photo from 1901 with Thomas H. Boardman as the head teacher.'

13 The Battle of Tsushima took place in May 1905.

14 James Cotton erroneously calls it 'Stott House' in his 2016 paper on Ellis. Magazine advertisements of the era later had the name of the college as Stott's Technical College. Stott's College exists to this day in Melbourne with other campuses.

15 It's not known what happened to Maisie Ellis, though Ellis did keep in touch with her. A photo-postcard from 1913 held in the Dick Ellis Papers in the NLA is addressed to 'My dear Maisie' with 'Best love, Charlie.' She is no relation to Maisie Ellis, the actress who appeared in the 1908 short *Lady Letmere's Jewellery*. Maisie would have been 11 years old in 1908.

16 Again, Cotton misnames the company, calling it Melville, Mullen and Slade. It was Melville & Mullen after 1900.

17 I contacted Caulfield Grammar School archivist Judith Gibson to access records of Ellis's enrolment at Malvern. She told me: 'I'm unable to confirm the enrolment of Ellis at Malvern Grammar School. When Caulfield Grammar School [CGS] affiliated in 1960 with Malvern . . . limited information and enrolment registers were located and passed across to CGS. So, no enrolment registers or academic cards are held for the years of 1890–1923, when Charles McLean was founder and headmaster. Nor [do] any published magazines exist in any comprehensive way, until the Malvern school magazine was established in 1936. So the gap with information is frustrating . . . [but] all around CGS were many small private schools.'

18 Now a hotel development in an area of the city called Southbank.

19 Ellis's papers at the NLA mention a 'Professor Rentoul' coaching Ellis for a scholarship; likely this was Irishman John Laurence Rentoul, a biblical languages and Christian philosophy professor at Ormond College. He died in 1926. Ellis was nominally a Presbyterian Christian. Writes Cotton, who had access to Ann Salwey: 'Though conclusive evidence is lacking, the most prominent figure in the teaching of both history and literature was John Laurence Rentoul . . . who, according to family sources, himself coached Ellis.'

20 In his entry in the 1965 edition of *Contemporary Authors*, Ellis wrote of his education: 'Melbourne Business College 1909–11, University of Melbourne 1912–13, St Edmund Hall 1914–15, 1920–21, Sorbonne University of Paris 1921.' As much as all this sounds impressive, Ellis never completed a degree. Melbourne, for instance, was not mentioned in Ellis's undergraduate application for Oxford. Nigel West wrote in his *Historical Dictionary of International Intelligence* (2006) that Ellis 'graduated from the Sorbonne' – this is not true. In the 2001 documentary *Camp X*, Ellis was called 'a Rhodes scholar' – this is also not true.

21 Hyde in *Secret Intelligence Agent* says Ellis 'joined an Australian troop contingent bound for England' but this would appear not to be the case when the first troop convoys left in October 1914.

Chapter 3   FRONT TO FRONTIER

1   Ellis's career was supposed to have also covered the Balkans and there is an essay about the Balkans in his collected materials at the NLA but there is no extant record (at least that I can find) of his service in that region of Europe. He mentions serving in the Balkans in his author biography in *The Expansion of Russia* (1965).

2 This contradicts Cotton's claim that 'he enrolled at St Edmund Hall, Oxford, for a course in languages, in the autumn' and that 'his studies at Oxford were cut short by volunteering for service in the Great War'.

3 Letter, Dick Ellis to May and June Henry, 20 March 1919.

4 Another Australian soldier with the name Charles Howard Ellis, a private in the 50th Australian Infantry Battalion of the Australian Imperial Force, was killed in action on the Somme on 5 April 1918.

5 According to James Cotton, Ellis 'experienced, according to family sources, nightmares about the war periodically for the rest of his life'.

6 Letter, Dick Ellis to May and June Henry, 20 March 1919.

7 Ellis writes in *The Transcaspian Episode, 1918–1919* (1963): 'My own participation in military operations in Transcaspia and Baku was fortuitous. After serving as an infantry officer for two years in France and Egypt I was posted to India, and in the autumn of 1917 found myself attached to a battalion of the South Lancashire Regiment stationed at Quetta in Baluchistan.' The timing of his deployment to Egypt and India in the book doesn't match with military records and other documents I have seen. The handwriting on the back of a photograph of Ellis in the Dick Ellis Papers at the NLA taken on the SS *Mutlah* while he was crossing the Red Sea clearly says, 'Jan 1918'. The *Mutlah* was a ship used to transport Indian labourers from India to British colonies such as Trinidad and Fiji. This suggests Ellis was on his way to India in early 1918 from Egypt.

8 See Ellis, *The Transcaspian Episode, 1918–1919* (1963).

9 *ibid.*

10 Not to be confused with Turkistan, a city in Kazakhstan.

11 Ellis is referring to Vladimir Liakhov's Cossack Brigade bombarding and then shutting down the Shah-opposing Iranian Parliament, the Majlis.

12 From Arthur Swinson's *Beyond the Frontiers: The Biography of Colonel F. M. Bailey, Explorer and Special Agent* (1971): 'Intent on forestalling a German-Turkish thrust from the Caucasus through northern Persia or Turkestan, towards Afghanistan and India, the Indian Government had set up two cordons. The first of brigade strength under General Dunsterville (and later known as "Dunsterforce") was sent to Baku. Here it succeeded in occupying the town but a few days later was driven out. However, the Royal Navy secured command of the Caspian Sea, a vital step should the Turco-German threat materialise. The second cordon under Major General W. Malleson (whose force also amounted to a brigade) was set up on the Meshed–Merv line, with orders to keep a close watch on the situation in Transcaspia, take action against enemy agents trying to penetrate Afghanistan or Baluchistan from the west, and take advantage of any opportunities to deny the use of the Central Asian railway to the enemy.

'Malleson, it should be explained, had served on the Intelligence Staff at G.H.Q. [general headquarters] Delhi, and on Lord Kitchener's staff, almost without a break from 1904 to 1914. He knew Persia and Afghanistan well and had made a study of communications throughout the whole Middle Asian area. Apart from a short period as bridge commander he had little experience of command, and indeed had been selected for the post at Meshed as a senior Intelligence Officer. As his role changed from Intelligence to operations, however, he came under a great deal of criticism, and he was certainly not the man to lead troops in battle. According to Colonel C. H. Ellis, who served on the mission, he had a dour personality, lacking "interest in society or the lighter graces of an army career". He was not an attractive man at all.'

13 From *Strolling About on the Roof of the World: The First Hundred Years of the Royal Society for Asian Affairs (Formerly Royal Central Asian Society)* by Hugh Leach with Susan Maria Farrington (2002): 'Dunsterforce eventually reached Baku in stages from Enzeli only to find local troops too involved in nationalist politics to offer any serious resistance to the Turks. By dint of subterfuge and with the help of [Commodore David] Norris's [British] Caspian flotilla, Dunsterville managed to

evacuate his forces to Enzeli, whence he was redirected to Krasnovodsk. Meanwhile, Malleson was ordered to carry out intelligence and military operations across the Russian frontier to prevent the Transcaspian railway being taken over by Turkish or Bolshevik forces. However, the collapse of Germany and her allies, and the temporary reoccupation of Baku by British forces, changed the strategic situation, and by March 1919 all British and Indian troops were withdrawn from Transcaspia either to Meshed or to Baku.'

The same book mentions Ellis was appointed a member of RSAA's editorial board for its journal in the 1960s: 'It was not until July 1961 that an Editorial Board was established, consisting of at least two members of Council, the remainder from the Society at large. Its first members were Lieutenant Colonel Geoffrey Wheeler, who became the Board's Chairman, Sir Gilbert Laithwaite (later to become the Society's Chairman), the journalist and broadcaster Mr Neville Barbour, Miss Violet Conolly, Colonel C. H. Ellis and Mr E. H. Paxton . . . an editor was appointed in October. Amongst those considered were Mr Stewart Perowne (husband of Freya Stark) and Colonel C. H. Ellis.'

Chapter 4   **STALIN AND THE KING'S MESSENGER**

1   A *verst* is a Russian measure of distance equal to 1.1 kilometres. Quoted from 'Some fresh news about the 26 Commissars: Reginald Teague-Jones and the Transcaspian Episode', Taline Ter Minassian, *Asian Affairs*, Routledge, Abingdon-on-Thames, Vol. XLV, No. 1, 14 February 2014.

2   *ibid*.: 'The director of the Institute of History at the Azerbaijan Academy of Sciences rightfully pointed out in February 2009 that the "Soviet story was entirely a falsification". Relying upon an Azerbaijani forensic medical investigation Yagub Makhmudov further insisted that 23 bodies were exhumed (which means that three bodies are missing) and that among the 26 Commissars there were as a matter of fact only eight real Bolshevik commissars (Shahumian, Azizbekov, Djaparidze, Fioletov, Zevine, Karganov, Vezirov and Petrov). He recalls that the others were not at all "commissars" (some of them were even train drivers) and not all of them were Bolsheviks – Amirian, for example, was a Dashnak nationalist Armenian.'

3   'Baku commissars', H. Montgomery Hyde, *Times*, London, 18 October 1961.

4   Knightley film pitch, *op. cit.*

5   Brian Pearce's letters to Chapman Pincher in the Chapman Pincher Papers held by King's College attest to this fact. In late 2022, Pearce's private archives were in the possession of Taline Ter Minassian and they contained a file on Ellis, which she generously copied for me.

6   'Ronald Sinclair: carrying his true identity to the grave', Peter Hopkirk, *Times*, London, 25 November 1988.

7   Letter, Dick Ellis to May and June Henry, 20 March 1919.

8   The book was translated into Persian, *Dikhālat-i niẓāmī-yi Brītānīyā dar shumāl-i Khurāsān 1918–1919*, in 1993.

9   From *The First Fifty Years: Soviet Russia, 1917–67* by Ian Grey, Coward-McCann, New York, 1967.

10 Ter Minassian made a startling claim in her book: 'Far from being a double agent in the service of Germany or the Soviet Union, Ellis was in fact completely cleared several years later.' When I contacted Ter Minassian, she explained that Margaret Thatcher's letter to Ellis's daughter, Ann Salwey, had given her the impression that the Ellis case had been cleared.

11 From Peter Hopkirk, *On Secret Service East of Constantinople: The Plot to Bring Down the British Empire*, John Murray, London, 1994.

12 In the letter, the name 'Bakeis' appears but there is no geographical record of a Bakeis. Ellis is either referring to Bathus or Bathys, the Greek name for Batum (Batumi), the Georgian port on the Black Sea, or Baku in Azerbaijan. It is not clear. Olik Ellis's timeline of his father's life mentions Batum in 1919, so it is most likely Batum.

13 Denikin was a White Russian military leader of the Volunteer Army and deputy supreme ruler of Russia during the Russian Civil War. He had supported the Transcaspian government in its fight with the Tashkent Soviet.

14 Letter, Dick Ellis to May and June Henry, 3 October 1919.

15 Letter, Dick Ellis to Alfred Brotherston Emden, 8 September 1920.

16 Sometime that year, a book by Ellis called *War and Politics in Central Asia* was also privately published, though I have not been able to locate a copy and it could be related to Ellis's article about Central Asia in *Stead's Review*. It is mentioned in the 1933 and 1934 editions of *Who's Who in Literature*.

17 James Cotton, *op. cit.*: 'Ellis's sympathies were socialist or socialist-liberal' and 'there can be little doubt that, in common with many of his generation, Ellis's life and outlook were moulded by the horrors of the Great War . . . Ellis's direct experience of Bolshevism first in Russia and then in the world of espionage seems to have inoculated him against placing any confidence in Leninist forms of internationalism.'

18 Stevenson expanded on Ellis's knowledge of Islam in *Past to Present* (2012): 'George Evans of the London *Daily Telegraph* . . . had done his military service in Afghanistan and learned local tribal tongues. His tutor was Charles "Dick" Ellis, who frustrated Russian efforts to control the region between two world wars. I know Ellis as Intrepid's former deputy. He authored *Transcaspian Episode*, a classic textbook on how to thwart Russian intrigues. Ellis outwitted Soviet enemies after his battlefield service in 1914–18. He studied Lawrence of Arabia, Mao, Tito, and the causes of France's 16 years of defeat in Indochina and Algeria. "Nothing rivalled The Great Game for control of the Muslim belt from Siberia to the Mideast," he wrote. "Nothing is more impossible to win than Afghanistan . . . our frontier officers all read Kipling's *Kim* and observed Uzbek traders who came to Peshawar through the Khyber Pass with their rugs, silks and lambskins."'

19 Letter, Dick Ellis to H. Montgomery Hyde, 26 December 1960. Interestingly, Ellis contributed a picture of Shamyl to *Hutchinson's New 20th Century Encyclopedia* by E. M. Horsley in 1964.

Chapter 5   A STRANGER IN A STRANGE LAND

1 Cotton gets this part wrong: 'In August 1920 [Ellis] arrived back in Australia, visiting family and staying until early 1921, when he returned to Britain and resumed his enrolment at Oxford.'

2 The Roberts family lived at 40 The Avenue, Highams Park.

3 As Rob Petre, college archivist at St Edmund Hall, Oxford, helpfully explains: 'Ellis was admitted to the *hall* on 7 October; matriculation is the ceremony in which students become members of the *university*, and you can only matriculate if you have been admitted to a hall or college.'

4 According to *St Edmund Hall Magazine* in 1951, A. A. Gordon died in June 1950.

5 Nigel West gets it wrong in *Unreliable Witness* (1984): 'Dick Ellis had originally joined His Majesty's Consular Service in Istanbul in 1921 but, in 1923, he transferred into SIS, having been recommended for recruitment by the Head of Station in Paris, Major T. M. Langton. His appointment to the SIS post of Assistant Passport Control Officer in Berlin was confirmed in a letter dated 24 October 1923 from the headquarters of the Secret Intelligence Service in London to the Foreign Office. Yet in his preface [to *A Man Called Intrepid*] Ellis states that he had been "twenty years in the professional secret intelligence service when in 1940 London sent me to British Security Co-ordination [sic] headquarters in New York". He had actually only been nearly seventeen years in the service by then. Perhaps this error can be explained by consulting *Who's Who*, which refers to "various consular posts since 1921". To someone familiar with the traditional diplomatic cover given to SIS officers, such a description might suggest that Ellis had indeed joined SIS in 1921. But the truth is that Ellis spent two years genuinely working as an acting vice-consul before his transfer to SIS.'

6   Ellis left Southampton and arrived on the *Olympic* in New York. Shipping records
    have his nationality as English. He gave his address as 'Oxford Unit, England . . .
    St Edmund Hall'.

7   Petre again: 'Typically all degree courses at that date took three years, but in Oxford
    it is usually counted as terms in residence rather than years; I think you had to have
    been up for at least nine terms before you could take a BA [Bachelor of Arts].'

8   For that reason, Chapman Pincher's claim in *Too Secret Too Long* (1984) that 'the
    files showed that Ellis, who was born in Sydney in 1895, had been an outstanding
    student of modern languages' makes you question what files Pincher was looking at.

9   James Cotton, *op. cit.*: 'Ellis's decision then to re-enter military ranks should
    be understood according to the prevailing standards. He had previously held a
    wartime commission. Now he was offered a post in the British Army (initially in the
    Territorials), which gave him entrée into the military caste, and potentially a future
    position in the national elite.'

10 That year he apparently published in Sydney a pamphlet called *Mozart and the
    Orchestra*, but I have not been able to find a copy. Ellis includes it in his author
    biography for *The Expansion of Russia* (1965).

11 Harington (one R) was the commander of Britain's occupying forces in Turkey and
    the Black Sea. See Olik Ellis, 'Charles Howard Ellis' timeline, 1994.

12 The line 'over-close relationships between SIS's Russian-speaking officers, using
    their own names, and their Russian agents, and the socialising between both groups
    which led to a most unprofessional level of interconsciousness' is attributed as a
    verbatim Ellis quote in the research paper 'Issues in British and American signals
    intelligence, 1919–1932' (2015). There are doubts about its accuracy.

13 Teague-Jones's reunion with Ellis in Constantinople is corroborated by Olik Ellis in
    his timeline.

14 'Abolition appointment of the Special Intelligence Officer, Constantinople. Case
    of Messrs. Vivian and Miller', File No. 96, Part III, Serial Nos. 1–11, Home
    Department (Political), Government of India, Simla, 1922. In 1921 Teague-Jones
    had apparently changed his name to Miller, which would become Sinclair the
    following year. This has not been mentioned in previous accounts of Teague-Jones.

15 An interdepartmental meeting at the India Office on 2 November that year
    recommended Teague-Jones have his contract renewed from 15 November 1920
    through to 31 March 1922. If Ellis arrived in Constantinople in late 1921, the two were
    reunited on Turkish soil after the 'Baku Commissars' incident and it stands to reason
    Ellis, an expert on Transcaspia, would work with his old colleague from Central Asia.
    Teague-Jones went to England in April 1922 and changed his name in May 1922.

16 Part III, Serial Nos. 1–11, Home Department (Political), Government of India,
    Simla, 1922.

17 Vivian, a career spy, kept a file on George Orwell in Paris in 1929, led the SIS
    interrogation of Walter Krivitsky in 1940 and recruited Kim Philby into the SIS in
    1941. He headed CE or Section V (counterespionage) of SIS from 1925 and worked
    for SIS until his retirement in 1951, the year Philby resigned. See Australian writer
    Darcy Moore's story on Vivian, Philby and George Orwell. Details in Bibliography.
    Philby had been working as a Soviet spy since 1934.

18 Britain's National Archives records the spelling as Elisabeth. But Elizabeth is more
    frequently seen. Phillip Knightley in his Ellis film pitch calls Lilia 'Irena', while Olik
    Ellis, her son, gives his mother's full name as Elizaveta (Lilia) Nikolaevna Zelensky.
    James Cotton also calls her Elizaveta. A record on ancestry.com has her as 'Lila
    Zelenski'.

19 Elizabeth (Lilia or Elisabeth) Zelensky was born in Kiev, Ukraine, in July 1905. She
    remarried in 1936, this time to Robert Gardiner, a consulting electrical engineer;
    he died in 1953. She remarried again, to a man called Robert Siddons, and died of
    cancer in West Cobham, Surrey, in April 1974, aged 68. Nelly Zelensky was born in
    1906 in Mariupol, Ukraine, and died in Paris in 1996. Aleksei Zelensky was born in
    1913 in Mariupol, Ukraine, and died in Paris in 1987. In *Secret Intelligence Agent*,
    H. Montgomery Hyde says his nickname was 'Sasha'.

20 This is confirmed in the book *Handbuch für das Deutsche Reich Bearbeitet im Reichsamte des Innern* by Reichsministerium des Innern (1924).

21 Now the Casino Wien.

22 It appears West took this snippet of information from Hyde's *Secret Intelligence Agent*: 'He remained based in Berlin on and off for the next 14 years or so.' Foley was the subject of Michael Smith's biography, *Foley: The Spy Who Saved 10,000 Jews* (1999).

23 Nelidov was well known to the Nazis. See KV 2/2467 and KV 2/2468.

Chapter 6   THE LEAGUE OF GENTLEMEN

1 There were claims that British envoy to the League, Konni Zilliacus – whom Chapman Pincher in *Traitors: The Labyrinths of Treason* (1987) calls a 'crypto communist' – was the real author of the book. James Cotton debunks this: 'A letter from Zilliacus himself to Walter Lippmann provides conclusive proof that Ellis was the author.' Cotton adds: 'That Ellis might also have been keeping an intelligence eye on Zilliacus is not completely improbable, given the latter's evident Russian sympathies . . . against the authorship of Zilliacus is the fact that the Ellis family always held that [Ellis] was the author, and indeed a copy of the book is to be found in his personal papers.'

2 Cotton again: 'Ellis was accredited at the League of Nations as a working journalist, though officially not in connection with the *Morning Post* but with *The Times of India*.'

3 A. M. Ross-Smith, 'New evidence on a spy that never was', *Daily Telegraph*, London, 19 April 1984.

4 'Meetings: Session 1932–1933', *The Geographical Journal*, Vol. LXXXI, No. 1, Royal Geographical Society, London, January 1933. Ellis was made a fellow on 21 November 1932 on the following grounds: 'Has travelled extensively throughout the world and has written several books on international affairs.' This was not true, clearly. He was recommended personally by Ronald Sinclair (Reginald Teague-Jones) and Captain C. M. Coleman of the Indian Army and resigned on 13 December 1937.

5 Ellis was reelected to a fellowship on 2 December 1957. 'Meetings: Session 1957–1958', *The Geographical Journal*, Vol. CXXIV, No. 1, Royal Geographical Society, London, March 1958. He was made a fellow on these grounds: 'Oriental language and history specialist; has lectured to universities in Australia and UK, most recently St. Anthony's College, Oxford. Writing a book on Central Asian expeditions 1917–19. Former Fellow of Society. Widely travelled and resident abroad in Middle and especially Far East.' Ellis resigned on 12 December 1960.

6 Ellis's *Who's Who* entry is illustrative of the gaps in his conventional biography and how difficult it is to get a clear picture of his life. Ellis appeared in the 1955, 1973, 1974 and 1975 editions and *Contemporary Authors 13–14* (1965). In the 1955 edition Ellis gives his address as 52 Coleherne Court, SW5:

Ellis, Charles Howard
CMG 1953; CBE 1946 (OBE 1919); TD 1953

Born 13 Feb. 1895; s of William Edward Ellis, Exeter, Devon, and Sydney, Australia, and Lillian Mary Hobday; m 1st, 1933, Barbara Mary Burgess-Smith (marr. diss., 1947); one s one d; 2nd, 1954, Alexandra Wood (née Surtees); died 5 July 1975

Retired from Foreign Office

Education:
Melbourne Univ.; Oxford Univ.; Sorbonne

Career:
Served European War, 1914–18; Middlesex Regt; France, Egypt, India, Persia, S. Russia; Afghan War, 1919; Caucasus and Black Sea, 1919–20; Foreign Office and Consular posts in Turkey, Berlin, Far East and USA, 1921–39; War of 1939–45;

Col on Staff of missions in USA and Egypt and Far East. Foreign Office and posts in Far East, 1946–53; retired, 1953. US Legion of Merit, 1946

Publications:
The Transcaspian Episode, 1963; *The Expansion of Russia*, 1965; *The New Left in Britain*, 1968; *Soviet Imperialism*, 1970; *Mission Accomplished*, 1973 [sic]

Recreations:
Music, drama, travel

Clubs:
Travellers, Royal Automobile

Address:
The Hollies, Hempnall, Norwich, Norfolk

His entry in *Contemporary Authors* makes no mention of Zelensky, refers to his son as 'Olik C' and spells his daughter's name as 'Salway'. At the time Ellis was working on a book called *Falsification of History*, which he expected to finish in 1966, but it never appeared anywhere.

7   Bill Ross-Smith asserted Aleksei Zelensky never existed but Aleksej Zelenski did. 'New evidence on a spy that never was', A. M. Ross-Smith, *Daily Telegraph*, 19 April 1984.

8   Chapman Pincher in a 29 April 1982 *Australian* article (also contained in a separate 29-page typescript in the Chapman Pincher Papers) claims Ellis told his interrogators he was blackmailed circa 1926–27 after going broke in 1926, throwing out all the conventional timelines for the alleged Ellis treason with the Abwehr. Ellis was employed and undercover in Vienna and Geneva at this time. Pincher omitted these dates when he reworked the same article for 1984's *Too Secret Too Long*. This shifting of dates suggests Pincher was not on solid ground with his accusations against Ellis.

Chapter 7   THE SPY FROM SANTIAGO

1   Now Rezidenza La Tanzina in Lugano.

2   See 'Otto Rusche v. Herbert Brownell, Jr., 244 F.2d 782 (D.C. Cir. 1957)'.

3   Given the similarity between the names 'Atle' and 'Attlee', it should be noted that Clement Attlee, who was British prime minister from 1945–51 and opposition leader from 1935–40 and 1951–55, is not known to have had anything to do with it either.

4   Writes William Stevenson in captions for *A Man Called Intrepid*: '[Stephenson's] Camp X became the staging area for Heydrich's assassination. Every available detail of his habits, daily schedule, and surroundings was studied. His regular routes were photographed, built into three-dimensional scale models, and in critical places actually constructed full size . . . the decision to proceed was soul-searing, but it was made.' In Bill Macdonald's *The True Intrepid* (1998, republished in 2001), Bill Ross-Smith says Heydrich's killing 'had nothing to do with British Security Coordination'. Ellis also never mentioned the assassination of Heydrich in his aborted literary works.

5   They were discovered by the US Army in the office of Wehrmacht Lieutenant Colonel Gustave Baetz in Köthen (Anhalt), Germany, on 14 April 1945.

6   See KV 2/2467.

7   See KV 2/2468. It's an interesting detail because of Vladimir von Petrov being called the head of a forgery 'factory' in Berlin in his file, KV 2/3858, which proves there is a clear link between Zelensky and Von Petrov in Germany and not France, as alleged by Nigel West and repeated by others. The idea that Ellis while in France was involved in passing any information to the Nazis can now be discounted. If it was taking place, it was happening in Berlin.

8 In Aleksandr Nelidov's confession, reproduced in West and Tsarev's *TRIPLEX* (2009), he says. 'London [MI6] gave an order for the fabrication of false documents, leaflets, propaganda brochures and a whole series of other documents calculated to incense the public by scaring peace-loving bourgeois citizens with the "Red Menace". The only success was the famous Zinoviev letter.' The Zinoviev letter was purportedly written by Comintern head Grigori Zinoviev to the British Communist Party and, in the words of the *Guardian*, 'called on British communists to mobilise "sympathetic forces" in the Labour Party to support an Anglo-Soviet treaty (including a loan to the Bolshevik government) and to encourage "agitation-propaganda" in the armed forces.' A copy of the letter was sent to the *Daily Mail* and published four days before the 1924 general election. Curiously, a 1966 *Sunday Times* clipping about the Zinoviev letter is contained in the Dick Ellis Papers at the NLA, though Ellis has never been linked to the letter.

9 See KV 2/2468.

10 See Abwehr report dated 16 February 1932 in KV 2/2467.

11 Reads the National Archives description: 'Helmuth KNOCHEN: German. KNOCHEN was a Gestapo chief in Paris, head of SD, and aide to the "Butcher of Paris", Karl [sic] Oberg.'

12 In Knochen's file (KV 2/2745), in a secret SIS document dated 2 May 1946, Von Petrov is said to have the alias PANNWITZ (possibly a confusion with Dr Heinz Pannwitz), which is not mentioned in the description for Von Petrov's file. He is also referred to as PETRO. It states he had a connection to Heydrich. In the file there is a list of questions SIS wants its interrogators to ask Knochen about Von Petrov.

'[Von Petrov] went to Rome in 1941, made trips also to Spain and Switzerland. In 1943 he was closely connected with [Hans] Josef Kieffer, Chief of Amt VI in Paris. Late in the summer of 1944 he went to Switzerland.' The file confirms Von Petrov worked for MI6: 'What else did he do for the SIS?' and 'What material did the SIS get from him there?'

13 See KV 2/96, statement dated 21 July 1945.

14 The reference to 'daughter of the diamond king' would suggest Elly was the daughter of Sir Bernard Oppenheimer, 1st Baronet Oppenheimer of Stoke Poges (d. 1921) and Lady Lena Oppenheimer (d. 1937). They had three children but none married Vladimir von Petrov. The two daughters were Elsie Rose Oppenheimer and Madeleine Hilda Oppenheimer. Elly could potentially be an abbreviation of Elsie or Madeleine.

15 Letter, 8 April 1945, KV 2/1009.

16 The book reveals that one of the 'Cambridge Five', Anthony Blunt, Surveyor of the Queen's Pictures from 1945–72, was recruited by 'a middle-class Eastern European whom he knew only as "Otto".' This 'Otto' met Kim Philby and John Cairncross. Otto von Bohl, perhaps coincidentally, was an alias of Vladimir von Petrov. But Von Bohl wasn't Von Petrov.

Peter Wright wrote in *Spycatcher* that 'Otto' had never been identified: 'Like [Maly], "Otto" was a middle-class East European, probably Czech, who was able to make the Soviet cause appealing not simply for political reasons but because he shared with his young recruits the same cultured European background. [Anthony] Blunt admitted to me on many occasions that he doubted he would ever have joined had the approach come from a Russian. For some reason, we were never able to identify "Otto".'

However, Ben Macintyre in his book *A Spy Among Friends* (2014) identifies him as Arnold Deutsch: a Czech Jew who'd grown up in Austria.

In *Alexander Orlov: The FBI's KGB General* (2002), FBI special agent Edward Gazur writes that Maly's 'operational codename was Mann. Mally [sic] was one of the best illegals who worked in the capitals of Europe during the early and mid-1930s.' Gazur says Maly met Orlov, 'the chief of the illegal *rezidentura* in

London for a time in the mid-1930s' in Paris in July 1937, where he was warned not to return to Moscow. But return he did and by November he had disappeared. Gazur's papers at Georgetown University in Washington DC describe Orlov as 'the highest-ranking Soviet officer to ever defect to the West'.

17 KV 2/1008.

Chapter 8   THE GENERAL

1   He was not a prince according to Czech historian Stanislav A. Auský. In a 2 December 1985 letter to Chapman Pincher, Auský writes: 'Turkul was not prince [sic]. He was even not a nobleman.' Auský died in 2010.

2   In the Walter Schellenberg file at the National Archives in London (KV 2/99) it names Turkul as working for Amt VI, the foreign political intelligence department of SD. Schellenberg refers to meeting Turkul in his interrogation. See KV 2/96. Schellenberg's relationship with Turkul is also detailed in Turkul's file. See KV 2/1591.

3   See 'Interrogation of Turkul' in KV 2/1592.

4   See KV 2/1591.

5   Aarons and Loftus in *Unholy Trinity* (1991) write the NTS 'had been created by Stalin as a means to infiltrate Hitler's Nazi Party in Germany. During World War II, the NTS and the Nazis worked hand in hand. In fact, NTS was virtually the sole source of German intelligence inside the Soviet Union. Under the direction of Prince Anton Turkul, NTS passed on reams of misinformation that crippled the Nazi military offensive on the Eastern Front.'

6   'Russian general protests French expulsion order', no byline, *New York Herald Tribune*, Paris, 26 April 1938.

7   In his 2 December 1985 letter to Pincher, Auský disputed Rosenberg's closeness to Hitler: 'Rosenberg was never close to Hitler and he was many times ridiculed by him . . . [he] sent a letter of resignation to Hitler in Nov. 1944.'

8   In *Mask of Treachery* (1988), John Costello calls the network 'Vansittart's Private Detective Agency', which appears to have been nicked from F. H. Hinsley's *British Intelligence in the Second World War* (1979), which carries the same description, word for word, as well as calling it 'virtually a private intelligence service'. Curiously there is no mention of Vansittart in Stevenson's books *A Man Called Intrepid* and *Intrepid's Last Case* but he is mentioned briefly in H. Montgomery Hyde's *The Quiet Canadian*, Phillip Knightley's *The Second Oldest Profession,* Peter Wright's *Spycatcher* and Chapman Pincher's *Their Trade is Treachery.*

9   From *The Siren Years: A Canadian Diplomat Abroad, 1937–1945* by Charles Ritchie (1974).

10 K. Gram-Skjoldager and H. A. Ikonomou, authors of the paper 'The construction of the League of Nations Secretariat: formative practices of autonomy and legitimacy in international organisations' (2017), call Ellis's book 'at once a historical–legal exploration of the League and a liberal-socialist manifesto for world peace'.

11 See KV 2/1591.

12 Rufina Pukhova, Kim Philby's late widow, denied this claim in her book *The Private Life of Kim Philby: The Moscow Years* (1999): 'The chapter titled "The Philby Connection" draws on a mix of primary and secondary sources from which the authors reach dubious conclusions. The comments regarding Philby's links to White Russian Prince Turkul and SIS officer Dick Ellis are unsupported.'

13 The description of Ellis as a 'horrible little man' was by Nicholas Elliott, the subject (along with Kim Philby) of Ben Macintyre's *A Spy Among Friends* (2014). A 29 July 1981 note by Pincher (in his papers, now held by King's College) confirms this. Elliott thought Ellis was 'a bloody traitor' and had known of his confession from 1965. 'All agreed on secrecy.'

14 The 'Skobline' Pincher referred to was in fact Nikolai Skoblin, most famous for the kidnapping and drugging of General Yevgeny Miller in Paris in 1937, who was sent back to the Soviet Union and executed in 1939.

15 See KV 2/1591.

16 'Questions, questions, questions: memories of Oberursel', Arnold M. Silver, *Intelligence and National Security*, Vol. 8, No. 2, Frank Cass Publishers, London, 1993.

17 'Drozdovians' (or 'Drozdovites') refers to the Drozdov division commanded by Turkul in the Russian Civil War.

18 Knightley writes in the footnote: 'There are many versions of the Ellis story. This one comes from an interview with one of Ellis's senior officers. The author will forward letters to him.'

Chapter 9   A DANGEROUS GAME

1 What these records are is not specified. Knightley in his pitch for a film on Ellis said Ellis's file in German secret-service records was found by the Soviets who blackmailed Ellis.

2 He was executed by firing squad on 9 April 1945 at Dachau concentration camp.

3 *Generaloberst* Beck was shot in Berlin (after attempting suicide with a pistol) on 20 July 1944 for his leadership role in the assassination plot against the *Führer*. Canaris was hanged in Flossenbürg concentration camp on 9 April 1945.

4 For a fuller account of this, see Eunan O'Halpin's research paper 'Small states and big secrets: understanding Sigint cooperation between unequal powers during the Second World War' (2002).

5 See *Their Trade is Treachery*. Ellis's friends H. Montgomery Hyde and Bill Ross-Smith were in agreement that Ellis did not become a full-time officer for MI6 until 1938, when, as Hyde writes in *Secret Intelligence Agent* (1982), 'the Nazi threat caused serious alarm at the time of the Munich crisis'. This is also mentioned in Hyde's letter to Chapman Pincher on 15 August 1984.

6 See Hooper, *Official Secrets: The Use and Abuse of the Act* (1987).

7 Z Organisation was tasked with intelligence gathering in Germany and Italy.

8 There is a mention by Kim Philby of Section X in *TRIPLEX* (2009), in which he refers to a Section X officer 'responsible for telephones, telegrams, liaison with the Post Office, telegraph companies, etc'.

9 West is particularly speculative about Ellis in his book *A Matter of Trust: MI5 1945–72* (1982); ditto in *Historical Dictionary of British Intelligence* (2005): 'Strangely, this particular source, once valued as a window in Joachim von Ribbentrop's activities, was compromised soon after Ellis had been indoctrinated into it.' Virtually the same wording appears in *The Faber Book of Espionage* (1993), edited by West.

Chapter 10   THE VENLO MYTH

1 As Nigel West points out in *A Matter of Trust: MI5 1945–72* (1982), James Ramsay MacDonald's son, Malcolm, was British high commissioner to Canada 'at the time of [Igor] Gouzenko's defection'. Malcolm MacDonald was later appointed governor-general of Malaya and Singapore, then commissioner-general for South-East Asia in Singapore at the same time Ellis was based in Singapore.

2 See Bill Macdonald, *The True Intrepid* (1998) and *Intrepid's Last Secrets* (2019).

3 Frederick Leathers, 1st Viscount Leathers, later Churchill's Minister of War Transport. He's described as Stephenson's 'English friend and business associate' and 'a close personal friend' in Hyde's *The Quiet Canadian* (1962).

4 See Olik Ellis, 'Charles Howard Ellis' timeline, 1994.

5 See entry for 13 September 1939 in *The Guy Liddell Diaries: MI5's Director of Counter-Espionage in World War II, Volume I: 1939–42* (2005). The second volume, also published in 2005 and edited by Nigel West, covers 1942–45.

6 A statement clearly sourced from Peter Wright, who wrote in *Spycatcher* (1987) that Stevens and Best 'were amazed how much the Abwehr knew about the organisation of MI6'.

7   John Costello in *Mask of Treachery* (1988) concludes similarly, writing that
     Ellis 'was responsible for the Venlo incident of November 1939'. Hyde's *Secret
     Intelligence Agent* (1982) oddly makes no mention of Ellis being connected to Venlo,
     though says Stevens and Best 'gave the Germans a more or less faithful picture of the
     operation of the SIS organisation in London'. Nigel West lays the blame squarely at
     the feet of Ellis, writing in a book review, 'A skewed survey of the UK's intelligence
     history' (2009), that Best and Stevens were victims of 'baseless charges' and 'that the
     true source of the leaks from inside the SIS was Dick Ellis, who was confronted after
     the war and confessed'.

8   Keith Jeffery in *MI6* (2010) says Dalton 'embezzled several thousand pounds' worth
     of visa fees'. No mention is made by Jeffery of Hooper. In the research paper 'Bill
     Hooper and secret service' (undated), the late Dutch intelligence historian Frans
     Kluiters states Hooper was not a blackmailer. He writes Dalton had been 'gambling
     in Belgian casinos, and debts forced him to dip into deposits for visas of travellers
     to Palestine. Dalton started to insist on Bill Hooper getting applicants to make their
     deposits in cash. Hooper became aware of the reason and urged Dalton to inform
     London. Instead, on 4 September 1936, Dalton chose to shoot himself through
     the head, leaving Bill a letter with instructions. In it he stated having committed
     suicide, and instructed Hooper to inform the British legation and MI6 of his death.
     Hooper was also to cooperate fully with Dutch police authorities in establishing the
     cause of death. Dalton concluded his letter: "Your only fault has been that you were
     too damned loyal."' However, Nigel West and Ladislas Farago have both painted
     Hooper in a far less flattering light.

9   See William B. Breuer, *Daring Missions of World War II* (2001).

10   *Operation Sea Lion: How Britain Crushed the German War Machine's Dreams of
     Invasion in 1940* (2014) by Leo McKinstry is an example: 'Schellenberg revealed
     under Allied interrogation that there had been a spy in MI6 by the name of Ellis.'
     Another can be found in Nigel West's *At Her Majesty's Secret Service: The Chiefs
     of Britain's Intelligence Agency, MI6* (2006), which says Schellenberg 'stated under
     interrogation that the Germans had received information from a certain Captain
     Ellis before the war'.

11   See A. M. Ross-Smith, 'Gross insult to SOE members', *Sydney Morning Herald*,
     11 May 1985. A story in the *Sydney Morning Herald* from 1984 held that Nigel
     West, in his book *MI6: British Secret Intelligence Service Operations, 1909–45*
     (1983), conjectured that the 'order of battle' was handed over to the Germans not
     by Ellis but by Lilia Zelensky: '[West] raises the possibility that [Ellis's handing over
     the SIS order of battle] was done by his first of four wives.' But this is not an accurate
     presentation of what West wrote. See Alex Sheppard, 'MI6 eventually muddled
     through', *Sydney Morning Herald*, 7 January 1984.

12   See Folkert Arie van Koutrik's file, KV 2/3643.

13   See KV 2/98.

14   See KV 2/95.

15   See Helmuth Knochen's file, KV 2/2745.

16   *ibid.*

Chapter 11   THE BLACK BOOK

1   Stephenson claims it was 10 May 1940 in his introduction to Hyde's *Secret Intelligence
     Agent* (1982), but in *A Man Called Intrepid* (1976) no date is mentioned, Stevenson
     referring only to 'the washed-blue skies that come in late May and early June'.
     F. H. Hinsley's *British Intelligence in the Second World War* (1979) puts the month
     of Stephenson's appointment to BSC as May 1940: 'In the interests of SIS's
     counter-espionage work in the United States, "C" had made contact informally, though
     with the President's approval, with the FBI, and in May 1940 the SIS had appointed
     Colonel Stephenson to be its liaison officer with the American intelligence services.'

2   Max Hastings has a slightly different take in *The Secret War* (2015): 'In the spring
     of 1940, [MI6 head] Stewart Menzies asked the Canadian businessman Sir William

Stephenson to try to open a link to J. Edgar Hoover, director of the FBI. Stephenson, eager for a top-table role for himself, set about this mission with a will, using an unlikely mutual acquaintance, the former world heavyweight boxing champion Gene Tunney, with whom he had sparred in France back in 1918. In those days the Canadian had been a fighter pilot, who went on to make a fortune before creating his own industrial intelligence network in the 1930s, from which he offered material to the British government.

'This opened a relationship with [Winston Churchill's adviser] Desmond Morton and Dick Ellis of Broadway, which continued after the outbreak of war. Hoover, before meeting the ebullient Canadian, took care to secure White House approval. Stephenson reported back to London that the FBI chief was keen to cooperate with MI6, and had suggested that his visitor should secure some official title to formalise his status in the US. Menzies promptly gave Stephenson a modest cover role as Passport Control Officer in New York, where he set up shop on 21 June 1940.'

Bill Macdonald tells a similar tale in *The True Intrepid* (1998), speculating that Stephenson met Hoover in the United States in April 1940, but says the dinner with Churchill in May in London took place at Stornoway House. In Hyde's *The Quiet Canadian* (1962), he writes that Stephenson was introduced to Hoover by Tunney but that Churchill met Stephenson 'in his old room at the Admiralty since he had not yet had time to move into Downing Street'. Michael Fullilove's *Rendezvous with Destiny* (2013) refers to Stephenson as Menzies's 'New York representative' and makes no mention of him being Churchill's 'personal representative'. According to a letter from H. Montgomery Hyde to Ellis of 7 October 1961, George Bernard Shaw and Winston Churchill apparently dined with Stephenson at New Cavendish Street in London in silence. Ellis's *The Two Bills: Mission Accomplished* (1972) paints a more heroic picture of Stephenson and his relationship with Churchill: 'With the outbreak of war . . . Churchill turned to those who stood by him in the pre-war years, among whom Stephenson had been . . . a close friend, whose mature judgment and energy had already been manifested.'

Major General Richard Rohmer, who wrote the foreword for *Intrepid's Last Case* (1983), writes in his autobiography, *Generally Speaking: The Memoirs of Major General Richard Rohmer* (2004): 'Jock Colville, Churchill's private secretary, took the position that William Stephenson had no such relationship with Churchill . . . Sir Jock maintained that contrary to all reports Sir William really never had any direct contact with Churchill, even though Sir William was given Churchill's full authority to act as the British spymaster in the United States and Bermuda during the crucial years of the war. My theory about Colville's position is that Sir William's meetings with Churchill were in keeping with the operation of a true spymaster. In other words, they were covert, without record, and away from 10 Downing Street, so that in the event William Stephenson was caught or otherwise exposed in the United States prior to or after the Americans getting into the war, there could be no track back to Churchill at all.'

3   The father of John F. Kennedy and Robert Kennedy. He served as ambassador 1938–40.
4   Writes Anthony Cave Brown in '*C*': *The Secret Life of Sir Stewart Graham Menzies, Spymaster to Winston Churchill* (1987): 'Stephenson . . . insisted upon taking with him a professional secret service officer, Colonel Charles H. Ellis. "C" [Menzies] opposed that request because Ellis was already employed on important diplomatic espionage work in London, and there was nobody to replace him. However, "C" relented largely because he had reasons for not wanting to keep Ellis inside Broadway – reasons that were not to emerge for several years – and Ellis was appointed as deputy to Stephenson.' Menzies having 'reasons for not wanting to keep Ellis inside Broadway' is a curious statement by Cave Brown, seemingly at odds with Cave Brown's defence of Ellis, though it can be interpreted in another way: Menzies was protecting Ellis. Intriguingly, Cave Brown, a Middle East correspondent in the 1960s, had been a friend of Kim Philby in Beirut. Philby's Arabist explorer

father, St John Philby, died in Beirut in 1960. Cave Brown's book about the Philbys, *Treason in the Blood: H. St. John Philby, Kim Philby, and the Spy Case of the Century*, was published in 1994.

5   Chapman Pincher in *Too Secret Too Long* (1984): 'American documents released under the Freedom of Information Act indicate that the US State Department was misled over Ellis's true function. He was officially listed as "His Britannic Majesty's Consul in New York", which gave him diplomatic immunity in the event of any clandestine activities to which the US Government would have objected . . . there is also FBI evidence that Ellis acted clandestinely in the US using the alias "Howard."' Again, what constitutes that 'FBI evidence' is unknown, as Pincher never footnoted anything. Ellis was registered as consul on 2 November 1940 and held the position for four years.

6   Writes Peter Hopkirk in *On Secret Service East of Constantinople* (1994): 'In 1941, at the age of 52, Teague-Jones was posted to the British consulate-general in New York, officially as a vice-consul, but in fact as an intelligence officer. It was at this time that Peter [Olik] Ellis recalled being startled to see him emerging from the New York headquarters of the British intelligence services, where he himself was then working. However, this was a world in which people came and went, and one learned not to ask too many questions.'

7   The VENONA project was a 1940s US–British cryptographic mission to decode Soviet cables. It ran until 1980. In 'Soviet espionage and the Office of Strategic Services' (1992), Hayden Peake claims 'the decrypts came from Soviet codebooks captured by the Finns and given to [William] Donovan. Reluctant to irritate the Soviets, the State Department succeeded in persuading the President to order Donovan to return them to the Soviets without making copies. Donovan gave them back, but copied them first. After the war they helped solve the [Klaus] Fuchs, [Julius] Rosenberg, and Ellis cases, among others.' The codename ELLIS actually appears as an unidentified Soviet agent in the 'Venona naval GRU US cables' (279–280, 316–317), but there is no suggestion this is Dick Ellis.

8   According to Thomas F. Troy: 'The date of Ellis's arrival is found in U.S. INS Form 1-404-A, a copy of which is located in Stephenson's INS file A6 762 816.' See Thomas F. Troy, 'The Coordinator of Information and British Intelligence', Central Intelligence Agency, Washington DC, Vol. 18, Spring 1974.

9   See Nigel West's introduction to *British Security Coordination* (1998).

10   'Little Bill' (Stephenson) and 'Big Bill' (Donovan) were nicknames for the 'Two Bills'.

11   See Brian Freemantle, *CIA: The 'Honourable' Company* (1983).

12   The Neutrality Acts of the 1930s (1935, '36, '37, '39) were passed by Congress to keep the United States out of the looming war. The 1939 Act allowed arms sales to Great Britain and France on a 'cash and carry' basis: paid for in cash and the purchaser had to organise their own transportation of the materiel (military equipment and supplies) back across the Atlantic and use their own ships. The Lend-Lease plan of 1941 allowed sales outright.

13   Letter, Dick Ellis to H. Montgomery Hyde, 17 August 1961.

14   See H. Montgomery Hyde Papers (Hyde 3/32) at Churchill College, Cambridge. It is undated and uncredited but likely from 1941. Its attribution to Ellis and Donovan is remarked upon in Mary S. Lovell's *Cast No Shadow* (1992).

15   See Nigel West's *MI6: British Secret Intelligence Service Operations, 1909–45* (1983). Amt IV E4 was the Gestapo department concerned with Counterespionage Scandinavia. Great Britain fell under Scandinavia for Nazi intelligence. Ellis's reputed friend H. G. Wells was also on the list.

16   Wilco Vermeer's article on the Venlo Incident at tracesofwar.com says, 'Mainly through . . . [Van] Koutrik the German Abwehr received all names of British secret agents.'

17   See Helen Fry's *Spymaster: The Man Who Saved MI6* (2021) and Kendrick's 'Black Book' entry at forces-war-records.co.uk. Kendrick's biographer, Fry, writes about Ellis in regards to an Austrian-born German double agent called Karl Tucek who

betrayed Kendrick to the Nazis, leading to Kendrick's brief arrest in August 1938: 'Tucek filed his report with his Abwehr handler, with devastating consequences. The Abwehr held onto the information, so that it could strike at Kendrick at a time of its choosing. The Tucek affair would soon have ramifications for Kendrick's whole network and for SIS agents in passport offices across Europe. For decades, speculation was rife that it was Kendrick's colleague Dick Ellis who had been the double agent who had betrayed him and the SIS network. Ellis always denied this, and it has never been proved. Ellis later argued that a lack of formal intelligence training had led him to inadvertently give away the SIS network to Berlin-based Russian agents, who (unbeknownst to him) were working for German intelligence. However, new research undertaken for this book clearly demonstrates that Kendrick was betrayed by Tucek, not Ellis.' Fry also claims Kendrick visited Ellis in New York and that he and Ellis were neighbours in Oxshott in Surrey in the late 1940s.

18 Pincher acknowledges his mistake in the Chapman Pincher Papers but makes it clear he drew the connection between Howard and Ellis solely from *A Man Called Intrepid*. This demonstrates Pincher's unique capacity for drawing a long bow when he has a target in mind, in this case Ellis.

19 The article 'Paul Manning, Civilian' at americanairmuseum.com reads in part: 'Manning was a war correspondent for CBS radio [who] worked closely with Edward Murrow throughout the Second World War. Manning was one of eight journalists of the Writing 69th who trained and flew [bomber] missions with the 8th Air Force . . . between missions Manning would broadcast CBS Radio from London and reported on Germany's surrender on VE Day. He transferred to the Pacific Theatre and trained as a gunner aboard B-29s in order to once again accompany bomber crews. He broadcast the Japanese surrender from aboard USS *Missouri*.

'Following the war Manning wrote articles for the *New York Times* and became a speech writer for Nelson Rockefeller. He turned his hand to historical writing, publishing books on Hirohito and infamously claiming that Hitler's secretary and Nazi Party leader Martin Bormann had faked his death and was pulling the strings in the postwar West German Government . . . Manning's wild claims in *Martin Bormann: Nazi in Exile* led to his marginalisation and even the murder of his son.' *Martin Bormann: Nazi in Exile* was published by Lyle Stuart, another fascinating character.

20 Ellis had also apparently denied Oberon a correct re-entry permit when the latter visited Canada the previous year. Higham calls Ellis 'one particular viper' and asserts that while in charge of the 'passport office in New York' Ellis not only white-anted Oberon but had the Germans 'track' the American actress Patricia Morison. There is zero evidence for both allegations. The book on Oberon was published in 1983, so not long after Pincher's *Their Trade is Treachery* had been in the newspapers: convenient fodder for Higham's fabricated, conspiratorial trash. In fact, Ellis appeared as the Nazi bad guy in *four* of Higham's books: *American Swastika* and his biographies of Merle Oberon, Cary Grant and Wallis Simpson. In the latter, Ellis receives a letter from the Duke of Windsor. Somewhat revealingly, Higham's dramatic description of Ellis as a 'Nazi agent' who had been 'planted' in New York was amended in an updated edition: Ellis was described as a 'British agent' and the word 'planted' did not appear. Higham died in 2012.

21 In an interview for another book, the same writer claimed Flynn – like Ellis, an Australian – had been given preferential treatment by Ellis in his role as consul 'because all the channels were open to Nazi sympathisers'.

22 See A Special Correspondent, 'Spies stranger than fact', *Canberra Times*, 29 March 1981.

Chapter 12 OUR MAN IN NEW YORK

1 Donovan was made a brigadier general in 1943.

2 Andrew Cook in *The Ian Fleming Miscellany* (2015): 'Fleming had discussed Donovan's plans and needed time to write his blueprint . . . Ian later told [BSC colleague] Ivar Bryce

that when he got to Washington he was "locked in a room with pen and paper". He produced a précis and a full 70-page document.' However, Cook concedes Ellis may have been the author: 'There is one odd postscript to Fleming's blueprint for the OSS. In July 1975 *The Times* claimed in its obituary of Dick Ellis (later suspected of having been a double agent) that Ellis had been decorated by the Americans for the OSS blueprint. Whoever wrote it, the contents must have boosted Donovan's campaign to start a secret service.'

Thomas F. Troy in 'Report on interviews with Sir William S. Stephenson in Paget, Bermuda' (1969): 'The late novelist Ian Fleming has been quoted as claiming a major role in the drafting of recommendations that led to the establishment of COI. Stephenson and Col. Ellis both ridiculed this, along with portions of McLachlan's *Room 39* as a "pack of nonsense". Ellis commented convincingly that Fleming's boss, Admiral [John Henry] Godfrey, the Director of British Naval Intelligence [sic, DNI], would have been "horrified" at the thought of [Lieutenant Commander] Ian Fleming being so engaged. Ellis further noted Godfrey's admission that the style of the recommendation did not square with DNI's. More importantly, Stephenson pointed to Ellis as the man Donovan turned to when details and charts were needed to show how an intelligence organisation could function.' Troy also wrote in 'The Coordinator of Information and British Intelligence' (1974): 'Ellis is particularly unhappy that promised changes in *Room 39* were never made.'

3   See Nelson MacPherson's *American Intelligence in War-Time London: The Story of the OSS* (2003) and Nicholas Reynolds's *Need to Know: World War II and the Rise of American Intelligence* (2022).

4   Yet Ellis fails to get a mention in Douglas Waller's biography of Donovan, *Wild Bill Donovan: The Spymaster Who Created the OSS and Modern American Espionage* (2011).

5   Bruce's diaries of the period, *OSS Against the Reich: The World War II Diaries of Colonel David K. E. Bruce* (1991), mentions Ellis in 1942. This from 20 May 1942: 'We left Botwood [in Newfoundland, Canada] at 6:35 p.m. on the 19th, and arrived in the greenery of Foynes, Ireland, at 7:35 a.m. on the morning of the 20th . . . I received a message from Dick Ellis, whom I had particularly intended to see, stating he was enroute to Egypt, and was spending the day at the Dunraven Arms at Adare. Thither . . . I lunched with Dick and had a long talk with him before boarding the 4:15 p.m. land plane for Bristol.' 20 June 1942: 'Interesting day and lunch in the Whaddon Chase country. Stopped at Major Cowgill's place, and saw Ferguson, Philby and Captain Mills. Taken around installations by Colonel Gambier-Parry. Bill Stephenson took us out to dinner at Sound Studios with Norman Loudon, Miss Preston, Dick Ellis and Jimmy Murphy.' 21 June 1942: 'Spent most of the day at office. Lunched with Colonel Donovan, Ellis, Howe, Murphy, Goodfellow, etc.'

6   Ellis's Legion of Merit recommendation at tracesofwar.com actually mentions this: 'During the period 1 January 1942 until the early part of 1943, Colonel Ellis, as liaison officer between the British Security Coordination in New York City and various intelligence services of the United States Government assisted in the firm establishment and growth of Secret Intelligence Branch of the Office of the Coordinator of Information (COI), predecessor of the Office of Strategic Services (OSS). He placed reservedly at our disposal his extensive experience with and intimate knowledge of the British Intelligence Service (SIS), of which he had been an officer for many years. He played a vital part in laying the foundation for an American counterpart of that organisation. Colonel Ellis's assistance during the above period of experimentation and growth was invaluable particularly in the absence of any American precedent in the initiation and operation of a clandestine intelligence organisation.

'Throughout the above period Colonel Ellis was a daily visitor to the COI (OSS) offices, where his helpfulness and advice were generously made available to the Secret Intelligence Branch. In addition he also furnished COI (OSS) many times of secret intelligence emanating from British sources. Such intelligence when turned over to the American Armed Forces and the various interested American Governmental Departments and Agencies proved to be of considerable value in the advancement of military plans and operations.'

It further says Ellis maintained 'a close and cooperative contact with various officials of the Office of Strategic Services, which has been of incalculable assistance to [the OSS]'.

Ellis's 'proposed citation' held by the National Archives in London (WO 373/148/259) reads: 'Colonel Charles Howard Ellis, British Army, in recognition of his material contribution to the success of highly important United States operations. Colonel Ellis was untiring in his efforts to further Anglo-American cooperation; and his enthusiastic interest, superior foresight and diplomacy were largely responsible for the valuable results achieved.'

His actual citation reads: 'Citation for the Legion of Merit, Degree of Officer. Colonel Charles Howard Ellis, O.B.E., British Army, performed outstanding services for the United States from August 1941 to May 1945. He gave unreservedly of his talent and wealth of information toward the development of certain of our intelligence organizations and methods. His enthusiastic interest, superior foresight and diplomacy were responsible in large measure for the success of highly important operations and to furtherance of Anglo-American cooperation.' It is signed by President Harry S. Truman on White House letterhead and can be found in the Dick Ellis Papers in the NLA.

7   See entry for 3 November 1941 in Nigel West (ed.), *The Guy Liddell Diaries: MI5's Director of Counter-Espionage in World War II, Volume I: 1939–42* (2005). Liddell is described by Richard Kerbaj in *The Secret History of the Five Eyes: The Untold Story of the International Spy Network* (2022) as the former 'deputy head of the agency's "B-branch", which specialised in rounding up, and sometimes recruiting, Nazi and Soviet spies. Liddell's division was the investigative heart of the security service: it ran operations involving informants, telephone and postal interceptions and physical surveillance.' Kerbaj writes: 'In 1933, two years into his career at MI5, Liddell anticipated a growing threat to Britain from Germany's military-intelligence agency, the Abwehr, as it evolved from a counterespionage service to an aggressive foreign intelligence force following Adolf Hitler's rise to power.' Ellis and Liddell worked closely with each other during this time and into World War II.

8   Bowes-Lyon was the younger brother of Lady Elizabeth Bowes-Lyon, later Queen Elizabeth The Queen Mother, mother of Queen Elizabeth II, so he was the late Queen's uncle. Political Warfare Executive was a secret propaganda unit formed by the Foreign Office to undermine Nazi Germany. Bowes-Lyon represented PWE in Washington.

9   See Stafford, '"Intrepid": myth and reality' (1987).

10 Popov quotes Pepper: 'Pepper shook his head. "Chain of command, old son. I'll give it to Colonel Ellis – Dick Ellis, our man in New York – and he'll see that [New York FBI head Percy] Foxworth gets it."' Pepper headed the economic warfare unit at BSC and later secret intelligence.

11 Monika Stevenson gave Hemming access to the Stephenson–Ellis correspondence held by the University of Regina. Stevenson denied my request.

Chapter 13   A SLEDGEHAMMER IN SEARCH OF AN ANVIL

1   It has been alleged that Hoover never met Popov and the FBI issued denials to this effect. But this is not true. A press release for Loftis's book reads: 'In August 1941 J. Edgar Hoover and the FBI were not only warned of a surprise Japanese attack on Pearl Harbor, but given documentary proof . . . Appendix 1 of the book, Loftis noted, includes two recently declassified documents never seen before in public: 1) an August 19, 1941 letter from FBI Assistant Director Earl Connelley to FBI Director J. Edgar Hoover; and 2) an attachment to that letter, identified by Connelley as "Exhbit C". In the letter, Connelley informs Hoover that the prior day, August 18,

he and FBI Special Agent Charles Lanman met with MI6 double agent Dusko Popov and British Security Coordination liaison Dick Ellis at New York City's Commodore Hotel.'

2   See Chapman Pincher, *Too Secret Too Long* (1984): 'When the US entered the war, after Pearl Harbor, in December 1941, BSC became much more important with a staff eventually numbering 1000.'

3   Bryden: 'Popov's ink was ammonium chloride, easily developed by passing a warm iron over the paper.'

4   Popov's own account of the meeting appears to be an error, according to Larry Loftis. 'In his memoirs Popov misremembered the details of the meeting, recalling by memory an event more than 30 years prior and confusing Earl Connelley with Foxworth, who later replaced Connelley as assistant director, New York.'

5   Popov is referring to the British Navy aerial torpedo attack on the Italian Navy base at Taranto, Italy, on 11–12 November 1940. Loftis: 'That . . . his assignment to investigate Pearl Harbor warned of a similar attack [to Taranto] by the Japanese . . . Popov swore to until his death.'

6   The Double Cross Committee, established by British military intelligence, was also known as the XX Committee (hence, Double Cross) or Twenty Committee. It ran hundreds of double agents against Germany. Chapman Pincher in *Too Secret Too Long* (1984) says Popov was 'being run by the British Double Cross Committee to feed false information to the Germans'.

7   Loftis: 'Unfortunately, however, Popov, Stephenson, [Ewen] Montagu, Ellis, and the entire staffs of British Security Coordination, MI5, MI6, and the Double Cross Committee were gagged by Britain's Official Secrets Act. The German questionnaire and Popov's warning would remain a secret until the release of [John Cecil] Masterman's *Double-Cross System* in 1972. Since then, both have been revealed by countless sources, including Popov himself, Lieutenant-Commander [sic] Ewen Montagu, British Security Coordination Director William Stephenson, BSC staffer H. Montgomery Hyde, and biographers of Hoover, Donovan, Stephenson, and Menzies.'

Masterman wrote in his book: 'TRICYCLE's questionnaire for America . . . contained a sombre but unregarded warning of the subsequent attack on Pearl Harbor.'

Bryden: 'The secret "BSC History" that Stephenson had compiled in 1945, and which only finally became available in the 1990s [as *The Secret History of British Intelligence* (1999)], makes only bare mention of Popov and says nothing of Pearl Harbor or his questionnaire, which Stephenson surely would not have missed including had he known of it . . . there is no mention in Montgomery Hyde, *Room 3604* [sic], either. Indeed, Stephenson disclaimed the Popov/Pearl Harbor story that author William Stevenson wrote into his controversial biography of him, *A Man Called Intrepid* (1976) . . . also, strangely, Ellis is referred to in the documents as "STOTT's assistant," rather than Stephenson's, but STOTT is a code name derived from Ellis's personal past. Stephenson is never mentioned by name.' STOTT, then, would clearly be a nod by Ellis to his old technical college, Stott & Hoare's, in Melbourne.

8   See press release '75 years after "the date which will live in infamy", declassified files reveal FBI director Hoover was warned of the Pearl Harbor attack in August 1941, new book shows', PRWeb Newswire, 16 November 2016.

Loftis's research about what happened at Pearl Harbor is particularly impressive: 'On October 5, 1943, the FBI sent MI5 a 24-page summary of Popov's activities . . . setting forth much of Popov's German questionnaire but omitting seven paragraphs. Ironically, it included all sections pertaining to Pearl Harbor and Honolulu.

'There were eight investigations concerning the intelligence failure at Pearl Harbor . . . *none* of them mention Dusko Popov or the German questionnaire. Dusko was never called to testify before any commission or other fact-finding committee . . . Hoover biographer Curt Gentry summarised the information quarantine: "As far as the FBI's role was concerned, the Pearl Harbor cover-up was completely successful, with one exception. The British knew."

Chapter 14   LITTLE WINDOW

1   Winks: 'Ellis apparently kept Downes at some distance, however, since he was not British and might well disapprove of some of the more ungentlemanly tricks which Stephenson and others thought up for discrediting anti-interventionist groups.'

2   Ellis never worked for the SOE, a point made in M. R. D. Foot's *SOE: The Special Operations Executive 1940–46* (1984): 'There were no known moles in SOE's headquarters in Algiers, Brisbane, Kandy, Kunming, Meerut or New York. (Whatever Charles Ellis, supposed by some to have been a mole, was doing in New York, he was not working for SOE.)' However, Burton Hursh in *The Old Boys: The American Elite and the Origins of the CIA* (1992) points out: 'On Ellis's recommendation, [William] Donovan retained Ellis's "old friend", the hardliner Polish Lt. Col. Robert M. Solborg, to build up his operations side. Solborg was pushed forward by Ellis as the ideal prospect to set up an SOE-style subversive-operations capability for the COI.' Solborg was also at one time accused of being a Soviet agent by American military-intelligence officer and spy-network head John V. Grombach in his book *The Great Liquidator* (1980).

3   See obituary by H. Montgomery Hyde, 'Mr C. H. Ellis', *Times*, 21 July 1975 and 'Mr C. H. Ellis', obituary by the *Times*, 16 July 1975.

4   Whether Ellis's role at OSS continued into 1943 is debatable. In his book *'C': The Secret Life of Sir Stewart Graham Menzies, Spymaster to Winston Churchill* (1987), Anthony Cave Brown writes that in September 1942 MI6 head Stewart Menzies told William Donovan he couldn't operate OSS agents at will in northwestern Europe, which 'produced almost a rupture in relations between Donovan and Menzies. Donovan cleared all British personnel from OSS headquarters, including Colonel Ellis, who had worked inside almost daily for eight to ten hours a day since January 1, 1942. At the same time, Donovan sent a directive to all headquarters that all OSS personnel were to prepare to terminate relations with SIS personnel, and he also examined proposals for the imposition of security procedures at OSS headquarters in London intended to prevent SIS men from visiting OSS installations and offices without invitation and also to guard against the possibility that "C" might seek to place agents inside OSS.'

5   As Troy points out, there is no footnote for this claim in Irving's book: 'According to Irving . . . it was Stephenson's deputy, Colonel Ellis, who "was sitting with Hoover and Donovan, and reporting directly to the President". Irving cites no proof for the statement, and reason renders it untenable: if a British officer were so positioned vis-a-vis Hoover, Donovan, and FDR, that officer would surely have been not a deputy but a chief.'

At time of writing the disgraced Irving, a Holocaust denier, was working on a third volume of his Churchill biography. He called Churchill 'a war criminal by any standard' in a 22 November 2022 Christmas newsletter message from St. Augustine, Florida, to his followers and claiming Heinrich Himmler 'did not kill himself as is the Allied version'.

'The British archives have finally revealed evidence that [Churchill] gave orders in 1944 for the immediate execution without trial, upon capture and identification, of fifty to one hundred top German officials including Reich Ministers and civilian *gauleiters* [regional Nazi leaders]. A British (or American) attempt was made on July 20, 1944, to assassinate Adolf Hitler, Germany's elected head of state; it failed, and the traitors were duly caught, tried and executed – and have puzzlingly been hailed as heroes by the Germans (i.e., U.S. government), ever since.'

Whether Ellis personally knew Prime Minister Churchill is unknown. Ellis's son, Olik, wrote in his timeline (held by the NLA): 'No record available of any direct contact with Churchill though latter proposed to submit CHE's [Charles Howard Ellis's] name for CMG [Companion of the Most Distinguished Order of St Michael and St George].'

6   See Thomas F. Troy, 'The Coordinator of Information and British Intelligence', Spring 1974: 'Letter from Col. Charles H. Ellis to the author, 13 November 1969,

Author's files. This writer talked about the matter with Ellis and Stephenson at the same time, 11 February 1969.'

7   See the OSS Society's film *Operation Overlord: OSS and the Battle for France* (2020), viewable on YouTube.

8   Antony Percy: 'One must posit the notion that perhaps [Guy] Liddell and [Dick] White were confident they had fingered ELLI already, but the nature of any disclosure would have been so embarrassing that they had to pretend that ELLI was an unsolved mystery.' See 'What Gouzenko said about ELLI', coldspur.com, 31 July 2021.

9   Cuneo provides no evidence of this.

10 The Sudoplatovs' book, *Special Tasks: The Memoirs of an Unwanted Witness – A Soviet Spymaster*, was released in 1994. Pavel, who died in 1995, was an NKVD lieutenant general. Anatoli is his historian son.

11 In *Unreliable Witness* (1984), Nigel West says Belfrage headed BSC's political warfare unit. There were five units: secret intelligence, political warfare, economic warfare, special operations and defence security.

12 See KV 2/96, statement dated 21 July 1945.

13 See KV 2/271, statement dated 28 June 1945.

14 Even Chapman Pincher conceded there was some weight to this, writing in the *Australian* on 26 April 1982: 'MI6 management . . . were prepared to believe that Von Petrov and other White Russians had convinced the Germans that Ellis had been their agent when in fact they had been his. This argument does not explain the haemorrhage of MI6 secrets.'

Chapter 15   PHILBY'S BLANK

1   It appears in the text as Honor, though there is no city by that name. MI6 did have a station in Hanoi.

2   Writes Nigel West in *Historical Dictionary of International Intelligence* (2006): 'Great Britain's postwar intelligence organisation in Singapore was created in 1945 to encompass the regional Secret Intelligence Service stations. Headed initially by C. H. Ellis, who would be succeeded by Courtenay Young, Alex Kellar, and then, finally, Jack Morton, CIFE included MI5's local Security Liaison Officer networks in Rangoon, Kuala Lumpur, and Hong Kong. The same organisation was also referred to as the Combined Intelligence Central Bureau and Security Intelligence Far East.'

3   See Roger Hermiston, *The Greatest Traitor: The Secret Lives of Agent George Blake* (2014).

4   Dansey thus became deputy to Stewart Menzies. He was described by Hugh Trevor-Roper as 'an utter shit; corrupt, incompetent, but with a certain low cunning'. He's the subject of Anthony Read's and David Fisher's biography *Colonel Z: The Secret Life of a Master of Spies* (1984). No mention is made of Ellis in the book.

5   Kim Philby, 'Report on SIS reorganisation', 6 July 1945, in *TRIPLEX* (2009).

6   Kim Philby, 'The reorganisation of SIS', 6 January 1947, in *TRIPLEX*.

7   H. Montgomery Hyde in *Secret Intelligence Agent* (1982) says he stayed with Ellis in Singapore in December 1951 on his way to the Korea Peninsula: 'I went to the front above the 38th Parallel to see troops in action. I also stayed with Ellis on my way back.'

8   Phoenix Park on Tanglin Road, in Singapore's Tanglin area, is a group of buildings that housed CIFE. It is now used for offices. In *Free Agent* (1993), Brian Crozier calls it 'a huge intelligence complex . . . staffed by career personnel from MI5 and MI6'.

9   See Phillip Knightley, 'Philby: Hollis? I just don't know', *Sunday Times*, London, 3 April 1988.

10 See Bill Chappell, 'Rare film emerges of double-agent Kim Philby speaking after defection', npr.org, 4 April 2016; 'British Cold War double agent Philby details life

of betrayal in Stasi video', reuters.com, 4 April 2016; 'Kim Philby: Unseen footage of Soviet spy – BBC News', BBC News, 4 April 2016.

11 Stevenson in *Intrepid's Last Case* (1983): 'Ellis had been credited with drafting the secret Corby Case report . . . when he was SIS Controller for the Western Hemisphere and Asia.' In *The Two Bills: Mission Accomplished* (1972), Ellis writes that William Stephenson 'happened to be in Ottawa at [the] time' of Gouzenko's defection and 'advised that the offer to defect be accepted and that Gouzenko be accorded protection against possible forceful measures against him and his family'. Ellis concluded that the Gouzenko case 'provided a foretaste of the continued hostility and lack of cooperation that was to be a marked feature of postwar Soviet policy'. Not what you'd expect from a long-term Soviet spy.

12 Confusingly, a Soviet mole called Kathleen Willsher, who worked in the British High Commission in Ottawa, used the codename ELLI. Many suspects have been put forward as the second, unidentified ELLI, including Leo Long, Anthony Blunt, Roger Hollis, Guy Liddell, Dick Ellis and Kim Philby himself. Intelligence expert and author Antony Percy fingers Stephen Alley, translator for Jane Archer during the Walter Krivitsky debriefing in London, and makes some interesting comments about Igor Gouzenko's reliability: 'He was by most accounts a difficult man, greedy, obstinate, peevish, litigious, and ill-mannered. While he impressed his interlocutors in Ottawa with his memory and clarity of thinking, his articulation was once described during earlier interrogations as incoherent. Irrespective of his personal faults, however, he displayed a willful [sic] contrariness in his testimony over the years, and it is hard to ascribe his inconsistences simply to a failing memory, or to the much-questioned fact of his alcoholism.' See 'What Gouzenko said about ELLI', coldspur.com, 31 July 2021. As mentioned earlier, Paul Monk suspects Hollis is ELLI. Phillip Knightley believed Gouzenko made it all up.

In *Spy Wars: Espionage in Canada from Gouzenko to Glasnost* (1990), J. L. Granatstein and David Stafford write: 'None of the books, none of the revelations, could definitively determine who was the mole, if indeed anyone was, in the British secret services. Unless they are caught in the act or confess, spies can rarely be definitively uncovered. And with Blunt, Hollis and Ellis dead and buried, no such final answer will be reached unless the Soviet archives are opened to research. The real point, however, is the way in which Igor Gouzenko's revelations of September 1945 have continued to reverberate. In the labyrinthine world of espionage, spies and defectors may die, but the echoes of their doings ring long after them.'

James Rusbridger in *The Intelligence Game: The Illusions and Delusions of International Espionage* (1989): 'Over the years Gouzenko was to change his story several times and, as is always the case with defectors, it was soon impossible to separate fact from fantasy in what he said.'

13 See Antony Percy, 'Litzi Philby under (the) cover(s)', coldspur.com, 31 March 2023.

14 See Pincher, *Too Secret Too Long* (1984) for the full statement.

15 If this is the case, ELLI would fit Guy Liddell, Kathleen Willsher and Dick Ellis.

16 See William A. Tyrer, 'The unresolved mystery of ELLI', *International Journal of Intelligence and CounterIntelligence*, Vol. 29, No. 4, 13 June 2016.

17 Section I was operational espionage and Section II was sabotage and political and military subversion. See CIA memo 'The German Intelligence Service and the war', undated.

18 'Vrinton' was actually Adrianus Johannes Josephus 'Aad' Vrinten, a 'former Dutch customs official' and spy for the British who got into counterespionage and 'who possessed two thick volumes in which were recorded the espionage agents of all countries, including Germany, England, Russia, Italy, France, as well as the agents of lesser countries'. He was considered a clear and present danger to the Nazis, who mounted a disinformation campaign against him. Vrinten, who worked with

Bill Hooper, employed double agent Folkert Arie van Koutrik, who fed intelligence to the Nazis before the Venlo Incident. See KV 2/3643. According to an article about the Venlo Incident by Wilco Vermeer at tracesofwar.com, 'Vrinten had been employed by GS III (Dutch Secret Service) and travelled frequently to Germany as a businessman. His company Zaal & Co. soon became a cover up [sic] for the operations of the [British] Passport Control Office. The company succeeded on short notice to acquire a large number of people that gathered intelligence as "spy" [sic] for the British. Unknown to Vrinten, the German Abwehr had already penetrated his organisation by the end of the thirties.' As I've said in the main text, it's very clear that Hooper and Van Koutrik could have been the primary source of the information contained in *Sonderfahndungsliste G. B.* and *Informationsheft G. B.* but which is commonly attributed to Ellis.

19 In KV 2/1741 there is a 22 September 1949 report from a redacted sender to Kenneth Morton-Evans of MI5: '"Capt. ELLIS" (cover-name), really a Russian sergeant of the RASVEDUPR, who worked against the U.K. from BRUSSELS, mainly on C.E. [counterespionage]. He worked through two Russian emigres, PETROV and MIZPOROSHNY. This went on until 1940 [not clear]. The British were warned against him.'

20 In his book *Traitors: The Labyrinths of Treason* (1987), Pincher writes: 'Philby was able to protect Pontecorvo and Ellis by concealing documentary information pointing to their treachery.' Bruno Pontecorvo, who died in 1993, was an Italian nuclear scientist and British citizen who defected to the Soviet Union in 1950 following an FBI investigation into his communist links. It's claimed he was tipped off by Philby.

21 In *'C': The Secret Life of Sir Stewart Graham Menzies, Spymaster to Winston Churchill* (1987), Anthony Cave Brown calls Canaris 'one of "C's" German adversaries during the war and then almost a collaborator in the ideological struggle against Hitler and National Socialism'.

Chapter 16 THE CLOUDS ARE PARTING

1 See Toohey and Pinwill, 'ASIS: Joke and dagger', *Sydney Morning Herald*, Sydney, 22 July 1989.

2 The MS *Willem Ruys* later became the MS *Achille Lauro*, which sank off the coast of Somalia in 1994.

3 Ellis's TD is mentioned in Arthur Swinson's *Beyond the Frontiers: The Biography of Colonel F. M. Bailey, Explorer and Special Agent* (1971).

4 In the book Pincher claimed, 'FBI papers available under the Freedom of Information Act have revealed that as early as January 1953 the FBI was making espionage inquiries into Ellis and that these continued through 1956. Almost all the information about Ellis in the papers, which are memoranda from the FBI office in New York to headquarters in Washington, has been blanked out for security reasons. Expert examination of the various numbers and initials still remaining suggest that the blanking out was done prior to declassification at the request of the CIA acting on behalf of MI6.' I made a Freedom of Information/Privacy Acts (FOIPA) request to the FBI and was told 'records potentially responsive to your request were destroyed'. Pincher refers to 'FBI documents. Letters to Hoover entitled "Dickie Ellis" dated October 1963 and 9 May 1956. While much is blanked out, the 9 May document states that the information is "being referred to the attention of the Espionage Section".' These could not be found, possibly because they were destroyed. In the United Kingdom, MI5 and MI6 are not subject to the Freedom of Information Act (FOIA) and therefore will not process Freedom of Information (FOI) requests. Pincher's papers at King's College do not include these memos but he includes a personal note that refers to their contents and says they were given to him by no less than celebrity trash peddler Charles Higham, which says a great deal about Pincher's lack of due diligence.

5 Horner misidentifies Von Petrov in *The Spy Catchers*: 'In 1984 the investigative journalist Chapman Pincher revealed that in early 1967 [sic] MI5 interrogated Ellis, who confessed to having passed secret information to the Germans before the Second World War, and that Ellis had passed the information via several White Russians, one of whom was named Vladimir Nikolayvich (not Mikhailovich) Petrov [sic].' In *The Protest Years: The Official History of ASIO, 1963–1975*, Vol. II (2015), John Blaxland calls him 'Vladimir Nikolavich Petrov'.

6 According to the *Canberra Times*: '[Frederick] Chilton recalled the easy charm that had led Casey to take [Ellis] in to a Cabinet subcommittee meeting, and Spry, of all people, to divulge the news of the impending defection of the Soviet diplomat and KGB operative Vladimir Petrov in 1954. On hearing this, Ellis promptly quit ASIS and left Australia for England, saying he was getting married. This was later established to be fictitious. Spry, accepting Ellis's reason, asked him to convey the latest on Petrov personally to London. The author, Chapman Pincher, has confirmed that Ellis contacted Philby immediately after he arrived.' See 'Did affable Aussie wreck Cold War for West?', 6 September 1998.

7 According to Blaxland in *The Protest Years* (2015), 'Spry discussed the Ellis case with other security officials. Spry spoke of the possibility that Ellis had confused the Petrov who defected with the Petrov who knew of Ellis's role with the Abwehr . . . Spry was concerned about the possibility that Ellis had been spooked by the name Petrov, believing him to be the agent who worked for the Germans before the war. It was believed that Ellis's quick departure from Australia in 1954 was due to his fear that the defector Petrov might have known of Ellis's RIS [Russian Intelligence Service] role. From this date, this became the dominant explanation, but this thesis downplayed Spry's reasoning that Ellis thought the Petrov defector was the same Petrov he had known in the 1930s.'

8 The EMERTON investigation is referred to as a 'Washington dossier' in *Intrepid's Last Case* (1983), suggesting it was CIA led, but Nigel West's *At Her Majesty's Secret Service: The Chiefs of Britain's Intelligence Agency, MI6* (2006) says on one page it was 'conducted' by William Steedman and on another it was 'conducted jointly by [Peter] Wright and [Bunny] Pantcheff'. When Chapman Pincher wrote his proposal for *Their Trade is Treachery* in 1980, he refers to Ellis only as '"Emerton" – the self-confessed spy of whom the public has never heard. (Now dead.)' Quoted in Malcolm Turnbull, *The Spycatcher Trial* (1988).

9 Pincher gives another account in *Too Secret Too Long* (1984): '[Ellis] claimed that he had decided to marry a woman whom he had met in England and had to return to do so. When asked for her name he gave it, and an address. Overnight MI5 traced the girl and found that she had married an American serviceman two years before Ellis's departure for Australia and was living, happily, with her husband in America. When interviewed she said that she had known Ellis but had never had any intention of marrying him. When faced with this Ellis said that he had been so upset by the accusations that he had given the wrong name and then gave another. When this girl was traced it was learned that she too had married before Ellis had left for Australia. Later in 1954 Ellis had, in fact, married a Mrs Alexandra Wood . . . he did not give her name to his questioners.'

10 ASIS's existence was only revealed publicly in 1977. Says its website: 'For over 20 years, the existence of ASIS remained a secret. The Service was first referred to in Parliament in 1975 and was not publicly acknowledged until 1977. The then Prime Minister, Malcolm Fraser, informed Parliament that "ASIS's capacity to serve Australia's national interest will continue to depend on its activities being fully protected by secrecy." This statement has been reaffirmed by successive governments.'

11 See Antony Percy, 'The hoax of the Blunt confession (Part 1)', coldspur.com, 31 January 2021.

12 See 'Did affable Aussie wreck Cold War for West?', *Canberra Times*, 6 September 1998.

13 Ellis's links to signals work in Australia are mentioned in John Fahey's books *Australia's First Spies* (2018), *Traitors and Spies* (2020) and *The Factory* (2023).

14 According to John Fahey's *The Factory* (2023), MI6 offered to send Ellis out to Australia during the war to investigate a leak of Allied communications by the Chinese Nationalist government in Chungking (Chongqing).

15 Letter, Dick Ellis to Richard Casey, 25 July 1962.

Chapter 17 CRYING TOWEL

1 *Hemisphere* ran until 1984.

2 The *Central Asian Review*, which ran from 1953–68, was published by the Central Asian Research Centre in conjunction with St Antony's College, Oxford University. Its principal, David Morison, was apparently 'convinced of [Ellis's] innocence', according to a 19 February 1982 letter from Brian Pearce to Chapman Pincher. A letter from Morison to Pearce, dated 18 May 1981, says he was 'distressed to read' Ann Salwey's 6 May 1981 letter to Pearce, 'and I can imagine how she must feel'.

3 Nigel West in *Counterfeit Spies* (1998): 'Perhaps significantly, Ellis was not referred to, but one controversial name was mentioned: that of Major General Sir Stewart Menzies, the SIS Chief who had retired a decade earlier.'

4 Part of BSC. Described by Keith Jeffery in *MI6* (2010) as existing to 'coordinate counterespionage and countersubversion work'.

5 Naftali: 'In the fall of 1963 [Ellis] wrote Stephenson requesting monetary compensation for losing this job. He said it carried a salary of £1000 a year.' See Timothy J. Naftali, 'Intrepid's last deception: documenting the career of Sir William Stephenson', *Espionage: Past, Present, Future?*, 1994.

6 See 'Dick Ellis: now even a defender has doubts', no byline, *Sydney Morning Herald*, 15 February 1983.

7 'BSC Account' refers to the manuscript republished as *British Security Coordination: The Secret History of British Intelligence in the Americas, 1940–45*, British Security Coordination (with an introduction by Nigel West), St Ermin's Press, London, 1998. Also sometimes referred to as 'BSC Papers'.

8 Ian Fleming writes in the foreword for *Room 3603*: 'Hyde has, for some reason, been allowed to write the first book, so far as I know, about the British secret agent whose publication has received official blessing.' According to Troy in *Wild Bill and Intrepid* (1996), Ellis 'cleared the first draft of the manuscript . . . with an MI6 security officer and offered to clear the final draft, but the offer was left to his good judgment'. The 'official blessing' mention by Fleming had catastrophic consequences for Ellis, as Troy explained: 'After his retirement, Ellis apparently had two jobs with the government, but they are not easily differentiated. He worked at one time or another with both the Home and the Foreign Offices, and the latter may have been cover for an MI6 job. Financially he needed both jobs. The "weeding" job was winnowing MI6 files. That he was on "the suspended list" (Ellis to Hyde, 12 Nov. 1962) he attributed to the "official blessing" matter. As for the termination news he could not explain it; Ellis to Hyde, 22 Nov. 1962. The "douceur" is in Ellis to Hyde, 26 Dec. [1962]. All in [H. Montgomery] Hyde Papers.'

9 Kim Philby's late widow, Rufina Pukhova, referenced this in her book *The Private Life of Kim Philby: The Moscow Years* (1999): '[Bill Macdonald quotes] the Dick Ellis comment that [H.] Montgomery Hyde's book, *The Quiet Canadian*, was "related to the defection of Soviet double agent Kim Philby". He then quotes author William Stevenson stating that *The Quiet Canadian* had nothing to do with Philby. Stevenson was right, but he gave no reason. Thus Macdonald goes on to say that "indirectly it is possible the release of *The Quiet Canadian* might have had something to do with the defection of Kim Philby and boosting the morale of the Western security services" . . . but that cannot be. As Nigel West pointed out in *Counterfeit Spies* . . . the Hyde book was published before, not after, Philby defected.' Wrote West in that book: 'Hyde's book had already been published when

Philby had fled from Beirut in January 1963. Accordingly, what is presented as SIS's motive in assisting Ellis is sheer hokum.'

10 See Timothy J. Naftali, 'Intrepid's last deception: documenting the career of Sir William Stephenson', *Espionage: Past, Present, Future?*, 1994. Troy on Naftali in *Wild Bill and Intrepid*: 'According to Naftali, Sir William was so driven by self-aggrandisement that from the early 1950s he deliberately deceived the world about himself and his wartime role as the BSC chief. He "was determined to reap some reward for his secret work and set in motion a plan aimed at widespread public recognition". He had a "dream of a big biography", of "a bestselling" book, even of making money out of it. To realise the plan he helped a string of writers . . . falsify and magnify the record of his wartime service . . . and ultimately apotheosise himself. The result, in Naftali's view, has been a "thicket of claims and counter-claims" and "a mess of contradictions".'

11 Ellis remarked: 'What a commotion over a couple of weekends with a tart.' See Lovell's *Cast No Shadow* (1992).

12 Letter, Chapman Pincher to Brian Pearce, 24 February 1982.

13 See *Too Secret Too Long* (1984).

14 See Scott-Smith's *Western Anti-Communism and the Interdoc Network: Cold War Internationale* (2011).

15 Virtually the same paragraph appears in *Too Secret Too Long* (1984): 'If Ellis was a Soviet spy at the time he might have had opportunities to destroy documentary evidence of his own misdemeanours and those of others whom he knew or thought to be Soviet agents or sympathisers. Fortunately there were documents which never reached him.' Again, a prime example of Pincher leading the witness.

16 This is referred to in one of the Ellis chapter endnotes in Pincher's *Too Secret Too Long* (1984): 'Confirmed by Stevenson, *Intrepid's Last Case*, who also records a letter from Ellis in which he states that, while doing his "weeding job" he took the opportunity to "slip a few bits of paper into the files".'

17 Ellis is not mentioned in Brian Lett's biography of Gubbins, *SOE's Mastermind: An Authorised Biography of Major General Sir Colin Gubbins KCMG, DSO, MC* (2016).

18 In *Counterfeit Spies* (1998), Nigel West reasons that it wasn't written by Ellis, largely on the basis of Ellis's error over the chronology of the Philby defection: 'Whoever concocted the "historical note", it could not have been Ellis, who, after all, had died on 5 July 1975, a year before *A Man Called Intrepid* was published. Unless what purported to be Ellis's preface had been written by him from beyond the grave, perhaps with the help of a clairvoyant, it must have been forged. Certainly it was not written before he died, considering the number of elementary mistakes contained in the short text, including details that Ellis might have reasonably been expected to remember.' West's checklist includes Ellis's length of service in MI6, but West got that wrong. As Ellis's foreword correctly states, he joined around 1920.

19 Macdonald even turns up evidence that Stephenson didn't want Ellis's foreword used in the final product but in the end it was. Which naturally begs the question: If Ellis were such bad news in 1975–76 why did Stevenson–Stephenson write *Intrepid's Last Case* in 1982–83? Did they write the book for Ellis or for themselves?

20 Roald Dahl sent a letter to William Stephenson on 21 February 1973, after talking to his literary agent, Murray Pollinger, about Ellis. Dahl notes: 'In both countries the book is now with a fourth publisher,' having been rejected by three publishing companies in England and three in the United States. 'I would have thought that a Canadian publisher might be the answer.' Dahl also says, 'Nobody over here [in England] has heard anything about pressure from the CIA.' Stephenson has scrawled on the letter: 'The fact is I think Dick is not well enough to do a job that publishers would go for.'

21 Naftali elaborates: 'Ellis asserted that Sir William had been Churchill's personal envoy, a claim he had not made a decade before. Also added were the claims that Stephenson and the Prime Minister had been "close friends" and that Churchill had

viewed sending Stephenson to New York as the first step in improving Anglo-American relations in the spring of 1940. The change that most set the tone for the next biography, *A Man Called Intrepid,* was Ellis's acceptance of the contention that Stephenson had played a decisive role in covert diplomacy before Pearl Harbor. Whereas Ellis had written in 1963 that Stephenson had had only an indirect influence on the process that resulted in the exchange of British bases for American destroyers; in 1972, Ellis asserted that Stephenson had represented Churchill in secret discussions of the "Destroyers for Bases" deal at US Secretary of State Cordell Hull's home. In the intervening decade, however, no new evidence had appeared to support a revision of Ellis's first version. Ultra was one subject that Ellis did not touch. His book was written in 1972, two years before the Ultra secret was revealed by [F. W.] Winterbotham. The honour of linking Stephenson with Ultra fell to the second biographer, a Canadian journalist named William Stevenson.'

22 Troy apparently agreed and was given permission by CIA executive director William Colby to do so: 'Mr Colby has, however, authorised Tom [Troy] to meet or talk with the TV producer, Mr William Stevenson, on an off the record and unclassified basis. Tom has also been given tentative approval to write a foreword for *The Two Bills* by Col. C. H. Ellis.' See Central Intelligence Agency, 'Memorandum for: Director of Training', Washington DC, 10 November 1972.

23 'A Man Called Intrepid: Sir William Stephenson', Canadian Broadcasting Corporation, Ottawa, 1973. Footage of Ellis from this documentary can also be seen in Jeremy McCormack's 2001 film, *Camp X.*

Chapter 18   NAILING ELLIS

1   Steedman is a shadowy character. In 'A better history of the SIS' in *International Journal of Intelligence and CounterIntelligence* (12 March 2012), Nigel West talks of 'William Steedman's epic search over a decade to track [Ellis] down'. In *Historical Dictionary of International Intelligence* (2006) he writes: 'In 1966, following a lengthy investigation codenamed EMERTON, William Steedman confronted [Ellis] with the allegation that he had sold SIS secrets to the Nazis through a contact in Paris before the war.' In *At Her Majesty's Secret Service: The Chiefs of Britain's Intelligence Agency, MI6* (2006), he says Steedman 'pursued the case through the German files since 1949, with gaps for his three-year tours of duty in Bonn and Berne [sic] in 1953 and 1960 respectively . . . Steedman went into retirement in December 1969. According to him, Ellis could have been caught 20 years earlier if successive SIS chiefs had devoted sufficient resources to checking on Schellenberg's allegation.'

2   See Frans Kluiters's 'Bill Hooper and secret service' (undated).

3   Sorge biographer Owen Matthews writes in *An Impeccable Spy: Richard Sorge, Stalin's Master Agent* (2019) of Sorge going to London in 1929 'to collect sensitive information from a top Soviet spy. Christiane, still on good terms with her husband despite their separation, joined him in London. She later reported that the purpose of their trip was to meet a "very important agent". The couple went together to the rendezvous on a London street corner. While the two men talked, Christiane kept her distance and a watch for signs of danger. Who Sorge's contact may have been was a mystery that worried British spycatchers for decades to come – notably Peter Wright, the Australian-born [sic] head of MI5 counterintelligence. Wright's theory was that Sorge's agent was Charles "Dickie" Ellis.'

4   Wright only refers to Pantcheff but various Nigel West books and Martin Pearce's biography of Maurice Oldfield mention that transcriber Ann Orr-Ewing was also present. Orr-Ewing retired from MI5 and became a cattle breeder. See Martin Pearce, *Spymaster: The Life of Britain's Most Decorated Cold War Spy and Head of MI6, Sir Maurice Oldfield* (2016). Writes West in *Historical Dictionary of British Intelligence* (2005): 'According to Wright, Pantcheff shared his opinion that Ellis had been skillfully [sic] manipulated as a high-level penetration by the KGB but this was an issue that was never fully resolved.' In other words, it was never proved.

5 Chapman Pincher in *Too Secret Too Long* (1984): '[Ellis] was put under surveillance by Special Branch to ensure, as far as possible, that he could not defect, and as an additional precaution his telephone was tapped without the formality of a Home Office warrant. The Post Office agreed on the understanding that the warrant would be applied for later when the interrogation was over, as duly happened. During the interrogations, which were tape-recorded, MI5 arranged electronic coverage of Ellis's office and discovered that he was in the habit of muttering to himself such remarks as, "They did not know about . . . they can't possibly know about . . . "'

6 Richard Deacon's biography of Maurice Oldfield, '*C*' (1985), puts the timeframe as '1965–66'.

7 West calls it a 'limited confession' in *Historical Dictionary of International Intelligence* (2006).

8 This was a fib. Pincher in *Too Secret Too Long* (1984): 'When he was sent home at the end of the day he was warned that if he failed to tell the truth he would be confronted with the German officer and that the case would be handed over to Special Branch, the arresting arm of MI5. That, in fact, was a bluff because MI5 did not know whether the officer was still alive and the management had no intention of staging a prosecution, whatever Ellis might confess. The policy of non-prosecution of intelligence and security officers found to be spies, which had been introduced by [Roger] Hollis, was being continued.'

9 Pincher gives a slightly different, more expansive – perhaps embellished – account of Ellis's alleged confession in *Too Secret Too Long* (1984). This is curious, as *Their Trade is Treachery* appeared in print three years earlier. Why not describe it fully the first time? Had something jogged Wright's memory? A highlight: 'Ellis's apologia was regarded as being an abject admission of spying not only for the Germans but for the Russians because at least one of his agents was trading with both and Ellis had known that. He was then asked four questions: "Did you hand over detailed charts of MI6 organisation just prior to the war which could have been used by the Germans in the interrogations of Stevens and Best after their capture in the Venlo incident?" He admitted that he had done so. When asked, "Did you betray our breaking of the Von Ribbentrop–Hitler telephone link?" he answered, "I must have been mad." To the question, "When you were providing the secret material, to whom did you think it was going?" he replied, "I don't know – the Germans, I suppose." Finally, when asked when he was last in contact with Zilenski [sic] or his associates he answered, "In about December 1939. I sent them an envelope via an MI6 officer who was going to Paris. He brought back a sealed package of money for me." This misuse of a brother officer, who had no knowledge of the contents of the packages, was regarded as particularly treacherous.'

A few points are worth making here. The confession was hardly 'abject'. As William Stephenson told Melbourne's *Herald* on 22 October 1983: 'I can imagine Ellis being a braggart, but never abject.' Said Ellis's daughter, Ann, in the same story: 'I cannot imagine my father ever being abject.'

I fully concur. Ellis's answers relayed to Wright and Pincher's secondhand account of those answers are best described as vague. To corroborate the Wright/Pincher story, we don't know what Ellis's motivations could have been (or if he was following instructions from a higher authority at MI6) – if indeed he actually did what is claimed – and we don't know the identity of the 'brother officer' who was carrying the envelopes. Whoever that man was, he was clearly coming from London, where Ellis lived and which demolishes the idea Ellis, in the words of West, 'sold out to the Germans in Paris'. No German money went straight into his hands in Paris. Could the 'brother officer' have framed Ellis?

10 This is Australian journalist Brian Crozier, who was involved in the setting up of Interdoc. On the typescript (held in the Chapman Pincher Papers), Pincher has marked Crozier's name in pen.

11 See Edward Jay Epstein, 'Intelligence and sometimes folly', *New York Times*,
    16 January 1983. There were only two mentions of Ellis in Cave Brown's *The Last
    Hero: Wild Bill Donovan* (1982). The first: 'The British . . . had left Commander
    [Ian] Fleming with Donovan and had sent in Colonel Charles H. Ellis, a career
    officer of the Secret Intelligence Service, to give WJD [Donovan] whatever help he
    needed in forming his organisation. Other British officers, experts in clandestine
    communications and training, arrived at Donovan's request, and as early as August
    1941 Fleming reported to London that WJD was "getting well into the saddle".'
    The second: 'After much discussion, Donovan acquired [Wallace Banta] Phillips's K
    Organisation, which gave the COI its start in espionage – a start, as Donovan put it,
    "from minus zero". With Intrepid's deputy in Washington, Colonel Ellis, keeping
    an eye on the new organisation, Donovan appointed Phillips Director of Special
    Information Service.'

12 Ellis features in Epstein's account of the Venlo Incident in *Deception: The Invisible
    War Between the KGB and the CIA* (1989): 'The Germans had recruited [Ellis]
    through a double agent in the late 1920s when he was stationed in Paris, and he
    had continued to sell them secrets when he was [sic] returned to England . . . [his
    information was] relayed back to German intelligence through the double agent in
    Paris who recruited him.'

13 Menzies is pronounced 'Ming-iss', with 'ming' rhyming with 'sing'. *Interview*
    magazine clearly misspelled his name based on Cave Brown's pronunciation.

14 See John Weitz, 'Anthony Cave Brown', *Interview*, April 1983.

Chapter 19 AMONG THE DRIPPING SHRUBS

1   Stevenson in *Intrepid's Last Case* (1983) claims Menzies recommended Ellis to
    Interdoc. Giles Scott-Smith, by contrast, says MI6 head Dick White recommended
    Ellis: 'Ellis entered the Interdoc circle through MI6 chief Dick White . . . in June
    1961 . . . White picked out Ellis as the most appropriate linkman due to his
    experiences in the 1930s, a move that had significance as well as repercussions.'
    See Giles Scott-Smith, *Western Anti-Communism and the Interdoc Network: Cold
    War Internationale* (2011). Chapman Pincher writes in *Too Secret Too Long* (1984):
    'The recommendation had been made by a former head of MI6 who had known all
    about Ellis's confession.' Among the Chapman Pincher Papers there are references
    to Dick White recommending Ellis. In the same papers, Pincher says Brian Crozier
    believed Ellis had spied for the Germans. In a note of 24 April 1981, Pincher writes:
    '[Crozier] told me that he knew, some six or seven years ago, that Dick Ellis had
    been a spy for the Germans and had been heavily suspected of being a spy for Russia
    later.'

2   Scott-Smith writes of an incident 'following an Interdoc meeting in Munich . . . [a]
    group went to see the musical *Hair* . . . this was not to everyone's liking, and Ellis
    "suffered terribly".'

3   Reproduced in Blaxland, *The Protest Years* (2015). Blaxland writes: 'Spry forwarded
    a copy of the letter to MI5. Beyond that, however, the matter remained unresolved.'

4   Troy: 'On registering at the hotel, I was astounded but delighted to be told, as
    if I had already been informed, that Colonel Ellis would be in the neighbouring
    room. That someone as well placed as Col. Charles H. ('Dick') Ellis, Stephenson's
    wartime deputy, as well as a veteran MI6 man, was on hand was an exciting
    prospect. We together taxied out to Camden House.' See Troy, 'REMINISCENCE:
    CIA's indebtedness to Bill Stephenson', *International Journal of Intelligence and
    CounterIntelligence*, Vol. 20, No. 4, 14 August 2007. The Princess is officially
    known as Hamilton Princess Hotel & Beach Club.

5   See Jefferson Morley's biography of Angleton, *The Ghost: The Secret Life of CIA
    Spymaster James Jesus Angleton* (2017).

6   These included his future biographer, Edward J. Epstein (who wrote the *New York
    Times* hit piece on Ellis in 1983), and Chapman Pincher. See Margaret Jones, 'Spy

revelations that are rocking Britain', *Sydney Morning Herald*, 28 March 1981. Pincher left a note in his papers at King's College, dated 21 December 1983, that says, 'Ed Epstein rang from New York about Ellis. Said that CIA contacts believed that Ellis had been a Soviet agent while in the US.' Those 'CIA contacts' are a clear reference to Angleton.

After Angleton's death, Epstein admitted he had used Angleton as a source in the book *Deception: The Invisible War Between the KGB and the CIA* (1989). This is corroborated by an internal CIA document titled 'A review of counterintelligence literature 1975–1992' (1992) by former CIA agent Cleveland C. Cram. Ellis is featured in Epstein's *Deception* in regards to the 1938 bugging of the German Embassy in London.

7   Letter from Chapman Pincher to Peter Wright, 13 March 1981, quoted in Turnbull, *The Spycatcher Trial* (1988).

8   In *The Defence of the Realm* (2009), Christopher Andrew calls Golitsyn a 'troublesome KGB defector' of 'passionately paranoid tendencies'. Even Peter Wright in *Spycatcher* (1987) concedes, 'The vast majority of Golitsin's [sic] material was tantalisingly imprecise. It often appeared true as far as it went, but then faded into ambiguity.'

9   William Stevenson claimed in a 1981 column for the *Toronto Sun* that Thomas F. Troy's 1981 book *Donovan and the CIA: A History of the Establishment of the Central Intelligence Agency* refuted the allegations against Ellis: Troy had quoted a statement by David K. E. Bruce that without Ellis 'American intelligence could not have gotten off the ground'. According to Stevenson, that was the CIA's way of 'entering the controversy . . . it would seem the CIA has joined in the debunking of a report dangerous to internal confidence'. However, this is debatable: Bruce's statement was first published internally in 1975, well before the Ellis allegations were made public. See William Stevenson, 'Patriot or spy?', *Toronto Sun*, 14 July 1981.

10   A variant spelling of her name is Aleksandra.

11   I spent nearly 18 months trying to obtain ASIO files about Ellis via the National Archives of Australia. As John Blaxland, ASIO's official historian, had gained full access to them for his book, I wrote to see if he had kept anything. Blaxland replied: 'Unfortunately, I was not allowed to keep any of the primary material I used in writing the ASIO history. All those documents are held by ASIO. But the footnotes [in the book] provide sufficient detail for the records to be requested. I understand that ASIO made a priority of clearing the documents we used so that people like yourself would be able to check them and use them as well.' Two months before my publishing deadline, 43 additional folios (sheets of paper) were transferred to the NAA – 31 were marked 'Open with Exemption' – so there were 74 folios in all. Exemptions had to be sought under paragraphs 33(1)(a), (d), (e)(ii) and/or (e)(iii) of the *Archives Act 1983*, which state:

'33. (1) For the purposes of this Act, a Commonwealth record is an exempt record if it contains information or matter of any of the following kinds: (a) information or matter the disclosure of which under this Act could reasonably be expected to cause damage to the security, defence or international relations of the Commonwealth . . . (d) information or matter the disclosure of which under this Act would constitute a breach of confidence . . . (e) information or matter the disclosure of which under this Act would, or could reasonably be expected to . . . (ii) disclose, or enable a person to ascertain, the existence or identity of a confidential source of information in relation to the enforcement or administration of the law; or (iii) endanger the life or physical safety of any person.'

12   Steeples had married Gordon Hatten in 1948.

13   An ASIO surveillance photograph of Ellis is published in *The Protest Years* (2015) with the caption: 'Charles Howard (Dick) Ellis, an Australian-born MI6 officer. In March 1971, information arose pointing to Ellis having been a Russian agent from as early as 1929.'

14 It's not clear what this invitation was. Giles Scott-Smith: '[I'm] really not sure what this might refer to. At that age I can't imagine it was anything substantial.'

15 See Chapman Pincher, 'Fact: Dick Ellis did spy', *Sydney Morning Herald*, Sydney, 10 February 1983.

16 This is not true. Pincher inserted a note, dated 3 September 1983 – see his papers on Ellis, held by King's College – which says, 'Elliott said he never liked Ellis and never trusted him, though without any sound reason. Agreed that if the KGB knew he had spied for the Abwehr he would have been put under pressure.'

17 Pincher wrote a note on 15 August 1981 that Cavendish, 'in trying to make an excuse for Ellis . . . said that Ellis's job was to liaise with the Abwehr . . . a kind of double role' but Cavendish had also called Ellis and Hollis 'idiots'. In another note, undated, Pincher says Cavendish considered Ellis 'grossly incompetent'. Apropos Hollis, Pincher's former colleague, *Daily Express* picture editor and later author Ron Morgans, left a comment under an online *Guardian* newspaper report following Pincher's death: 'Don't be so dismissive of the Hollis conspiracy. I worked on it in the '70s and know without doubt that Hollis was given a traitor's burial by the Establishment. I've been to the little church where it happened and met a mourner who saw it. His widow Val Hollis tended the churchyard where his unmarked ashes were stowed behind a flint in the churchyard wall.' The source for this is a screenshot from James Bruce's (@Marys_Miles) Twitter account, 8 February 2018. The comment was made on 7 August 2014 under the handle 'Kindleer'. The 6 August 2014 report by Richard Norton-Taylor was titled 'Spycatcher defence correspondent Chapman Pincher has died, aged 100'.

18 According to Frank Cain's entry for Ellis in the 1996 edition of the *Australian Dictionary of Biography*, Ellis was cremated. I could find no record of Ellis's gravesite.

Chapter 20   A BREAK IN THE SILENCE

1 Hugh Trevor-Roper said Hyde was approached to write the book but declined. See Trevor-Roper, 'The faking of Intrepid', *Sunday Telegraph*, 19 February 1989.

2 Letter, William Stevenson to William Stephenson, 9 October 1975. Stevenson mentions Olik Ellis again in a 15 October 1981 letter to Chapman Pincher. Olik allegedly 'tried to put the bite on' Stephenson: ask him for money. 'I think you'd find Ellis Jr is in a sensitive Candn [sic] govt post.'

3 See Joe Ritchie, 'Washington writer cites role in unmasking British spy; writer says he unmasked spy', *Washington Post*, 26 March 1981.

4 Giles Playfair, a writer recruited by Ellis, worked for BSC. Playfair was one of the co-writers of the 'BSC Account' or 'BSC Papers' later published as *British Security Coordination: The Secret History of British Intelligence in the Americas, 1940–45* (1998).

5 See Stewart Tendler, 'Mrs Thatcher refuses to comment on man named as spy', *Times*, 22 April 1981.

6 Ann Salwey later wrote to Ernest Cuneo to thank him for his support: 'Thank you for your strong belief in my father. It is a very deep hurt and hard to live without being able to do anything constructive.' The letter is contained in the Ernest Cuneo papers and dated '23 March', presumably 23 March 1981.

7 Letter, Ann Salwey to Brian Pearce, 6 May 1981.

8 In his memoir *A Bigger Picture* (2020), Malcolm Turnbull argues the British government in fact secretly abetted Pincher by not stopping its publication: 'The government had had copies of the manuscript prior to printing . . . Thatcher was directly responsible for encouraging Pincher to write a book about [Roger] Hollis.' Turnbull makes no direct mention of Ellis in *A Bigger Picture* or *The Spycatcher Trial* (1988), in which he argues both Peter Wright's *Spycatcher* (1987) and Nigel West's *A Matter of Trust: MI5 1945–72* (1982) were 'covertly authorised' by the British government. However, there is a reference to Ellis by Chapman Pincher in the earlier Turnbull book as 'Emerton'.

9   Nicholas Elliott again. See 29 July 1981 note by Pincher (in the King's College papers).

10 See Chapman Pincher, 'Treachery', *Sydney Morning Herald*, 30 August 1981.

11 Pearce's grandson Ray Toye laments Pearce's lack of recognition despite 'having done so much to help Russian intellectuals endeavouring to criticise the Soviet Union . . . he was rejected by both the English left, the academic establishment, and others.'

12 See Richard Hughes's untitled column on Ellis in the *Far Eastern Economic Review*, 17 November 1983.

13 Pincher claims the dates of the FBI's inquiries into Ellis – including memos to the head of the Russian desk, Bill Branigan – were 17–23 January 1953, 16 October 1953 and 9 May 1956.

14 McDonald raised Ellis's name once more: on 2 June 1983 in the House. McDonald and 268 other passengers and crew were killed months later, on 1 September 1983, after missiles fired by the Russian military brought down Korean Air Lines Flight 007. The plane crashed in the Sea of Japan near Sakhalin, Russia.

15 Stevenson wrote: 'Stephenson did not want a stranger walking through the gates of Camp X. He wired London: "Sending back your man by next available transport." He would assign trusted SIS men of his own: men tested by himself on wartime assignments, who could be depended upon to steer Gouzenko through the weeks of detailed debriefing . . . he had done all he could to keep Gouzenko safe from intruders.'

16 In *A Web of Deception: The Spycatcher Affair* (1987), Pincher claims '£5000 of the first instalment [of the book advance for *Their Trade is Treachery*] came to me and £5000 went to Wright. There were other consultants but Wright was the only one who had insisted on payment.' In Pincher's autobiography, *Dangerous to Know: A Life* (2014), he further claims Wright 'had shared half the royalties earned by my book, which had been a bestseller, but wanted more. So, without consulting me, he had written an extended version, called *Spycatcher*.' Pincher says their relationship had ended in 1983 after Wright stopped replying to Pincher's letters and Wright had pocketed a sum of £31,827 in royalties from publishers Sidgwick & Jackson. Wright admitted this under oath in court. Ellis fails to get a mention in Pincher's autobiography, which is odd considering the latter devoted two bestsellers to impugning his memory. Pincher claims that after the *Spycatcher* trial in Australia, Wright's sister Elizabeth branded her brother 'a compulsive liar and a vindictive mischief-maker prepared to betray secrets for money'.

17 Turnbull writes about Wright in *A Bigger Picture* (2020): 'I visited [Wright] in the shack south of Hobart that he and his wife, Lois, called home. The fences were falling down, and the few horses looked as miserable as their owners. Peter and Lois were broke. Peter was 74, frail yet with an intensity about him, almost a fanaticism, that must have been unnerving for all those traitors and suspected traitors he'd interrogated during the dark days of the Cold War.'

18 This is demonstrably true. William Donovan's Office of Strategic Services is bizarrely referred to as the 'Overseas Security Service', which makes you wonder if anyone edited the manuscript.

Epilogue   THE ELLIS IDENTITY

1   Count Carl Magnus Torsten Armfelt was a Finnish-American who served in the US Army Air Corps and worked as a CIA agent. He died in 2005. See Giles Scott-Smith's *Western Anti-Communism and the Interdoc Network* (2011) for more on Armfelt. Scott-Smith writes: 'Armfelt, attending a dinner with Margaret Thatcher in 1992, took the opportunity to thank her "for putting a lid on the Dickey [sic] Ellis rumours and charges" (in relation to her opposition to Peter Wright's *Spycatcher*).'

2   Wright's biography of Teague-Jones, *Centurion of the Inner Circle: The Secret Service of Ronnie Sinclair, 1889–1988*, was on submission to publishers at time of writing.

3   Keith Jeffery refers to it in *MI6* (2010) as the Ship Observers Scheme.
     H. Montgomery Hyde in *The Quiet Canadian* (1962) and Ellis in *The Two Bills: Mission Accomplished* (1972) call it the Ships Observer Scheme.

4   According to West's biography at Israel-based speakers' agency Spy Legends, he was voted thus 'by a panel of other intelligence historians in the *Observer* in November 1989'.

5   He even did so in the House of Commons, in 1994 when he was an MP, under his real name, Rupert Allason: 'The Secret Intelligence Service . . . has sometimes been described, perhaps unfairly, as the second oldest profession. When one is working at the coalface, hostile penetration is almost inevitable. We have the cases of Kim Philby, George Blake, John Cairncross, Dick Ellis and the unnamed victims of the molehunts in the 1970s. All those cases are occupational hazards of secret intelligence.'

6   Pincher had said, '[Ellis] was a pal of Philby's, who must have known of his past.' See McDonald, 'Treason of British spy has serious effects on American intelligence', House of Representatives, 26 April 1983.

7   Nigel West took a different view in *The Faber Book of Espionage* (1993): 'The tragedy of Best's case was that he was innocent of the charge that he had cooperated with his Nazi interrogators. It was only much later that the SIS learned that another SIS officer, Dick Ellis, had passed on secrets to the Abwehr . . . Ellis confessed to his treachery.'

8   See Dilks (ed.), *The Diaries of Sir Alexander Cadogan* (1971). Cadogan's entry for 3 May 1939 talks of a 'telephone intercept, which looks as if No. 10 were talking "appeasement" again'. David Dilks, the diaries' editor, also writes: 'On 28 November [1938] an officer of the Intelligence [sic] service brought Cadogan material which seemed to show that someone at 10 Downing Street was in contact with Ribbentrop through Fritz Hesse, press adviser to the German Embassy in London.'

9   Distinct to a *blockführer* (block leader), the supervisor of a barracks in a concentration camp.

10   Stevenson elaborated: 'There was, in a prewar British edition of *Mein Kampf*, a definition of *Volksgemeinschaft* that sought to stifle any alarmed criticism. The word meant "folk community" and applied to the whole body of the people, without distinction or class. "Volk" was a primary word that suggested the basic national mood after the defeat of 1918, the downfall of the monarchy and the destruction of the aristocracy. It was "the unifying coefficient which would embrace the whole German people".' The Nazis introduced racial purity into the meaning of *Volksgemeinschaft*.

INDEX